UX Design for Mobile

Design apps that deliver impressive mobile experiences

Pablo Perea
Pau Giner

BIRMINGHAM - MUMBAI

UX Design for Mobile

First published: July 2017

Production reference: 1260717

Published by Packt Publishing Ltd.
Livery Place
35 Livery Street
Birmingham
B3 2PB, UK.

ISBN 978-1-78728-342-8
www.packtpub.com

Credits

Authors
Pablo Perea
Pau Giner

Reviewer
Lisandra Maioli

Commissioning Editor
Ashwin Nair

Acquisition Editor
Divya Poojari

Content Development Editor
Roshan Kumar

Technical Editor
Murtaza Tinwala

Copy Editors
Shaila Kusanale
Dhanya Baburaj

Project Coordinator
Ritika Manoj

Proofreader
Safis Editing

Indexer
Mariammal Chettiyar

Graphics
Jason Monteiro

Production Coordinator
Shraddha Falebhai

About the Authors

Pablo Perea has been working as a designer for many years, mainly focusing on user experience, user interface, and mobile and web design for companies such us Embarcadero Technologies. His daily work includes researching, prototyping, designing, and testing new ideas and solutions.

He graduated in computer engineering and has a deep knowledge and understanding of different programming languages. As a devotee of technology, he is always learning and investigating new working fields and methods.

He is an adaptable and flexible person who welcomes change and loves meeting new cultures and teams.

Pau Giner is a designer. He likes exploring and prototyping new ideas, and always has a pen to hand.

As part of the design team at the Wikimedia Foundation, he has been designing for Wikipedia and other open projects to ensure that millions of users can easily access the sum of all human knowledge. His design work has explored new ways to contribute, from translating Wikipedia articles to reviewing content with the help of artificial intelligence.

He has organized several design workshops, he got a PhD from the Universitat Politècnica de València for his research on mobile workflows, and he has also published a number of short stories.

Acknowledgments

We would like to thank the effort and support that Torquil Harkness, María Pérez, and Patricia Caballero have given us, helping us find the right words and providing helpful feedback in the way that only friends can.

About the Reviewer

Lisandra Maioli is a UX Specialist with B.A. in journalism, specialization in marketing (UC Berkeley), digital marketing (UCLA) and UX design (General Assembly Santa Monica). With over 17 years of an international experience working for large agencies and portals, as well as for small companies, start-ups for clients based in Brazil, US, Italy, Ireland, China and Netherlands, in different positions in Digital Communication--journalism, social media strategy, content strategy, community management, digital marketing, and digital products. Passionate about UX, she has been organizing events and giving online workshops and lectures on this topic. She is also the author of the *UX for High Performance* chapter for a digital marketing book published in Brazil, and is currently writing the book *Fixing Bad UX*, Packt.

www.PacktPub.com

For support files and downloads related to your book, please visit www.PacktPub.com.

Did you know that Packt offers eBook versions of every book published, with PDF and ePub files available? You can upgrade to the eBook version at www.PacktPub.com and as a print book customer, you are entitled to a discount on the eBook copy. Get in touch with us at service@packtpub.com for more details.

At www.PacktPub.com, you can also read a collection of free technical articles, sign up for a range of free newsletters and receive exclusive discounts and offers on Packt books and eBooks.

https://www.packtpub.com/mapt

Get the most in-demand software skills with Mapt. Mapt gives you full access to all Packt books and video courses, as well as industry-leading tools to help you plan your personal development and advance your career.

Why subscribe?

- Fully searchable across every book published by Packt
- Copy and paste, print, and bookmark content
- On demand and accessible via a web browser

Customer Feedback

Thanks for purchasing this Packt book. At Packt, quality is at the heart of our editorial process. To help us improve, please leave us an honest review on this book's Amazon page at `https://www.amazon.com/dp/1787283429`.

If you'd like to join our team of regular reviewers, you can e-mail us at `customerreviews@packtpub.com`. We award our regular reviewers with free eBooks and videos in exchange for their valuable feedback. Help us be relentless in improving our products!

Table of Contents

Preface

In this book, you will be introduced to a pragmatic approach to designing mobile apps that will delight your users. You will learn to explore new ideas and turn them into mobile app solutions that meet real user needs. The proposed techniques can be applied early in the process, resulting in less time investment, reducing risks, and saving time during the construction process. Each chapter will focus on one of the general steps needed to design a successful product according to both the organization's goals and the user needs. For each step, the book will detail hands-on pragmatic techniques to design innovative and easy-to-use products.

During the book, you will learn how to test your ideas in the early steps of the design process--picking up the best ideas that truly work with your users, rethinking those that need further refinement, and discarding those that don't work properly in tests with real users.

This book will show a working process to quickly iterate product ideas with low and high fidelity prototypes, based on some professional tools from different software brands. It will explain the pros and cons of each kind of prototype, when you should use each of them, and what you can learn at each step of the testing process. It will further show the basic testing approaches and some more advanced techniques to connect with and learn from your users.

Thanks to step-by-step guides, you will learn how to start exploring and testing your design ideas, regardless of the size of the design budget. Additional considerations based on real-world experience will be provided to help you cover the gap between theory and practice, in order to apply what you learn to your own projects.

What this book covers

`Chapter 1`, *Design Principles and General Design Planning*, teaches you the basic design principles that will lead you to a clear understanding of the book's content. It will cover evolutionary aspects that largely determine the way humans perceive the world, showing principles for good design aimed at real people. In addition to general design principles, you will understand the importance of adapting the design solutions to the environment and to the final scenario in which the solution is used.

A general overview of the design process will introduce the context of the book and the journey it proposes. Each chapter of the book works as a coherent unit, describing one step of the process, but it will also work as a complete solution when read as a whole.

`Chapter 2`, *Research - Learning from Your Users,* explains the need for a deep understanding of the problem before jumping in to solve it. A good study of potential users' mental model will allow you to express the interactions of your app in users own terms.

Finding patterns and conventions will help the designer take the right decisions when exploring possible solutions. Also, it will explain how to put useful methods into practice to learn key aspects from your users behaviors.

`Chapter 3`, *Exploring Ideas - Sketching,* explores how to create quick sketches to explore innovative ideas and present them to the team and other stakeholders. Using pen and paper, you'll be able to find new directions for your solution you had never thought of before. This chapter contains tips, examples, and a working process to guide idea exploration.

`Chapter 4`, *Mobile Patterns - Web App, Android, and iOS Best Practices,* details how to create a multichannel product. The current approaches will be presented in an easy and structured way. The chapter will cover the main mobile platforms based on the number of users, and it will further explain the key differences the designer must know about to design a successful cross-platform product.

`Chapter 5`, *Detail Your Solution - Wireframes and Mockups,* proposes a working process to explain your solution in detail, creating detailed documents that will help the development team understand and follow the design concept. You will learn how to create the right specifications for both Android and iOS developers, and also how to create sets of assets for different screen resolutions and different platforms. The chapters will highlight the importance of motion in today's designs and how it affects user perception.

`Chapter 6`, *Prototyping - Bring Your Ideas to Life,* describes how to create a testable version of your ideas in the early stages of the design process. It will provide general guidelines for planning your prototyping process. It will also explore different prototyping tools and discuss their pros and cons. You will learn how and when you should use each approach, based on the project requirements and the complexity of the proposed project features.

`Chapter 7`, *Prototyping with Motion - Using Tumult Hype*, outlines how to create an application prototype with a timeline-based prototyping tool. You will learn how to use motion to support your ideas, showing interactions in a visual way, and its advantages and what it represents to the process. For this step-by-step guide, you will use one of the best tools in the market, Tumult Hype, a keyframe-based animation system. Tumult is a company founded by two Apple veterans, and the tool has received awards and tremendous praise from its users.

`Chapter 8`, *Prototyping with Code - Using Framer Studio*, focuses on how to create a prototype using a programming-based tool. Readers with coding experience will be able to apply the prototyping mindset to a familiar environment. It will cover the step-by-step process with Framer Studio, a design tool of reference. Framer Studio is used by top designers at tech start-ups and design schools worldwide.

`Chapter 9`, *User Testing*, dives into how to test your prototypes with real users and learn by observing their interactions. The chapter contains a plan to follow for moderated tests. It will explain how to plan and develop a testing session and also cover general details on unmoderated tests. The chapter also gives a clear view about the importance of testing at scale for big and growing projects, covering aspects about the definition of metrics and A/B testing.

What you need for this book

Even though most chapters in this book do not need any specific software to follow the proposed workflows, the prototyping chapters make use of design and prototyping software to create testable versions of your ideas. It is recommended to have at least Bohemian Sketch, Tumult Hype, and Framer Studio to get the most from this book. Additionally, Adobe CC will allow you to make use of some provided assets and test some ideas.

Who this book is for

This book is for designers, developers, and product managers interested in creating successful apps. This book will provide them with a process to produce, test, and improve designs based on best practices.

Conventions

In this book, you will find a number of text styles that distinguish between different kinds of information. Here are some examples of these styles and an explanation of their meaning.

Code words in text, database table names, folder names, filenames, file extensions, pathnames, dummy URLs, user input, and Twitter handles are shown as follows: "We can then add the image to the second scene and rename the scene `Activity Details`".

New terms and **important words** are shown in bold. Words that you see on the screen, for example, in menus or dialog boxes, appear in the text like this: "Make sure that you leave **Apply changes to all scenes** selected."

A block of code is set as follows:

```
# STEP 3
# Step 3 states
sketch.Step_3_Artboard.states.out =
 x: 1080
 animationOptions:
 time: 0.3
 curve: Bezier.ease
```

Warnings or important notes appear in a box like this.

Tips and tricks appear like this.

Reader feedback

Feedback from our readers is always welcome. Let us know what you think about this book—what you liked or disliked. Reader feedback is important for us as it helps us develop titles that you will really get the most out of.

To send us general feedback, simply e-mail `feedback@packtpub.com`, and mention the book's title in the subject of your message.

If there is a topic that you have expertise in and you are interested in either writing or contributing to a book, see our author guide at `www.packtpub.com/authors`

Customer support

Now that you are the proud owner of a Packt book, we have a number of things to help you to get the most from your purchase.

Downloading the example code

You can download the example code files for this book from your account at `http://www.packtpub.com`. If you purchased this book elsewhere, you can visit `http://www.packtpub.com/support`and register to have the files e-mailed directly to you.

You can download the code files by following these steps:

1. Log in or register to our website using your e-mail address and password.
2. Hover the mouse pointer on the **SUPPORT** tab at the top.
3. Click on **Code Downloads & Errata**.
4. Enter the name of the book in the **Search** box.
5. Select the book for which you're looking to download the code files.
6. Choose from the drop-down menu where you purchased this book from.
7. Click on **Code Download**.

You can also download the code files by clicking on the **Code Files** button on the book's webpage at the Packt Publishing website. This page can be accessed by entering the book's name in the **Search** box. Please note that you need to be logged in to your Packt account.

Once the file is downloaded, please make sure that you unzip or extract the folder using the latest version of:

- WinRAR / 7-Zip for Windows
- Zipeg / iZip / UnRarX for Mac
- 7-Zip / PeaZip for Linux

The code bundle for the book is also hosted on GitHub at `https://github.com/PacktPublishing/UX-Design-for-Mobile`. We also have other code bundles from our rich catalog of books and videos available at `https://github.com/PacktPublishing/`. Check them out!

Downloading the color images of this book

We also provide you with a PDF file that has color images of the screenshots/diagrams used in this book. The color images will help you better understand the changes in the output. You can download this file from https://www.packtpub.com/sites/default/files/downloads/UXDesignforMobile_ColorImages.pdf.

Errata

Although we have taken every care to ensure the accuracy of our content, mistakes do happen. If you find a mistake in one of our books—maybe a mistake in the text or the code—we would be grateful if you could report this to us. By doing so, you can save other readers from frustration and help us improve subsequent versions of this book. If you find any Errata, please report them by visiting http://www.packtpub.com/submit-Errata, selecting your book, clicking on the Errata submission form link, and entering the details of your Errata. Once your Errata are verified, your submission will be accepted and the Errata will be uploaded to our website or added to any list of existing Errata under the Errata section of that title.

To view the previously submitted Errata, go to https://www.packtpub.com/books/content/supportand enter the name of the book in the search field. The required information will appear under the Errata section.

Piracy

Piracy of copyrighted material on the internet is an ongoing problem across all media. At Packt, we take the protection of our copyright and licenses very seriously. If you come across any illegal copies of our works in any form on the internet, please provide us with the location address or website name immediately so that we can pursue a remedy.

Please contact us at copyright@packtpub.com with a link to the suspected pirated material.

We appreciate your help in protecting our authors and our ability to bring you valuable content.

Questions

If you have a problem with any aspect of this book, you can contact us at questions@packtpub.com, and we will do our best to address the problem.

1
Design Principles and General Design Planning

"If you can design one thing, you can design everything."

- Massimo Vignelli

Every day we interact with many elements in our environment, for example, turning off the alarm clock, opening doors, greeting our neighbors, or brushing our teeth.

Some of these interactions are positive, whereas other interactions can become really frustrating. We enjoy a fresh drink while relaxing on a sunny day. However, nobody likes waiting in a queue, getting lost in a building, or filling in long forms. Well-designed products and services result in positive interactions.

A saucepan with handles like the one shown in the preceding image is hard to lift when it is full. This is part of *The Uncomfortable,* a collection of deliberately inconvenient everyday objects, designed by Athens-based architect Katerina Kamprani. Unfortunately, finding uncomfortable objects around us is not that unusual (refer to the source available at `https://www.flickr.com/photos/colalife/14624508474/`).

The **User Experience** (**UX**) of a product or service is defined by how we perceive the summary of our interactions with it. A positive UX is the result of a careful design that is centered on the user needs. This perspective represents a big departure from the classical technology-driven approach that has produced many unusable products throughout history.

This book provides real-word guidance for a user-centered design process. The process described is based on both sound design theory and practical experience. We shall describe the steps to create successful mobile products and provide advice on how to apply these steps in the real world.

In this chapter, you'll learn the following essential aspects of a user-centered design:

- How to adopt a user-centered perspective
- The principles that make a product well-designed
- The basic steps in the design process
- The general challenges you'll find when you apply the concepts learned in the real world

All of these aspects are important for the design of mobile apps, but they are also useful in the design of other products.

Switching your perspective to focus on the user

All products are made for their users. So, what does a user-centered perspective mean, and what is special about it?

Two taps that have been designed from opposing approaches (source: https://www.flickr.com/photos/phrawr/6655550583/; source: https://www.flickr.com/photos/afoncubierta/3003286245/)

The taps shown in the preceding image represent two different approaches in design. The one on the left is the result of a technology-driven design, whereas the one on the right is the result of a user-centered design.

The first tap has two handles--one controls hot water, and the other controls cold water. The two-handle design is dictated by the pipe technology, which comes with separate pipes for hot and cold water. By adding a handle to each pipe you can control everything you need from a tap. The temperature can be adjusted by opening or closing the hot and cold handles to different degrees. However, once you find the ideal temperature, adjusting the flow of water requires to manipulate both handles in coordination to keep the temperature constant. This may not be convenient in many of the uses of the tap, such as filling a glass or washing your hands.

The second tap design starts instead from the user needs. Users need two different kinds of adjustments while operating a tap, that is, adjusting the water flow and the temperature. These independent needs are mapped to two independent movements of a single handle. Move the handle left or right to adjust the temperature. Move the handle up or down to control the water flow.

This makes it easy to keep the temperature constant as the water flow is adjusted, and even keep the preferred temperature every time you use it.

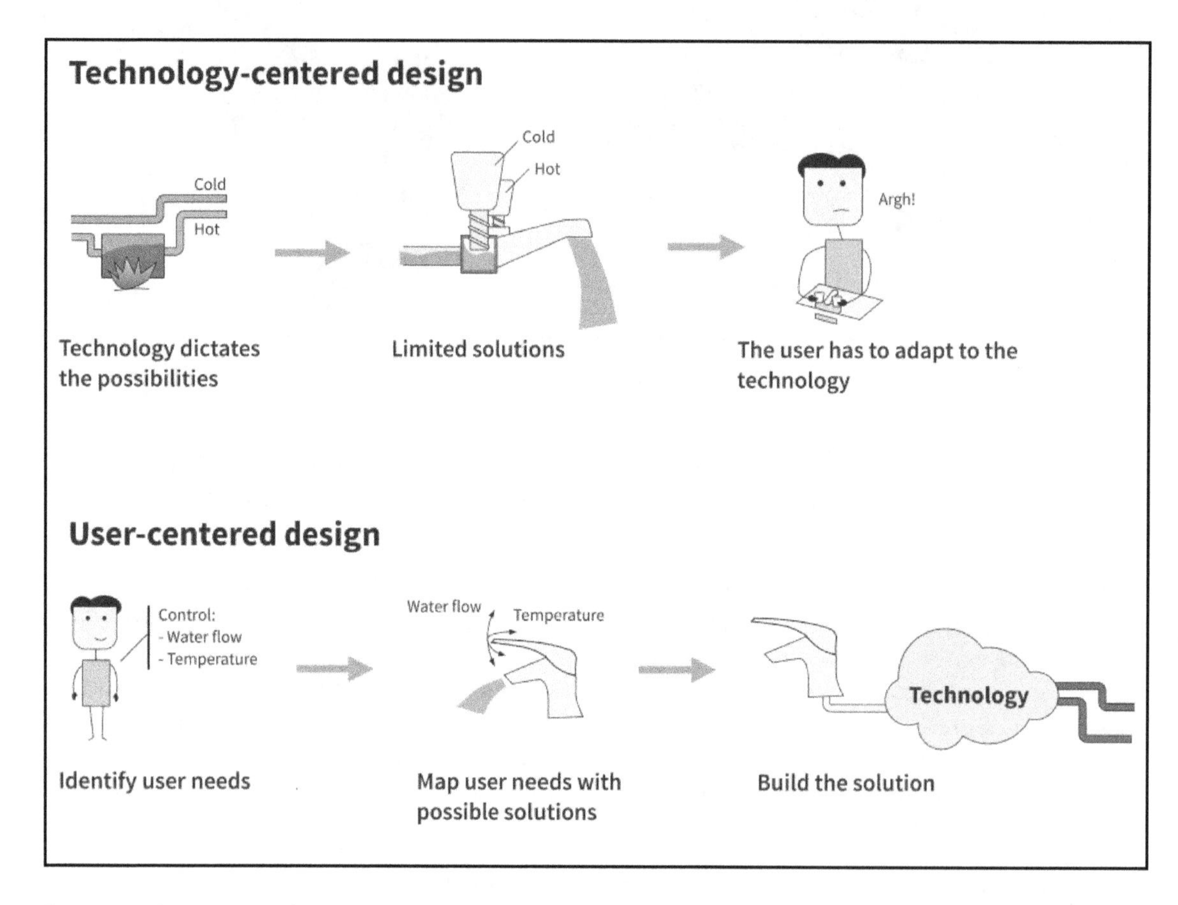

Starting the process from the user needs' perspective allows us to focus on what is easier for the user, as opposed to what is simpler for the technology. The second tap is easier to use, resulting in a better UX when you are washing your hands.

Shifting the complexity from people to technology makes life easier for your users. The drawback of shifting the complexity to technology is that this often represents more work for those building the product on the technical side. In the preceding example, connecting the second tap with the usual two-pipe technology requires a more elaborate mechanism.

People building a solution must understand the importance of providing a good experience to the users. Instead of understanding technology as a limiting factor, we need to understand technology as the magic that could support the best user experience.

Getting organizations to adopt a user-centered perspective

UX design has become a central part of many companies. From big organizations to small start-ups, many companies have adopted design techniques as part of their daily processes. However, the design process is not well-supported in all organizations.

The Z-89, a computer from 1979, with a monochrome text-based user interface (source: http://www.flickr.com/photos/ajmexico/3281139507/)

During the initial stages of computing, software was written by developers, for developers. The introduction of mobile devices changed this idea radically. In 2010, the global sales of PCs were surpassed by smartphones and tablets. In the following years, the number of mobile users grew fast, and for many people, the mobile device became their main tool to access the digital world, or even their only one--mobile-only internet users accounted for 15% of all internet users globally in 2017, and represented more than 30% of internet users in countries such as Thailand or Malaysia.

People who were not technology savvy entered the digital world in large numbers, thanks to the wide adoption of mobile devices. People who were afraid to put their hands on a computer mouse previously were suddenly sharing pictures with their friends through social networks. This stressed the importance of making intuitive products that are simple and easy to use. If your product is too complex, users will be eager to look for an alternative.

Mobile devices, such as smartphones, tablets, or smart watches, opened a new world of possibilities and restrictions. Users were now capable of interacting with their devices with natural gestures and voice, but at the same time, they had to use a much smaller screen and care about the device's battery life. Compared to the old days of monochrome text-based terminals, the increasing diversity allowed and demanded more creative solutions.

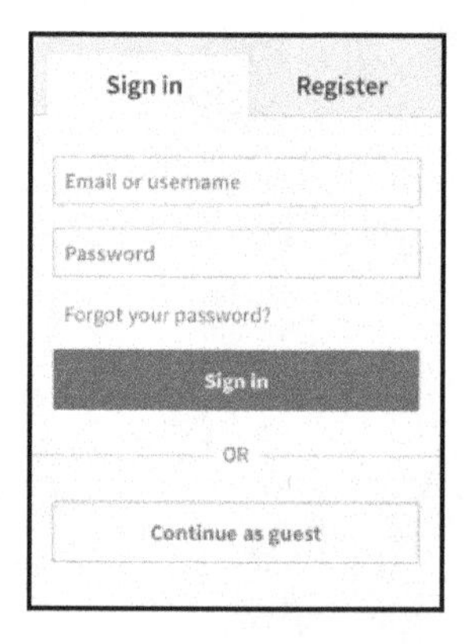

A recreation of the sign in step before the checkout step in an online store, with a convenient option to skip it

Creating positive experiences benefits the user, but ultimately it is also beneficial for the organization that creates such products. There is a commonly known story in the design sector that illustrates this:

An online shop was forcing users to register with them before buying products. They discovered that most of the users who forgot their password never completed the process. Users were able to request a new password through the usual **Forgot your password?** link, but they never returned. Since this affected users who had already decided to purchase their products, this meant that many sales were lost. The solution was simple: a button to complete the process without registering. Providing such an option was technically easy, and it resulted in sales going up by 300 million dollars. The difficult part in this case was not building the solution, but identifying the needs of the user and picking a solution that met them.

Design principles

Many different factors contribute to the user experience. Imagine that you are using an e-book reading app. Your experience reading a novel can be ruined by different factors, for example, the use of a tiny font that is uncomfortable on your eyes, an inconvenient way to move through pages that makes you wait too long, or the app forgetting the page where you stopped reading.

Each of these issues is problematic, but each one fails to meet needs of different kinds. A well-designed product responds to user needs at different levels:

- Needs from our human condition
- Needs from general expectations
- Needs from the specific context of use

We'll provide more details on each of those needs.

Needs from our human condition

As humans, we probably experience our world very differently than bats, octopuses, or the fascinating water bears (half-millimeter-long animals that can survive in outer space) do. We experience the world through our human senses; we process information in a visual, auditive, and to a lesser degree, olfactive way--we use our hands to manipulate elements and our voice to communicate.

After a process of millions of years of evolution, our human capabilities have been shaped as a key factor for survival in the physical world. However, when using digital products, our experience is heavily influenced by these same senses and the way our brain is wired to process them.

Understanding how our senses work can help us to design solutions that better fit our natural behavior as humans. For example, our peripheral vision allows us to identify movement at the edges of our vision field. Although we cannot recognize shapes or colors perfectly in that area, we can quickly notice any movement. The evolution theory suggests that this may have been useful to our primitive ancestors to quickly react to predators.

Nowadays, we use our peripheral vision to note the notifications that many apps show us as moving boxes at the top of the screen of our mobile devices. Designers of such interaction patterns took advantage of our capability to detect movement in the surroundings of our focus area. They decided that notifications should appear by moving in--as opposed to fading in--so our eyes notice them more easily.

Incoming call notification appears by moving in from the top

We have intuitive reactions to different stimuli. Even the most basic aspects--such as shape or color--bring their own implicit meaning when we process them. We describe these effects as their psychology.

A simple experiment shows the **psychology of shapes** in action. When people are shown two apparently random shapes like the ones in the subsequent image and are asked to name them as either *Bouba* or *Kiki,* most people will pick the same names for the same shapes. Most people will associate the rounded shape figure with the *Bouba* name and the spiky figure with the *Kiki* name.

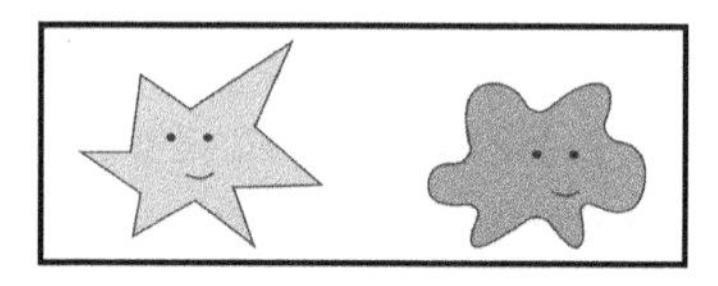

Given the names Bouba and Kiki, most people assign them consistently to each of these shapes

The psychology of shapes can affect many elements in the design of your app. For example, the use of straight corners or rounded corners in the interactive controls can help to provide a more serious or a more playful feel to it.

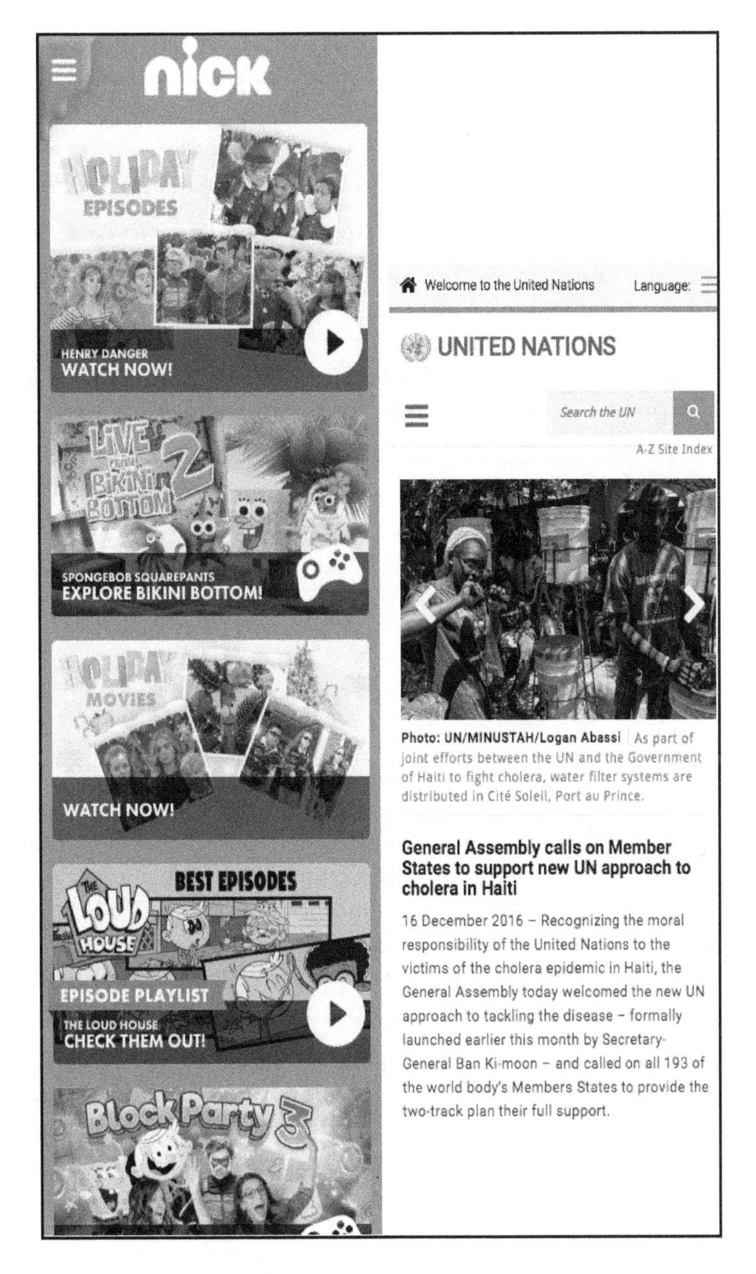

Rounded shapes are predominant in the child-oriented Nickelodeon website, whereas straight shapes are more common on the United Nations website with more serious content. (Source: Source: http://www.nick.com/, Source: http://www.un.org/)

The **psychology of color** is another widely researched area. Technically, color is just a representation of light at different wavelengths. However, when classifying colors, we use temperature (warm or cold colors) based on some of their associations. Marketing and branding has studied how these associations affect the sales of products and the perception of the companies selling them. While red is associated with excitement, blue is associated with relaxation.

These implicit reactions should not be the main force driving our design decisions, but we should be aware of possible contradictions that can confuse users. These confusions may occur when the meaning we try to convey contradicts the implicit meaning of those elements. For example, a red text will catch the user's attention, so it may not be the best choice for an e-book app as the main text color for reading a book comfortably.

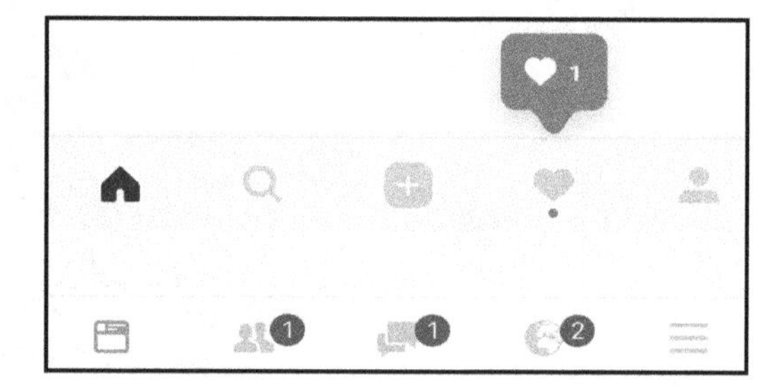

Instagram and Facebook use red for calling the user's attention to specific areas when there is any new relevant content (source: Screenshot from Instagram, source: Screenshot from Facebook)

Beyond the perception of individual elements and their properties, it is interesting to think about how we understand them together to form our experience. *Gestalt* (*form* in German) psychologists studied human perception and defined a set of properties that have been influential for many designers. They described how our brain identifies individual elements and is eager to find meaning of those elements. In particular, *gestalt* principles for grouping have many applications in the design of digital products.

For example, **the law of proximity** dictates that elements that are close to each other are perceived as a group. By adjusting the space around elements, we can control how those are related to each other by our brains. Consider a photo gallery app; by adjusting the relative distance between pictures, we can make all photos look like a single group (keeping a uniform separation) or break them into rows or columns (increasing the vertical or horizontal space to guide our eyes).

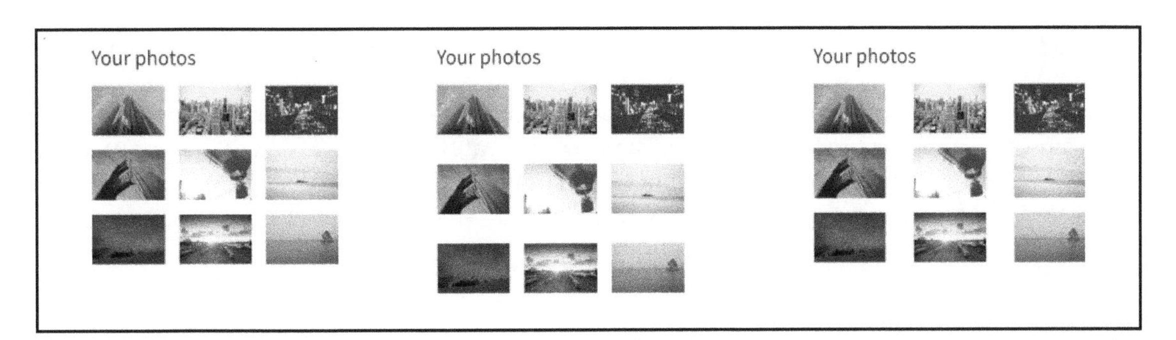

We don't need to enclose elements in a box to organize them in groups

Other gestalt principles suggest that our brain also groups together elements that look similar (law of similarity), move in the same direction (law of common fate), are connected without abrupt overlaps (law of continuity), or form a simple pattern (law of good form).

One of the main underlying ideas of these and other gestalt principles is the *tension between similarity and contrast*. This tension can occur in different dimensions (space, proportion, time, motion, and so on) and contributes to our perception of order.

When designing a product, we want to present physically connected what is conceptually related. Adjusting these different properties in the right way allows us to guide the eyes and the brain of our users to understand such organization as intended.

The Human Computer Interaction (HCI) community has been modeling many different human behaviors. For example, Fitt's law is a predictive model for human movement. In short, it states that the time it takes to hit a target (such as tap on a button) depends on how far away the target is and its size. This means that a small button far away will be harder to access than a big button you can access nearby.

The size of the targets, such as buttons and other controls, have evolved in mobile design thorough history, affecting their ease of use. The first mobile devices adopted the stylus as a pointing device and required users to be precise when choosing their targets. The iPhone challenged the idea that a smaller screen required smaller targets. Increasing the size of the targets made it comfortable to use with fingers, resulting in more intuitive interactions.

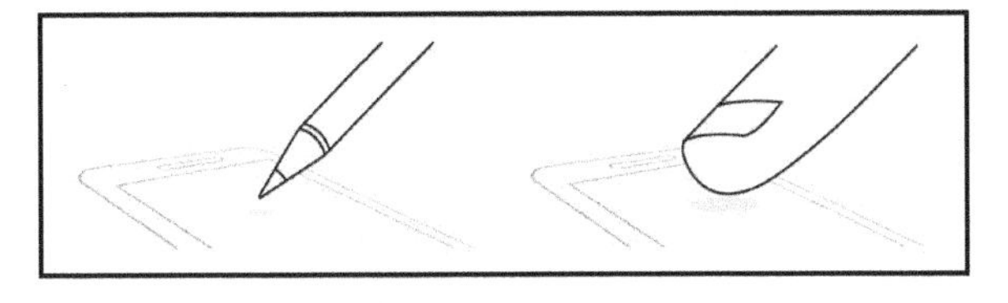

Different touch pointers need different sized targets

Our bodies and brains are the platform we ultimately run our products on. There are many disciplines and much research that provides us with valuable information about this platform. You don't need to be an expert in psychology, medicine, or biology to design great products, but understanding how humans work at their basic level will help you to design better for them. Being curious about human nature and observing people's most intuitive and visceral reactions can help you to identify relevant behavior that, being a core part of our nature may otherwise go unnoticed.

Needs from general expectations

Even if our body and brain are capable of doing many activities, it does not mean all of them are convenient, comfortable, or pleasing for us. Regardless of the specific type of product, users have general expectations when using them. Failing to meet those expectations when designing our products will negatively affect the resulting user experience. Users will be confused to see a product not behaving as they expected, which is breaking the **principle of least astonishment**.

Each interaction the user performs with a product requires some mental effort. This mental effort is often referred as the **cognitive load**. For example, a navigation app can ask your destination during your vacation trip in different ways. It would be easier for you to indicate the destination by the name of the place (*Eiffel Tower*) rather than the specific address (*Champ de Mars, 5 Avenue Anatole France, Paris*) or using the exact coordinates (48° 51′ 29.6″ N, 2° 17′ 40.2″ E). The cognitive load could be reduced further if the app were capable of ignoring potential typos, allowed voice input to just say the destination, or could suggest the destination in the first place, anticipating your needs.

A well-designed product should demand as little effort from the user as possible, reducing the points of friction where the user has to stop and think, reorient, or gets confused. Reducing friction often requires moving most of the complexities--such as translating the name of a place into coordinates--from the user into the computer.

The effort to use a product can be divided in two stages--understanding how the product works and operating it. Design considerations are key in both stages.

Explaining how a product works should be the job of the product itself. Designing a product that is obvious to use is essential since no one is going to read the instructions.

Donald Norman described the elements that communicate the possible actions of an object as **affordances**. Door handles are a classic example of affordances. They are placed at the hand reach and shaped to be manipulated by our hands. They are the way for the door to tell us how to open it. When affordances are applied wrong, they result in confusions about the possible actions. As a result, people find themselves pushing a door that should be pulled instead--those cases of badly designed doors are known as *Norman Doors,* named after the well-known designer.

A post-it note was added as an attempt to clarify how to operate the door (source: https://www.flickr.com/photos/chrisandhilleary/153059898/)

Affordances can use different properties to suggest their intended use such as shape, position, color, or movement. That helps users to interpret their meaning, but their meaning is also reinforced by previous experiences. The direct or indirect associations with previous uses of similar cases helps with the learning of new ones. Products do not exist in isolation, and the use of existing products will influence our expectations of new ones.

The digital world also has its own conventions that millions of previous products have help to establish. For example, many users will identify an "X" icon to represent an action to close or discard.

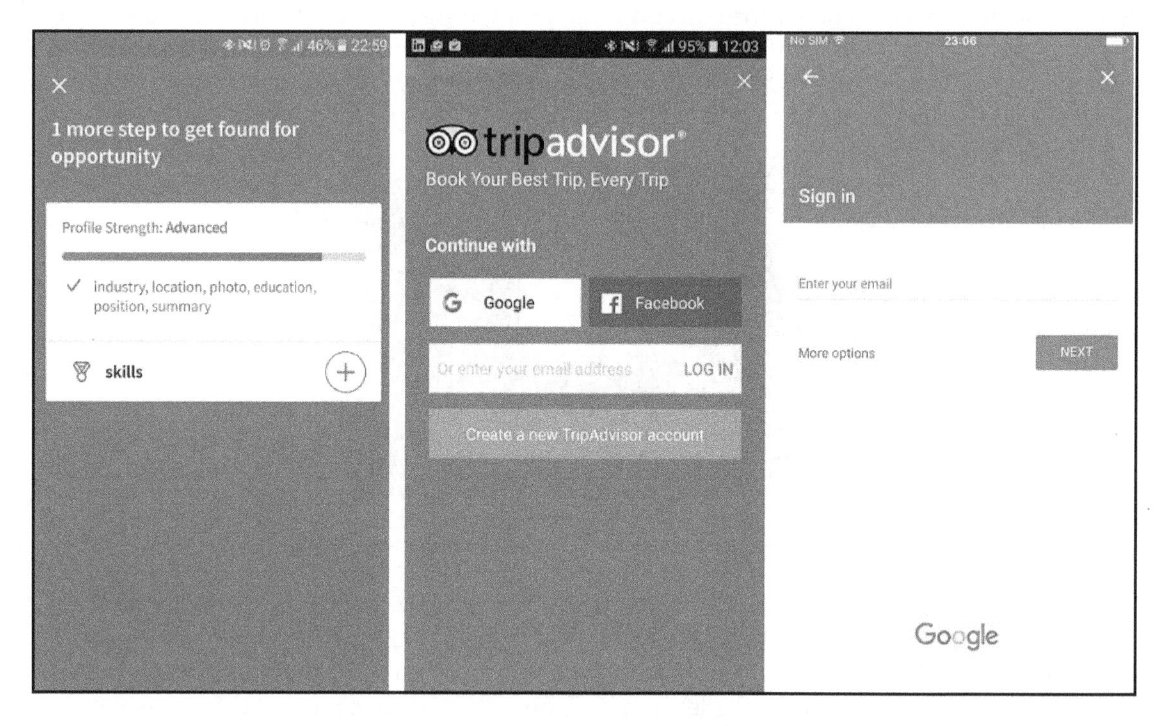

LinkedIn, TripAdvisor, and Google using an "X" icon as a way to discard (source: Screenshot from LinkedIn, source: Screenshot from TripAdvisor, source: Screenshot from Google)

Metaphors can help users connect the dots between a known concept and an old one. The digital concepts of *desktop*, *folder*, or *windows* rely on some of the aspects of their physical counterparts. A shopping app can use a shopping cart icon to signal the place where your selected products are.

However, we need to be careful and avoid mimicking the original concepts. It won't make much sense to use a 3D recreation of the shopping cart where you need to make the space to place each product in the cart as you would in a real supermarket. Avoid transferring the limitations of the physical world into the digital one. The digital space is better suited for many actions such as finding the products you bought last week. You don't want to follow a metaphor so literally that it limits the possible solutions.

Design guidelines capture important conventions to consider when you design for a specific platform, organization, or family of products. In this way, your solutions can reuse concepts that are familiar to users in the exact way they are used to interacting.

Breaking conventions may be needed at times, but it should be done only for a really good reason. We need to make sure that the benefit provided to our users is much greater than the potentially negative effects of possible confusions.

Social and cultural conventions also have their influence on what people expect from products. A hand gesture that means approval in one culture can be an offensive gesture in another, when found as an icon. Similarly, languages bring their own conventions. Concepts associated with directionality will be represented differently depending on the language direction. For example, a *forward*, *next*, or *reproduce* action in English--a left-to-right language--can be represented with a triangle or arrow pointing to the right, whereas it needs to point to the left for languages, such as Arabic, which are written in the opposite direction to keep its *forward* action.

In addition to understanding how products work, we want them to require minimal effort when they are used. The following principles contribute to a positive user experience for all kinds of products:

- **Require minimal intervention**: The fewer steps we need to solve a problem, the better. Our designs should avoid unnecessary steps for people when using our product. This can be supported by the following different strategies:
    - **Allowing flexible input**: Information can be provided in many different ways. Some people use spaces, parenthesis, or dashes to group telephone numbers or monetary amounts in a transaction, others do not. Instead of imposing a specific format to meet the needs of the technology, allow your users to provide the information in all the ways that are most natural to them.
    - **Providing smart defaults**: When asking users for information, we should avoid open questions, and provide options instead. Recognition is a much simpler mental process than recall from memory. Thus, anticipating possible answers will save time for the user. If any of those options is likely to be what the user needs, setting it as the default would save time in most cases. For example, navigation apps can assume that your current position is your starting point. That is not always the case, and you may need to change those defaults, but overall it will avoid an additional step to go through most of the time.

- **Support direct manipulation**: For a long time, the mouse was one of the most common input devices. Users moved the mouse on their desk to move the cursor on their screens in order to act on a digital object. The arrival of touch screens allowed users to tap the element directly, reducing indirection steps. Indirection steps require users to make mental efforts to go through them. For example, it is simpler to use a hand gesture to zoom a picture than accessing a separate zoom menu that is disconnected from the picture it affects.

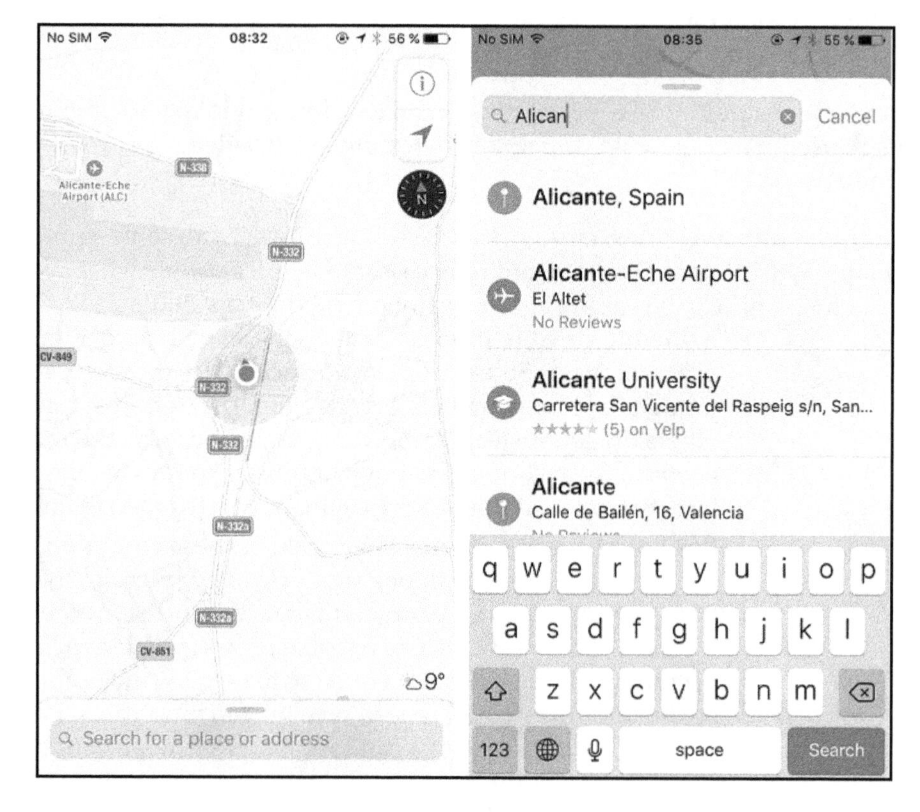

iOS Maps assumes that you are interested in knowing your current location (left) and provides suggestions as you look for destinations (right) (source: screenshots from iOS Maps)

- **Inform users in relevant terms**: Users want to know what is happening when using a product, but this feedback needs to be meaningful. Some aspects to consider:
    - **Make users feel in control**: Regardless of the level of automation a product can provide, users want to feel in control. A user trying to send a message to a friend will be more comfortable when they are sure that the message is sent and has reached the destination. This confirmation can happen in many different ways, from a simple visual cue to a more explicit feedback text. Choosing the right level of prominence for feedback according to each case will allow users to feel in control without the system being perceived as annoying.
    - **Explain by comparing**: Information is better understood when compared. During a car trip, knowing the distance to the destination can be useful. This distance is useful in your favorite distance unit--miles or kilometers--but it is even more useful when presented compared with the car speed as the time to reach your destination. Given a piece of information, it is important to identify the purpose it serves for our users in order to decide which is the most meaningful representation for it.
    - **Communicate in the user's terms**: The closest we represent concepts to the way users understand them--what is referred to as the user **mental model**, the more fluent their interaction will be. We should avoid messages that refer to internal aspects of the system or using technical jargon. A user looking for a taxi will be confused to hear that *no records were found*. It is easier to understand instead that *no taxis are available in the nearby area.*
- **Don't waste the user's time**: Time is a precious resource. When helping users to solve their problems, they will always appreciate solutions that require them to use as little time as possible. These are some relevant concepts to be considered:
    - **Keep tools at hand**: Providing the tools people need where they need them helps the user to avoid spending time looking for them elsewhere. After you call a telephone number that is not in your contacts, it is convenient to have an option to save it as a new contact. Identifying the next logical step and looking for ways to facilitate it will help you come up with these convenient shortcuts. Separating actions (the operations you commonly use to manipulate information) from configuration (the preferences you have and rarely change) also helps users to have the most needed options at hand.

- **Performance**: Nobody likes waiting. We should aim for our products to respond to user interactions as fast as possible. Anticipating the user next steps, caching, and other technical optimizations can help you to keep the user interactions under a reasonable response time. Regardless of the real time it takes to complete an action, even more important is how long the wait is perceived by the user. The **perceived performance** can be improved in many ways. Using placeholders similar to the content that will be loaded or communicating long waits with an adequate loading indicator will help the wait to feel shorter than what it actually is.
- **Reduce interruptions**: Asking the user to stop what they are doing will force them to switch context and break their flow of actions. Modal dialog and alerts can become annoying. We should aim to communicate relevant circumstances, such as the username proposed not being available or the internet connection being lost in a non-blocking way. Make your users aware of the information, but let them to decide when to act about it. Similarly, when waiting for some information, keeping the blocked elements to a minimum will help to reduce interruptions. For example, on a map application, it is convenient to make it still possible to manipulate the map--moving or zooming it--while the map tiles are being loaded with images.

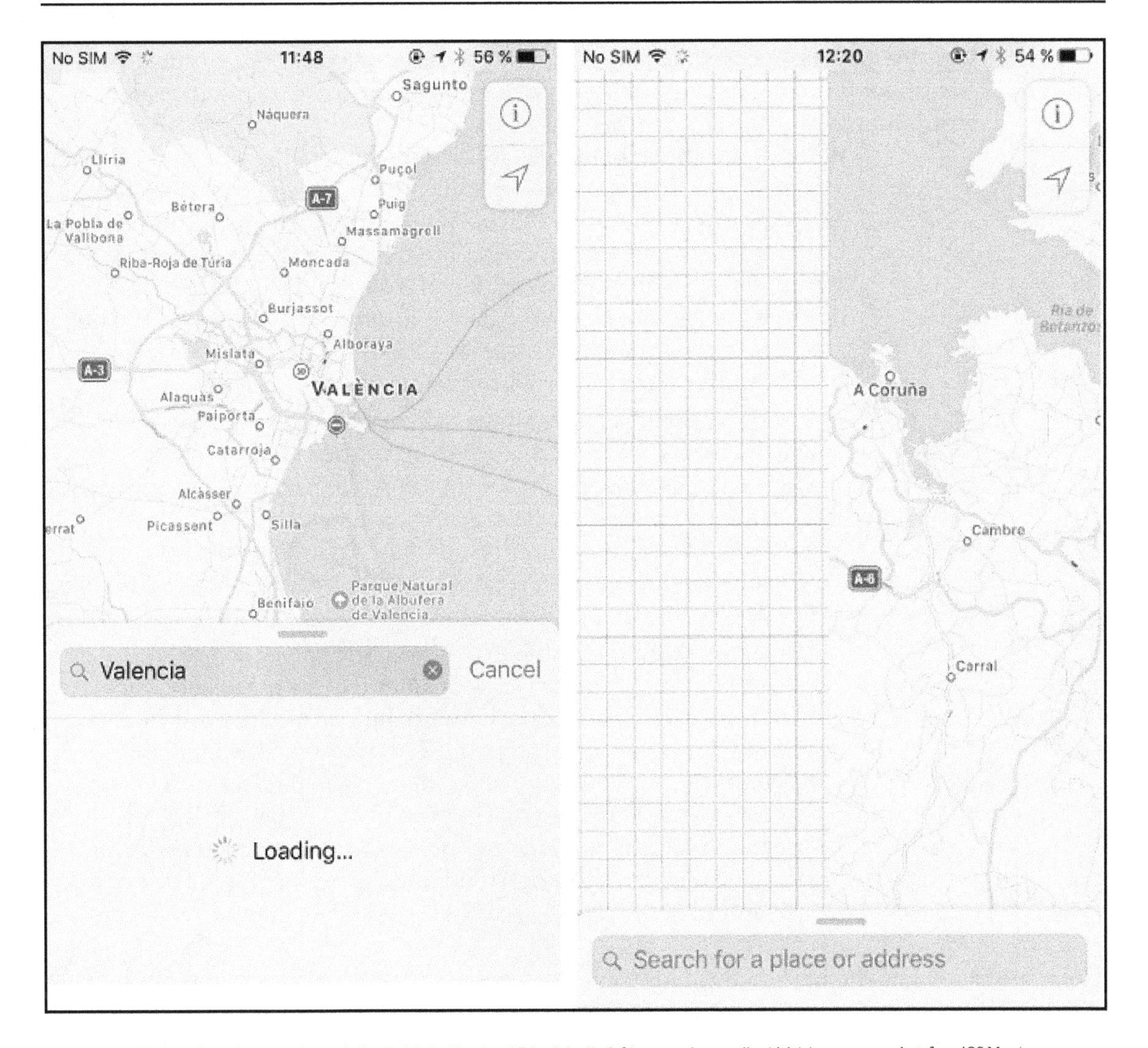

iOS Maps allows the map to be manipulated while loading the additional details (left) or even the map tiles (right) (source: screenshots from iOS Maps)

- **Avoid mistakes**: People feel bad when they make mistakes. Your products should not harm the user or make them feel stupid. These are some possible approaches:
    - **Make it impossible to use it incorrectly**: Ideally, a product should be designed in such a way that it is impossible to use it improperly. For example, using the appropriate controls, you can communicate that the range of dates for your hotel reservation can only include future dates. Preventing accidental side-effects and confusing errors contributes to creating an environment of **safe exploration**, where users are welcome to move around and find their way without the fear of messing things up.
    - **Avoid dead-ends**: Users should always have a way forward to achieve their goals. We should avoid putting them in situations where there is no apparent way to move forward. For example, if there are no results for a user search, some alternatives can be suggested based on similar results--similarly spelled results--or you can provide alternative ways to find content--such as browsing by categories.
    - **Alleviate the unavoidable**: In cases where mistakes are unavoidable, our product can consider ways to correct or alleviate those issues. For example, a network failure can be fixed by retrying the operation automatically without bothering the user. If the connection remains unavailable for a longer time, informing about the issue and keeping the pending changes locally to be saved later would help. In any case, never blame the user. Avoid messages that can be understood as an error being the fault of the user, since users only do what the system lets them do.

There are many general design and usability heuristics and pattern libraries and guidelines. These provide recommendations on important aspects to consider when designing positive interactions for all kinds of products. Following them will help your products to be more usable. However, these are not enough to guarantee that your solution will satisfy all the needs of your users.

Needs from the specific context of use

In addition to our needs as humans, and our general expectations as users, there is another set of needs that are specific to the context of use. These are defined by the purpose and goals of people using a product.

The video editing needs of a casual consumer documenting their last vacation trip are very different from those a professional filmmaker may have for a film. Therefore, a video editing app will be very different depending on which of these audiences we design the app for.

Conversely to the previous sets of needs, you can only learn about context-specific needs on a case-by-case basis. The users you will be designing for will be very different from yourself. There is no specific advice that applies to all kinds of products. Nevertheless, the design process will help you with the mindset and provide a set of activities to guide you to learn more about your users, identify their needs, and solve their problems.

In order to solve a user need, first you have to recognize what a need is. This may sound simple, but the distinction between a need and a solution is not always obvious.

Imagine that you live in a town next to a river. The town mayor calls and tells you: "*We need a bridge. Can you design one for us?*". At that point, you may be tempted to start thinking on how to design the perfect bridge. However, *a bridge* is not a need, the real need is to cross the river.

A bridge is just one of the many possible ways in which the underlying need of crossing to the other side of the river can be addressed. Other possible ways to cross the river are creating a ferry service, a cable car, or a zip-line. Failing to identify the underlying need limits the possible solutions you may consider.

Limiting the range of possible solutions too narrowly can lead you to suboptimal solutions, ignoring interesting ideas and limiting your capabilities to innovate. Asking "*why?*" is a good way to identify the underlying needs.

Asking *why* allows you to make the problem scope wider--maybe the town inhabitants don't need to cross the river if they have a food delivery service or if the course of the river can be diverted. The different constraints, priorities, and conflicts will limit the scope of the problem and will inform the selection of possible design solutions.

Design rarely happens in an environment with unlimited resources. There are many constraints we need to take into account instead. These constraints may come from different areas such as budget, law regulations, social conventions, and more. It is part of the designer's job to understand and consider those when looking for solutions.

In a constrained environment, not all needs have the same priority. It is important to consider how they impact the user since we'll have to support them at different levels. The model described by Noriaki Kano defines different patterns of user satisfaction:

- **Must-haves**: This indicates the basic needs users expect to be supported by a product. Failing to properly support these generates frustration for users. However, there is a certain point where improving the support will have diminishing returns. For example, users of a navigation app will expect to have some zoom capabilities. Providing no zoom at all would be frustrating for users to pick their destination; however, they don't need the app to compete with a NASA telescope in zoom capabilities and additional levels of detail won't improve the user experience significantly.
- **Linear needs**: This indicates the needs that add more value as they are better supported. In our navigation example, the time it takes to find a route will impact the user experience. There will be a point where the time is considered too long to be usable, and another point where it will be considered fast enough, but the faster it finds the best route, the more value it will bring to the user.
- **Latent needs**: These are needs that users do not realize they have. For products that don't support them, users won't miss them. Therefore, they don't get frustrated by their absence. However, as soon as a product solves those needs, they will greatly benefit from the new possibilities. A navigation app that suggests good places to eat when lunch time approaches can be helpful for many users, but it may not be something they ask for if it is not common in other apps. Latent needs are hard to discover since users cannot easily articulate them. Research techniques will help you to identify behavior patterns that can signal these needs.
- **Indifferent aspects**: Some aspects from a product may not be serving any particular user need. You would want to identify and remove those.

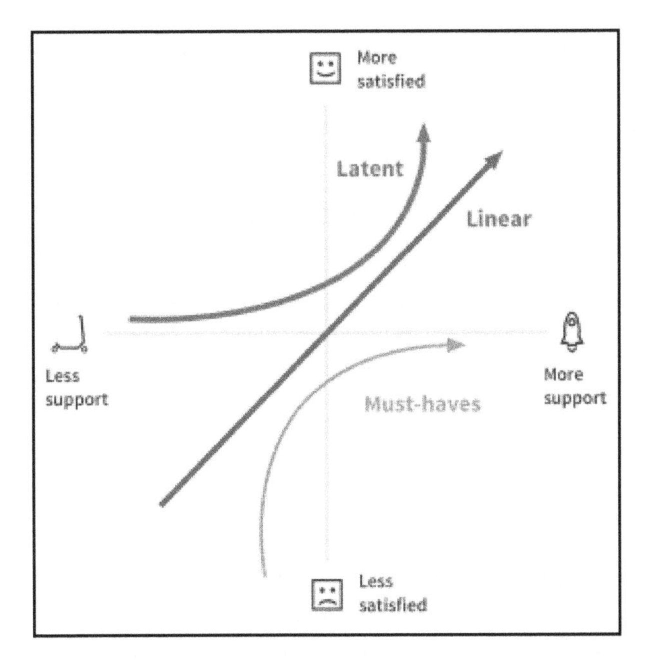

Kano model classifies the needs based on their impact in user satisfaction as they are better supported

When designing a product, it is common to find **conflicting needs**. Users of a camera app may need it to be quick to shoot with. However, they may also need a high degree of control to adjust many different parameters. Design is about finding optimal balances between conflicting interests. Some useful considerations when dealing with conflicting needs:

- **Adjust the prominence level based on frequency and impact**: When satisfying multiple needs, the designer acts as an orchestra conductor. Supporting in a more prominent way--bigger, in an easier to find location, with a contrasting color, and so on; these needs occur more frequently or have a bigger impact on the user. Functionality, such as the shutter button of a camera, which is often used, should be more prominent than controls that are used infrequently or have a much lower impact.
- **Identify what to optimize and what to just allow**: When you cannot satisfy multiple needs to the fullest extent, you need to identify the ones you want to optimize your product for. Consider how to fully support the essential needs while still providing basic support for the secondary ones. It is often better to prioritize support for the critical needs at the expense of other less critical needs rather than providing mediocre support for all of them.

- **Keep things simple**: Between two solutions that solve a given problem well, you should prefer the simple one. Simple solutions are easier to understand and operate. Don't be afraid to drop some capabilities in favor of supporting the main needs better.

Solving design problems requires a deep understanding of the context of use. Every problem is different. Fortunately, the design process can be applied to different contexts.

The process we present in this book will guide you through the steps to identify different user needs, find solutions for them, and verify that your ideas work in practice. The great Italian designer Massimo Vignelli (more about his perspective on design can be found in his freely available Canon at `http://www.vignelli.com/canon.pdf`) said, *"If you can design one thing, you can design everything."*

General design planning

The design process can be summarized in three simple steps: learn about the problem, explore possible solutions, and verify the solutions that work in practice.

The following chapters will elaborate on those steps to detail specific activities that can help you move through the process:

- **Research**: You cannot solve a problem if you don't understand it well. Learning about your users, their needs, and motivations is essential in order to solve their problems. Research techniques will help you get this knowledge and analyze it.
- **Explore ideas**: Given a problem, there is no single possible solution. Problems involving people normally have many potential solutions. Innovative ideas can be found quickly with an exploration process based on sketching.
- **Mobile patterns**: In order to meet the basic expectations of your mobile users, you'll need to follow the conventions on the different mobile platforms.
- **Detail your solution**: Communicating your ideas clearly is essential in a team. Design tools allow you to move your idea from the abstract to a more detailed representation.
- **Prototyping**: Design solutions are not static. To evaluate your ideas, you need to recreate how users interact with them. The prototyping process allows us to simulate our ideas without the effort needed to build them. Picking the right tool for the job is also part of the process.
- **Prototyping with motion**: Visual tools that embrace the concept of time are powerful prototyping tools. They provide control on how to communicate with motion by defining transitions and animations with great detail.

- **Prototyping with code**: Another perspective of prototyping is using code. Translating the prototyping concepts to code is a powerful approach to prototype your ideas.
- **User testing**: You don't know whether things work or not until they are used in practice. If you are able to recreate how an idea will work with a prototype, you can put it in the hands of a user and learn how well it will work.

This process is iterative in nature. Although it is described as a sequence of steps, you'll experience many different iterations for different parts of the product. Moving back and forth is totally expected and the results of each step will inform the next move.

For example, based on the results of testing a prototype of the general idea for your app, you can go back to learning about the problem, exploring more solutions on the drawing board, looking for a completely different approach, or further detailing your existing solution focusing on a specific aspect.

As with all chapters in this book, a *Being pragmatic* section will provide some advice in applying the design process in practice.

Being pragmatic

User experience design sounds like a simple process. Ideas such as understanding a problem before trying to solve it may not sound very radical. However, the number of badly designed products we encounter every day shows that this process is not always well applied in practice.

There are many challenges when following the design process in the real world. You may be tempted to consider these to be political issues caused by someone else or the result of a general lack of design culture in society. However, that perspective is not going to help in practice. Applying a proper design process in a team requires the efforts of the team to understand the benefits. You are in charge of helping them to change their mindset for the process to work in practice.

Design is not about making things look nice

Design is a process of finding solutions, and it starts before the problem is clearly defined and understood. However, many people identify design only with the aesthetic aspect of an object. They expect designers to come at the end of the process to make an existing product look good with few cosmetic adjustments. Although aesthetics definitely contribute to the user experience, that is just one component, and it won't help to fix the big usability issues in your product if those already exist.

You need to make sure that you are involved in a project from the very beginning. Emphasize in your team the need to understand the problem well before jumping into a solution in cases where they are already considering a predefined path of action. If you arrived late in the process, it is still useful to present alternative solutions. This will illustrate how design can be more valuable at the beginning of the process the next time.

Users are not able to tell you what they need

> *As Henry Ford put it, "If I had asked people what they wanted, they would have said faster horses."*

He was referring to the latent need for better transportation and the way people communicate those needs based on the solutions they already know, as opposed to potential solutions that do not exist yet, such as a car.

People are not good at describing their needs or predicting their future behavior. That does not mean you should be arrogant and ignore what people tell you. This means that you get feedback from them based on observing actual use, and make an effort to understand which are the underlying issues behind a user suggestion.

You (or your team) are not your users

People in your team, including yourself, may project their own needs or personal preferences onto the products. These opinions may not help solve the real needs of your users, and often lead to fruitless discussions among people with different preferences.

In these situations, it is important to change the perspective of the conversation--instead of discussing about what people in the team like, focus the conversation on what will work for your users. This encourages people to connect their feedback to the product goals and provide more context.

A complaint such as *I don't like this drop-down menu* is not very helpful. Framing it as *I don't think this drop-down works since users are provided with too many options when making a quick decision* brings more context and it is presented as an hypothesis that can be checked--you can ask for a situation in which such a problematic case would manifest, and recreate this when testing. This perspective change helps to focus on the user goals, and turns feedback into opportunities for learning more about your users. Making sure that the team regularly views real users using your products and prototypes will help with this shift of perspective.

User experience is not a list of features

Products are often described as a list of their features. However, that does not reflect the aggregated experience users have when using all those features combined in a product.

A great feature may be worthless if users cannot find it or they get confused when trying to use such a feature. Thinking only about adding more and more features often leads to ignoring how easy or hard is for users to use them.

Similarly, teams may be willing to cut corners of a product for an initial version or a **Minimum Viable Product** (**MVP**). A complete product with a small scope is preferred to an incomplete product with a wider scope. A small focused product is more useful than a bigger half-baked solution. Addressing many different needs poorly is not going to generate a very positive user experience. At the end of the day, a bike is much more useful than half a car.

Your goal is not to make your client or boss happy

As a designer, your goal is to find the best possible solution to a user problem. You are giving voice to the users of the product, who otherwise would have little room at the table.

While having a positive working relationship with clients and teammates is good, it is your responsibility to flag anything that negatively affects the users even if that leads to some serious conversations. Some of the user needs may conflict with the needs or interests of your organization. While it is part of your work to consider the different constraints such as production costs when solving a problem, you also need to make the organization understand that going against the user interests won't be good for the organization in the long run.

For example, an airline website that hides the option to opt-out from travel insurance to trick users into getting it will get some monetary benefit in the short term, but it will negatively affect the trust the users have with the brand in the long run. Tricks that make products hard to use on purpose are known as **dark patterns**, and you should never use them.

Summary

In this chapter, we introduced the importance of adopting a user-centered perspective when designing your products. Designing a positive user experience is the key to successfully addressing the needs of your users.

Throughout the chapter, we described different types of needs based on our human condition, general expectations, and the specific context of use. We introduced a set of basic design principles for you to consider when addressing these different types of needs.

We provided an overview on the general steps of a user-centered design process and provided advice on how to apply the process in practice. Each of the following chapters will focus on one specific step in this process.

In the next chapter, we'll present key research methods for you to discover, understand, and capture the specific needs of your users. Your understanding of the problem will inform many of your design decisions for your product. Having a deep understanding of the user needs will allow you to meet those needs more accurately.

2
Research - Learning from Your Users

"If the user is having a problem, it's our problem."

- Steve Jobs

User research is the phase where we get into the user world. We have to learn as much as we can from the way they do their activities, because it is for these activities that we will create new design solutions. Learning what user motivations are, and the goals they pursue when performing those tasks will help us make better decisions in the creation process.

The most successful companies, platforms, and brands are usually those that know how their users think. They know their needs and how to better support them. Companies like Apple, Muji, and Dyson have user needs in mind when designing their great products. When customers buy a product from a brand and their user experience is satisfactory, they remember and relate the brand with that experience, and the possibility of a second purchase in the future increases greatly.

It is the same with applications; every time a user interacts with your application, it is a golden opportunity. Giving an incredible first experience to your users is one of the key points to being successful as a designer or product manager. So, it is vital to analyze their needs and test your prototypes with real users before launching your product to the market.

Learn as much as possible about your users and design for them. Think how they will feel and what they will think, and you will have a solid foundation to create a successful design solution.

How we will do that?

We will use different methods and tools to understand how users are actually doing their tasks and how we can improve their different processes. Our objective, as user experience designers, is to offer a solution for an existing problem. The first thing we have to do is to learn as much as possible about the experience of our users when doing their tasks, in order to know which points are especially tedious and which are simple and productive.

In this chapter, we will cover everything from planning to the implementation of this process using different techniques that can be applied according to the needs of the project and the information that we want to obtain.

Getting to know your users

Our system needs to speak the same language as our users, not a language based on the technology field. Our users are not, or may not be, technicians, so we should not design as if all our users were experts in technology.

The good news is that the workflow of development teams is changing and the user-centered design is gaining more importance in most companies. If we plan according to this work philosophy, we will have room to learn about our users before getting into the development phase. This will affect the whole development process, and it will be positively reflected in the results.

As decisions are taken with a better understanding of the problem, the solution becomes more effective in solving the user needs, saving costly development hours.

Mental model - understand how your users think

Kenneth Craik talks about mental models in *The Nature of Explanation*, where he introduced the concept in 1943 (`http://uxmag.com/articles/the-secret-to-designing-an-intuitive-user-experience`).

The mental model describes how the user understands a system or how a thing works. Mental models are built upon experiences and interactions that the user has had in the past. It gives the user a personal perspective and a way to understand what is happening at each moment. This personal point of view gives the user an idea about how to interact with the system and how to solve future situations.

In some cases, your future users will not have any previous experience with your system, but even in those cases, the users will have a personal view about how it should work. This understanding emerges from experiences with similar systems, and generates user expectations. Users will feel lost if the system does not act as they expect.

You can close the gap between the user mental model and how the product is designed by explaining how the product works to them before they get lost during their first use. Welcome processes and 'just in time' tips can help the user learn how the product works as they interact with the system, adjusting their mental model as they experience their first steps with your product.

Skeuomorphism has been used in mobile app design for years to reduce the gap between the new devices that were emerging and the previous user experiences. This technique consists of introducing elements of real-life objects in the product user interface, so the user recognizes them even before beginning to use the application (`https://en.wikipedia.org/wiki/Skeuomorph`).

It has its advantages and disadvantages. While it may assist the user in recognizing the operation of certain controls by past learned behaviors, it may also be that these controls are more difficult to handle as they pass from the real world to be represented on a touchscreen. We have to evaluate whether it is worth using this technique, or if we show other controls more adapted to the platform for which we are designing. Also, keep in mind that touchscreens have been around for a long time, so the operation of many controls is already familiar to our future users.

For example, if we are designing a music player app, we can use the levers and buttons that we would find on a real radio. When the users find radio controls, although these controls are displayed on a screen, they already know how to interact with the system. Once the user becomes familiar with the location of the elements and their functions, we can substitute the physical aspect of the elements for others that are more minimalist, obtaining gradual learning.

There is a well-known example of this kind of evolution in Apple's operating system. When Apple launched the release of iOS 7, many of the elements that gave a realistic touch to the user interface were removed, but users already knew how to interact with a mobile after years of experience. Touchscreens were already something common for most users, and therefore not a strange device anymore.

Example of skeuomorphic user interface
(source: https://commons.wikimedia.org/wiki/File:Redstair_GEARcompressor.png)

What is the conceptual model?

Once we understand our user's mental model, we can capture it in a conceptual model. The conceptual model is a representation of the mental model using elements, relationships, and conditions. Our design and final system will be the tangible result of this conceptual model.

When you design a new user interface, you are doing so based on a conceptual model. The closer our conceptual model is to the mental model of the user, the easier it will be for the user to understand the system. As each user has his own mental model, it is not possible to match all the users' needs, but we will use different techniques to understand and create successful experiences for our target users.

For example, a mechanic has a very different mental model about a taxi than the one a passenger has. While a mechanic sees a set of parts that form transport:

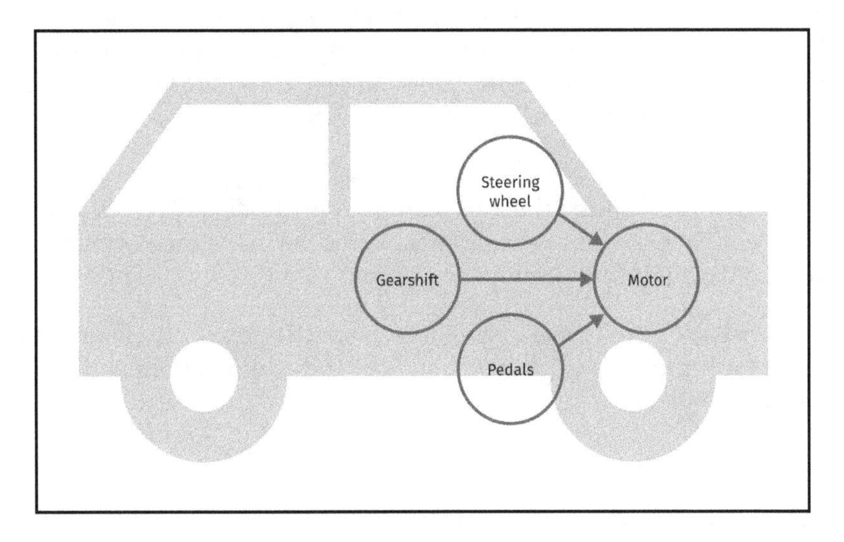

A mechanic sees the car as a set of pieces

A passenger sees it as a service that allows him to move from one place to a destination, paying according to the distance or the time of the displacement:

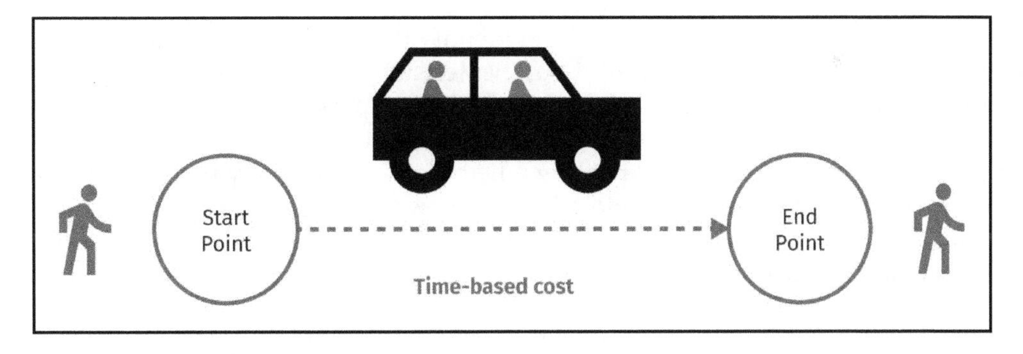

A passenger sees a taxi as a service that transports them from one place to another for a cost based on the time or distance

Researching methods

There are a lot of methods that you can use to gain a deeper understanding of how your users think. In this chapter, we will explain how to apply different methods to understand your user's mental model. Different techniques will give different results; therefore, some methods will be more useful for some objectives than others. Practice with all of them and create your own set of tools.

In this chapter, we will go through the most common methods used by many user experience designers. They are easy to implement and the investment in time will be justified by the quantity of information you will get.

These methods consist of small tasks to give to your participants. Allowing them to use their own terminology will help us understand how they think and how they expect the system to interact with them.

Observation and interviews

One of the simplest and most effective ways to learn about the processes our future users perform is to observe them doing these tasks and let them explain how and why they are doing each of the actions they perform. This can be really interesting and fun if we get the user to feel comfortable with us.

Before starting a research session, you should identify the key questions you need answered. It is very important to think about the decisions that each piece of information will help you make and how it is connected to the overall project goals. Human curiosity is unlimited but resources are not, so you'll have to prioritize the questions you ask, to pick the most useful ones. For example, knowing whether users frequently travel to the same destinations or not can inform many decisions in the way we help users find and suggest destinations. However, knowing the user's favorite hairstyle may not be the most relevant information for a travel app.

Once you know what you need to learn, you can talk with your participants. Observing user activities in their own environment is a big learning experience. To maximize the benefits, act as an apprentice who is trying to understand how your users do their tasks. Ask questions as you observe anything that requires further details, but ensure that the user feels as if they are the expert.

One of the first things we should do is to explain the purpose of our experiment, and ensure that the participants understand that we are not evaluating their ability or whether they are doing the task right or wrong. We simply want to collect information about how they are doing the task in the moment of the experiment, and to find points where technology, or our application, can help make their life easier.

It is important that we try to collect data from people who exercise different roles in the organization. Each position in the organization has different priorities and objectives, and therefore the people who work on each position develop their daily tasks differently. By understanding these differences, we can adapt our solutions to each of the profiles, improving the user experience for all of them.

Before making an interview, and especially if you will record a user, ensure that the user understands the purpose of that recording. Explain that the recording will be used only inside your team. Try to keep only the information you need for the study and ensure that you delete all files when they are no longer needed. Each country has its own laws about personal data protection, so ensure that you meet all the legal requirements of the country you are developing the experiment in.

Affinity Diagram

The Affinity Diagram is a method that helps you organize concepts and data, creating connections between the elements that the user considers related. The term Affinity Diagram was created by Jiro Kawakita in the 1960s (`https://en.wikipedia.org/wiki/Affinity_diagram`).

This diagram is really useful when we have lots of different ideas that can come from a brainstorming session, user interviews, or surveys. At the end of the process, we will have different groups of concepts connected in a manner according to how our participants understand that they are related.

The method steps

The process consists of typing each idea on a sticky note or a piece of paper. All the ideas will be randomly situated on a board or table. This board will be visible by the whole team, so everybody can participate and improve the organization during the following steps.

We will describe a step-by-step guide to create an Affinity Diagram. You can follow these steps or adapt it to your needs. Understanding the general purpose will be enough to create your own version and get good results:

1. **Brainstorming**: The first step is to get the ideas that we will later classify into groups. Let the participants say anything or everything for a particular topic or task; any idea is welcomed at this time. You should provide them with some sticky notes or pieces of paper. Sticky notes will be especially useful in the next steps, and this is the reason why the Affinity Diagram is usually represented with a dashboard full of sticky notes:

   The objective of this method is to know more about how our users think and how they relate ideas into a field, so you should avoid taking part while the participants do this step.
   If participants get stuck or stop working, we can try to guide them, but remember that it is important that they create as many ideas as possible. Any personal contribution we may have can have an impact on the results. So, limit yourself to reminding the participants of the objective of the process and try to set them in motion again.
   This is a fun activity, and usually, the participants start feeling comfortable after a few minutes. As soon as the participants start creating ideas, you will be able to discover many new concepts and thoughts. Feel free to take notes at this stage.

2. **Grouping the ideas**: The next step is to group all the ideas into different categories. The participants will now have time to group the ideas from the preceding step into groups. All participants should take part in this process, moving elements into groups and creating associations:

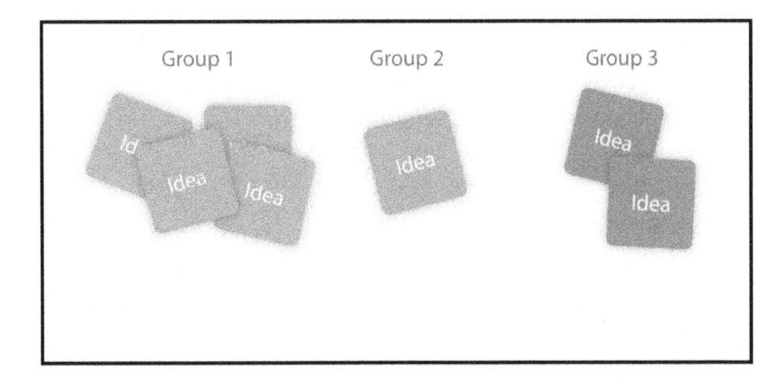

The best results are usually obtained when all the components of the study participate and when these components come from different fields with respect to the project. The experience is much more enriching and thus, more points of view are involved in the research.

If we are creating an online store, we will try to have participants who buy and sell different types of products. Choose participants who access the platform with different devices, and whose frequency of use is also varied, which will improve the spectrum of information.

An idea can go from one group to another if the new group makes a better match for that person. The participants can collaborate and give their reasons for their associations. If one idea is clearly associated with two different groups, we should create a new note so that both the groups will have the complete pack of ideas.

3. **Creating subgroups if necessary**: If we are creating a few groups with lots of ideas in each of them, it can be interesting to create subgroups in some of them. This is an optional step, and it will have sense only for some of the groups:

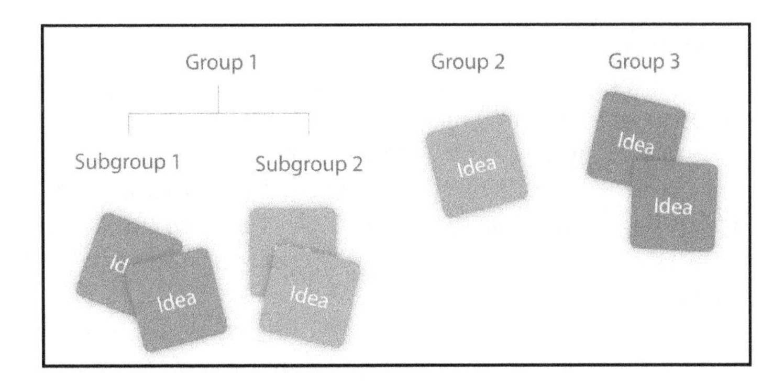

Allow the participants a second round with the objective of dividing the groups into smaller groups. At the end of the activity, one group can have elements inside the main group and other elements inside deeper-level groups.

For example, we can have a group of *electronic devices* with items such as smartphones, smartwatches, tablets, TVs, and a Chromecast. The participants may find it logical to group all the items with a screen into the same group, but may find that the Chromecast has no relation with the other items. Finally, Chromecast can sit with *electronic devices* and the other elements belong in the new *devices with screen* subgroup.

4. **Naming the groups and subgroups**: Once we have the ideas and concepts classified in groups, we will ask the participants to choose one idea that represents all the elements inside the group. If the participants do not find one element that represents the relationship between all the elements, they can create a new one:

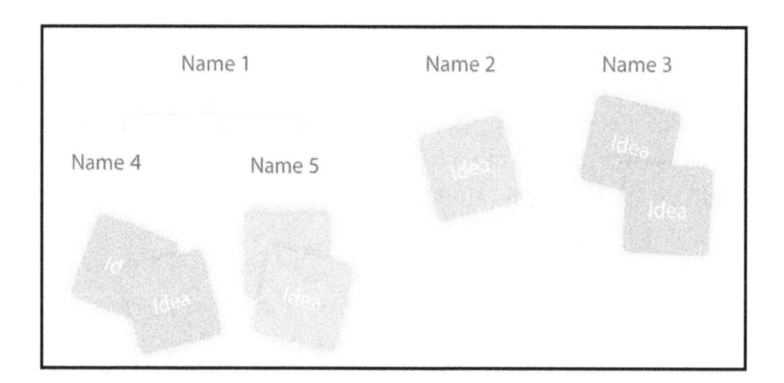

Move the sticky notes chosen as the group label, or the label created for this group, to the top of the groups. The participants can move elements from one group or subgroup to a new one as many times as needed.
With these groups, and a few ideas in each of them, it should be easy to see the relationships between the different groups and their elements. If we find that several groups have a relationship with each other, we can add these new relationships as a higher-level group, giving proper names to the new classifications.
In this kind of method, the objective is that the groups and categories come from the ideas, from inside to outside, trying to avoid the creation of categories based on previous thoughts.

Even if the ideas obtained are not directly applicable to your design solution, learning how your users organize them in their heads will provide valuable insight into how they think:

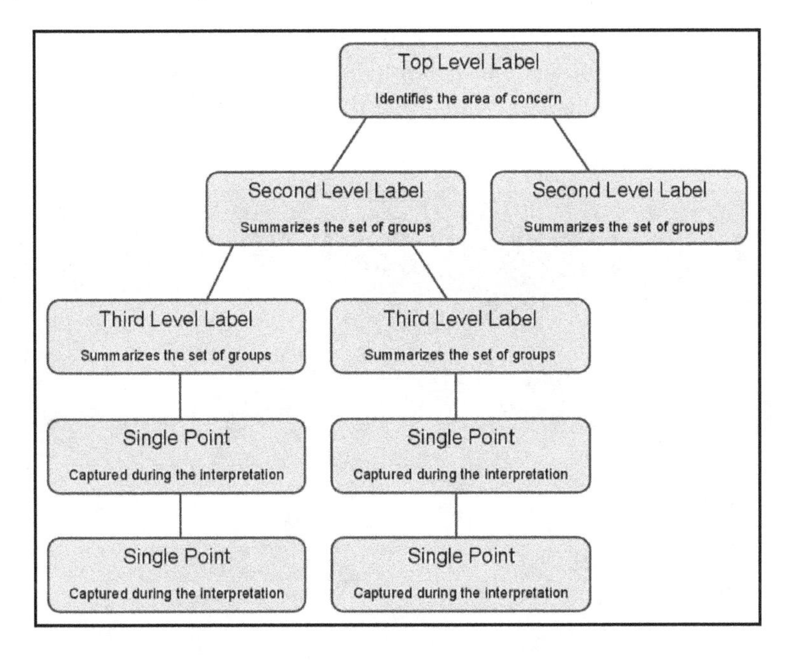

Affinity diagram example (source: https://commons.wikimedia.org/wiki/File%3AAffinity_wall.png)

Card sorting

Similar to the affinity diagram process, the card sorting method tries to find the relationships that the participants find between a set of topics. It will help us improve the findability in our web or app solutions.

We can distinguish three versions of this method: open, closed, and reverse, also known as **Tree Testing**. We will talk about the two first here, and we will look at Tree Testing later in the chapter. Both the open and closed versions consist of participants arranging a set of cards--each representing a different concept--into groups. The main difference between the open and closed versions is that in the open version, the participants name the groups after grouping the cards while in the closed version, the participants have the cards and groups names from the beginning.

This kind of method can be helpful in organizing the content of your application into a small set of sections. Imagine that you are creating a music application, and you want to introduce various functionalities, but you do not know how to group them in a logical way. Using this method, you can have a set of elements to sort, such as these:

Get recommendations, find old groups, publish your own music, see what others are listening to, listen to music in the car playlists, send music through bluetooth, choose audio quality, artists, and *albums* and create groups for the user to arrange them into, such as *discover music, my library, create, listen,* and *settings*.

Image from Wikimedia Commons (source: https://commons.wikimedia.org/wiki/File:Grouped_Post-Its.jpg)

Open card method steps

1. **List all items on cards or sticky notes**: As an organizer, you should write all the ideas, concepts, or products that you want to include in the experiment. A packet of sticky notes or pieces of paper will work perfectly for this.
2. **Organize the cards into groups**: The participants will receive the complete set of cards, and they will be asked to group them based on the relationships they find between the elements.
3. **Name the groups**: The participants are asked to write a name or concept that summarizes the content of the group.

Closed card method steps

1. **Write the items and groups on cards or sticky notes**: Write the items and groups on cards, pieces of paper, or sticky notes. Use a different color for the group names as they will be used to classify the other cards.
2. **Organize the cards into groups**: The participants are asked to organize the elements into groups. Each of the groups will be headed by one of the different color cards, those that correspond to group names.

The participants will classify each of the elements into one of the groups.

Perhaps, a participant can feel that some cards do not belong to any of the groups. These cards can be grouped separately. Identifying new groups will help you to analyze why those cards do not match the user mental model and whether to incorporate new categories, discard or adjust the concepts.

When is it convenient to perform this method?

This kind of method is useful when we have some understanding of the user mental model and that we want to confirm it with user input. We want to clarify our conceptual model in order to get the best findability for our content.

This easy method can be very useful in different phases of our project, although we will need to apply it slightly differently depending on the current stage of the development process. When we start designing the structure of our application we can apply the method with a reduced set of cards, that correspond to the main functionalities with which the first versions of the product will be launched. We can perform this method with 10 or 15 cards and let the participants propose different organizations and groups that fit their mental models. Conversations can lead to interesting insights that you will be able to apply in your design solutions.

If you have different options to organize the sections of your application, you can perform the method several times and evaluate the results as you apply different organization schemes. You can give a set of cards with features and a few groups that match the suggested organizations. You could then propose the organization of your application based on groups of content according to their nature, for instance in an application about recipes. Another way of planning our application navigation is according to the relationship that these contents have with your users, for example in a magazine and newspaper application you could create groups according to the user interests or behavior whilst using the application. You could also think of an application that offers a set of actions the user can perform, for example in a camera application the users could open the app and take some pictures, edit their preferred ones or print some of them on paper. By having several options and letting your participants express their thoughts when they see the proposed organizational options, you can get an idea of which structure works the best, or how you can improve it to better meet the needs of your target user groups.

In more advanced phases of a project or if our application covers a larger set of content, you can have more elements to organize. Although it is better to limit the number of cards to avoid overloading your participants, you can increase the number of cards to 30 or 50, thus obtaining a broader spectrum of conversations and reasoning on which to work to create new ideas that improve your application. You can even apply this method to organize just a section of your application to improve how intuitive your app feels for your users when they are exploring the content of that specific section.

Tree Test

This is also called *reverse card sorting*. This is a method where the participants try to find elements in a given structure. The objective of this method is to discover findability problems and improve the organization and labeling system.

The organization structure used should represent a realistic navigation for the application or web page you are evaluating. If you don't have one by the time the experiment is taking place, try to create a real scenario, as using a fake organization will not lead to really valuable results.

There are some platforms available to perform this type of experiment with a computer. One example is `https://www.optimalworkshop.com`.

This can have several advantages: the experiment can be carried out without requiring a physical displacement by the participant, and you can also study the participant's steps and not just analyze whether the participant succeeded or not. It can be that the participants found the objectives but had to make many attempts to achieve them.

The method steps

1. **Create the structure**: Type or create the navigation structure with all the different levels you want to evaluate.
2. **Create a set of findability tasks**: Think about different items that the participant should find or give a location in the given structure.
3. **Test with participants**: The participant will receive a set of tasks to do. The following are some examples of possible tasks:
    - Find some different products to buy
    - Contact customer support
    - Get shipping rates
4. **The results**: At the end, we should have a success rate for each of the tasks. Tasks such as finding products in a store must be done several times, with products located in different sections. This will help us classify our assortment and show us how to organize the first levels of the structure better.

How to improve the organization

Once we find the main weak points and workarounds we have in our structure, we can create alternative structures to retest and try to find better results. We can repeat this process several times until we get the desired results.

The **Information Architecture** is the science field of organizing and labeling content in a web page to support usability and findability. There's a growing community of Information architecture specialists that supports the Information architecture Institute--`https://en.wikipedia.org/wiki/Information_architecture`.

There are some general lines of work in which we have to invest time in order to improve our Information architecture.

Content organization

The content can be ordered by following different schemes, in the same way that a supermarket orders products according to different criteria. We should try to find the one that best fits our user needs. We can order the content, dividing it into groups according to nature, goals, audience, chronological entry, and so on. Each of these approaches will lead to different results and each will work better with different kinds of users.

In the case of mobile applications, it is common to have certain sections where they mix contents of a different nature, for instance, integrating messages for the user in the contents of the activity view. However, an abuse of these types of techniques can lead to turning the section into a confusing area for the user.

Area naming

There are words that have a completely different meaning for one person to another, especially if those people are thinking in different fields when they use our solution. Understanding our user needs, and how they think and speak, will help us provide clear names for sections and subsections. For example, the word *pool* will represent a different set of products for a person looking for summer products than for a person looking for games.

In the case of applications, we will have to find a balance between simplicity and clarity. If space permits, adding a label along with the icon will clarify and reduce the possible ambiguities that may be encountered in recognizing the meaning of these graphic representations. In the case of mobiles, where space is really small, we can find some universal icons, but we must test with users to ensure that they interpret them properly.

In the following examples, you can find two different approaches. In the Gmail app, attach and send are known icons and can work without a label. We find a very different scenario in the Samsung Clock app, where it would be really difficult to differentiate between the Alarm, the Stopwatch, and the Timer without labels:

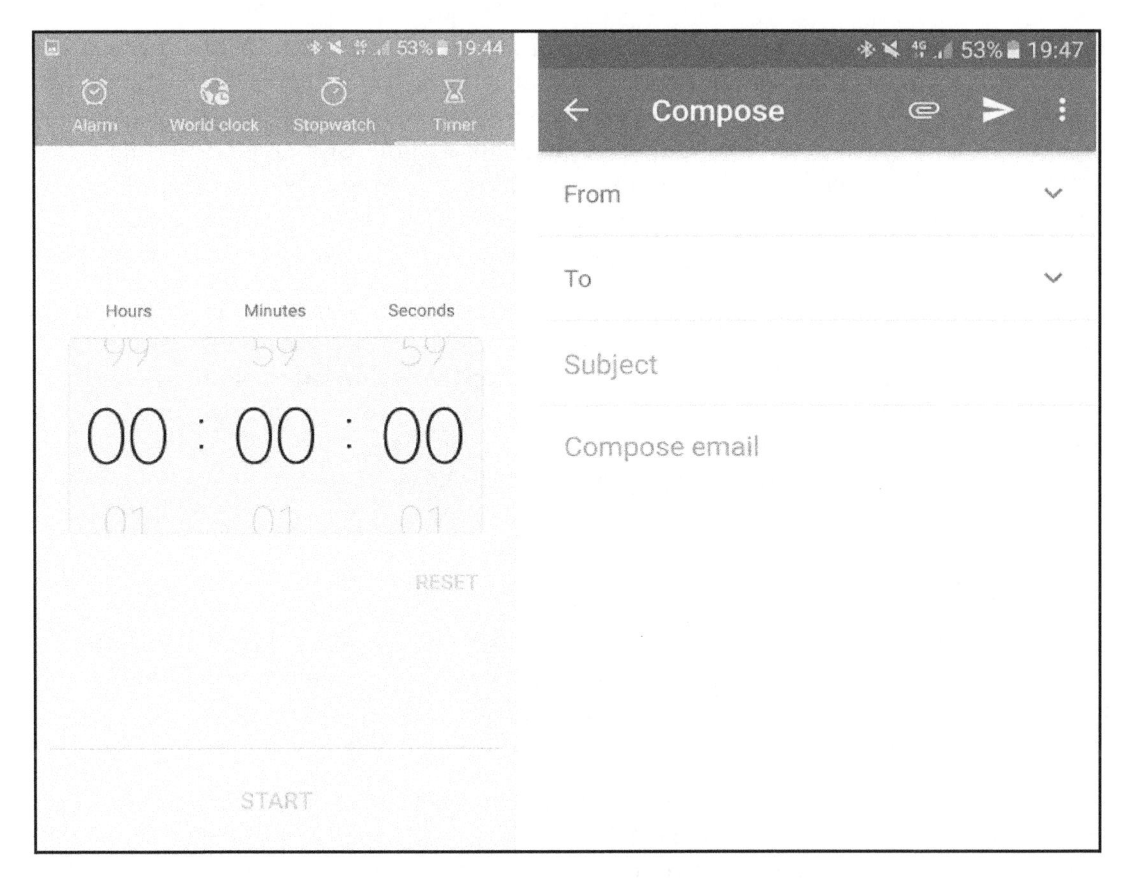

Samsung system and Google Gmail App screenshots (source: Screenshot from Google Gmail App, source: Screenshot from Gmail App)

The working memory limit

The way the information is displayed to the user can drastically change the ease with which it is understood. When we talk about mobiles, where space is very limited, limiting the number of options and providing navigation adapted to small spaces can help our user have a more satisfactory experience.

As you probably know, the human working memory is not limitless, and it is commonly thought to be limited to remembering a maximum of seven elements (`https://en.wikipedia.org/wiki/The_Magical_Number_Seven,_Plus_or_Minus_Two`). Some authors such as Nelson Cowan suggested that the number of elements an adult can remember while performing a task is even lower, and gives the number of reference as four (`https://en.wikipedia.org/wiki/Working_memory`). This means that your users will understand the information you give them better if you block it into groups according to their limitations.

Once we create a new structure, we can evaluate the efficiency of this new structure versus the last version. With small improvements, we will be able to increase user engagement. Another way to learn about how the user understands the organization of our app or web is by testing a competitor's product. This is one of the cheapest ways to create a quick prototype. Evaluate as many versions as you can; in each review, you will find new ideas to organize and show the content of your application or web app better.

Surveys

Surveys allow us to gather information from lots of participants without too much effort. Sometimes, we need information from a big group of people, and interviewing them one by one will not be affordable. Instead of that, surveys can quickly provide answers from lots of participants and analyze the results in bulk.

It is not the purpose of this book to deal in depth with the field of questionnaires since there are books devoted entirely to this subject. Nevertheless, we will give some brushstrokes on the subject since they are commonly used to gather information in both web pages and mobile applications.

Creating proper questions is a key part of the process that will reduce noise and help participants provide useful answers. Some questions will require more effort to analyze, but they will give us answers with a deeper level of detail. Questions with pre-established answers are usually easier to automatize, and we can get results in less time.

What we want to discover?

The first thing to do is to define the objective for which we are making a survey. Working with a clear objective will help the process be focused and will get better results. Plan carefully and determine the information that you really need at that moment.

We should avoid surveys with lots of questions that do not have a clear purpose.

They will produce poor outcomes and result in meaningless exercises for the participants. On the contrary, if we have a general leitmotiv for the questionnaire, it will also help the participants understand how the effort of completing the survey will help the company, and therefore it will give clear value to the time expended.

You can plan your survey by following different approaches and your questions can be focussed on short-term or long-term goals. When you focus your research on **long-term planning**, your purpose is to understand your users expectations and their view about your product in the future; this will help to plan the evolution of your application and create new features that match their needs. For example, imagine that you are designing a music application and you are not sure about focusing on mass majority music or maybe giving more visibility to amateur groups. Creating a long term survey could help you understand what your users need to find in your platform and plan changes that match the conclusions extracted from the survey analysis. When you think of **short-term planning**, the purpose of the questions are more related to operational actions. The objective with these kind of surveys is to gather information for taking actions later with a defined mission. These kind of surveys are useful when we need to choose between two options, that is, whether we are deciding to make a change in our platform or not. For example, it could help to decide which piece of information is most important for the user deciding which group to listen to, so we can decide to make the music genre or other users' ratings more visible. We will take better decisions by understanding which are the main aspects our users will expect to find in our platform, and how they let the users explore the content.

Find the participants

Depending on the goal of the survey, we can use a wider range of participants or reduce their number, filtering by their demographics, experience, or the relationship with our brand or products.

If the goal is to expand our number of users, it may be interesting to expand the search range to participants outside our current set of users. Looking for new niches and interesting features for our potential users can make new users try out our application. If, on the contrary, our objective is to keep our current users loyal, it can be a great source of improvement to consult them about their preferences and their opinions about the things that work properly in our application. This data, along with the data of use and navigation, will let us see areas for improvement, and we will be able to solve problems of navigation and usability.

Determining the questions

We can ask different types of questions; depending on the type, we will get more or less detailed answers. If we choose the right type, we can save analysis effort, or we can reduce the number of participants when we require a deep analysis of each response.

It is common to include questions at the beginning of the questionnaires in order to classify the results. They are usually called filtering or screening questions, and they will allow us to analyze the answers based on data such as age, gender, or technical skills. These questions have the objective of getting to know the person answering the survey.

If we know the person answering the questionnaire, we will be able to determine whether the answers given by this user are useful for our goals or not. We can add questions about the experience the participant has with general technology, or with our app, and about the relation with the brand.

We can create two kinds of questions based on the type of answers the participant can provide; each of them, therefore, will lead to different results.

Open-answer questions

The objective of these types of questions is to know more about the participant without guiding the answers. We will try to ask objectively for a subject without providing possible answers. The participant will answer these type of questions with open-ended answers, so it will be easier to know more about how that participant thinks and which aspects are proving more or less satisfactory.

While the advantage of this kind of questions is that you will gain a lot of insights and new ideas, the con is the cost of managing big amounts of data. So, these types of questions will be more useful when the number of participants is reduced.

Here are some examples of open-answer questions:

- How often have you used our customer service?
- How was your last purchase experience on our platform?

Questions with pre-established answers

These types of questions facilitate the analysis when the number of participants is high. We will create questions with a clear objective and give different options to respond. Participants will be able to choose one of the options in response. The analysis of these types of questions can be automated and therefore is faster, but it will not give us as detailed information as an open question, in which the participant can expose all his ideas about the matter in the question.

The following is an example of a question with pre-established answers:

- **Questions**: How many times have you used our application in the last week?

  Answers:
  1) More than five times
  2) Two to Five
  3) Once
  4) None

Another great advantage is the facility to answer these types of questions when the participant does not have much time or interest to respond. In environments such as mobile phones, typing long answers can be costly and frustrating. With these types of questions, we can offer answers that the user can select with a single click. This can help increase the number of participants completing the form.

It is common to mix both the types of questions. Open-answer questions where the user can respond in more detail can be included as optional questions. The participants willing to share more information can use these fields to introduce more detailed answers. This way, we can make a quicker analysis on the questions with pre-established answers and analyze the questions that require more precise revision later.

Humanize the forms

When we create a form, we must think about the person who will answer it. Almost no one likes to fill in questionnaires, especially if they are long and complex.

To make our participants feel comfortable filling out all the answers on our form, we have to try to treat the process as a human relationship.

- **Make the participant be part of the process**: The first thing we should do is explain the reason of our form. If our participants understand how their answers are going to be used in the project, and how they can help achieve the goal, they will feel more encouraged to answer the questions and take their role seriously. Filling a survey can be a tedious process, but knowing that a team will work with the provided data to create a better project can motivate your participants.
- **Focus on the goal and ask appropriate questions**: Ask only what is strictly necessary for the purpose you have set for it. We must prevent different departments from introducing questions without a common goal. If the form is going to answer concerns of different departments, all of them should have the same goal. This way the form will have more cohesion. We should not go beyond the limits of indiscretion with our questions, or the participant may feel overwhelmed. Especially if the participants of our study are not users of our application or our services, we must treat them as unknown.
- **Use a friendly tone and humanize your vocabulary**: The tone used on the form should be friendly and clear. Being respectful and kind is a key point in getting good participation levels. Avoid the use of complex and technical vocabulary, even your application will be done using programming languages and will be involved in taking complex decisions, your users will have their own language and you should try to match their needs to create a successful experience.

Research documents

We will go over some of the most used documents in the research stage. These documents will make the gathered information accessible and easy to use for the whole team, so all the different people included in the development process will benefit from them. Connecting with your users' needs is easier when you can imagine them as real people, and therefore these documents will try to create a real person in the development team's mind.

Once we have collected all possible information from our users, we will try to classify and represent our users as real people with needs and circumstances. The same application will not be used in the same way by all our users, so we have to try to understand the different contexts that affect the user experience we are designing. We will work with different types of users in our head, trying to make our solution effective for all of them.

Although these documents can work as independent documents, they work better as a whole. We will describe and give some tips about documents--personas, scenarios, and user journeys. Mapping the connection between them is a key point to understanding the motivations and circumstances that make a user interact with our system a little bit deeper.

These are the research documents we will cover in this book. They are some of the most commonly used ones by all kinds of teams:

- **Persona document**: We will create a fictional character for each of the user groups we target, and select or invent a set of motivations, characteristics, and circumstances that match the general characteristics of the group it represents. We will work with this character as a reference for our design tasks, with the aim that our designs meet the needs of the members of the group.
- **Scenario**: In each scenario, we will find a different set of circumstances and motivations that will affect the user experience of our character when using our application. The level of detail may vary according to the needs of the project. You can simply tell why the character uses the application and when, or you can detail each step and interaction of the character with the app, from the beginning until the final task or set of tasks.
- **User Journey**: The User Journey document is mainly focused on the interactions, feelings, and thoughts that the user has while doing a specific task. As in the scenario, the level of detail can be different on each project. While in some stages of product development it could be enough working with the main steps and interactions, we should give information about all the aspects that can modify the user experience in other stages. In this document, we can also study all the possible alternative scenarios that can occur when the task moves away from the most usual scenario.

The Persona Document

Different kinds of people need different kinds of solutions. The Persona Document is a tool used to classify the characteristics of a group of users in an easy-to-handle document. It will give a clear vision about the users for whom you are designing your application. It will work as a summary of the user research phase, allowing the team to work over a closed set of characters, instead of thinking about millions of different users, each with their own needs.

The Personas will be the base characters that we will use in the description of our user scenarios. These characters will have different goals, objectives, and skills and therefore, they will need different design solutions to achieve their purposes while using our application or piece of software.

How should I create a persona document?

Usually, a Persona Document is a one- or two-page long document where we summarize the knowledge we have about a group of people with similar interests, goals, and difficulties. This document is focused on what we know from those users regarding the task we want to solve with our design solution. Personas Documents are also used on the marketing field, as a way to strategize the marketing actions. For our purpose, demographics and status can impact our classification, but we will also need to focus on all the aspects that change the way that a person, or group of people, interact with our system or platform.

Try to find those aspects that really affect the user behavior in your platform and create groups based on these characteristics. For example, if you were drawing up personas for an educational platform, the user experience with computers could be a key skill to interact with the system. Try to group people that have similar goals and difficulties into the same group. For instance, following the same example, for the same platform, we could distinguish between young users, very accustomed to using technology daily and another group of users with more experience in non-technological tools and perhaps of an older age. Each group will be represented by an imaginary person who complies with the general lines of each group. Adapting our solution properly, we can achieve satisfactory results for both the groups and therefore for the common objective.

Better with an example template

The Persona Document can be represented in many ways, being adapted to the needs of each work group and each project. However, they all follow a similar general line. We have created a downloadable template with some very common sections so that it can be modified and adapted to the requirements of each project:

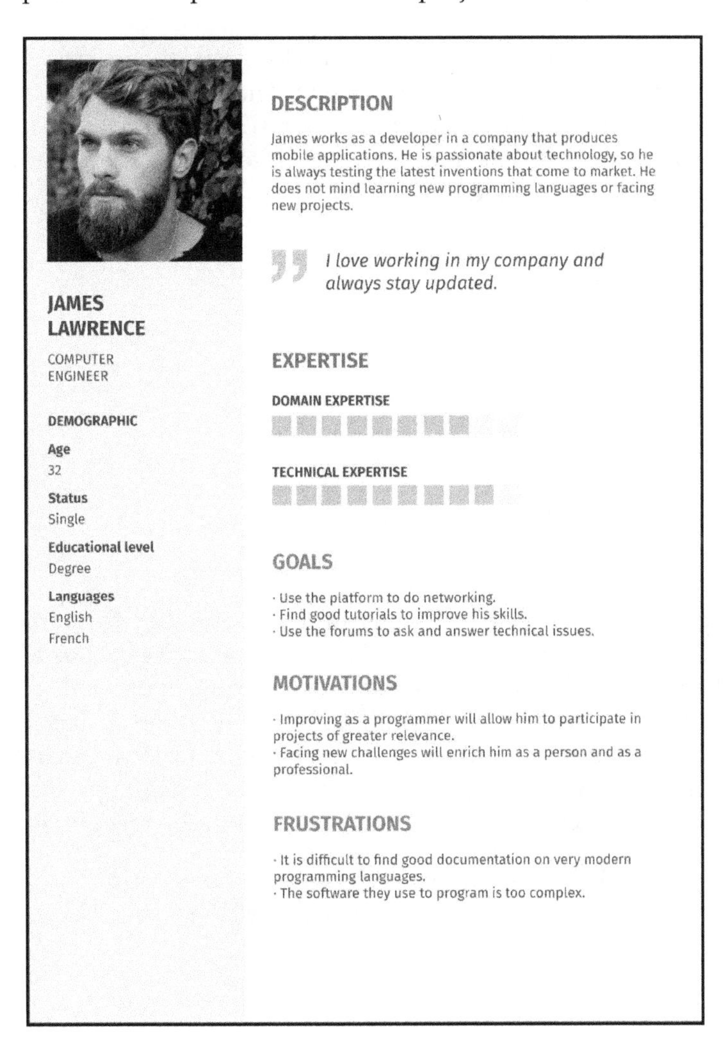

Persona document example.

(Assets from https://pixabay.com/en/man-red-hair-beard-red-beard-1848452/)

You can download this template from the code bundle. Feel free to adapt it to your particular needs; `[Asset_A6462_A02_A01_Persona_Template]`, this is present with the code files that have been provided with the book.

Demographics

In this section, we will give some details about the character, such as age or gender. We want to attach some personality to our persona as it will help the team to interpret better how this person acts and feels when using the design solution. Try to create a character that makes sense with the rest of the data and attributes described in the persona document. For example, a person with high field knowledge must be old enough for the time it takes to become an experienced professional.

Here are some examples of possible demographic values:

- Age
- Gender
- Education level
- Native language

Picture

A picture can help the team to imagine the person represented by the persona document. Although each persona represents a group of users, the objective will be to imagine a real person as it can help the team understand how that person behaves, how that user feels when he achieves his goals, and what frustrations and difficulties he has to overcome while achieving them. We should try to find a picture that matches the values in the document. We don't need to necessarily get a picture from one of our research participants as this is only a way to put a face attached to the data we will find in the rest of the page.

There are several pages where you can get pictures for a cheap price or for free. At the time of writing this book, you can find pictures at Pixabay or Unsplash (`https://pixabay.com/` or `https://unsplash.com/`).

Description

While some people can imagine the users behind a Persona Document without a narrative that describes the fictional person in detail, some people will find it very inspirational. The objective of this description is to create a character in the reader's mind. Try to catch the essence of the information gathered in the rest of the document. In some cases, it can be helpful to find inspiration in real users or film characters, but take into account that the general purpose is to understand the motivations and goals of the group of persons that this document represents.

Adding a quote about the goals or frustrations that these kind of users feel will give reality to the description, but it is not required in most cases.

Domain and technical expertise

The domain expertise corresponds to the knowledge the user has about the system and the process itself. A person who has been working for a company for many years will probably have a deep knowledge about the methods and steps to get a task completed. Technical expertise refers to the skills a person has in a solid field. For example, a person can have lots of experience using the computer or surfing the net.

Each user will have some technical expertise and some background about the domain itself, and both will work together when the user starts using our system. A user with a lot of domain experience will have more ability to recognize specific field vocabulary, and he will try to solve problems by following learned procedures.

The **progressive disclosure** technique allows you to adapt the system to different levels of expertise, giving more complex tools for advanced users. New users will find a reduced number of tools that will be expanded according to the progress in our system.

Goals

Each kind of user will interact with our system trying to develop different kind of actions. If we have a clear vision about the goals of each persona and therefore of each group of users, we will be able to evaluate the effectiveness of our system when used for that specific goal. Our system will work better for some goals than others, and we need to have a clear idea of the users we will support with our solution.

These are some examples of possible goals:

- Get contact information from a colleague
- Generate more leads and traffic for the business

- Get support from the technical service
- Analyze performance numbers and create summaries for stakeholders

Frustrations

Technology has evolved really in the recent years, but users are still learning how to carry out tasks with a computer. Even those who use technology on a daily basis may find certain tasks too complex or tedious. All users have frustrations that affect their daily work. Knowing and understanding their frustrations and how those frustrations impact their progress with the system is a key point to research at this stage. If we understand why the system is not easy to use, or why the user feels that the system should be nicer or quicker, we will be able to redesign or improve how it interacts with them.

Here are some examples of possible frustrations:

- The process is too complex or too long for a simple task
- The language used in the system does not match the field language
- I do not have help or indications when I need them
- The system is always changing

Motivations

Understanding the motivations that lead the user to use our platform will give us tools to create a satisfactory experience for the user. In a process in which diverse people interact, each of them will have a different interest. For example, while a person buying a product in an online store may be motivated by wanting to give a gift to another person, the seller behind the store may be trying to reach the end-of-month sales quota. We will, therefore, be able to offer information about the state of the system in an appropriate way to each one of them.

The following are some examples of possible motivations:

- Increasing the business revenue
- Connecting with teammates and working as a whole
- Doing the job well to get paid
- Making world knowledge accessible for everybody

Scenarios

In terms of UX design, a scenario describes the context where the group of users represented by a Persona Document use the application in order to complete a task. It should be mainly focused on why the user opens the app and which kind of action the user develops. One Persona can use the application in different scenarios for different tasks.

It will be easy for the development team to understand why the users spend their time using the application. It is easier to visualize the frustrations and problems a user can find using an app when you know more about the reasons and circumstances surrounding the user. For example, one user can have a very different experience using a health app when booking an appointment for a routine checkup than when trying to find a doctor for a emergency assistance. In the second case, the user will be stressed and can run into problems with relatively easy tasks, which may not be an effort in a calm situation.

This kind of document allows us to illustrate the problem without jumping to the solution. The scenario will set a context for you to later explore possible solutions for it. Working with a higher-level perspective will give you a clearer view about the problem, and will let the team evaluate different possibilities to solve the user needs.

A scenario can represent a use case from a very superficial point of view, or it can analyze the user interaction in detail. When this scenario is very detailed, it can overlap information with the user journey. The main difference is the kind of information you try to transmit with each of them. The scenario document is more focused on the set of circumstances that lead the user to perform the actions, while the user journey focuses on the different steps and the feelings the user has on each interaction with the system.

Here are some possible scenarios:

- John is a 30-year-old guy who habitually buys on the internet, so he is familiar with pages such as Amazon or eBay. His motivation is to find a great product with a good price. The delivery time is not first in his preferences list, but the sooner the better. John always buys from his mobile, and before buying any product, he often finds reviews on YouTube.
- Margaret has never bought through the internet, but she knows that prices are better on some internet sites. She wants to find a good deal, but she only knows how to find things on the internet using Google. If she finds too many options, she will not be able to decide between all of them, so she prefers something easy and clear. She always uses a laptop to access the internet, and usually, she uses the internet at work while doing other things and without paying a lot of attention.

When you have a complete set of scenarios, the design team will be able to create a solution keeping in mind all that the different users need. One by one, all the specific needs can be checked in the system, and the team will be able to take confident decisions.

Usually, the scenarios are connected with Personas Documents, so it is easier to understand all the circumstances that are involved in the process. With the pair of Persona and Scenario, it is easier to imagine how that person will interact with the system, and the team will be able to find the limitations and difficulties that the user will encounter. Also, the team will be able to determinate the external elements that can impact the whole process and anticipate the possible solutions.

User journeys

A user journey shows how the user completes a particular task. We will describe all the steps the user takes inside and outside of our platform, and we will also add the thoughts and feelings that the user has at each moment:

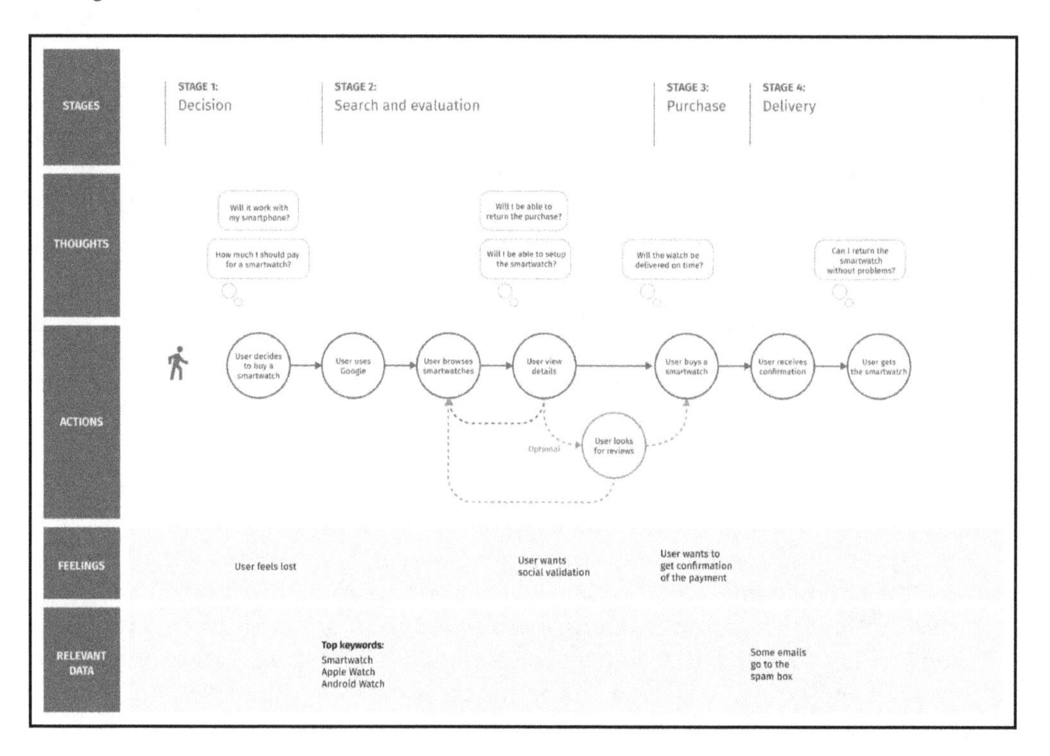

User journey example

A user journey can be created using different techniques, and each of them can work better for some projects than others. While some designers prefer to create storyboards, others may use narratives, but any other method may be useful if it creates a clear picture about the process the user takes to accomplish the task at hand.

For example, some users can be willing to buy on Amazon because their shoes are worn away. This user will open Amazon in order to find some nice shoes, and he will try to find them at the best price. As this user wants to buy a great product, reading good comments will give the user confidence about the purchase; he will review all the available information for each of the shoes the system offers and finally, if everything goes well, he will decide to buy a pair of shoes. This person will use a credit card to pay for the product and will review his email to find all the information about the purchase.

Create a User Journey

To create a user journey, we should follow these steps:

1. **Define the main steps**: Find the steps that represent the normal course of events without too many details and focus on the key points that the user is required to accomplish for the task until he completes it.
2. **Complete the steps**: Add the intermediate steps that describe the accomplishment of the task in detail, and consider adding new lines of temporary development in case of an action that must be done several times or if there are steps where the user has to make decisions.
3. **Add the feelings and thoughts**: Now, add the thoughts and feelings that our user can have when performing the different actions. For example, in times of uncertainty, if we understand what the user is thinking, it will be easier to provide useful information.
4. **Add secondary data**: Now, add any notes that you think can help you understand the process in depth. In this section, you can add technical notes that help you understand the accomplishment of the task from a more technical point of view.

Competitors' analysis

Whether our purpose is to create a new application or improve an existing one, making use of competitor applications in the research phase will provide us with a valuable and inexpensive research tool.

Performing user testing on competing applications is one of the most inexpensive ways to have a functional prototype. Without investing hours in development, we can draw a lot of information that will help us develop our product.

Functionality analysis

If our application will compete in a field where there are already many applications performing a similar task, analyzing the functionality of our competition will help us focus on differential factors.

This study of functionality can be done with different levels of detail. In the first instance, we may find it interesting to know what functionality is already being developed by our competitors. We can focus on the functionality that our competition is not developing and we consider interesting. Thus, we will get a unique product with a clear differential factor.

On a deeper level, we can analyze the flows that follow to perform certain types of tasks so that we can produce more effective and simple tools for our users.

Vocabulary analysis

The same action or process can be called a different thing, depending on the field we are working in. If we adapt our vocabulary to future users of the application, their learning will be faster and therefore they will feel that they have control of the situation earlier, allowing the actions to be developed.

To realize a complete analysis of the vocabulary usually used within a specific field, we can first list the tasks that our users can perform with our application. Once we have the detailed tasks, we will do a step-by-step analysis of the vocabulary that is used in the descriptions, buttons, and messages, and we can place all of them in a grid.

After analyzing as many applications as we can, we can find some words that are repeated more than others and therefore will be more familiar to the users of our application.

Modern testing techniques can allow us to test different labels and terms for the same button or label with our users. With the results, we can choose the ones that show better conversion rates based on the goals we set for the study.

Target users, supported users, and non-supported users

With all the documents created, we can make a further analysis of the users we support and those who will be out of our platform solution.

When you are creating a solution, it is very difficult to satisfy all the potential user needs, so it may be necessary to know who you are working for. You can classify the users into three groups, and those will determine the importance of focusing on their needs when creating the design:

- **Target users**: This is the main group for us. All included personas that are in this group should find their needs covered if possible. We will study the scenarios that affect this group of people and will try to ensure that all the required tasks can be completed with our design solution.
- **Supported users**: In this group, we will have the users who, even if they are not the main objective of our platform, should be taken into consideration when designing the project. If we have the possibility to match some of their needs without affecting the needs of the target group, we will try to cover these tasks in the best possible way.
- **Non-supported users**: Everybody else will be in this group. As mentioned earlier, and especially for complex tasks, sometimes it is not possible to solve the needs of every kind of user. So, we need to make the team understand that some users will not be taken into account when designing our solution and therefore some great ideas will not be considered correct for a complete project:

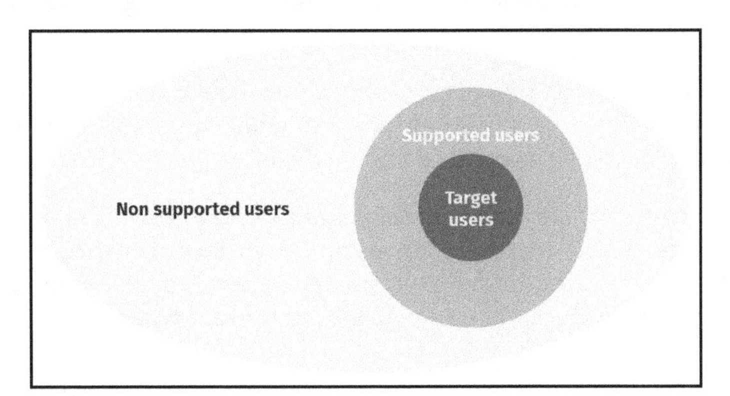

Being pragmatic

Performing research tasks may be unworkable at first because of the lack of resources or budget. However, some of the proposed processes can be carried out without investing a large amount of resources.

Without knowing the problem well, it is very difficult to provide an adequate solution. If it is not possible to perform a detailed study of the tasks for which we will provide solutions, try to analyze the behavior of a small group of users. A fieldwork vision is always fruitful and helps us understand the way the user thinks, avoiding solutions that, while they may be effective, are not suitable for the specific environment of your users.

A competition study will be very useful for all departments besides the design department. It will give us an interesting insight into the effectiveness of certain types of solutions and helps us place ourselves in the market with an interesting and competitive product.

Recruiting participants

When it comes to deciding the number of participants for our experiments, we will have to take several factors into account. We have to create manageable groups that produce valuable results and, at the same time, we also need to keep in mind that the budget will be limited.

Keep in mind that design is an iterative process. If you have a budget to recruit 15 users, it may be better to organize three rounds of 5 participants where you can adjust each round based on what you learned in the previous one rather than having a single round with all users.

If possible, you should contract the services of professionals for the recruiting process. They are experts, and they will save you a lot of time that you can spend elsewhere, creating the assets you will use to develop the method and analyze the results.

The goal will be to cover the maximum possible range of users within our target group. We should try to reach users who represent large groups within our platform. In order to do this, we can try to take into account demographic data, levels of experience, technical capabilities, and all those aspects that we consider important when interacting with our platform.

Avoiding biases

When talking to your users, you need to be neutral. You need to avoid leading questions in order to get reliable information. If you ask "*Do you think the text is too big?*", you would influence the user answer toward the negative aspects of the product.

Users also come with their own biases. You may find users who have a tendency to agree or be nice, and may not be comfortable with sharing negative feedback. You should ensure that the users are comfortable and relaxed.

Users are not good at predicting their future behavior. You should not ask for their opinion on a feature; making questions about past activities helps get the answers connected to the existing behavior. For example, instead of asking how often they would travel if your app was available, you can ask how often they traveled last year or how many times they considered doing so but didn't.

Looking for the signs

Users are often not able to tell you the full story. They may take some aspects for granted. Don't be afraid of asking obvious questions. People like to talk about what they do, and you may discover that some of your assumptions were not exactly as you expected.

In many activities, there may also be a gap

It is also important to look for clues in the environment. For example, a user making use of a post-it to keep some information may indicate the lack of a more convenient way to move information around. Users may not even notice the problem if they have found a workaround, but fixing it with your better solution will make the experience much more fluent.

Summary

In this chapter, we talked about the need for carrying a good study of the mental model of your users in order to create effective solutions, that is, how discovering patterns and conventions helps the designer take better decisions later when exploring the possible design solutions.

We also presented some useful research methods and documents to present your findings. The whole team will benefit from this information, making it easier to create a user-friendly application.

In the next chapter, we will talk about sketching, a technique that will allow us to explore possible solutions and present ideas quickly and efficiently.

3
Exploring Ideas - Sketching

"Design is practical imagination: Imagining possibilities and making them real."

--Matias Duarte

Design problems rarely have only one solution. Basic human needs, such as sitting comfortably, have been approached in many different ways throughout history. These diverse solutions include different kinds of products such as couches and chairs, and they also include many variations of each of those products.

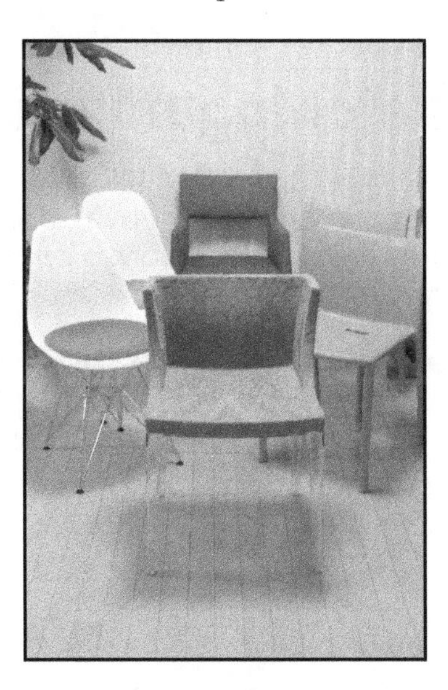

The diversity in the design of a chair illustrates that there is more than one solution to our problem of sitting comfortably (source: https://www.flickr.com/photos/bygenejackson/3112404581/)

Designing great user experiences requires you to explore a wide set of possibilities. From the general idea of your app to the smallest details of each screen, each problem can be solved in many different ways. Approaching each design decision with an open mind helps you to find more innovative solutions that may be ignored otherwise. Your first intuition is not necessarily the best. Even if you already have an initial idea in mind--or someone else suggests one to you--it is essential to avoid rushing into a predefined direction without considering other alternatives first.

All possible solutions for a problem define the **design space**. As a designer, you will be navigating this space to look for the best solutions for your users. In order to achieve an effective exploration, you want your process to be as follows:

- **Fast**: To explore as many options as possible and avoid spending too much time on solutions that won't work
- **Organized**: To avoid blind spots that prevent you from discovering great, but less obvious solutions

Sketching is a common tool used to support design explorations. In this chapter, you'll learn how sketching can help you to explore possible solutions in a quick but organized way. You'll see how to communicate and discuss the ideas you explore in order to improve them.

Adopting the sketching mindset

Sketching is a common technique used to visualize your ideas and help you think about them. It forces you to transform the abstract idea present in your mind into a more concrete and tangible form that captures its essence. This process helps you to consider how your solution may be used by your target users and whether it fulfills the different design goals.

Pen and paper are the most commonly used tools for sketching. The simplicity of these tools is ideal to focus on capturing your ideas and iterating them quickly. They also represent a very low entry barrier to the sketching process. You can sketch anywhere, alone or with other people.

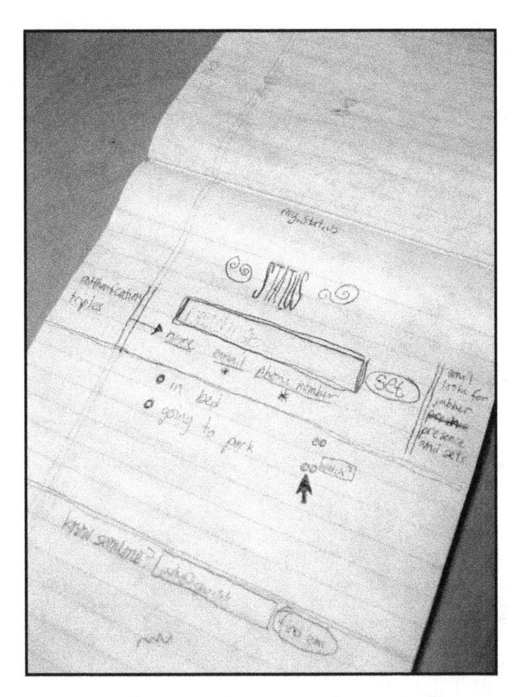

Sketch by Jack Dorsey capturing his initial ideas for a micro-blogging service named stat.us, which later became Twitter (source: https://www.flickr.com/photos/jackdorsey/182613360/)

Sketching takes advantage of our visual processing capabilities and uses paper as an extension of our limited working memory. However, despite visual skills being a common way of expression for kids, not all adults are comfortable using them. In addition, making the most of sketching requires practice.

Sketching helps you in different ways to find great design solutions:

- **Think more about your solutions**: Sketching helps you find better ideas that you have not considered before and also helps you to analyze what makes one solution better than the others.
- **Experiment**: The low investment required for sketching encourages experimentation. You can consider risky ideas with very little time investment.
- **Communicate**: Sketches represent potential approaches that you can discuss with others to get their valuable feedback. This is also helpful as historical documentation, capturing discarded paths you may want to reconsider in the future or useful to explain expected drawbacks when someone proposes similar ideas.

The sketching process is iterative. It combines cycles of **idea generation** with cycles of **idea synthesis**. When generating ideas, you will focus on quantity, exploring as many ideas as possible. When synthesizing ideas, you'll focus on quality, evaluating the ideas to identify the most promising ones. You will discard many ideas, and select a few promising ones to iterate on next, thus starting the process again.

Sketching basics

A sketch captures the essential aspects of an idea visually. When you sketch, you should not aim for precision, completeness, or beauty. Your main focus should be on simplicity and clarity. You should express the central aspects of how your idea works in the clearest way.

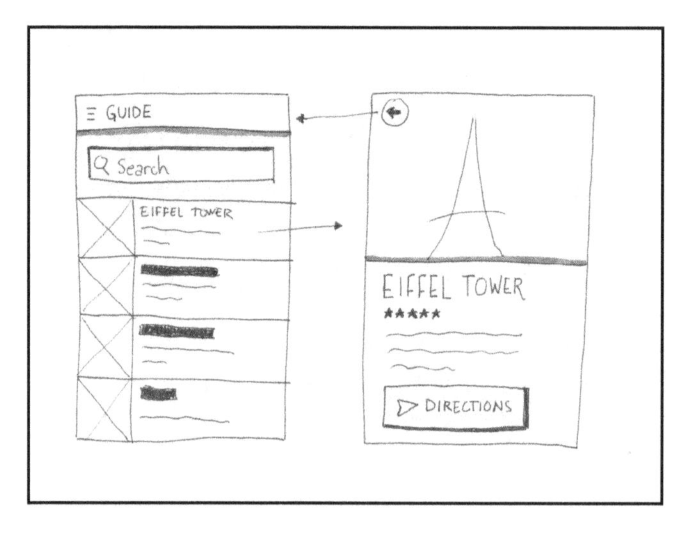

A sketch illustrating the navigation between a list and a detail view

Sketching is different from drawing or painting. You only need a very small set of basic elements to communicate your ideas effectively:

- **Simple shapes**: Lines, squares, circles, and triangles are enough to communicate most ideas. Combining these simple shapes, you can recreate most user interface components well enough to be recognizable.
- **Text**: Headings, labels, or paragraphs help to exemplify the content users will find. Adjusting the style of the text--text size, color, use of bold face or underline--will help to communicate the purpose of such text.
- **Annotations**: Arrows and text notes can help to describe possible interactions, transitions, or relevant details that need further clarification.

- **Shadows**: The use of shadows or filling lines can help to clarify the spatial relations of some components. Buttons are often presented as raised, whereas input boxes are presented as embossed. Shadows are only optional elements to be used if they add clarity and take little time.

With these basic ingredients, you can pick your favorite mobile app and capture an essential part of it. This can be a good practice to improve your sketching skills. Describing solutions that do not exist yet presents some other challenges that we will address later in this chapter.

Sketching tools

A black pen--or marker--and paper is all you need to start sketching. Pencils can be used too; however, since they can be erased, it may be tempting to waste time correcting non-essential details. That will only slow you down.

Sketching tools fit in a small case: a ruler, blue pencil, black pen, black marker, and gray marker is more than what you need for most sketches

Making your sketches in black and white is enough. Blue and red pens for different text colors or highlighted elements can be helpful too. Similarly, a pencil or a gray marker can be useful for adding shadows or deemphasizing some elements.

You don't need to make perfectly straight lines. Making lines with a controlled and fluid motion is enough to contribute to the clarity of the sketch, but it is totally fine for lines to look hand-made. In the case you really need some guides, you can use a ruler or a business card.

You can sketch on any writing surface. Different formats can be useful, depending on the context:

- A notebook helps to keep all sketches together, which is convenient to move them around and find them later. Plain paper pages allow you to focus on the sketch, but you can also consider using a notebook with squared or ruled pages for extra guidance.
- Using separate sheets of paper provides you flexibility on the surface to use. You can fold the paper, cut it, and rearrange multiple pieces.
- Sketching on post-its note helps keep sketches in smaller spaces and makes it easy to cluster them.
- Sketching on whiteboards is useful when discussing ideas with others who may want to contribute to the sketch. In these cases, remember to take pictures of the whiteboard if you don't want some of the good ideas to get lost.

Sketching happens mostly on paper, but there are also digital tools that can help with the sketching process. When you need to share or organize your sketches digitally, you can still start the process on paper and scan or take a picture of the results.

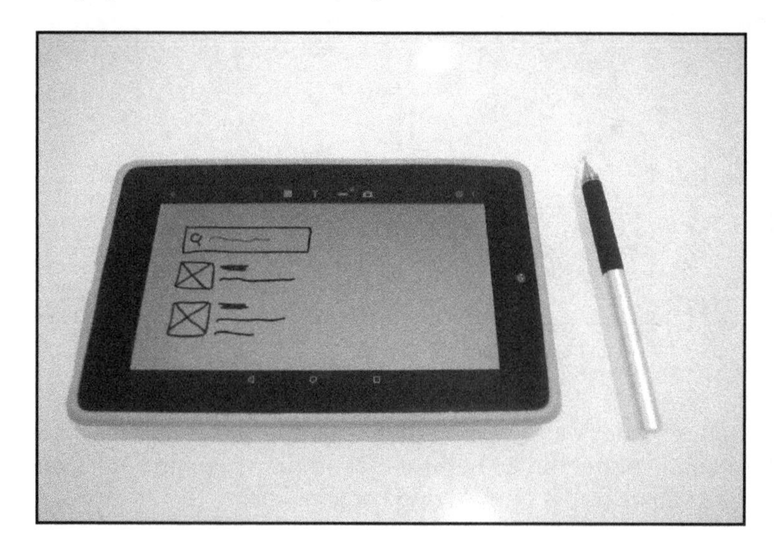

A tablet with a stylus can also be a digital alternative to sketching on paper; many drawing apps available can be re-purposed for sketching

It is also possible to directly sketch using digital tools. Graphic tablets or digital tablets allow for stylus input that simulates the interaction with paper. There are many different apps available for painting or drawing that can support the sketching process.

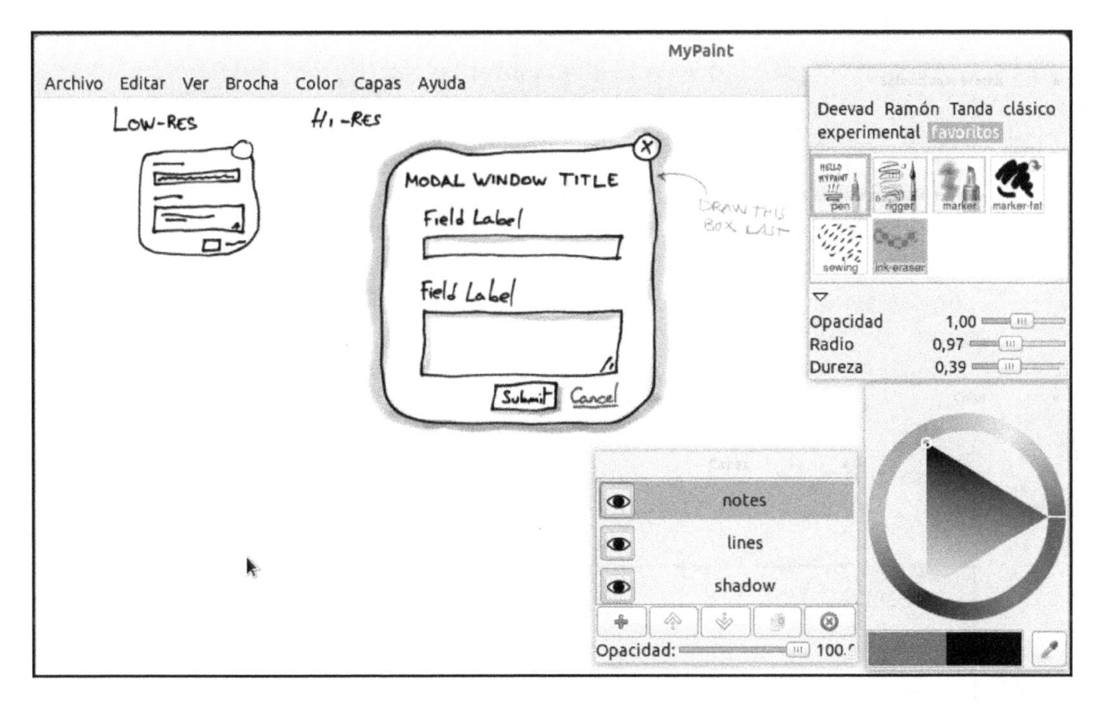

MyPaint screenshot (source: Screenshot from MyPaint)

Digital tools can provide the unique advantages of a digital medium such as having infinite art-boards or the possibility of real-time sharing with remote collaborators. It is also possible to use digital tools to sketch on top of existing solutions using a screenshot of your current product as a background in order to communicate variations on them. However, all these additional capabilities present the risk of providing too many options and causing distraction or encouraging you to get lost in the details.

Producing results fast

When sketching, you will want to move quickly through the design space. Avoid getting lost in the details; adding limits to your time can help you to keep a fast exploration pace.

Adjusting your focus

While sketching, you should skip anything that is not essential to move faster. Focus on the main elements of your idea or those elements that add relevant context to provide clarity.

Identify the problem you need to solve with exploration clearly; this will help you to avoid getting lost in the details that are irrelevant or that you can address later. Before you start the exploration, it is better to write the following:

- You can write the problem statement. Phrasing your problem as an open question is helpful to encourage multiple answers. For example, you can define your problem as "in which way might we quickly select a vacation destination?".
- You can also write the parts of the user scenarios that are relevant to provide context to the problem. If you already have a scenario describing a user buying some shoes, you don't need to spend time thinking about a product to illustrate your sketch; just use that scenario.
- Write down the design goals you expect your solutions to achieve. Defining general properties for your solution, such as being "quick to operate", can act like a checklist to later compare competing solutions.

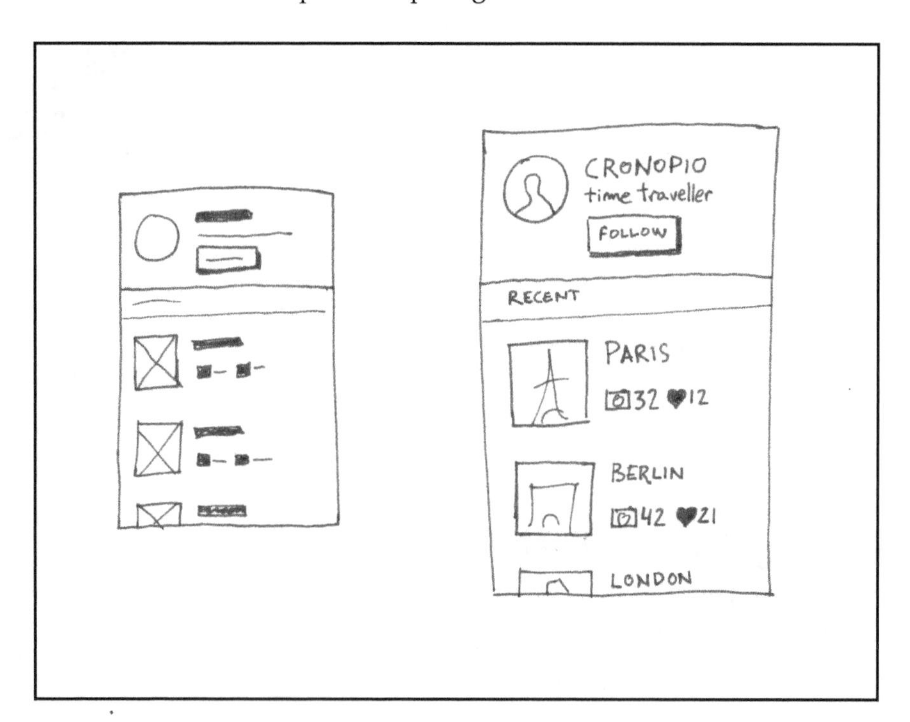

Two sketches of the same idea at two different levels of detail. There is no correct level of detail. It depends on which aspects you are exploring

Even for the aspects you want to include in your sketch, you need to decide how much detail they need. Different aspects of your sketch can be represented with different levels of detail. For example, you can write realistic text copy or use a few parallel lines to quickly represent a paragraph instead. You need to consider the right fidelity level for these elements based on how relevant they are to understand the idea.

Decisions can slow you down. When you are in doubt about two possible solutions, it may be better to just go ahead and sketch both of them instead of spending time deciding which one to choose.

Timeboxing with the Crazy Eights technique

You can limit the time of your exploration with the Crazy Eights technique. This will help you to keep moving fast in short iterations.

First, you start by selecting one problem and stating the design goals. The problem can be more general, such as defining the steps of a checkout process, or more specific, such as the details of the mechanism to pick the delivery date in the checkout form. Regardless of the abstraction level, it will be one single problem to focus on. Once the problem is defined, you can start the exploration.

Fold a piece of paper in eight parts and try to solve your issue in at least eight different ways. Set a timer to just five minutes; it is okay to add a few extra minutes when you are doing the exercise for the first time. The time limit forces you to keep moving forward without getting lost in the details, sketching one solution after another until the time is over.

Part of a Crazy Eights exploration; the sketches have very low fidelity since there is no time to add details

Finally, you evaluate the solutions against the design goals. You want to identify the aspects that seem to work well, those that don't, and other areas that you would like to detail further. Based on this, you'll select the most promising solutions to iterate them further in another round of the exercise.

The Crazy Eights technique is aimed at teams, but it is also useful when applied individually. When doing it with more people —normally organized in groups no larger than 10 people to keep the session under 1 hour—you get a higher number of ideas, and you will receive feedback from other people. Even if you sketch on your own, getting external feedback is always very useful.

Organizing your exploration

Ideas may occur at any time--a brilliant idea may surprise you while in the shower, during a walk in the forest, or while sleeping. However, your sketching process should not rely on good ideas to randomly appear; you should look for them.

As you organize your exploration better, you will not only get more ideas to explore but also cover the space of possibilities better, reducing the chances of missing interesting ideas.

Design exploration sessions are not like brainstorming exercises. While brainstorming usually involves many people speaking their ideas out loud as they come to mind, a design exploration normally involves participants exploring many possibilities silently in an organized way, for them to be shared with others later.

Decomposing your problem

When sketching different ideas, it is useful to pick one specific scenario at a time. In this way, you can focus your exploration on one particular context in detail, before moving to the next. If you are focusing on the *business trip* scenario, you can ignore *how to handle sports equipment* until you move to the *family skiing trip* scenario.

You can move through as many scenarios and personas as you want in your exploration, but going through them one at a time avoids unnecessary distractions.

Even when focusing on a specific scenario, there are many more aspects that you can explore. Often, it is convenient to identify those aspects in advance and then focus on one at a time.

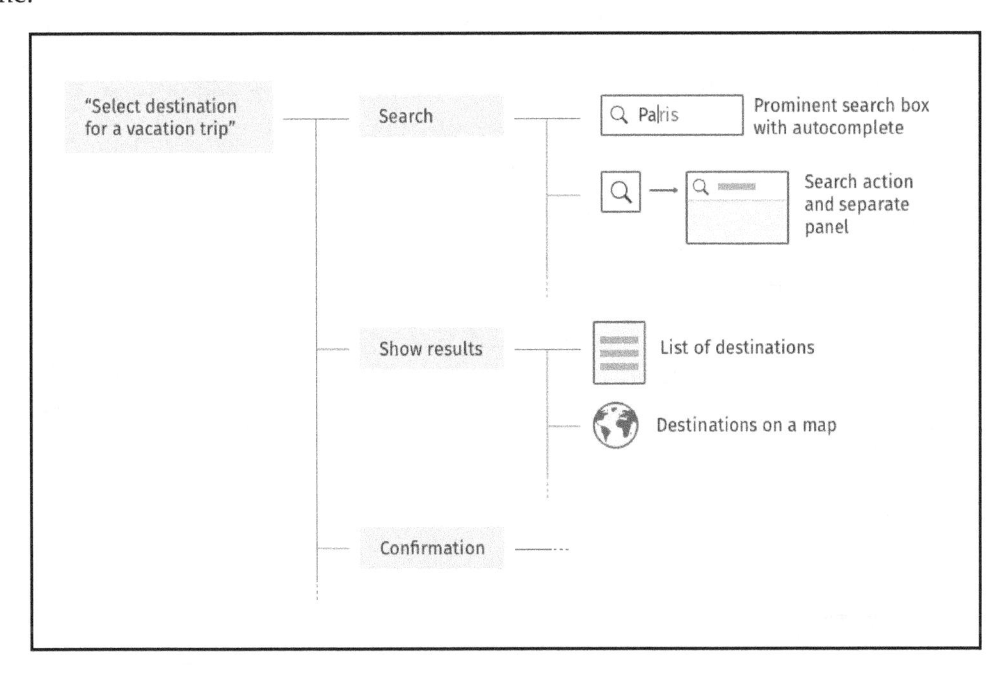

A problem decomposed in several steps with the exploration of different ideas on how to support those steps. How to prominently support the search function and how to display the results or communicate the successful selection are some aspects among many more that you can explore one at a time

This decomposition can be based on different criteria.

You can decompose your problem horizontally, based on the sequence of steps--in terms of acting or thinking--which the user goes through. For example, the "**Selecting a destination for a vacation trip**" scenario requires the user to search for a destination, view possible results, and get some feedback about the selection among other steps. For each of these aspects, you can explore different possible solutions.

You can decompose your problem vertically, in terms of the different layers present across all steps. You can focus on the layout, the wording, the visual style, or the order in which the different steps can be combined--each of these may deserve its own exploration.

There are many ways to divide your design space to organize the exploration. Depending on your resources, you can decide how many aspects to explore; however, identifying these possible directions in advance will help your navigation to be less erratic. Once you have explored multiple ideas, you need to explore the ways in which you can combine the most promising ones into a single solution.

Identifying conflicts

Constraints may be perceived as something negative, but they are helpful to encourage creative solutions. Without them, it is hard to know what you are looking for. Imagine that you are designing a chair, but you don't know whether the chair will be used for working in an office or eating on an outdoor terrace. You need this information and the associated constraints to conclude your design decisions about whether it is important for the chair to be stackable and water resistant or not.

As you sketch possible solutions, you may encounter conflicting aspects. For example, while designing an app to create a video summary of your vacations, you may identify *user control* and *automation* as a conflict.

Making these conflicts explicit may help you with the exploration. You can think of these conflicts as a spectrum with multiple possibilities that go from a fully automated solution to a fully controlled one. From those, you can explore many intermediate steps and pick the right balance for your context--not necessarily in the middle of the spectrum.

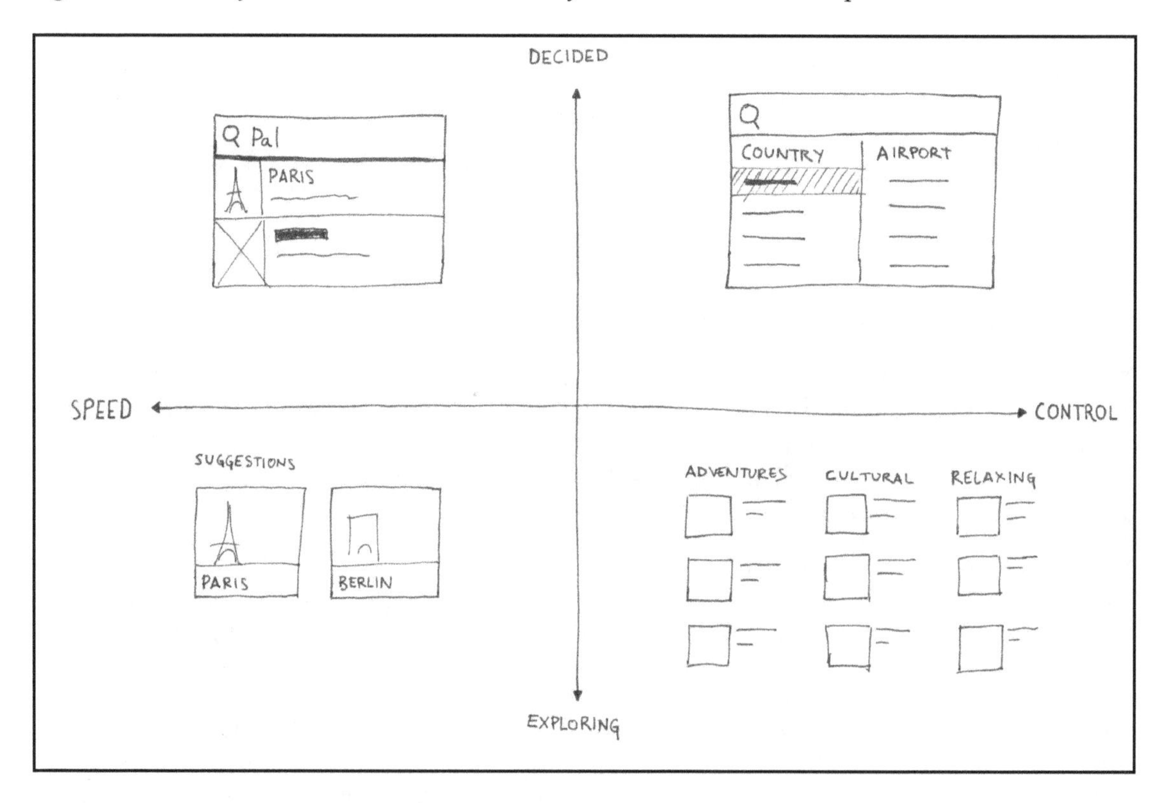

Two exploration axes defined by two conflicting pairs of aspects. You can explore intermediate solutions along one axis or explore them in combination with more

You can visualize those exploration axes. This is very useful to identify gaps that force you to explore less obvious areas of the design space.

When creating an app to make a trip reservation, users can find their destinations in different ways; some of these represent conflicting aspects. For example, the following are two possible axes of exploration in this case:

- **Speed versus control**: Finding a destination can be a process led by the system--happening as automatically as possible--or led by the user, with many options to adjust
- **Decided versus exploring**: Users may have already decided their destination--they just have to select it--or they may be still considering possible destinations

Each axis of exploration represents a gradient of options where not only opposing solutions exist but many more in-between solutions are possible. When multiple axes are defined, it is interesting to think how those axes can intersect. This will encourage you to explore non-obvious combinations.

Communicating your ideas

When ideas are discussed in the abstract, it is very possible for different people to interpret them differently enough to create misunderstandings. By capturing ideas in a more specific way--using sketches, for example--we can help to avoid misunderstandings. Sketches are very useful to communicate ideas, but they are not going to do it by themselves.

Capturing a good design solution in a sketch and sharing it is not enough; you need to communicate fully. The best solution for a problem is useless if it never gets built, and you'll need to convince many people along the way:

- Other designers with feedback on how to improve your design
- People building the product, thinking how to turn the idea into reality
- Decision-makers such as your client or your manager, considering whether the solution will fit in their budget
- Users sharing their opinions on what works for them

A big part of the designer's job is to explain the merits of a proposed solution. You need to take responsibility for this part of the job and make sure that you communicate your design solutions clearly, having productive discussions that lead to better solutions.

You'll be discussing your designs throughout the whole design process. This section focuses on some guidance that can help you with early discussions during the exploration stage, where your ideas are more fragile and have a greater risk of being discarded too early.

Creating storyboards

When a sketch is presented in isolation, it may be hard to understand how it fits into the broader story. Storyboarding is a useful technique to do so.

This storyboard shows a user interacting with a car sharing app. It illustrates the problem of recognizing the car in a street and a possible--although noisy--solution

Storyboards have been used in the cinema industry for a long time. The basic idea is to present a sequence of images to explain the basics of a story. You can combine several sketches to illustrate your scenario in a similar way as comics do.

The sketches included may not only illustrate the product you are designing but also include representations of the context. For example, illustrate the moment a taxi arrives after the user requests it using your app.

Organizing critique sessions

Sharing ideas early provides valuable input for the exploration process. You can organize a **critique session** to share your solutions with other people in your team in order to get feedback. However, you cannot just throw a number of sketches at them and then expect to get valuable feedback in return. For any group larger than four people, you'll need to make an effort to stop the conversations going off-track.

When presenting a sketch, the attention of the audience often goes toward the most superficial aspects. It is easy for them to focus on what they immediately see, without considering deeper implications. This results in nonproductive conversations about very minor details, such as the placement of specific buttons, or other unexpected tangent topics.

In order to have a more productive exchange, you need to guide the conversation onto the right path. Ensure that you start by providing the necessary context to the audience:

- **Introduce the persona you are designing for**: Explain why you want to focus on a particular kind of user as opposed to others
- **Describe the scenario you aim to solve**: Highlight any problematic areas that may need to be addressed
- **Identify the design goals**: State what you want to achieve with the solution

Ensure that you check whether there is an agreement on the initial context by asking the audience. In this way, you can identify earlier if anyone in the audience has different expectations--such as considering that a different problem has more importance.

Sketches shown in the preceding image capture different ideas from the participants of a workshop we organized on the IxDA Interaction conference. We arranged the ideas around different areas first, to keep the discussion focused.

Before presenting solutions, communicate the specific kind of feedback you are interested in. For example, indicate whether you want people to focus on the general idea, the information clarity, the process fluidity, or another specific aspect.

At this point, the audience is ready to view some solutions. You can ask for feedback. Try to be specific about the kind of feedback you are interested in, although you may still get feedback of any kind.

When you receive their feedback, identify the level that the feedback is targeting. You can ask follow-up questions to determine whether the feedback is about the problem context, the approach you followed, or the specific execution.

Transform the feedback to hypotheses in order to make it actionable. For example, if you are told to "move the search button to the top", you may find that the intent behind that request is to make the search more obvious, since search is assumed to be the preferred or most often used entry point.

Consider the hypotheses for your next exploration to find alternative solutions--exploring how to make search more prominent--or as part of your research to validate if they are true for your particular target audience; do users prefer using search or do they have difficulties when finding it with the proposed approach?

Being pragmatic

Capturing and discussing ideas through sketching improves your designs. However, you need to make an effort to keep the process productive. Here are some considerations to speed up your exploration of ideas.

The perfect is the enemy of the good

Your sketches should not be intended to be presented at a museum. Sketches look unfinished because they capture evolving, unpolished ideas. You can spend time making sketches reflect your idea better--adding annotations and even highlighting some elements--but you should spend no time on purely aesthetic or style considerations.

If you are a perfectionist, you'll need to practice being comfortable with lines not being straight. You need to remember that moving fast will save you time that you can spend on polishing the details of the most promising solutions later.

Don't try to preselect only the best ideas in advance. When exploring ideas, don't be afraid of bad ideas. A bad idea can lead to a really good one in the next iteration. Make sure that you analyze ideas and try to identify what works and what does not work about them as input for another iteration.

In environments like big serious corporations or in other organizations less familiar with design practices, sketches may not be considered serious enough. That should not stop you from introducing them, but you may want to do it in a gradual way. You can start by using sketches in individual conversations as supporting material for your explanations, to make people around you more comfortable with them. As people become more aware of the value that sketching brings, you can move your sketches to a more central part of the process and start involving more people in activities, such as design critique or the Crazy Eights.

This is not about inspiration

Design work is often associated with the idea of creative inspiration, as if good ideas come magically to the designer. This passive perspective is not very helpful for you or the general understanding of design in the industry.

Design is about solving problems. In order to solve them, you need to deeply understand your user needs, explore many different possibilities, and evaluate what works in a given context. Your intuition and taste will definitely help, but you cannot rely only on those.

The techniques presented in this chapter allow you to explore the design space in an organized way, based on what you know about the users, and identify and check various hypotheses. Conveying this process will help those who are receiving your ideas understand that they are not just coming out of the blue.

Connecting the conversation to the design goals

A sketch represents a particular solution for the user needs in a given context. People unaware of such context will provide feedback based on their personal opinions or the scenarios that they imagine. You need to move the conversation from what people like about a drawing to what they expect to work--or not--for the users, in the presented idea.

You need to make a constant effort to connect the discussion with the goals. As mentioned for the critique sessions, it is important to introduce the goals before you present a solution. In addition, you need to be careful to keep the conversation connected to those goals when you describe the solution and receive feedback.

Avoid presenting your solution by just describing its parts. If you just describe individual pieces, it will be hard for the audience to understand the role those pieces have in supporting the user needs. Instead of saying "here is the search bar", you can indicate that "since data shows that searching is the most common activity for our users, we provided a quick way to search".

Even if you make an effort to present the context of your design connected to the goals, you may still get feedback that is too specific or based on personal opinions. In those cases, you need to reinterpret the specific feedback that people provide.

When anyone in your team asks for a specific change in the designs--such as adding an icon to that button--you need to understand the underlying issues that the suggestion is trying to address. By asking in which way that change is going to help the user achieve their goals, you can separate the proposed solution from the underlying issue in a better way, which can potentially be better solved with other alternative solutions.

You need to make sure that you do not discourage a person from asking. You don't want them to feel they are asking stupid questions since that will demotivate them from providing more feedback in the future. You want to express your honest interest in learning more about the root cause of their concern.

Making tradeoffs visible - you cannot emphasize everything

As you present sketches, you may get contradicting requests. This often happens when people focus on a particular perspective, ignoring the overall picture.

For example, making something more prominent results in making the rest less prominent. People normally understand the idea that you cannot make everything more prominent at the same time--like highlighting every sentence of a book. However, you may often be asked to make one particular aspect more prominent. In those cases, it is important to communicate the idea that emphasizing something a bit more means to de-emphasize the rest a bit too. That highlights the hidden costs of emphasizing a specific aspect.

Highlighting the conflicts you identified during the exploration can help to find the desired balance. It also helps to remind you of the difference between optimizing and supporting. While you want your solution to be optimized for the most common or important cases, other less frequent cases should be supported only to the point that they don't interfere in providing the best possible support for the main ones.

Even if priorities are not yet clear, making the conflicts visible will help everyone get a better understanding of the proposed point in the spectrum in which the feedback suggests to adjust.

Summary

In this chapter, we introduced sketching as a powerful tool to explore possible solutions for a given design problem. We provided guidance on how to produce results fast while also keeping your exploration organized so that you can find innovative ideas.

In addition to idea generation, we provided advice on how to present and discuss your ideas based on your sketches. This will allow you to act on the audience's feedback and improve your ideas.

The next chapter introduces mobile patterns for you to consider as reusable solutions that are recommended for each mobile platform. Knowing common building blocks on mobile platforms can help you to solve recurring problems in ways that are familiar to your users.

4

Mobile Patterns - Web App, Android, and iOS Best Practices

"Simplicity is the ultimate sophistication."

- Leonardo da Vinci

For many years, the access to information was dominated by desktop computers. This has marked the evolution of digital design until today. The emergence of mobile as the dominant platform to access the online world has changed the way we design our products. It is paramount for any project to understand the different options mobile devices provide to better support its users. Many of our users will access our service by touching a small screen, and that will drastically affect how they interact with the interface and the content displayed.

Originally, mobile phones were aimed at the basic tasks of calling and sending short text messages. At that time, the manufacturer's goal was to reduce the size of the device as much as possible. Before the growth of application stores and platforms such as Google Play and the App Store, some mobile phones had internet access, but the experience of accessing a website was not very intuitive. Some web pages were adapted, providing a very limited versions of their desktop counterparts. It was not until the arrival of the smartphones with tactile screens, when the growth of the access to web pages from mobile phones began to take off (`http://thenextweb.com/mobile/2011/12/06/the-history-of-the-smartphone/`).

Thanks to touchscreens, the need for a physical keyboard on smartphones vanished and the size of the display area grew up to 3.5 inches and higher. As a result, it was possible to create mobile-specific products that resulted in satisfactory user experiences.

Today, most of the major companies are focused mainly on two approaches with respect to mobile users: those users who access their services from a mobile web browser and those who make use of native applications, although some users belong to both the groups. Both the options have advantages and disadvantages; while the native applications make use of all the features of the device, we require an extra step, that is, the installation of the application.

When you create a web application, it is generally aimed at users of different platforms, and therefore you have to design a satisfying experience for users who access it from different mobile operating systems and various screen sizes.

In addition, when the users access your content from a mobile browser, the browser controls may take some space, leaving less space for your content. The menus and controls of your content will be at a second visual level. Even those browsers that hide their controls when you start browsing the content will show the controls again with certain reserved gestures or when moving in the opposite direction to the content flow. However, new hybrid models are trying to blur the differences between these two models of mobile programming.

Progressive Web Apps are a new trend that change the user experience when visiting a web page from a mobile device. These web apps try to make the most of both the worlds, being web pages, visible for search engines, but that have many of the native applications' advantages (`https://en.wikipedia.org/wiki/Progressive_web_app`).

By reducing the number of steps to access your app, you can increase the conversion rate, since the users can use the application without installing it on their mobile device.

Web application approaches - responsive, adaptive, and flexible

If you want to support a large diversity of devices which your users may have, your website or web application should be adapted for different types of screens and resolutions. In this book we will talk about some of the most used design techniques to adapt web pages to different screen sizes. Each of them tries to approach the problem in different ways and understanding them will help you to choose the right one for each type of project.

Responsive behavior

A page with responsive behavior uses media queries to manage the position and size of the elements that form the web page.

A media query is a CSS instruction that sets a different style based on the properties of the user device, such as the screen size. In the following example, we use media queries to change the size of the content according to the screen size, making the content go full width on 640 px-wide screens or smaller, and making content narrower for screens wider than 1024 px:

```
@media only screen and (min-width:1024px) {
    .content {
       width: 80%;
    }
}
@media only screen and (max-width:640px) {
    .content {
       width: 100%;
    }
}
```

Media queries allow you to easily define different layouts that target different devices. We can make content appear in three columns when users access from a desktop, and display the same content in a single full-wide block when they access from a mobile:

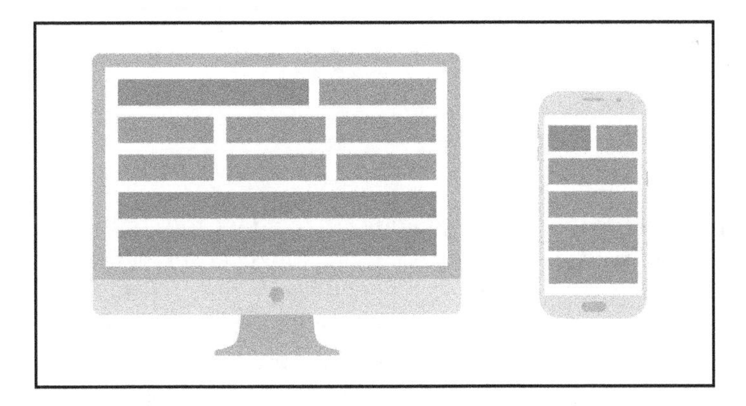

Responsive example--the desktop experience (left) has a new layout in a smartphone (right). The purple elements move from occupying a third each of the desktop version to occupying the entire width in the mobile version.

Fluid

A fluid page defines the size of your objects by percentages. This way, when content is shown in a smaller screen, the elements will be adapted to occupy the same percentage of space they would occupy if the screens were bigger. This type of solution can be effective for very simple pages, but it is difficult to adapt the experience properly with this type of technique when the web page is complex and has many elements in one area. For its simplicity, it is sometimes used in emails:

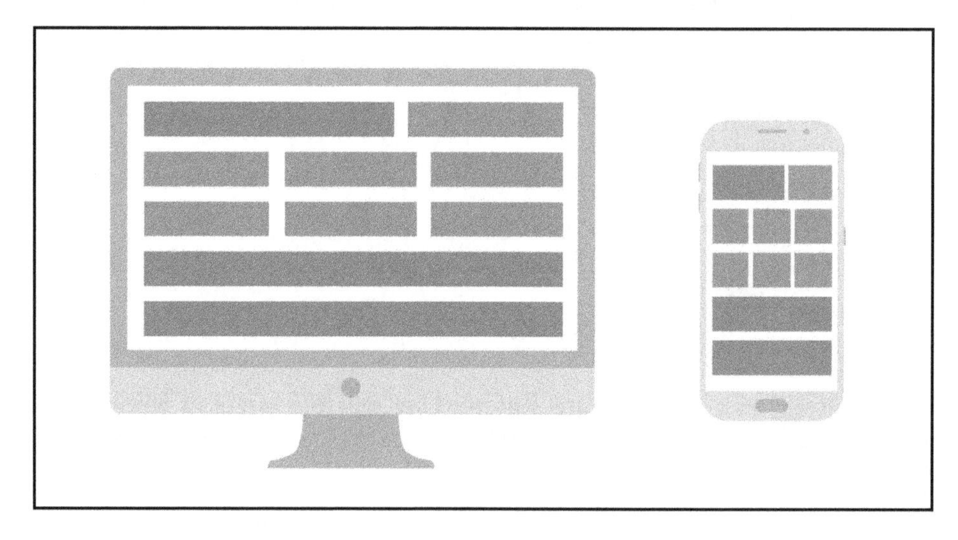

Fluid example--the desktop experience (left) is adapted to mobile, expanding the objects (right)

Adaptive

A page with adaptive behavior uses media queries to adapt the complete experience to the device the user is accessing the web page on. It is really useful when we consider that it is better to offer a completely different page, depending on the capabilities of the tool they use to access. For example, we can offer a complex web page for users looking for insurance through a desktop computer, showing tables and graphs, and at the same time, showing a very simple application of search for insurance with a few steps and elements for users who are accessing from a smartphone:

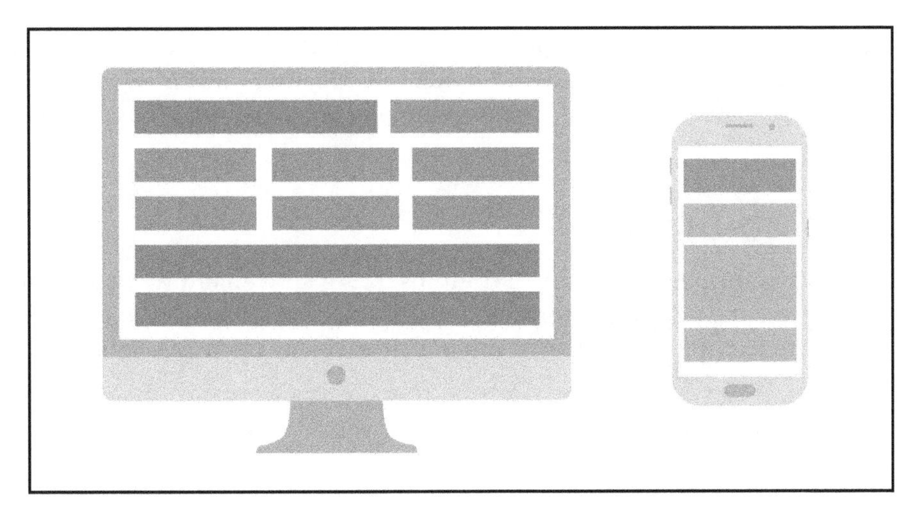

Adaptive example--the desktop experience (left) is transformed completely in smartphone (right)

Hybrid

Many companies are making use of mixed strategies, taking advantage of the benefits of each solution. For content pages, where functionality is not so fundamental, we can make use of more flexible approaches, such as fluid or responsive, and for those areas of the application that're more important, we can completely adapt the user experience to the limitations of the device being used to access.

Frontend frameworks

Maybe the most popular design technique is the responsive behavior. In the last few years several HTML/CSS frameworks have appeared to make programming tasks much easier for frontend developers.

As designers, it is useful to know how these frameworks function in order to provide the correct specifications to the developers. A grid system provides a common reference to communicate the layout aspects of your designs.

Two of the frameworks most used at the time of writing this book are Zurb Foundation, which also has a reduced version for emails, and Bootstrap, a project that was originally created by two Twitter workers and is currently open source. Both the systems are based on the use of columns and have a strong community that supports them, in addition to numerous tutorials and examples that explain how to use them.

It is worth following the evolution of standards such as Flexbox (`https://www.w3schools.com/css/css3_flexbox.asp`), a new layout mode in CSS3, and CSS Grid (`https://www.w3.org/TR/css-grid-1/`), which introduces a two-dimensional, grid-based layout system.

Design in columns

Both the frameworks support design in 12 columns. It is a convenient way to spread the content on the screen and adapt it according to the size of the screen of the device that is used to access the web application. The number 12 is divisible by 1, 2, 3, 4, 6, and 12, which makes this number very versatile:

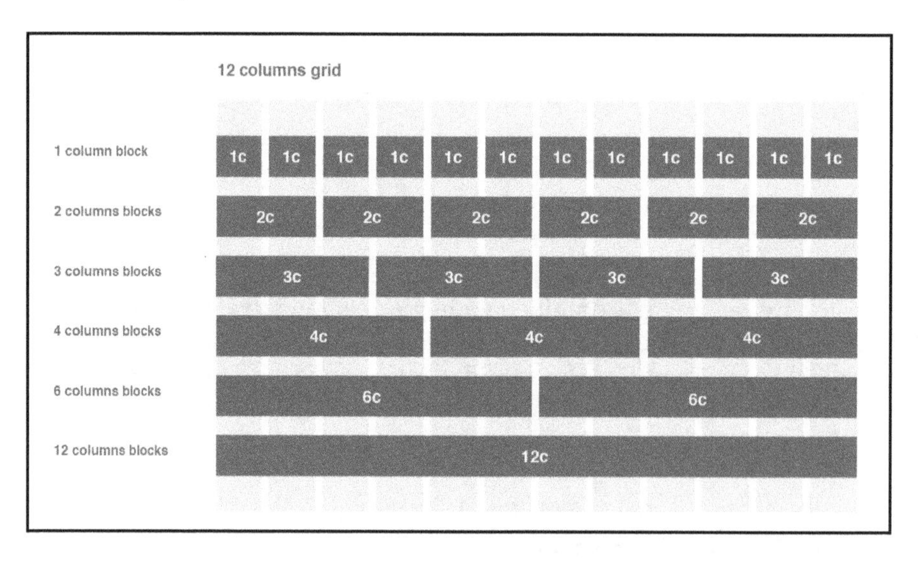

12 columns grid layout system

Our objects will occupy a set column size when accessed from desktop, tablet, or mobile phone. We can start designing both from desktop to mobile or vice versa. You should take into account that an object that occupies 4 columns in width on the desktop should occupy 12 columns on mobile so that it is usable and does not leave the content truncated or too stretched.

In the following example we can find two blocks of text that occupy 6 columns when displayed on a desktop, but when displayed on mobile they occupy 12 columns. Using the full display width on mobile avoids compressing the text too much, that on a smaller screen would be difficult to read:

DESKTOP

6 columns

Lorem ipsum dolor sit amet, consectetur adipiscing elit. Nam fermentum odio eu fringilla molestie. Sed id iaculis orci. Curabitur a lacus mauris. Nam pretium augue dolor, eget porta lectus suscipit nec. Fusce nec ipsum diam. Nullam vitae eros in metus vehicula mollis id non ex. Pellentesque in convallis orci. Etiam imperdiet odio dui, quis blandit sem fermentum sed.

6 columns

In facilisis fermentum lorem, non pretium quam accumsan in. Aliquam sapien orci, hendrerit in leo non, facilisis convallis libero. Proin laoreet a est eu euismod. Cras maximus quam at imperdiet ullamcorper. Phasellus et vehicula ligula. Quisque sem massa, fringilla id finibus ac, elementum ut enim. Aenean vitae ante at magna fringilla scelerisque nec eget velit. Morbi in orci consequat eros pellentesque scelerisque.

MOBILE

12 columns

Lorem ipsum dolor sit amet, consectetur adipiscing elit. Nam fermentum odio eu fringilla molestie. Sed id iaculis orci. Curabitur a lacus mauris. Nam pretium augue dolor, eget porta lectus suscipit nec. Fusce nec ipsum diam. Nullam vitae eros in metus vehicula mollis id non ex. Pellentesque in convallis orci. Etiam imperdiet odio dui, quis blandit sem fermentum sed.

12 columns

In facilisis fermentum lorem, non pretium quam accumsan in. Aliquam sapien orci, hendrerit in leo non, facilisis convallis libero. Proin laoreet a est eu euismod. Cras maximus quam at imperdiet ullamcorper. Phasellus et vehicula ligula. Quisque sem massa, fringilla id finibus ac, elementum ut enim. Aenean vitae ante at magna fringilla scelerisque nec eget velit. Morbi in orci consequat eros pellentesque scelerisque.

Lorem ipsum dolor sit amet, consectetur adipiscing elit. Nam fermentum odio eu fringilla molestie. Sed id iaculis orci. Curabitur a lacus mauris. Nam pretium augue dolor, eget porta lectus suscipit nec. Fusce nec ipsum diam. Nullam vitae eros in metus vehicula mollis id non ex. Pellentesque in convallis orci. Etiam imperdiet odio dui, quis blandit sem fermentum sed.

In facilisis fermentum lorem, non pretium quam accumsan in. Aliquam sapien orci, hendrerit in leo non, facilisis convallis libero. Proin laoreet a est eu euismod. Cras maximus quam at imperdiet ullamcorper.

Columns responsive behavior from desktop and mobile phone

Zurb Foundation for Emails, formerly known as Ink, allows you to use this technique for the design of emails that work well in both desktop and mobile. Although not all email readers support media queries, there are many who do, and in 2016 Gmail joined this group. (`https://developers.google.com/gmail/design/`).

Mobile application design patterns

Over time, different patterns have become common for most mobile users. Designing solutions that make use of these patterns is an effective way of creating experiences that are natural to your users.

Other patterns are not so universal, but knowing them can help you understand which solutions work in a specific context and which ideas to test with your users. Improving the user experience is an ongoing process that is fed by testing, reading, and listening to your users.

In the next few pages, you will learn about some of the most common design patterns, separating them into two groups, those which can be associated with the user interface, and those patterns associated with the behavior of the application. This division has been made with the intention of helping you in understanding the usefulness of each one of them and to guide you in their use. However, the classification of some of them can be subjective.

Mobile user interface design patterns

In this section, we will discuss some of the most common design patterns related to the user interface. We will also analyze why these patterns work, and what are their advantages and disadvantages. These patterns propose solutions to common problems that we encounter as designers.

Navigation

Your app may have different parts, tools, or spaces that users can move around. As it happens with real spaces such as roads or buildings, facilitating navigation with clear signals is key for people to not get lost. Designing the navigation of your application can be really complex. You will have to decide aspects such as location, number of elements, and their behavior. Navigation menus are one of the elements of the interface that will be used more often, so each detail will affect the user experience. The most common menu types are sliding drawer, upper area menu, bottom menu, and no menu.

Sliding drawer

Sliding drawer is also known as "hamburger menu". Designing an application with a hamburger menu is perhaps the simplest option. All elements will be in a tray that will open when the user clicks on the menu icon, usually represented by three parallel lines. This approach leaves almost all the principal screen space for the main content your users are looking for, but it hides all the navigation options.

One of the advantages of this type of menu is that it allows you to have an indefinite number of elements without cluttering the initial experience. This kind of menu is very popular to create mobile versions of web pages since it allows you to keep all the elements that you find in the desktop version. It is also very useful for complex applications as email browsers with tags and folders.

However, you should carefully analyze whether this solution is the most effective for users who access your application using a smartphone, or if a different experience that is tailored to their needs might work better.

A sliding drawer menu can be a good solution in applications where many sections have equal importance or when your application has a section in which your users spend most of their time, all the other sections being secondary based on the user behavior.

Nevertheless, if we can prioritize the most important sections of our application and organize the content neatly, we can make use of other menus such as the tab bar or bottom navigation that can always be visible and allow quick access without having to previously make a tap to open the menu. The mobile first philosophy suggests starting with mobile users in order to give importance to the really essential elements of our solution (`http://www.lukew.com/resources/mobile_first.asp`).

In addition, we can create sections and groups if the app has a lot of menu items, sorting them into a logical structure. Another advantage of having enough space in each menu entry gives the option of having additional information on the side, for example, we can indicate the number of items added since the last opening or if a section is new since the previous release:

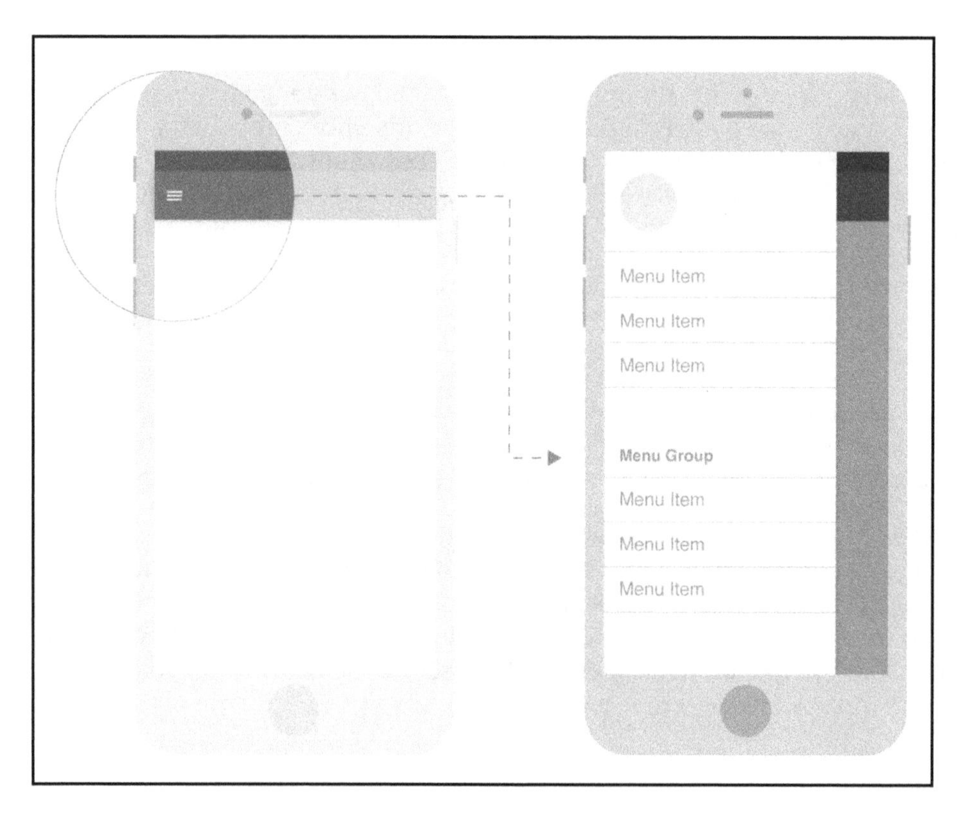

Three lines icon (left) and sliding drawer (right)

Upper area tabs

The menu in the upper area uses the normal read direction of the user to display the information as most languages in the world use a top-to-bottom direction for writing. This arrangement can be especially useful for users not accustomed to the mobile interfaces:

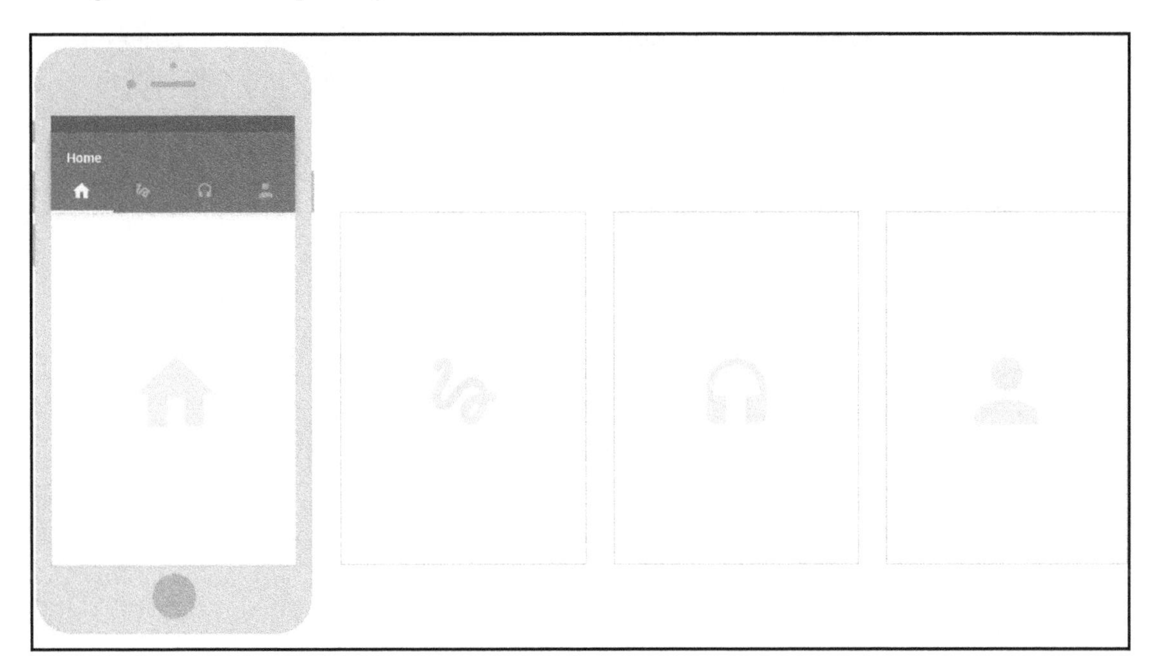

Tabs are displayed in an upper area menu, dividing the application into four main sections.

This type of menu is used in both web apps and native applications, being more common in Android applications. It can coexist alongside hamburger menus, usually the hamburger being the main menu, and the upper menu a selection of menu entries or simply a division of the active screen into subsections.

Bottom menu

This is the most common layout for iOS apps. In Android, we have spent several years where this distribution was not the most popular; however, the current trend of many applications is to use a bottom menu in both the versions: Android and iOS.

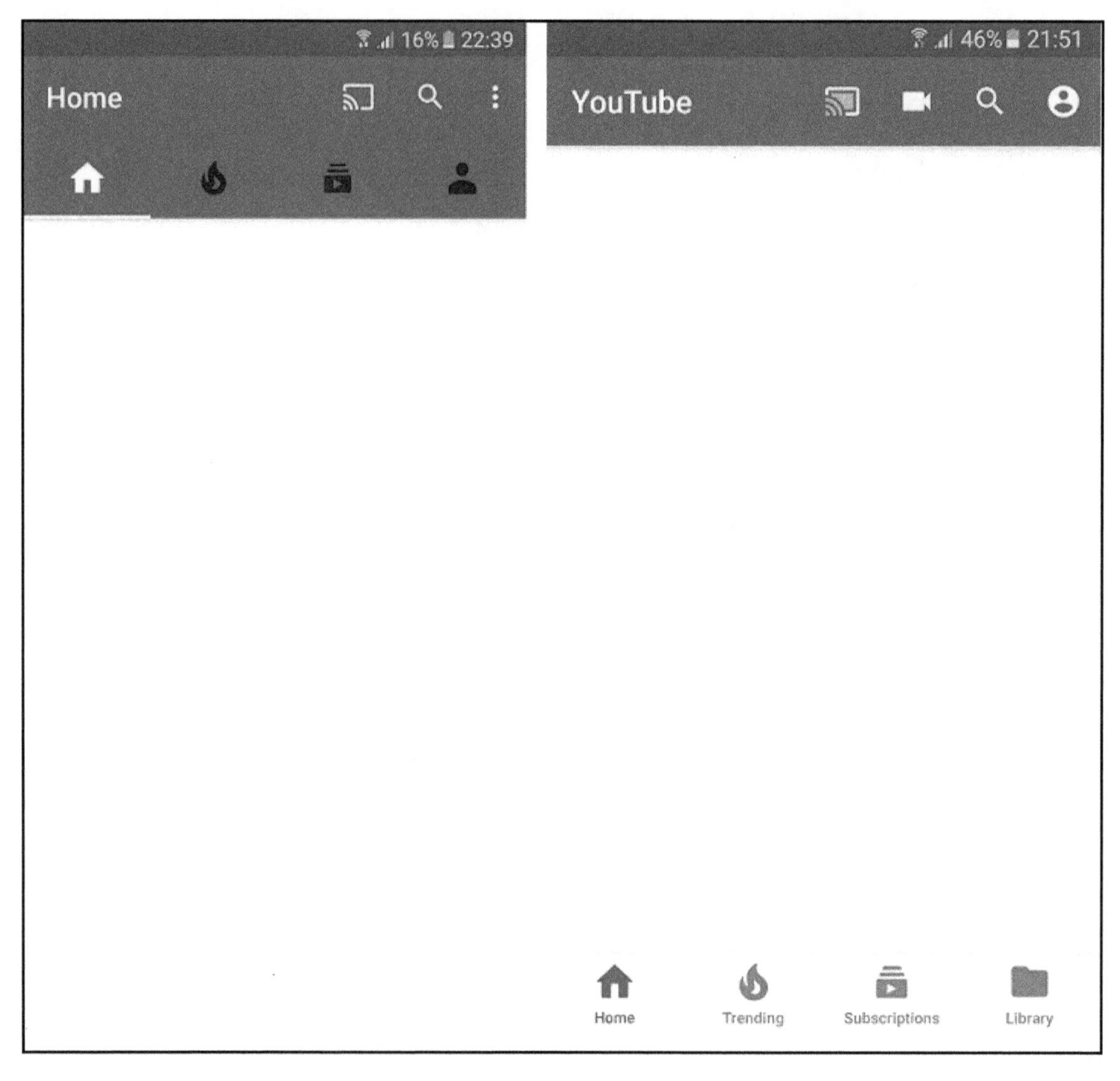

Some applications such as YouTube are testing different versions of the menu; in the upper area (left) and at the bottom (right). Edited screenshots from the YouTube application to remove content (source: Screenshots from YouTube App)

The bottom menus are close to the user's thumb, so they allow them to change sections without too much effort, which is a big advantage over the menus located at the top of the screen. The content of your app does not have to be pushed down by navigation structures at the top, making it more visible for your users from the beginning. Also we have to take into account that many mobile users work with one hand, so placing the menu within reach of the thumb will allow the user to get a better experience, reducing the effort and creating engagement:

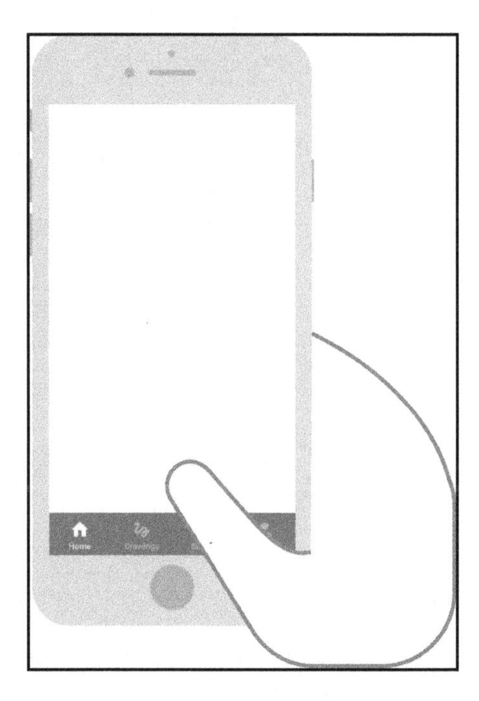

Bottom menu is easily reachable with the thumb.

They are usually designed by dividing the content of the application into a maximum of five sections in order to have all the sections always visible on the screen. If possible, this will be the recommended option as it will give enough touchable space for each of them.

Some more complex applications need more sections, and one of the five options includes access to additional sections. Usually, the text *more* or three dots is used for this section since it is quite popular and generally understandable. However, by including a *more* section in our application, we will force the user to make additional touches to find certain sections of our application.

Placing actions in the screen to facilitate navigation

Mobile screens are generally getting bigger over the recent years. While the first iPhones had a screen of 3.5 inches, new iPhones and Android devices have screens of 5 inches and more. That makes it more important to locate the most often used actions near the thumb area:

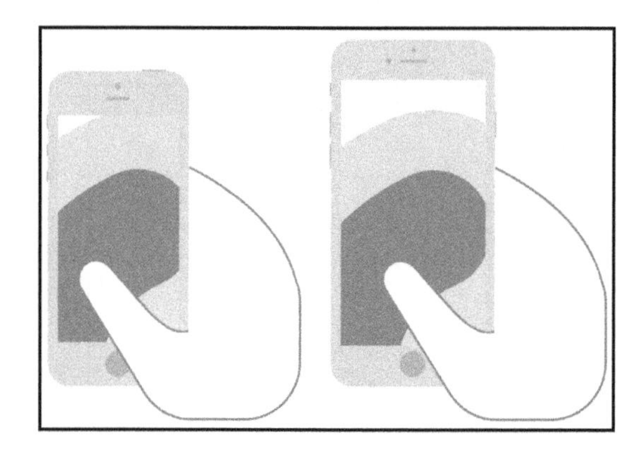

Bigger screens (right) have difficult access to the upper area when the mobile is used with one hand

On a research, Steven Hoober discovered that 49% of the people use the mobile with one hand (`http://www.uxmatters.com/mt/archives/2013/02/how-do-users-really-hold-mobile-devices.php`).

Back button

The back button allows the user to return to the previous screen, in the same way that a breadcrumb can store the path traveled by the user in desktop. This button is used both in complex processes with several steps, and when a user visits a detail of any item found in a previous screen:

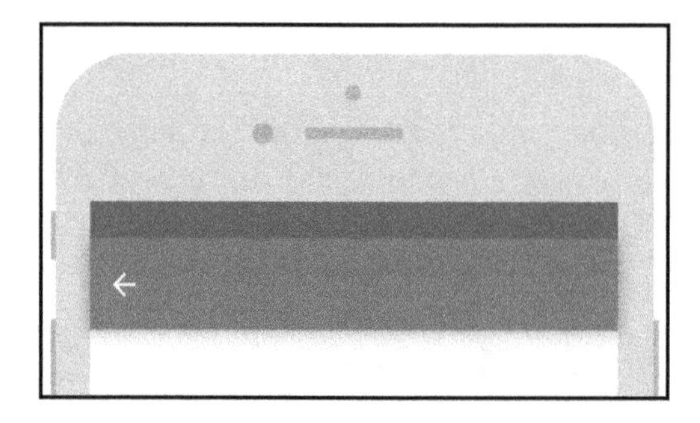

The back button should be located in the top-left corner

The backward-facing function is usually placed on the top-left, in the same way that it is usually placed in desktop browsers. For languages written from right to left, such as Arabic or Hebrew, the arrow will be placed and pointing to the right-hand side. Both Android and iOS have icons and style guides for this functionality; following their specifications will help the user quickly understand what it is for.

Multiscreen task

In mobile, it is common to break complex processes into smaller simple steps. Users will move through several screens to perform a task that is too complex to be completed in a single screen. Despite the linear nature of those processes, we should provide users with a freedom of exploration. Users should be able to move back and forth to correct their mistakes or leave the process incomplete to return to it later. If the work done is costly, and leaving the funnel will make the users lose their created content, we must ensure that they understand the consequences of the action. If possible, it may be helpful to save a draft so that they can retrieve it later.

Explore navigation

It is possible that your application allows free navigation to the user, allowing them to go from one content to another without following a tree content structure. In the same way that a web browser allows you to go backward as many steps as you want regarding your browsing history, your application should manage the visited screens to allow the users undo as many steps as they want.

If the user does not want to retrace his steps, he will want to access a new menu option and start a new exploration. If your application does not allow the user to retrace his steps, ensure that your menu is easily accessible.

Floating buttons

Floating buttons are commonly used in applications to highlight a functionality over the other elements on the screen. The Floating Action Button or FAB is a component featured in the Material Design style guide, making it very popular in Android applications.

This component is presented in several areas of the screen and is popular in maps. It is common to locate this button in the bottom area of the screen because of its proximity to the thumb area. In that position, it offers very fast access to the main action of the active screen. It is really useful when our main navigation menu is located at the top since we can significantly reduce the number of times the user has to stretch their hand to perform the next action.

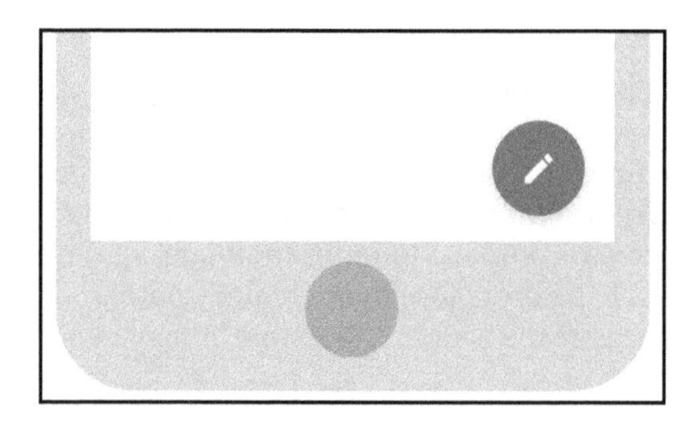

A FAB located in the bottom-right corner with an elevated shadow style

It is recommendable to use this functionality for actions that really stand out from the others on a screen, making them really useful and eye-catching for the user. In some cases, the **FAB** (**floating action button**) can function as an access to a set of related actions. It is the so-called **Speed dial** in the Material Design guide.

Notifications

Well-used notifications are a very effective user engagement tool. Before using them, we will need to ask for the user permission. Notifications can cause unnecessary distraction to users and become very annoying, so it's important to study what our users value as interesting and provide them with valuable content.

Movement in notifications

Humans easily detect movement with the peripheral vision, which is why many designers make use of moving or flashing elements for notifications. Our brain interprets these movements as important and makes us pay attention.

Circle hint

A fairly accepted design pattern is the circle to indicate that something has changed. It is used both in menu items and tabs, and in other elements. An overuse of notifications, especially if the content we offer is not usually of interest to the user, can cause your users to stop responding to notifications. If we insist on this behavior, we risk that the user decides to revoke the notification permissions of our application.

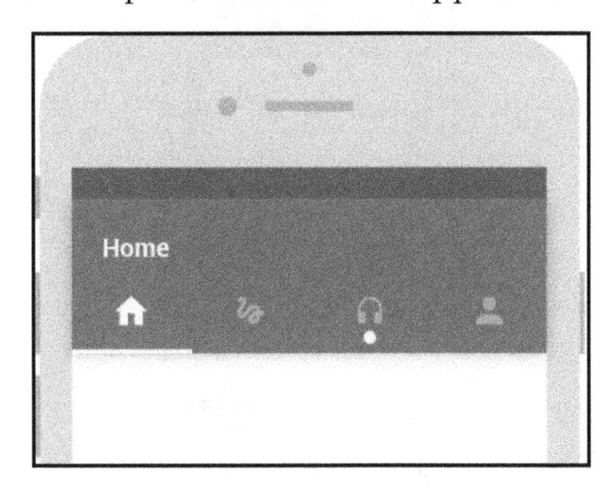

Something new inside a tab is indicated with a circle

It is common to find it both with a number inside and without any other element apart from the circle itself. When it has a number, it represents the number of new items that we will find if we click on the highlighted element of the indicated interface.

Count notifications app icon

Usually called badge app icon, the application icons found on the home screen of our mobile can use this type of circle in one of the corners, with a number, to indicate the number of notifications that have reached the application since the last time it was opened.

Dialogs

Dialogs allow for a quick response from the user. They block any other user activity forcing users to reply immediately. This makes dialogs quite intrusive and annoying, so they should be used only when our application can not continue without the user's interaction, or when we want to confirm an action that could lead to unexpected results, such as deletion of some important info or cancellation of a long process in progress.

Before using a dialog, consider whether there is any possible non-blocking alternative that does not get in the way of the user.

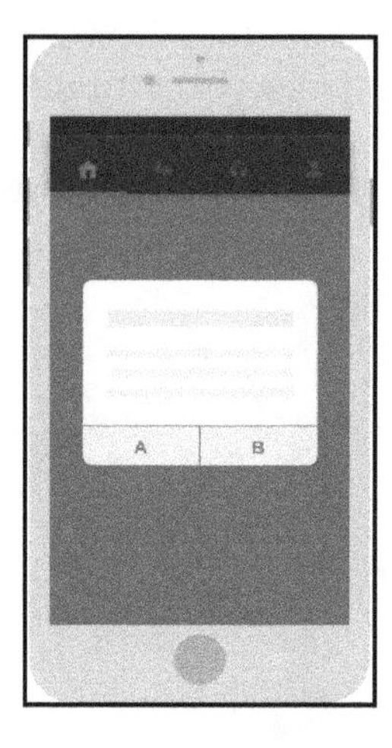

Roadblock notification with two options; the user needs to interact with the dialog to keep using the app

Both the iOS platform and Android have different design options to interact with the user and get such responses. From central dialogs, to options that appear from the bottom as bottom sheets.

Following the style guides of the platforms is usually a good idea since the user is accustomed to interact with these types of dialogs and will quickly recognize their functionality. This will help avoid an irritating situation for the user. In case you create your own design, ensure that you clearly convey the objective of the dialog and try to avoid designs that are too alarmist, especially if the situation is not urgent.

Galleries with miniatures

Image galleries are a very useful design component for displaying listings of items in a graphical way. They are used both in applications and the mobile system itself and therefore cause the user to expect component behaviors from their previous learning.

Items shown as thumbnails should be interactive. If your gallery shows the images in a small size that does not allow you to see the details comfortably, the user will probably understand that interacting with the object will show a zoom of the image.

Arrows

There is a natural relationship between the arrows and the movement that the user expects when tapping on an object that contains it. Usually, the up and down arrows are used to scroll or display content, especially in Android, while the side arrows are often used to indicate forward and backward movement between screens. In iOS, it is common to find them in menus of options:

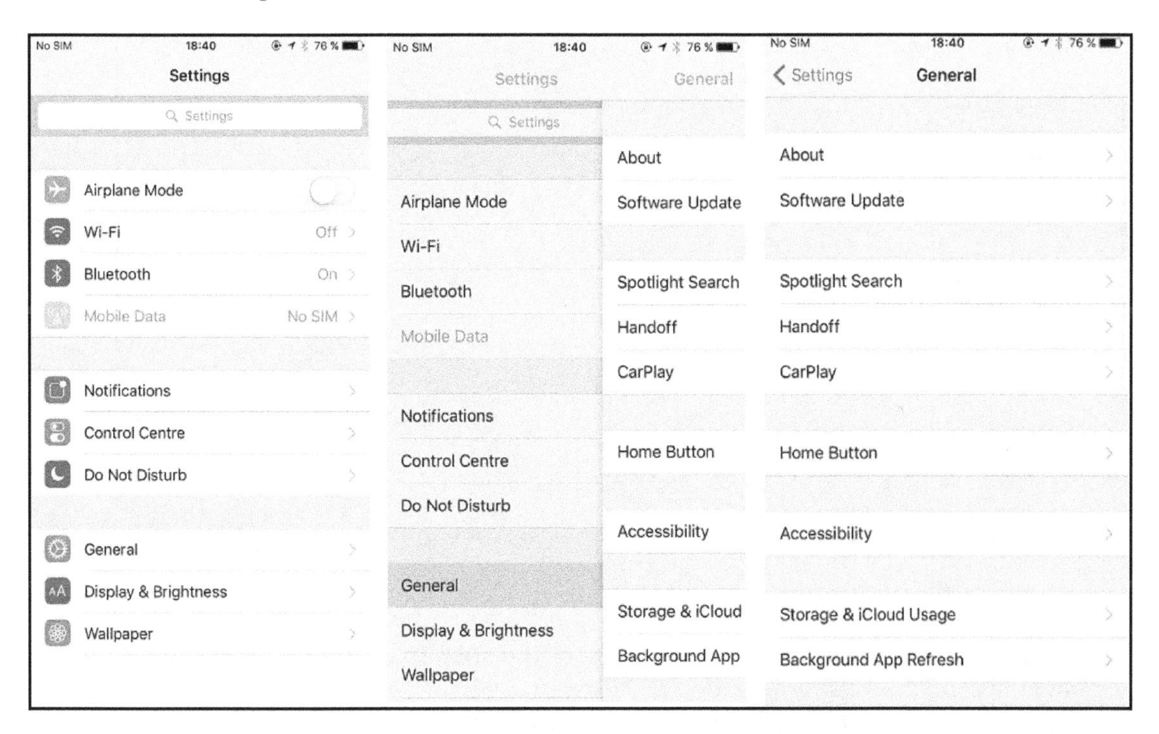

iOS Settings uses arrows to access submenus. The screens appear from the right. Back button shows an opposite direction arrow (source: Screenshots from iOS Settings)

Note that not all languages follow a left-to-right reading direction, usually written as LTR. Those languages whose direction of reading is RTL can interpret the arrows as contrary to the expected one.

Portrait (vertical) and landscape (horizontal) orientations

Modern smartphones can use the accelerometer to detect the orientation of our devices. Most users use their mobile in portrait position. Generally, this approach allows use of the mobile with one hand, so it is not surprising that it is the most popular.

However, some applications may take advantage of the use of the landscape position. Applications such as games, which seek greater maneuverability, allow the user to make use of both their hands in a horizontal position:

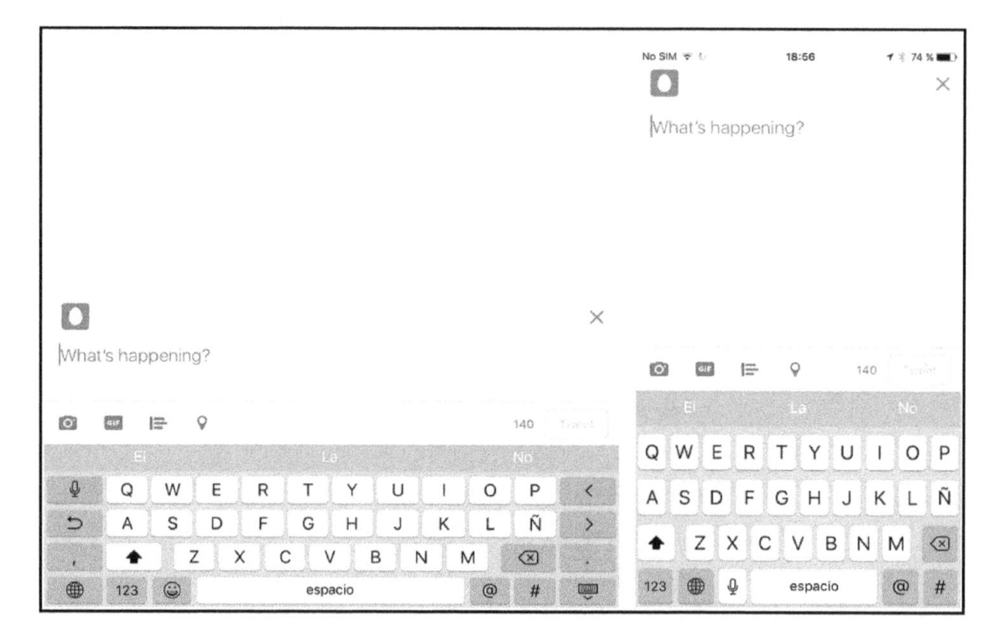

Twitter app on landscape position with bigger keyboard and less typing area (left) and on portrait position with bigger typing area and smaller keyboard (right) (source: Screenshots from Twitter App)

In our applications, we can take advantage of this position to introduce new ways of viewing the content of our application or different methods with which to interact with our application that take advantage of two-handed use. Applications such as Twitter show a larger keyboard in the horizontal position, with larger keys, but hardly accessible with a single hand. Other video applications use the landscape view as a secondary screen to show the video in full screen and fewer controls.

User interactions

Creating engagement in our application is a progressive process. From first use, we have to offer the user different levels of interaction and different levels of reward. These rewards can come in many different forms, from better recommended results to interactions with other users or prizes.

We will describe a few insights about some of the most common interactions.

One-tap interaction

The simplest action a user can do with our app is a tap. Almost all applications aimed at engagement usually have an action as simple as this. It is common to see it as a heart or a thumbs up:

Commonly used one-tap interaction icons

Its functionality is highly effective. Thanks to a small contribution of our user, it allows us to offer better results in the future, based on your preferences. In addition, it allows us to know what contents of our application are really interesting for the majority of our users.

Share functionality

We are social by nature, and this affects our way of seeing the world. People like to be connected. Group feeling is closely related to our evolution as a species, and this also affects how we interact with applications. This is represented in those applications in various ways; following somebody, connecting, making friends, or sharing content are some of them.

Each app can develop its own social terms depending on the purpose of the app. Sharing is one of the core terms often found in all kinds of social applications, but it may be represented in different ways. Each platform has created its own design patterns for this functionality, which means that we find different icons that mean the same thing. However, not all of them will be just as effective for your users.

In Android, the most common icon is the three connected dots, while iOS users are accustomed to seeing a box with an up arrow. In addition, we can find others, such as the box with the arrow to the right, formerly used in iOS, or the arrow to the right with nothing, used in Material Design, that we can find in some Google products:

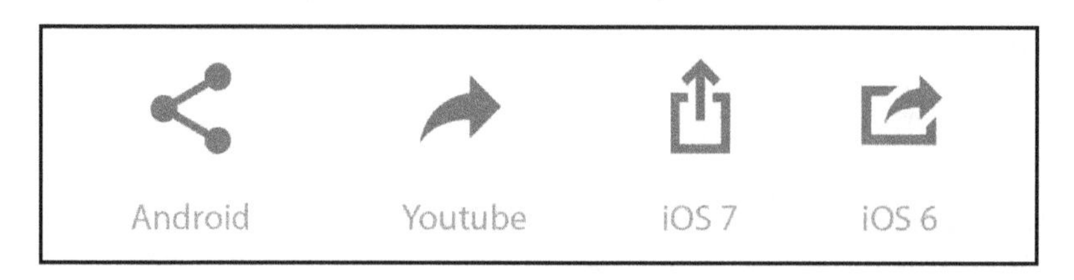

Commonly used share icons

When choosing which icon to use, several factors come into play. While an option is to try to find the icon that has better acceptance among all your users as a group, another option is to use the icons that work best on each platform, customizing the experience for subgroups of users.

Comment and review

Comments allow us to create interaction between users. In a timeline, we can analyze how a conversation has developed and participate in it. Including these kinds of interactions will give credibility to a product or a video, capturing the attention of users and inviting them to interact with the platform.

If you want to capture your user's attention, include an image of the person that is doing the comment. People remember images better than words, it is called the Picture Superiority Effect (`https://en.wikipedia.org/wiki/Picture_superiority_effect`), and they are especially appealing to us if they are images of other people.

Secondary actions

In desktop solutions, we can show contextual actions when the mouse is positioned on top of an element or when the user right-clicks on an item, but it is more complicated to create different types of secondary actions on mobile.

Brands such as Samsung and Apple are testing new ways to interact with the mobile screen. Samsung's Air View technology detects a hovering finger before it touches your mobile screen, while Apple's 3D Touch technology allows you to detect different levels of pressure.

Also, at the software level, developers test different solutions to enrich the user experience. The gestures allow us to explore new options to show secondary actions, the long tap is one of the most used. In return, these gestures are usually hard to discover and require some learning for users since there is not always a simple and reliable way to signal that an element can be swiped, pinched or rotated.

Gestures can become convenient shortcuts, but you need to be careful not to rely on them as the only way to support a key action for the user. For example, long-tap can be used in grid views to enter multiselection mode. If you use the long-tap gesture or 3D Touch functionality, it is advisable to offer an alternative way to perform the same actions with common menus accessible with taps on the screen following user-interface elements. Those more advanced users will be able to benefit from these additional functionalities, and those with less experience will still have a way to perform the same actions.

Handling errors

We try to ensure that our applications do not fail and our users always find the way to do their tasks easily, but both people and systems fail. When any of these circumstances occur, what we must do is inform the user properly about the situation and provide useful information to solve what went wrong.

Errors are interruptions for the user and nobody likes things going wrong, but it is something that happens continuously in real life. We should try to handle these situations as humanly as possible, and we can try to turn a negative situation into an enjoyable experience for the user.

Here are some tips to create error messages:

- **Humanize errors:** Users do not speak the language of servers, nor do they understand codes, especially if we are talking about a mobile phone application. We should phrase the errors in the same way we would speak to another person. Avoid technical terms that could confuse the user and make the problem seem more important and complex to solve.
- **Use proportional language:** Not all errors are equally serious, and this should be reflected in the explanation of the error. The seriousness with which we express an error situation affects the users perception of the error. We must use language that is soft and reassuring in those errors that do not convey a serious application failure.

- **Avoid interruptions when possible:** Use interface elements to display the errors that match the severity of the problem. When we have to inform the user of an error that prevents the operation of the application, the error can interrupt the user and request an action in order to continue. For example, an application might not work due to a malfunction of the servers that support the application. However, errors that do not affect the overall operation of the application should be displayed locally and allow the user to continue with the rest of the application. Some applications allow the user to continue despite having a malfunction in some parts of the application. For example, an application might report poor internet access, but allow the user to continue browsing the local content or content that has already been loaded.
- **Provide a solution if possible:** Users will appreciate that the message, in addition to explaining what is wrong, tells them how the error can be solved. We can include tappable actions in the error itself, so that the user is guided to solve the problem from the error message. Guiding users in resolving an error will help make the experience more satisfying, reducing any feelings that an application is complex or requires prior learning.
- **Allow a user to explore or cancel:** Those errors that do not need to be solved straight away, should allow the user to explore and get further information, or undo the action to resolve the problem later. We can inform the user that a section of our application needs action by the user in order to function properly. Through a visible action the user can get more information about the problem to solve, but decide to fix it later. Keep the user navigation history when possible, so the users can recover the task they were doing previously.

Overlay tips

When you are designing a new flow for users, the objective should be that it is self-explanatory, although sometimes it is not easy or even possible. Help messages at the right time can prevent our users from being lost.

You can also use this component to explain a new functionality that has been recently added to your application, or to highlight a feature that has not been explored by your users. An application that improves over time is a live application, but the changes must be handled with caution, avoiding the possibility that users do not find functionality in a way to which they are accustomed to.

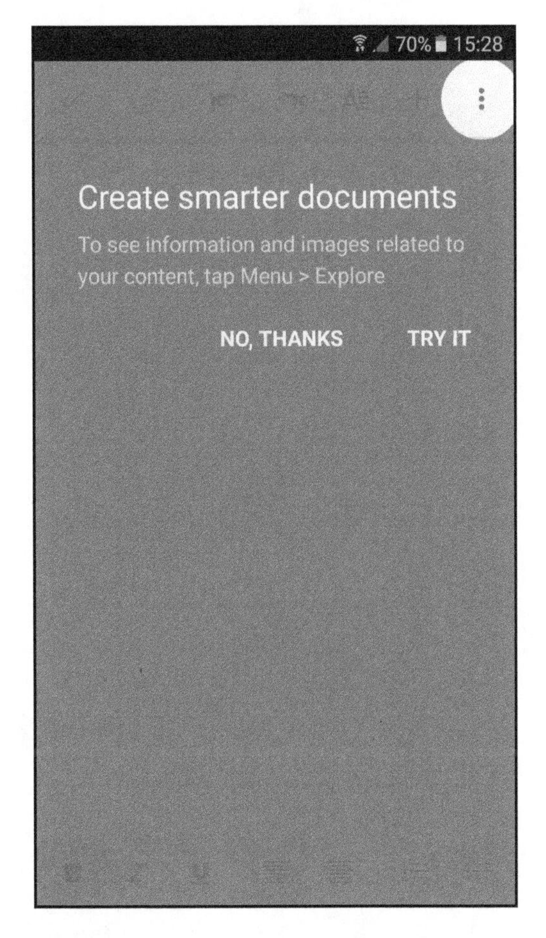

An overlay example explaining the functionality of the three dots icon (source: Screenshot from Google Drive)

Including too much information in the welcome process can be cumbersome for the user, while a message when you first find a new icon will help the user understand the interface.

Roadblocks

Roadblocks are a type of dialog to display a message to the user. They usually occupy the entire screen, and have an X or a skip to close them if the user does not want to read them. Like any interruption, it must be used with great caution.

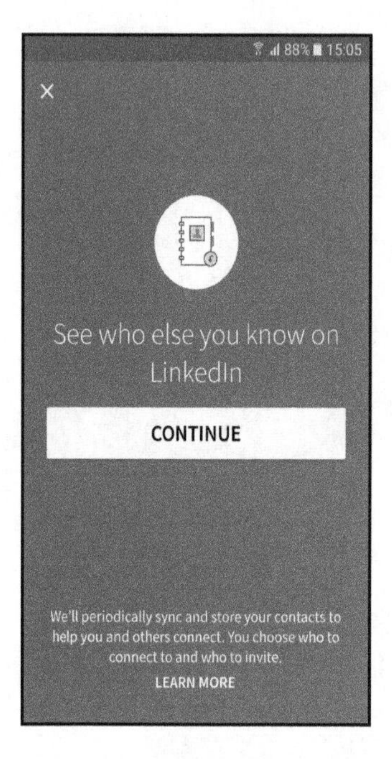

Roadblock message to introduce new functionality to the user (Source: screenshot from LinkedIn app)

Whatever the purpose, it is advisable to include a button at the end of the message in the reading order. If the message does not prompt the user to choose between several options, a button with a **Got it** or **Ok** will help the user to avoid confusion about which is the next action to perform. In a case of inciting the user to take some action, it is highly recommended to include an alternative option to exit the roadblock without forcing the user to perform it. For example, we can use a button with the **Not now** text, which the user will activate if he does not want to continue with the suggested process.

This technique will be useful when the message that we have to show is of great importance or when we consider that it will be highly accepted by the user and therefore it will improve the user experience. As always, it is best to try with real users. Today's analysis techniques will allow us to see the operation of these components, and even let us compare the effectiveness of different texts.

In-content messages

A less intrusive option to request the user interaction are **in-content messages**. This technique consists of integrating messages between the content of a section of our application.

For example, if we are designing a music application, we can introduce a message to connect with other users with the same interests between the music selection list. Finding the right place and not introducing an excessive number of these messages is key to avoiding too much intrusion that can make the content itself meaningless.

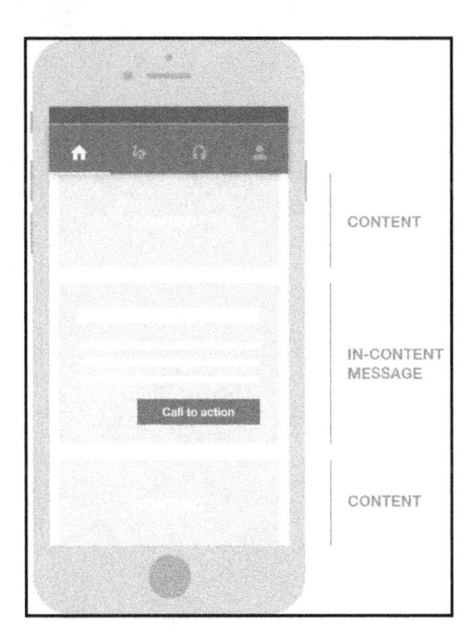

In-content messages are displayed inside the content of the section

This technique will allow us to help the user take the first step to use a new functionality that we have launched with the last release, or to introduce users to areas of your app that they do not usually explore. We can also use it to request new user data in order to improve the application customization and finally, the user experience.

Displaying a message as the first block of content

In an intermediate point between a roadblock message and an in-content message, we can find messages placed as the first element of the content of a section or as a sticky box. While they are not as intrusive as a roadblock, they are highly visible and will interfere with the results expected by our users.

It is convenient to use these types of messages when the message that we want to convey to our user greatly affects the user experience. The perception that our user will have with these types of interactions will follow a similar logic to those they would have with an interpersonal relationship. If the distraction performed offers something of value to the user, such as a better adaptation of the application and a customized user experience, the user will better understand its use.

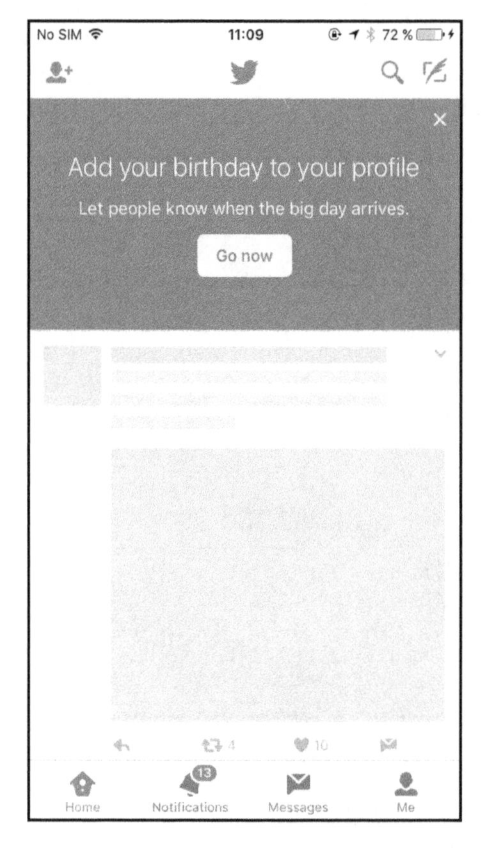

In-content messages displayed as the first element of the content in Twitter application. Edited screenshot to highlight the message box. (source: Screenshot from Twitter App)

Other mobile user interface design patterns

We strongly recommend that you carefully read the style guides of the two platforms covered in this section and other mobile platforms.

They are full of examples and ideas that you can use in your applications and will solve the common problems that every designer faces when designing an application. Many interface design patterns are widely covered and studied by these guides, and they offer examples of how to create a good user interface and list the typical errors that should be avoided.

However, each application is unique, and each user group responds differently to a design solution. Therefore, with your designs, we recommend that you test, test, and test again. With their behaviors, users will tell you whether a design solution is effective or not. While following a design guide will help you organize your interface in a clear and natural way for your users, finding the little details that your users prefer is a task of testing and learning. Every mistake will take you one step closer to the ultimate solution.

Mobile design behavior patterns

In this section, we will include some behavioral design patterns and how we can use them to optimize certain processes or adapt the user experience to be more effective. Each project is unique, and choosing which of them fit our circumstances is a key decision in the design process.

There are many studied design patterns, and reading about them and studying them yourself is key to understanding your users. New interfaces are constantly being tested in thousands of applications, so keeping up with the ones most often experienced by our users is an indispensable tool to have as a designer.

Progressive disclosure

This technique consists of adapting the functionality of the application to the technical skills of the user. Inexperienced users will see a simplified version of the application, while more advanced users see a more complete and complex set of functionalities. We will ensure that all users find an application adapted to their needs. New users will become experts in time, discovering new functionalities with their progress.

The same technique can be applied with respect to other parameters. For example, we can request more interaction from the users who normally make use of the full set of offered features, whereas those users who only use the application sporadically will receive a different treatment aimed at achieving higher engagement levels.

Lazy login

Registration in applications is evolving. Just as it was normal to request a mandatory registration to access content earlier, today, the first few seconds our users come into contact with the application are considered critical, and adding a barrier before viewing the content may cause us to lose conversions in the registration process. That's why many applications make much more use of a flexible registration, allowing anonymous visitors to use the application and see the content, registration only being required when it is completely necessary.

There are several ways to decide when it is a good time to apply for mandatory registration. Some applications request registration when the users want to interact with the platform, whilst others allow such interaction, leaving them associated with a group of unregistered anonymous users until such time that the user decides to register on their own initiative.

The choice of one system or another will mainly be based on the nature of the application since some interactions hold more credibility when associated with a specific user. This is the case of reviews, where a review with a name and a photo will be more credible and influential than an anonymous review. However, other interactions, such as liking a product, can work perfectly with a percentage of anonymous users.

Swipe down to refresh

This is a design pattern widely used and expected by our users. In the same way that a web page is updated when we press *F5* on the desktop, users expect to be able to update the results by stretching the screen down.

To add visual feedback to the user gesture, we must include some kind of spinner, which follows the movement of the user's finger while stretching the top of the screen:

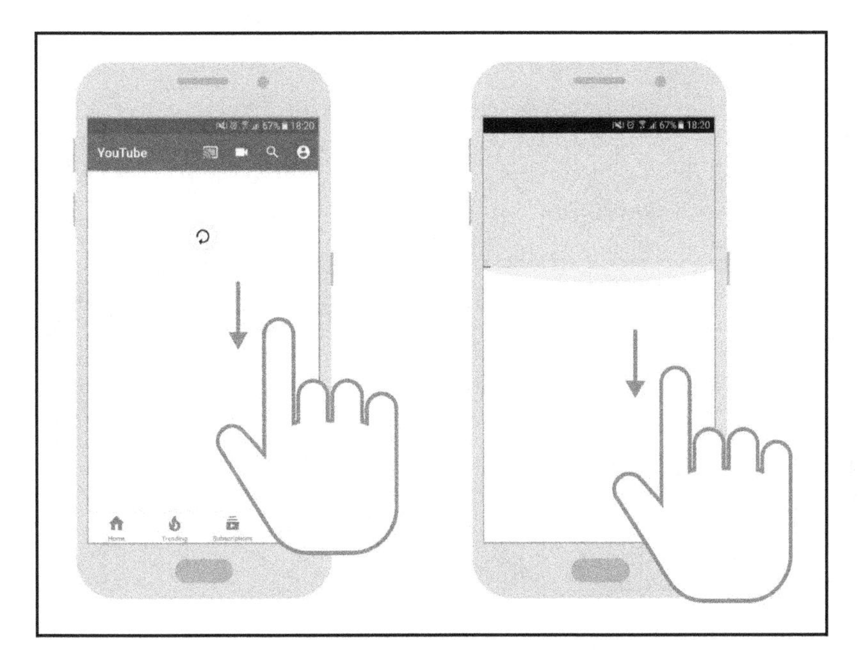

Swipe down spinner (left) and feedback to user (right). Screenshots have been edited to remove content and focus on the user interface (source: Screenshots from YouTube)

It is also important to take this pattern of design for those screens of our application that do not support this type of behavior, but, by their nature, can lead the user to try to update. If this is the case, it is convenient to add clues to make the user understand that his gesture has been received, but does not produce results intentionally.

Some applications add a shadow that is stretched when the user swipes down, or stretch the top element of the screen to produce a similar effect.

Search suggestions

It is important to organize your application properly to match the mental model of our users as it is providing a suitable search system. In applications with a lot of content such as YouTube, it would be practically impossible to reach all the content just by browsing through menus.

The moment a user taps on the magnifying glass or the search box, we can start working on the user experience of the search process. It is generally a good idea to clean the screen of any other item with the aim of focusing the user on the task he is doing, avoiding distractions.

If we can, we should offer intelligent suggestions, with the objective, in the best case, of reducing user input. For example, if we are in a video application, we can offer common categories or results of general interest. In applications where the user searches for the same content several times, we can offer previous searches' suggestions.

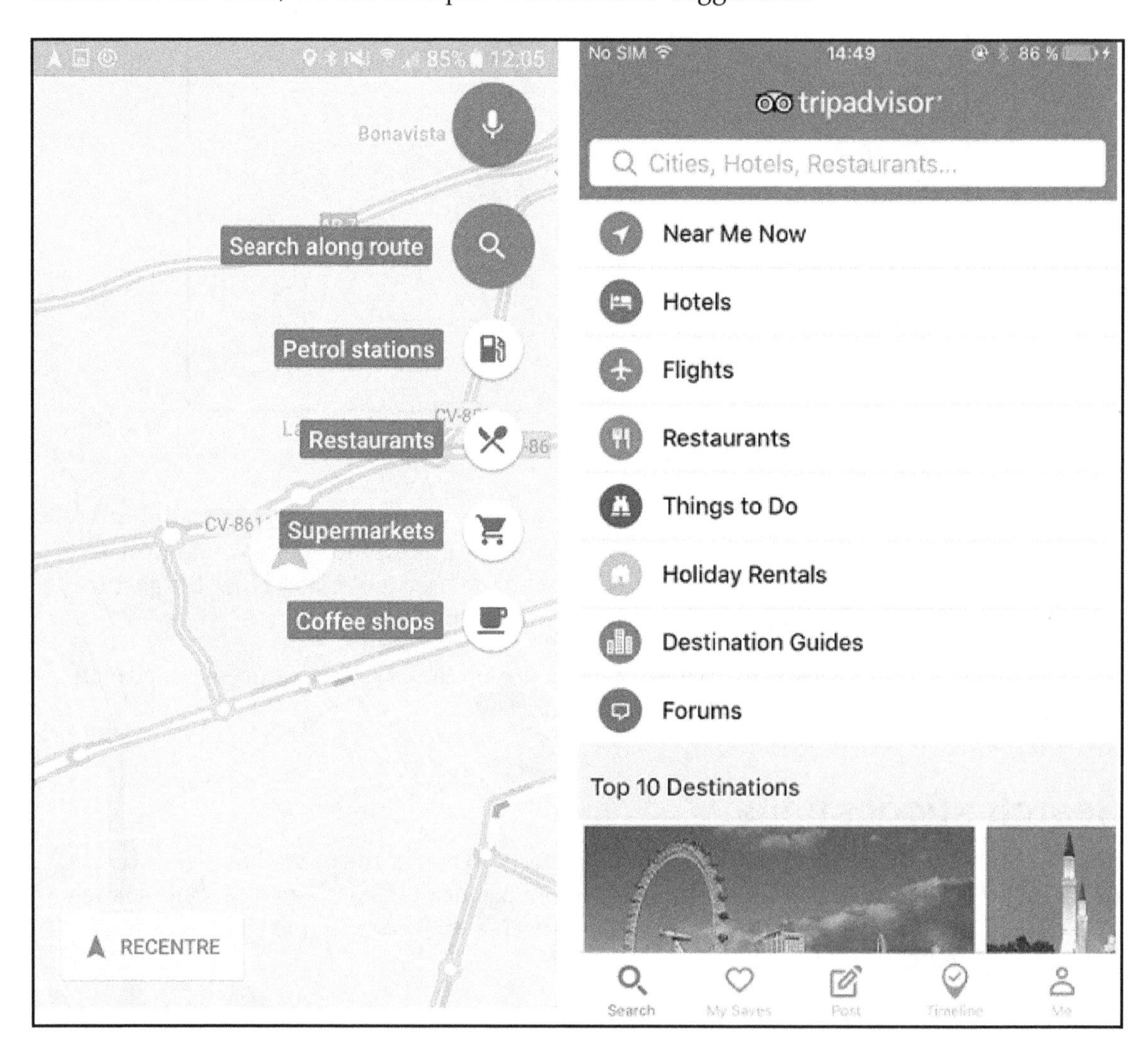

Google Maps (left) and TripAdvisor (right) suggest common categories (source: Screenshot from Google Maps, source: Screenshot from TripAdvisor)

At the moment the user begins to write, we can offer both writing suggestions and results with the information we have. If the users find what they are looking for ahead of time, we will save some typing effort for them.

If no results are found, it is a good idea to offer pivoting options so that the user can start a new search journey.

Reciprocity

Some behaviors are highly linked to our human nature, and one of the behaviors we can expect is the reciprocity effect. When one person does a favor for another, the other normally feels forced to return the favor. It is easy to imagine how this type of behavior has allowed our species to survive and collaborate for a common good for thousands of years.

This is also true in the virtual world of your applications. If a user feels that our platform is giving something of value, that user will feel more willing to interact with the platform.

We can take advantage of this behavior to get our users to interact with our application. Before asking for an effort on their part, we offer them something of value. If we ask for an interaction later, the user will be more willing to participate. For example, if our app recommends a good restaurant when users are going out for dinner, later these users will be more willing to give their opinion about this or other restaurants.

Android and iOS differences

At the beginning, each of the platforms had a very different style. In the recent years, both the platforms are tending toward a common and simpler style, with flat elements and minimalistic interfaces. However, there are small differences that we can apply as minor design adjustments if we want our experience to be more native for each platform user.

It is important to read and understand the style guide of each of the platforms. In Android, we found the design guide Material Design (`https://material.io/guidelines/`), while Apple has **iOS Human Interface Guidelines** (`https://developer.apple.com/ios/human-interface-guidelines/overview/design-principles/`). Both offer solutions to general problems of content organization and interface design. We have to look for a balance between the visual identity of our application and the application of style guides.

Physical buttons

The iOS system is only used by Apple products while Android is a system that was acquired and powered by Google to introduce to a large number of devices from different companies.

The iOS devices are distinguished by having a single round button on the front of the smartphone; this is located below the touchscreen of the device when in portrait mode, aligned in the center. Actions such as going back or hiding the virtual keyboard will be actions that will have to be handled by the application itself.

However, in Android devices, we can find different configurations. Brands such as Samsung bring three buttons, some physical and other tactile, on the front of the device, below the screen: a home button, a back button, and a functional button. Other brands, such as Motorola, produce some devices whose buttons are integrated in the display itself. We can also find Android smartphones with four controls, as some add a quick access search button. This will affect how Android users interact with your application, for example, the back button is widely used by Android users to undo steps or dismiss the keyboard.

If these differences are unfamiliar to you, it is highly recommended that you have at least one device from each operating system and use them extensively. Appreciating the differences of the same application in both the systems will help you see how developers of the best companies solve small adaptations, and what paths they take to make the experience more friendly for all their users.

Screen density and features

Although development for mobiles with different screens and hardware features is quite standardized nowadays, your designs and functionality will need to be adapted for different resolutions and aspect ratios. Testing the final application in different devices will be necessary to ensure the quality of your solution.

Whilst in iOS you will need to test your application on devices from Apple, with Android you will need to test on devices from different manufacturers. Each manufacturer creates products based on different market standards that match their target customers, and can modify the operating system to adapt it to their specific needs.

Nor can we forget that our end users will have different versions of these operating systems, which can affect elements of the user interface. When using native system elements, the user experience can be better integrated with previous knowledge of our users, but it must also be taken into account that it will add an element of variability that should be checked.

UI elements

The following are some of the UI elements that enhance the UX:

- **Menus**: While iOS has always been distinguished by having the menu of their applications at the bottom of the screen, Android developers have been somewhat more flexible in creating their applications. It is common to find applications with menus both in the lower area and in the upper area in the form of tabs or drawer. The latest trends indicate that many applications are including bottom menus in Android applications, and Google has already contemplated this trend in its Material Design guidelines.
- **Look and feel**: Material Design guides are distinguished by elements such as the virtual height denoted with shadows, the FAB, or movements associated with the sensation of gravity. iOS is usually more subtle in the use of shadows, making a mixture of flat style with translucent effects for menus and dialogs.

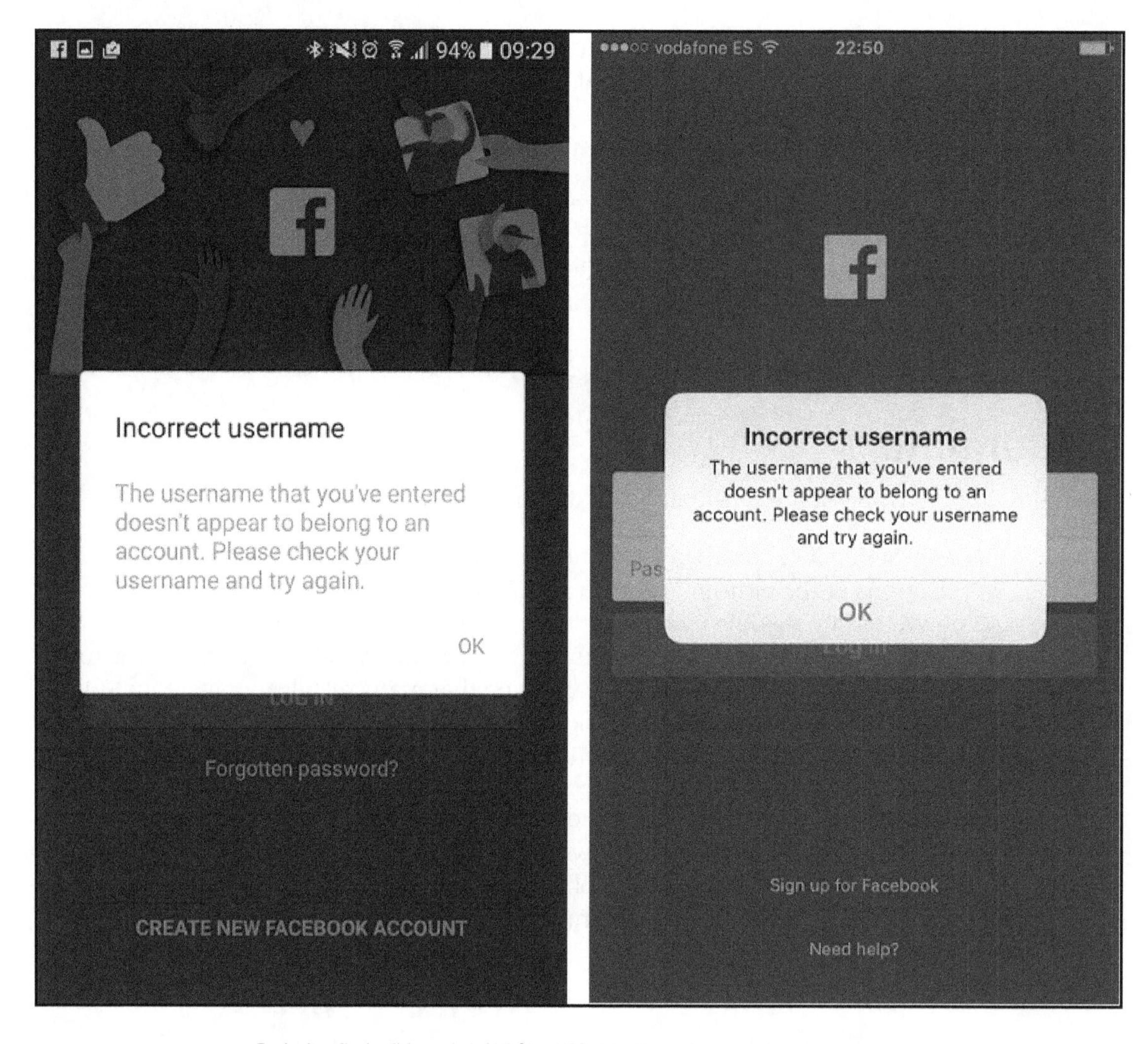

Facebook application dialog on Android (left) and iOS (right) (Source: Screenshots from Facebook Apps)

- **Icons**: When your application is supported on different platforms, you need to decide whether to create a set of icons and graphics that are specific for each platform or use a common visual style for all platforms. You can find these two different approaches in apps from leading companies.
  Those that do not distinguish between platforms use commonly simple solid icons or hollow icons with thick lines, as this kind of icons work very well on different screens sizes and resolutions. The applications that adapt their icons based on the platform, tend to use thinner icons on iOS, using inverted solid icons for selected states in tab bars and some functionality, and use solid and hollow icons with thick lines on Android, using the color and the opacity to represent different states.
  If your project will be developed for different platforms, you will have to find a balance between the native style of the platforms themselves and the one of your brand identity. Depending on the nature of your project, your users could be changing from one device to another. By providing a common visual design your users will recognize the functionally easier when they use their other devices.

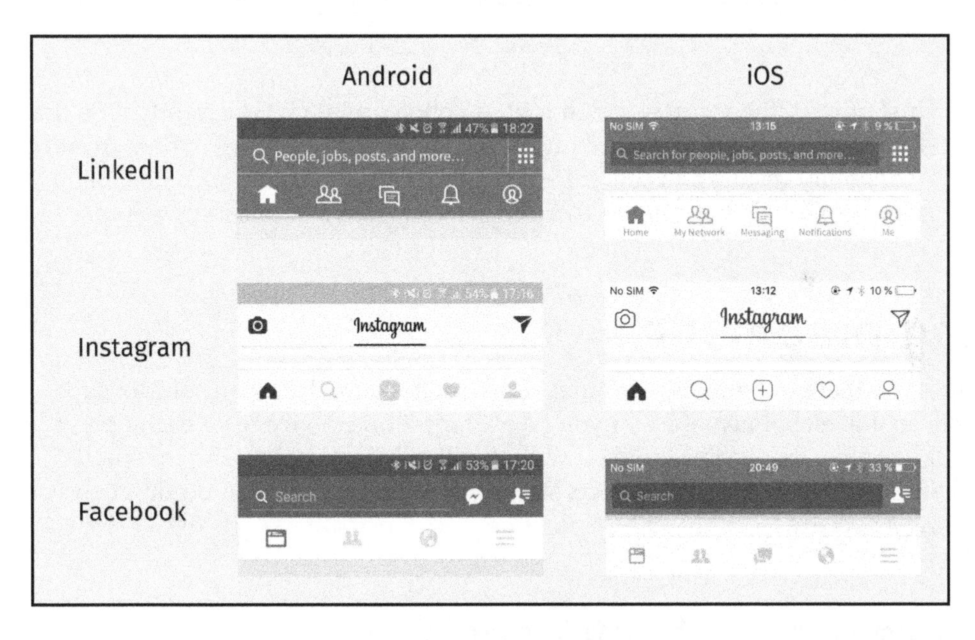

How different apps adapt their icons to each platform--cropped screenshots to focus on the user interface elements (source: Screenshots from LinkedIn, source: Screenshots from Instagram, source: Screenshots from Facebook)

- **Fonts**: Choosing the font that we use in our application will mark the user experience drastically. Readability on mobile screens is often more complicated due to the need to distribute the space between all elements of our user interface. The choice of the font can also be influenced by our brand image, so we will have to look for a balance between functionality and design.
  Both the operating systems have highly optimized fonts for good readability, and it is advisable to use them, at least in contexts where a less optimized font family produces difficult readability scenarios.

Roboto
Lorem ipsum dolor sit amet, consectetur adipiscing elit.

Helvetica Neue
Lorem ipsum dolor sit amet, consectetur adipiscing elit.

SF UI Display
Lorem ipsum dolor sit amet, consectetur adipiscing elit.

Roboto, Helvetica Neue, and SF UI Display fonts are highly adapted to multiscreen environments

In Android, the recommended font is Roboto, while iOS currently uses the San Francisco font, but previously used the Helvetica Neue. All of them produce good readability results and therefore can be extremely useful when designing our screens. Google Fonts and other services offer help in pairing two types of fonts.

Being pragmatic

It is important that you know the technologies which you will design solutions for firsthand, so it is recommended that you have at least one device from each operating system. If possible, familiarize yourself with the devices and use them personally throughout the day, since many aspects are appreciated by chance and not when you are performing a specific task.

Explore different solutions

Investigate and compare how applications are adapted to different platforms. Carefully analyze the operating systems of both Android and iOS as they apply a lot of design patterns and solve complex problems.

Explore your own solutions and evaluate them according to the goals for which you are creating your solution. Some solutions will work for large groups of people, while others will work better with a smaller or specific group of users. Adapt your solutions to the target group of users who will finally use the app.

Summary

In this chapter, we saw how web applications can be adapted with media queries to different screen sizes. Also, we saw some common design patterns and how they can help solve typical problems that are recurrent in the app design process.

We also showed some of the differences between the two main mobile platforms that dominate the market today.

In the next chapter, we will see how we can provide details of our design solutions with wireframes and mockups and how to create accurate specification files.

5

Detail Your Solution - Wireframes and Mockups

"If you can't explain it simply, you don't understand it well enough."

- Albert Einstein

While quick drawings are the most effective tool in the early stages of exploring ideas, you need to capture your solutions in more detail. You can capture a more detailed design solution in a schematic way with wireframes or in a more realistic way with mockups. Each technique is adequate to cover specific objectives, and you may prefer one or the other depending on the type of your problem.

Some teams will find no benefit in creating detailed wireframes from sketches. They feel comfortable discussing ideas as sketches and move directly to produce mockups. Other teams may use wireframes to focus on functionality and behavior in great detail, leaving the graphical visual aspects for a later stage. Being familiar with both tools will let you find the one that best suits you and your team.

Understanding wireframes

A **wireframe** is a technical representation of a screen using skeletal lines. By similarity, they are also known as user interface blueprints. Each type of element in a wireframe must be represented in a clearly differentiable way. We do not have to follow a specific visual style when designing our wireframes, but we must make sure that they are clear and easy to understand.

For example, actionable elements can be represented as button shapes, icons, and underlined texts, but colors can also be used for this purpose. The general structure of the screen can be represented with lines or zones in a range of colors that is in contrast with the actionable elements.

It is also possible to indicate the transitions and gestures that the users do in order to move from one screen to another. When different wireframes are connected, they offer a perspective similar to that of a flowchart, so they are also known as wireflows.

Wireframes can be very useful as a communication tool between people from different departments. You can apply your wireframing process to all kinds of platforms, and you can create wireframes at different levels of details, depending on their purpose.

You can create a **low-fidelity wireframe** with dummy texts and boxes as content. This is useful to represent the structures of the screen in a very basic way and the main transitions between different screens. With this level of detail, creating a wireframe will have an outcome very similar to drawing a sketch, but with cleaner lines. So the choice of technique will depend more on which technique and tools you feel most comfortable working with.

By increasing the level of detail of your wireframes, you can isolate the functionality of your application in a **high-fidelity wireframe**. These wireframes accurately capture the basic structure of your app without considering aspects of visual design, that is, aspects that you can deal with later in more detail using mockups. To do this, they should include contents and elements that are a clear representation of the behavior of the application and the interactions users can have to navigate and perform the different actions within the application.

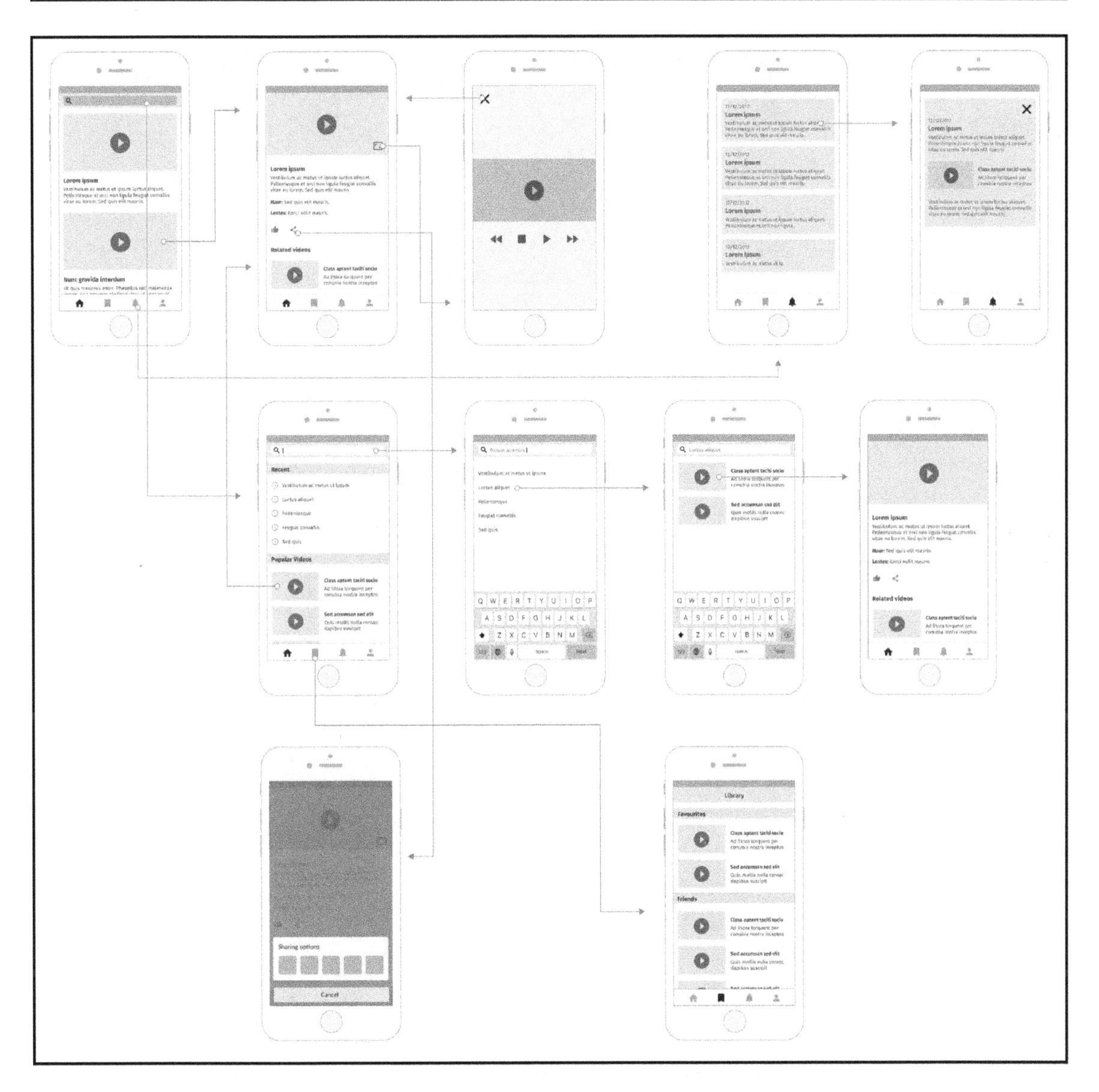

A wireframe example created using Adobe Illustrator with a workflow of different screens connected.

Wireframes as a functionality specification document

When using a wireframe as a technical specification tool, it should be as detailed as possible. Any developer looking at the wireframe should have a clear vision about the flow of the application, including the gestures that bring the user to another screen, the layout and status of the controls, and the transitions that occur between each screen.

Although some types of transitions can be represented by icons or small drawings, other transitions will require small prototypes where we will show the developer the final result that we are looking for. In this prototype, we can show factors such as the order and time in which the elements move.

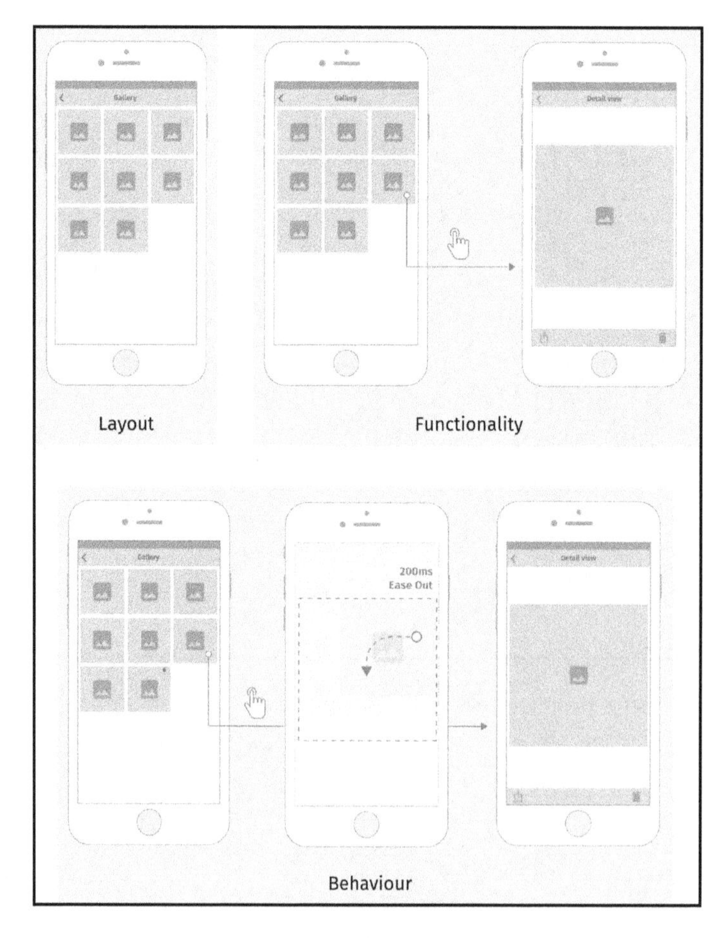

This image depicts different levels of details; you can go from layout to functionality and also include behavior

Design details can be specified in other types of documents along with the mockups. Using a different document for the detailed version of our designs will help us in not repeating design aspects for screens that visually do not present anything new.

Layout

The layout defines the general structure of the application and where each item is in relation to others on the screen. Whether a button should be at the top or bottom of the screen or whether it belongs to a tab bar should be reflected in the wireframe. Aspects like the font family can be specified in another kind of document, so we can isolate the functionality here without any noise. We should also represent whether a heading or a button is bigger than another and it belongs to a group, in order to provide a clear hierarchy to the view we represent. You can use colors to highlight important elements of your wireframe. They are very handy in driving the reader's focus towards those areas that need further attention.

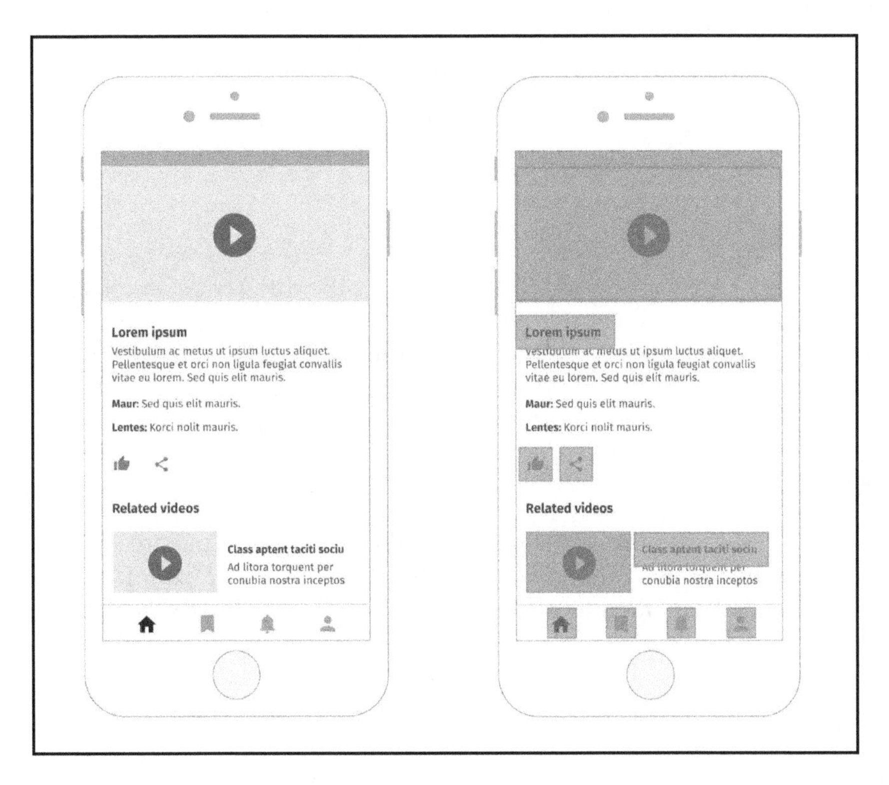

Using colors (right) to represent the actionable areas of a wireframe.

Gestures

An application may react to different types of gestures. These gestures can be represented with hand icons or with labels. In this way, dynamic interactions can be captured in a static image and describe what triggers each transition between two screens. In addition to navigation, you can also represent interactions happening in a single screen. You can indicate that the user is able to zoom in an image or the functionality behind a force touch or a long press. In the following link, you have a set of gestures that you can use and freely modify in your projects `[Asset_A6462_A05_A01_Gestures_Assets.ai]`.

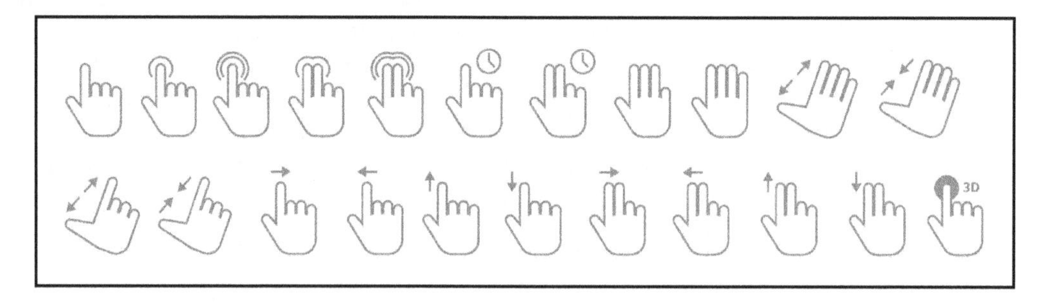

Gesture assets set

Transitions

When we design our applications, we choose the way the different elements and screens appear and disappear. We need to define elements such as movement trajectory, speed, duration, and timing since they affect the user's perception of what is happening. By adjusting these parameters, we can achieve a natural and predictable movement.

Trajectory

The simplest path is the straight line; displacements in a straight line are effective for moving elements when they shift on only one coordinate axis. For example, we can use a completely horizontal movement to introduce a new view from one side of the screen.

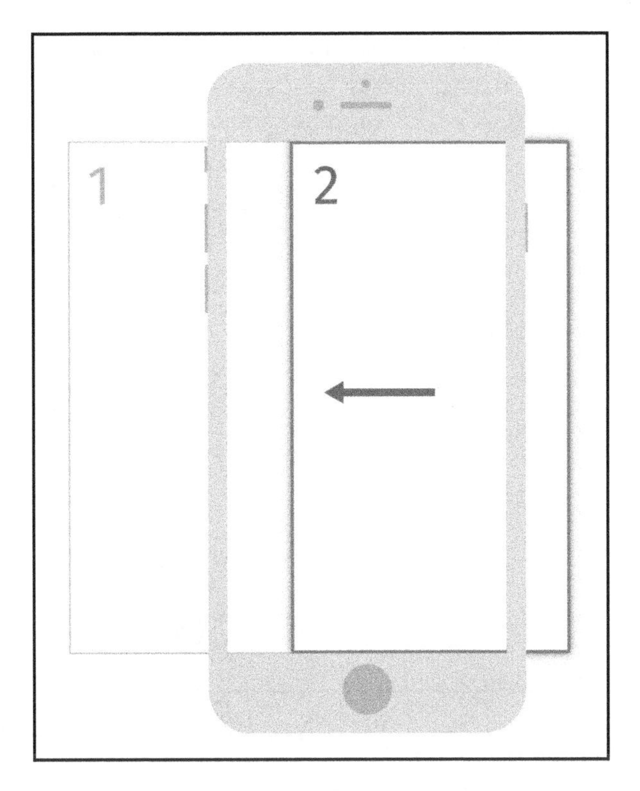

Screen number 2 replaces screen number 1 with an horizontal movement from the right to the left

Avoid complicating trajectories with fancy movements for something that should be easy and quick, as the result will be more difficult to understand. You will be able to use more sophisticated trajectories to catch the user's attention when necessary or to represent actions that involve complex processes.

Some movements, such as changing the location of a card onscreen, can have a more natural effect if we apply a slight curve to trajectory. In the real world, objects have weight and gravity affects them, so our brain is more accustomed to such movements.

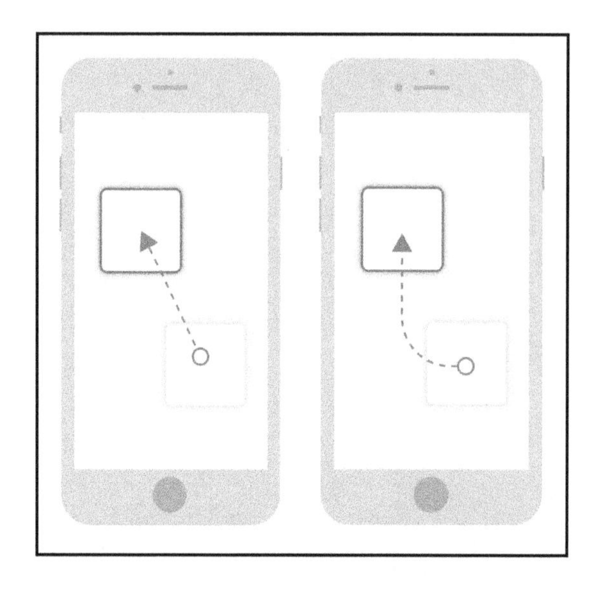

Relocating elements that move in two edges (left) can feel more natural when moving with a curve trajectory (right)

Complex transitions can be chaotic when their elements act independently. The number of elements that change their location or shape from the initial to the final state of your transition will affect the perception of the user. If each element moves independently, all of them will catch the user's attention, generating a transition that is too complex to process. We can follow different techniques to make our transition more natural and enjoyable. It is always recommended that you try different timings and combinations in order to find the perfect and most elegant transition that you are looking for.

Generally, you can try to reduce the complexity of your animations by organizing how the elements synchronize with the other elements in the transition. If you choose an item or group of items to focus the attention of your users, the transition will be organized neatly, and your users will have a clear point on which to focus their attention. The rest of the elements must accompany this movement, and if that is not possible--as some elements are changing their shape or position dramatically--you can try fading effects so that they do not cross their trajectories on the screen, which may make the transition feel unorganized.

Timing

Sometimes, the transition of one element can be handled with one single step. However, this transition can affect different values of the element, and we can move different elements in the same transition if the focus and attention of the user is maintained on a single focal point. Many elements moving in a disorganized manner can cause our perimeter vision to be distracted, as we are receiving stimuli from different areas of the screen.

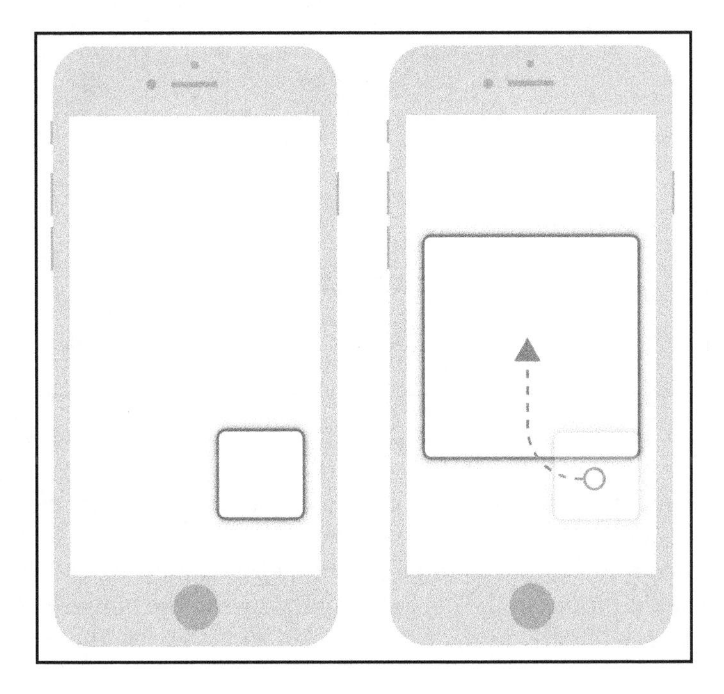

Transition of an element that scales while relocating

If your transition includes several elements that will cross their trajectory while moving at the same time, and vanishing some of them is not the desired transition, try to match how they would move in the real world. Users will naturally expect some real-world physics to be in effect in the digital world, for example, it will feel unpredictable if elements pass through other elements.

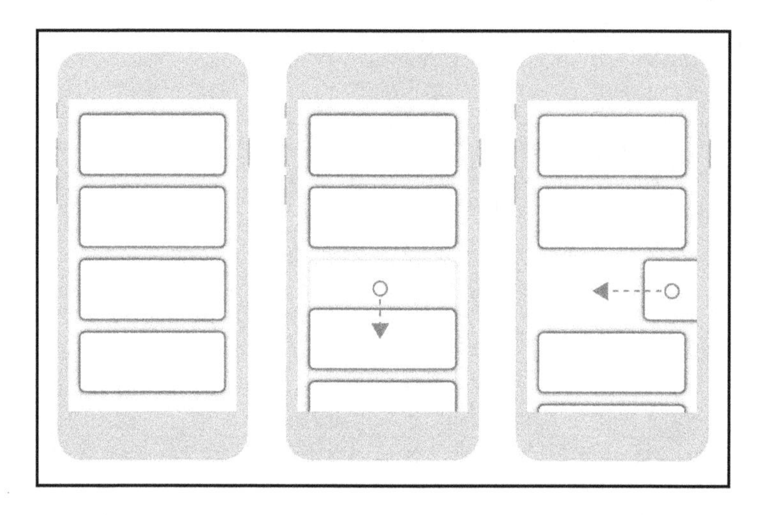

Transition in two steps--the element, first, move to open a space where a new element is placed in a second movement

In the preceding example, a new element appears on the screen to occupy the third position of a list. Moving the five elements at the same time will make the new element hit or cross the elements that currently occupy the final position of the new element. We can get a more ordered move by making room in the list before introducing the new element. In the first step, we create a space, while the new element takes its position on the screen in the second step.

Take into account that although the system can take some time to perform a process, the user will expect an instant reaction of the user interface when making a gesture. If we show a reaction before 100 microseconds, the user will perceive the sensation immediately, creating a more satisfactory control experience. With buttons, you can change their color while in other areas you can highlight the tapped area, or you can use an expanding effect centered on the position of the tap, as Android suggests with its radial reaction.

Duration

Very slow transitions may go unnoticed by users. It is in our nature to detect quick movements so any fast movement is highly noticeable, but an overuse of them could be stressing for your users. Also, our perception has limits, and some really quick movements could be interpreted as a flash without being able to appreciate in detail what is happening. We have to find a balance that allows the user to perceive the changes in a pleasant and easy-to-understand way.

The ideal speed of a transition will depend on various factors, such as the length of the displacements and the number of elements involved. On mobile phones, average times are recommended that work for most users, ranging from 200 microseconds to 500 microseconds. Transitions with a single element and short displacements will be located near 200 microseconds and transitions with several steps or with elements displacing longer distances will be around 500 microseconds.

However, if your users belong to a group with different perceptual abilities, such as people of advanced age with a slower perceptual capacity, you will have to evaluate if the proposed times should be adjusted.

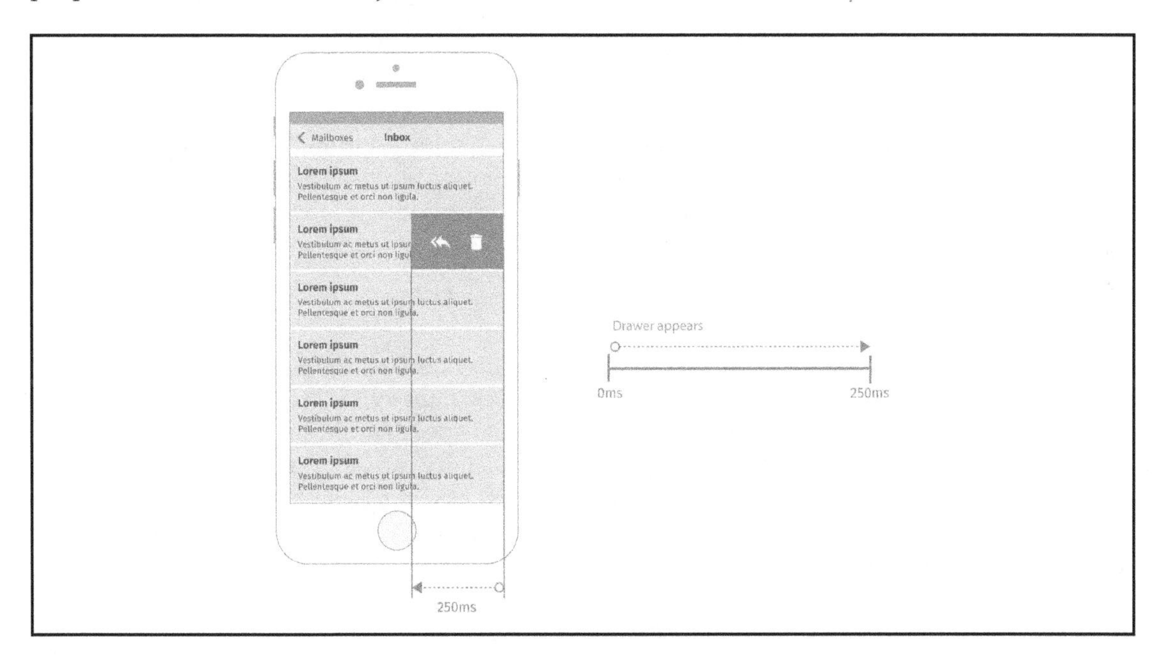

The transition between two near points develops in 250 microseconds

A simple transition that reacts to the user swipe should be fast and following the user movement, as it will give the user the feeling of control and reactability.

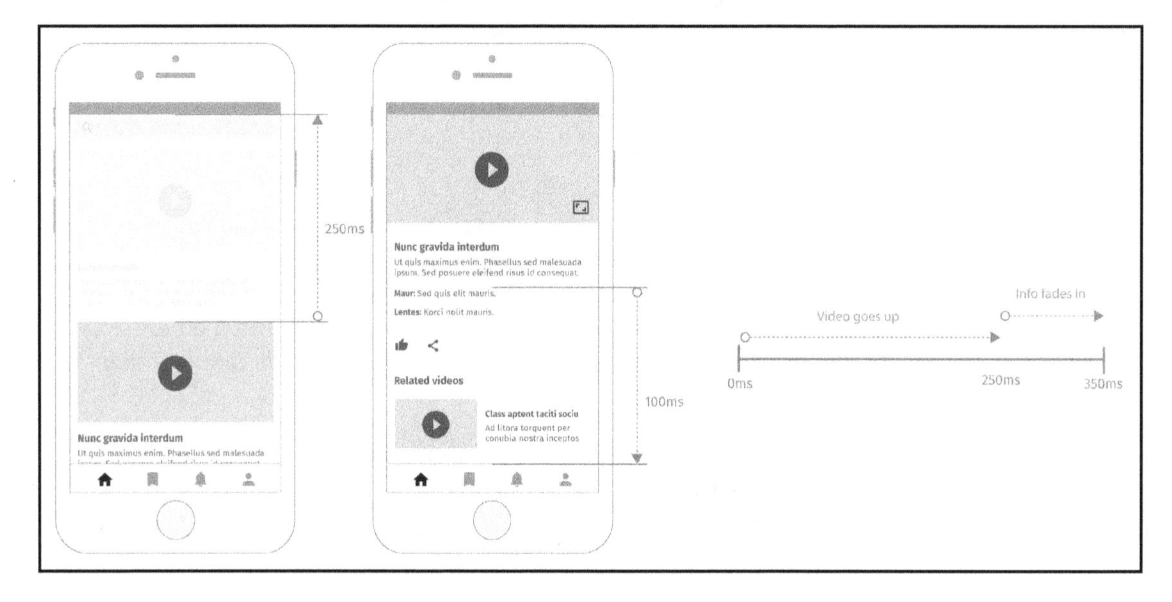

Complex transitions with steps can take longer

In the preceding example, the transition first moves the selected item to its final position, and when that transition is finished or the space for the content is available, a second transition occurs, with the content appearing on the screen with a fade-in effect.

Speed

In real life, objects move in different ways according to their nature. A train that moves on tracks without stopping will have an approximately constant speed. However, when a train arrives at the station where it should stop, it reduces its speed, braking gradually. The same thing happens when moving objects--objects do not usually move at one speed from one point to another. When a person lifts an object, the first effort is usually faster at the beginning than when it is reaching its final position, and more precision is required when it's near its final position.

Almost all working frameworks have different types of movement available to give your application transitions that feel predictable and natural to the user.

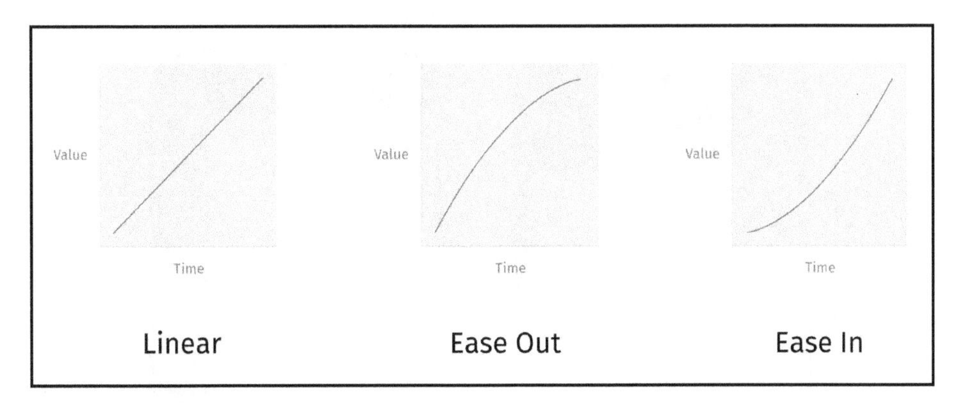

Bézier curves are traditionally used in motion design to represent the speed an object has at each time

The evolution of the value we are "easing" over time is usually represented by Bézier curves. Some common examples are Ease In, which changes the value to be slower at first, Ease Out, which changes the value to be slower at the end, and Ease In-Out, which starts and ends at a slower pace than at its midpoint. You can find some examples at `http://easings.net/`. They will be very useful when it comes to detailing how an animation should behave. The development team will normally have the means to include these types of curves in their projects, as they are widely supported by different development environments.

Mockups

Mockups are replicas of the final design of the product. When you make a mockup you must capture the same functional aspects that you have described in a wireframe, while also giving the elements the proper visual characteristics and affordances to represent that they are actionable.

While design has to be visually effective, it is even more important that it clearly represents its functionality and its comprehension is easy for your users.

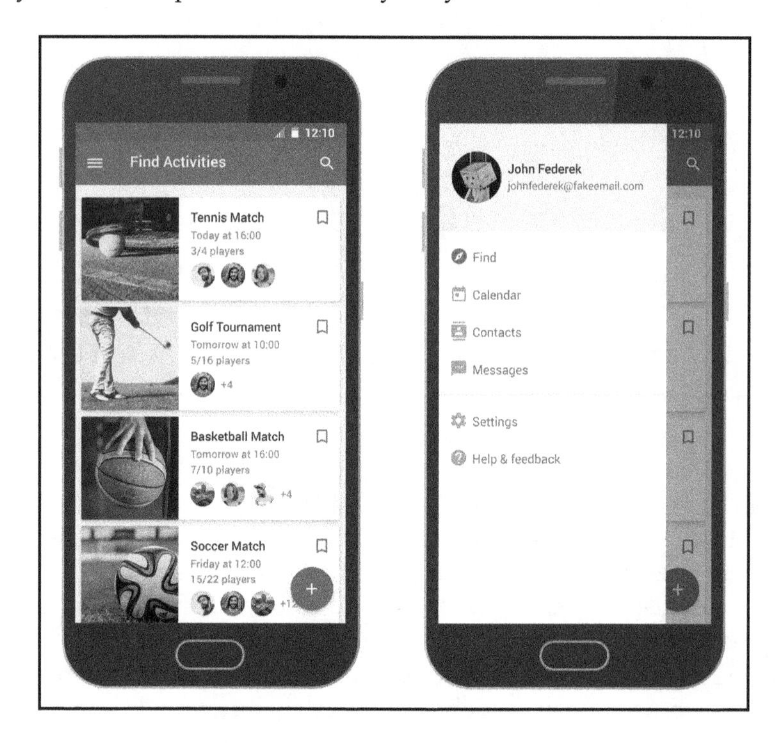

App mockups (assets from https://www.pexels.com and https://pixabay.com)

When considering the visual treatment for your mockups, you should clearly represent the hierarchy of elements and unequivocally differentiate actionable elements from the static content. When choosing colors, you should reserve certain colors to highlight actionable elements and to highlight elements that have a greater weight in the content. Links, sections, and titles must be clearly represented in the design. Annotations will be useful to indicate specific properties and measurements.

Testing your designs with real content

Mockups are an effective tool to represent the product before it is developed. Using real content in your mockups is important to avoid surprises when those are transferred into code. Focusing too much on mockups may lead you to use photos that look great but do not represent the actual content of the application, or use content that is more complete or more homogeneous than the content that the application finally will have.

If you have real content available--because you are redesigning an application or showing previous content in a new view--test your designs with that content, as you can show a version closer to reality. When the application is new, test your designs with heterogeneous content within the limits that may be introduced later. Do not assume that your users will have a certain type of behavior. You can also use the content from similar applications in the market for this phase, but remember that if you take a popular application as a reference, your content will represent users in a phase of relationship with an application that is much more advanced than the users you will have in an early stage of adoption of your application.

It is always better find layout problems in the design phase than when developers have already invested hours of work. Small adjustments right now can save a lot of work in the future.

Specifications and assets for multiple screens

Once your designs move to the development phase, it is necessary to provide complete specifications if you want to get precise results. For this purpose, you can use mockups and wireframes, as each document will compliment the other.

Generally, for each object or text, you will have to define attributes such as colors, sizes, fonts, and alignment, and you will also define the different states each object has when the user interacts with them. If you have a style guide where some of the standard components are already defined, you can just refer to it and avoid repeating the information for each instance of a standard component.

Due to the large amount of smartphones with different characteristics we can find on the market, our application will be seen on devices with very different screens in both size and resolution. That is why we have to know some conventions in measures and terminology that will help us have a common framework in which to create our specifications.

Understanding units and pixel densities

Pixels (**px**) are the smallest physical squares we find on digital screens. These are addressable, and we can define their color in an image or an application. As we now have devices with different concentrations of pixels per inch, if we define our assets with reference to these pixels, the icons or elements we design will be rendered in very different sizes according to the screen where they are displayed. A 24x24 px icon will be the correct size on a mobile with a low-density screen, but will appear very small when displayed on a mobile with a high-resolution screen.

If a file is not created taking into consideration the size at which it will be displayed, or if it is scaled in the rendering process, blur effects may appear. That's why mobile developers have created a system so that designers can provide the assets suitable for each of the **pixel density resolutions** that will have the devices.

On Android, generalized densities are as follows:

- `ldpi` (low) ~120dpi
- `mdpi` (medium) ~160dpi
- `hdpi` (high) ~240dpi
- `xhdpi` (extra-high) ~320dpi
- `xxhdpi` (extra-extra-high) ~480dpi
- `xxxhdpi` (extra-extra-extra-high) ~640dpi

Further information can be found at `https://developer.android.com/guide/practices/screens_support.html`.

On iOS, generalized sizes are as follows:

- `@1x` ~160dpi
- `@2x` ~320dpi
- `@3x` ~480dpi

Further information can be found at `https://developer.apple.com/ios/human-interface-guidelines/graphics/image-size-and-resolution/`.

This means that you will provide your assets adapted to these resolutions, and different devices will use the correct assets according to their resolution, making them look nice and smooth. You can design your icons at the baseline resolution in a vector format and export them later for the required resolutions on each platform. Although you can use a program such as Photoshop to produce the icons of your application, with a vectorial tool, such as Illustrator or Sketch, you can make use of the features designed for this purpose. For example, you can design your icons at 24x24px or 25x25px artboard sizes, the commonly used sizes, and export them later for higher and lower densities with options for exporting at different resolutions.

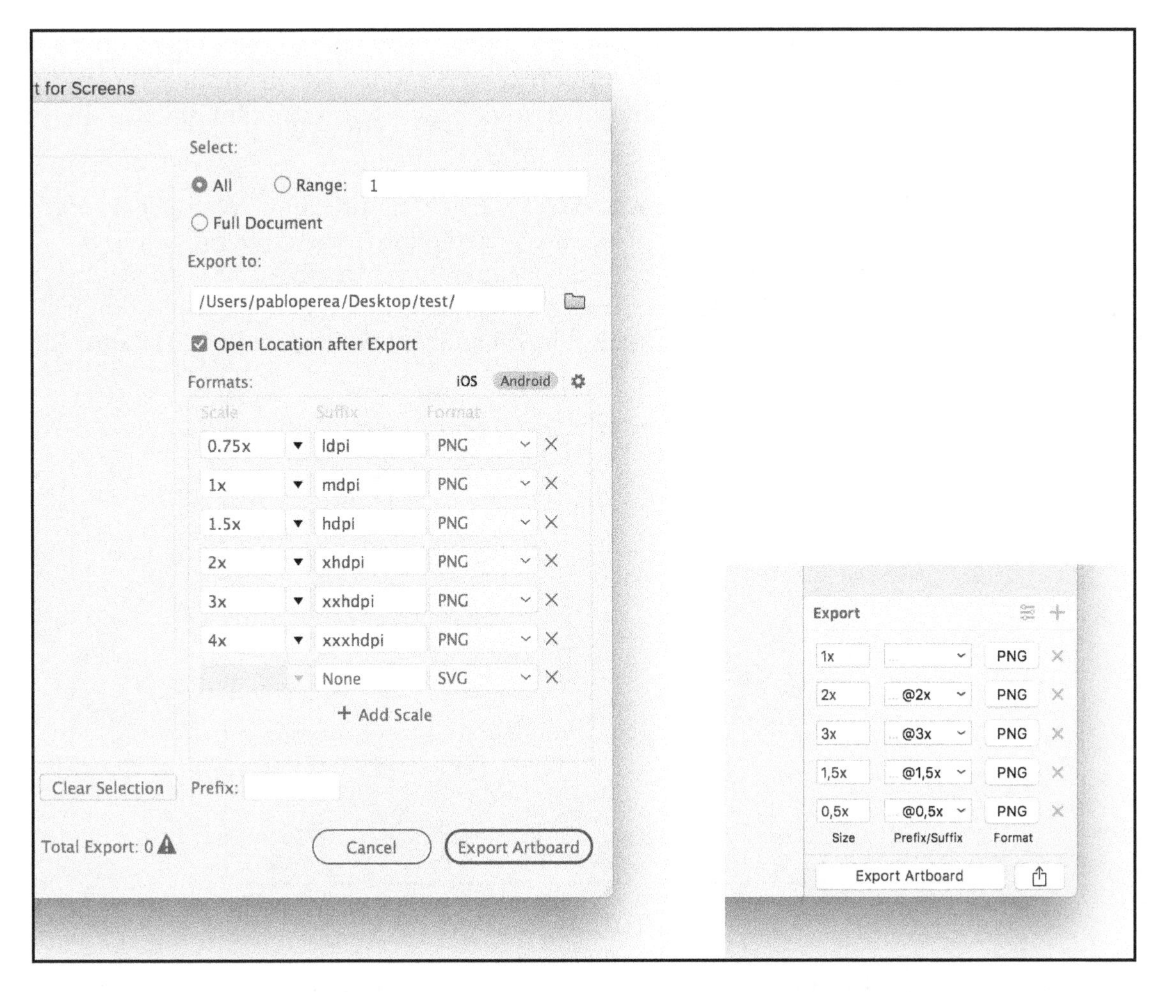

Export for screens in Illustrator(left) and export with slices in Sketch (right) (source: Screenshot from Illustrator; source: Screenshot from Sketch)

Similar to how we provide assets for the different resolutions, we need to provide measures for all of them and for all the elements displayed in each view. As providing pixel sizes for each resolution will be an ineffective method, you can use generalized units for all the different pixel densities.

On Android, it is common to use **density-independent pixels** (**dp**) for graphical elements and **scaleable pixels** (**sp**) for fonts, whereas on iOS the generalized unit is the **point** (**pt**). A dp will be 1 pixel on medium density screens, scaling from 1 pixel for the other densities and the same happens with pt--that will be a pixel in a `@1x` density screen (1 pixel equals one point (1/72 of an inch) on a standard resolution screen). The sp are similar to dp, but are also affected by the user's font settings.

For example, if you indicate that a button will measure 48dp, it will measure 48px on a smartphone with a screen with mdpi, and 96px on a smartphone with an xhdpi (2x) screen. The same will happen with iOS measurements, if you define a button as 44pt, it will measure 88px at a `@2x` resolution or 132px at a `@3x` resolution.

Does it mean that iPhone 7 Plus will use @3x assets without modification? Well, that is not exactly true. Some devices use downsampling and upsampling in the rendering process. That means that the iPhone 7 Plus creates the information using the size @3x as a reference, but shows the final content on the screen making a small adjustment. For example, iPhone 7 Plus shows the final content with a downsampling adjustment equivalent to 1.15 (Value equivalent to 1242/1080=2208/1920=1.15).

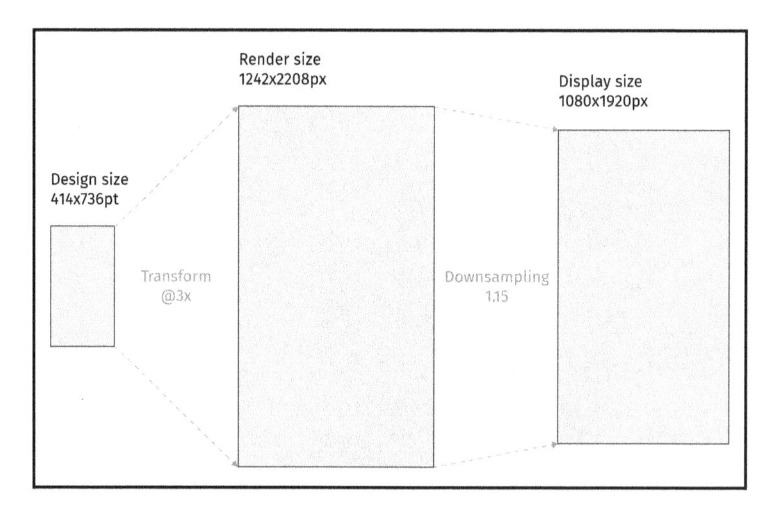

Design and rendering process on an iPhone 7 Plus

In the preceding image, we can see the design and rendering process for an iPhone 7 Plus resolution. We will design at **414x736pt**--the artboard will be first rendered at 1242x2208px and then it will go to the display after a downsampling that will bring the design to 1080x1920px. You can find other examples at `https://www.paintcodeapp.com/news/ultimate-guide-to-iphone-resolutions`.

Specifications file

We can find different plugins on the market to make specifications in our designs. While we will have to make small adjustments to suit our projects, tools such as Sketch, Photoshop, and Illustrator have specific solutions to perform this function. In the following examples, we have used two plugins that are free and can be downloaded at the specified addresses.

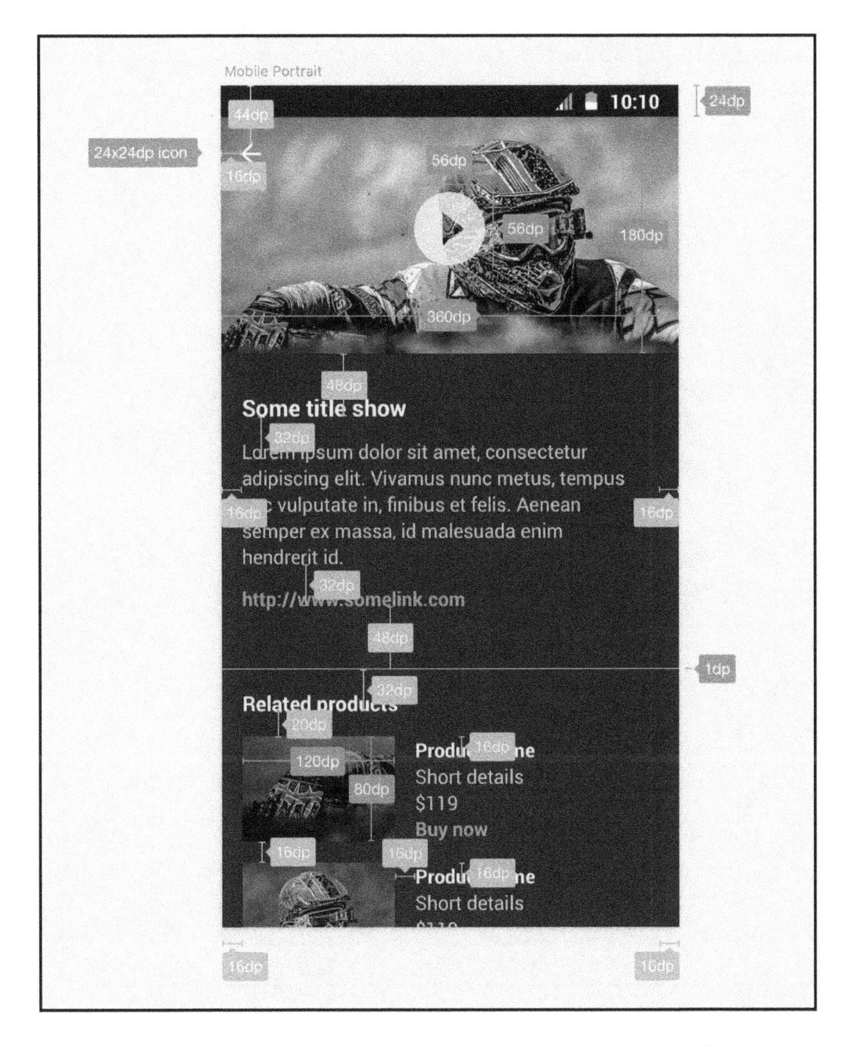

Measurements specs with Sketch Measure as a base; some elements have been added or modified

(assets from https://pixabay.com/en/sports-games-fun-holiday-parks-679594/, source: screenshot from Sketch with Sketch Measure)

Sketch Measure can be easily installed from the Sketch Toolbox plugin. This plugin will allow you to install different plugins to get the most out of Sketch. With Sketch Measure you can measure distances, sizes, and fonts, making it very easy to create a useful and well-presented specification document. The measurements are editable, so you can make adjustments if necessary.

You can download Sketch Toolbox from `http://sketchtoolbox.com/`, and Sketch Measure from the Toolbox or from `https://github.com/utom/sketch-measure`.

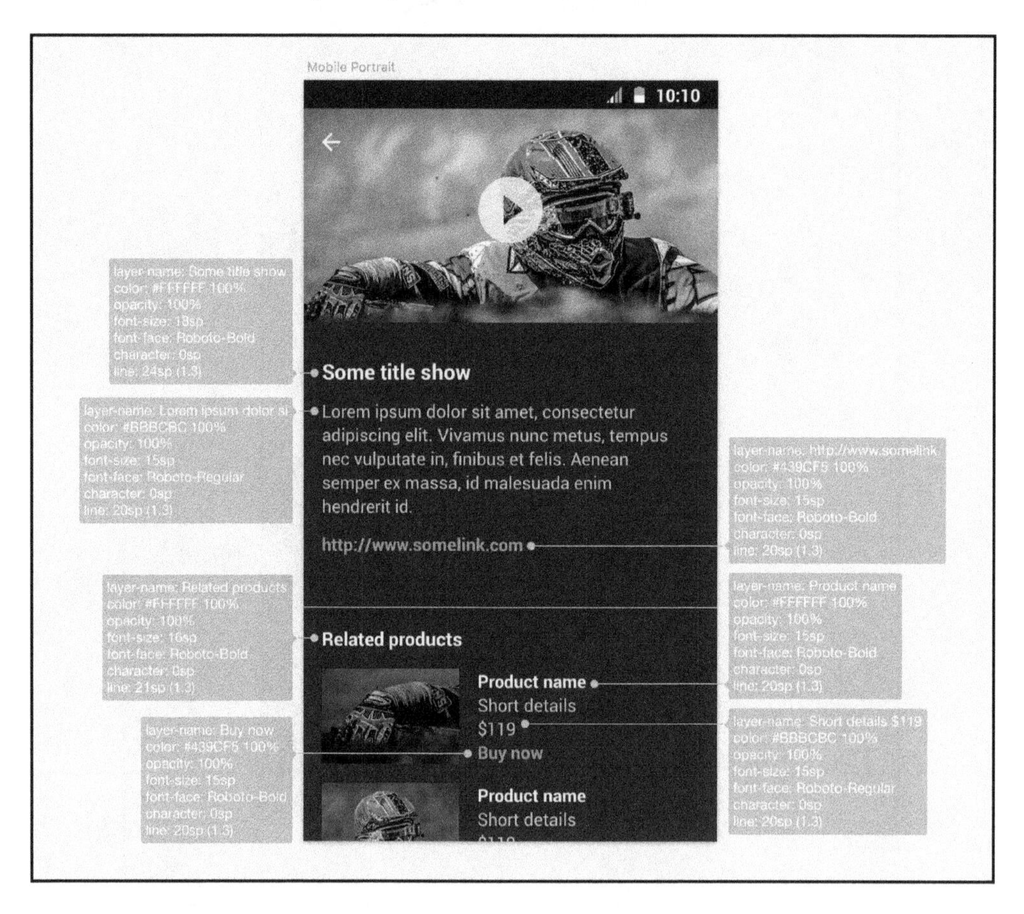

Fonts specs with Sketch Measure as a base. Some elements have been added or modified (assets from https://pixabay.com/en/sports-games-fun-holiday-parks-679594/, source: Screenshot from Sketch with Sketch Measure)

In this example, we have divided the measurement indications and the attributes of the texts into two documents, but you can create only one and use more space to include all the specifications in a single document. Make sure that all measurements are easily understandable by the development team.

The following example is made with Photoshop using the Ink plugin. Similar to Sketch Measure, it allows you to indicate measurements and text attributes. You can download Ink for Photoshop at `http://ink.chrometaphore.com/`.

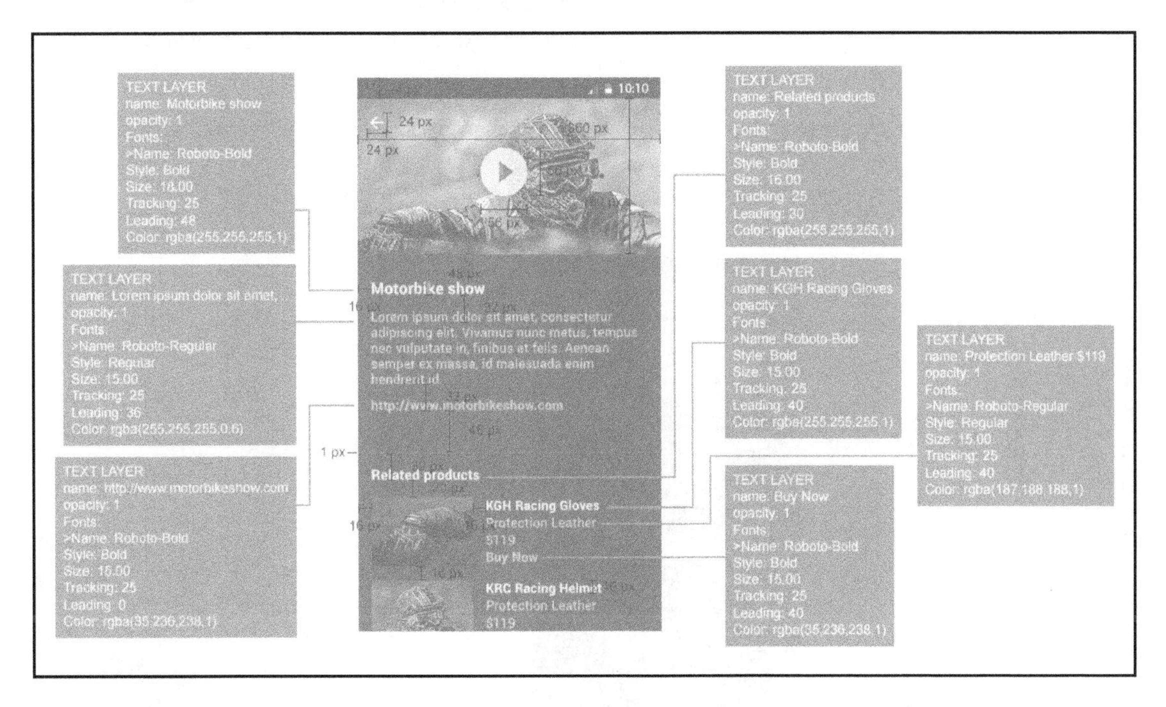

Fonts specs with Photoshop Ink as a base; some elements have been added or modified (assets from https://pixabay.com/en/sports-games-fun-holiday-parks-679594/ source: Screenshot from Photoshop with Ink)

In case you want to include some missing parameters, you can edit the measurements, as they will appear as editable layers in the layer inspector.

Automated solutions

You can also find some automated solutions that can improve your specifications creation workflow. Zeplin at `https://zeplin.io/` or InVision Inspect at `https://www.invisionapp.com/` have plugins that directly connect your designs with software that provides specifications for the development team.

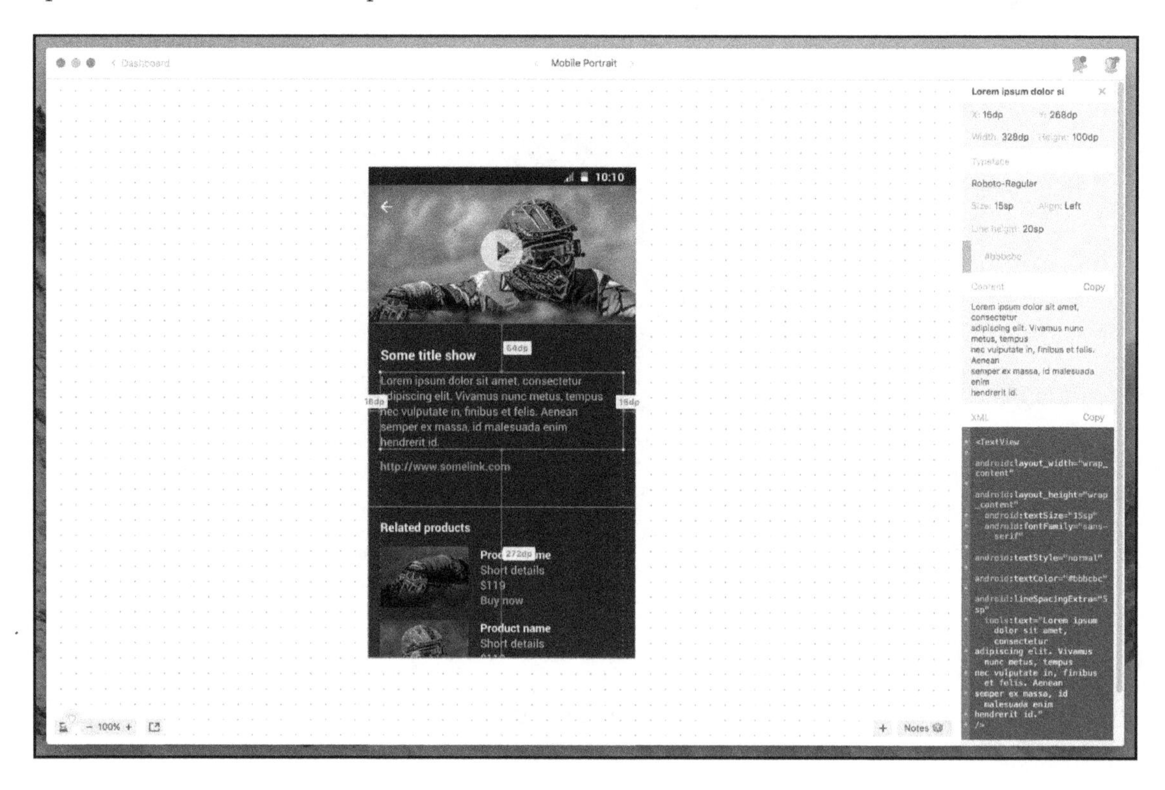

Screenshot from Zeplin Desktop

Touch target

The touch target is the area the user can tap on the screen in order to perform an action. The recommended size is between 7mm and 10mm. As we define our sizes in points and density-independent pixels, Android and iOS guidelines have recommended sizes in these units to get good results on the different devices. In Android, the recommended touch target is minimum 48dp x 48dp, whereas the recommended touch target is minimum 44pt x 44pt in iOS.

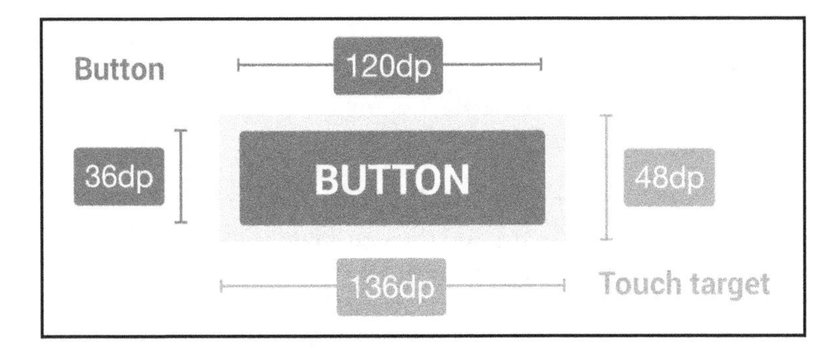

The touch target should have a minimum size of 48x48dp on Android, regardless of the visual representation

It does not mean that buttons should be 48dp tall; it depends on your design and also on their nature. For example, you could have a button of 36dp in height and 70dp in width, and its touch target still should be 48dp tall or more. Having an active area bigger than the visual representation of a component is a way to balance the contradicting requirements of mobile devices--limited space but using controls that are comfortable to operate with your fingers.

Images with good resolution

The backgrounds and images that you use in your application should be adapted to the different densities where they will be shown. The images you use in your application can be vector or bitmap. Bitmap images are a collection of ordered pixel colors in a grid, and vector images are defined using polygons with attributes as to their color or shape. That means that vector images are scalable without loss of quality; simply increasing the numbers in their mathematical specification, changes them to the new size, but bitmaps can show blurred areas when scaled. There are some projects, such as Google RAISR, that try to mitigate this loss of quality in bitmap images.

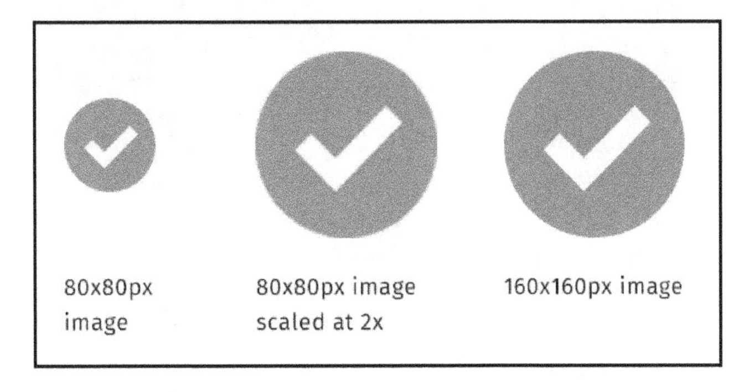

Scaling effect in bitmap images; graphic gets blurred when scaled at 2x (middle)

If your image is vectorial, you can use different vector formats to provide developers with a single asset that will scale properly when it is displayed in a different density. Some formats that support vector information are **Scalable Vector Graphics** (**SVG**) and **Portable Document Format** (**PDF**).

If your image is in bitmap, for example, **Portable Network Graphics** (**PNG**) files, **Joint Photographic Experts Group** (**JPEG** or **JPG**) files, or **Graphics Interchange Format** (**GIF**), make sure that you provide assets adapted to the different resolutions in which they will be shown. A larger image than necessary will occupy valuable space in your application, and a low quality image will make your application look unpolished--not all the assets will suffer in the same way.

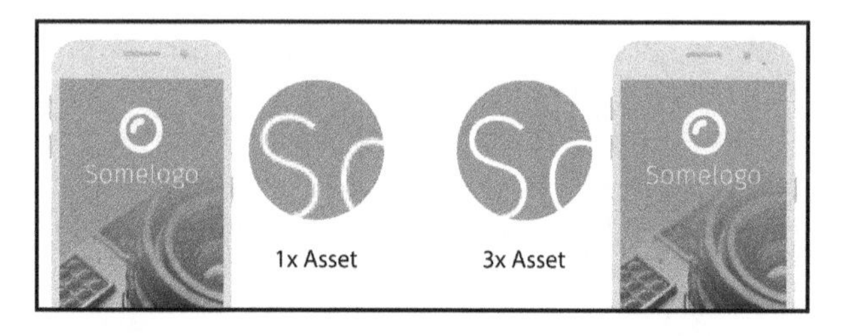

Scaling effect on a thin font logo. Small details can be visually poor.

(assets from https://pixabay.com/en/camera-photography-lens-equipment-801924/)

Busy backgrounds will not suffer as much from using a lower resolution compared to some logos, icons, and geometric artworks. Keep that in mind when making concessions on the quality of your assets.

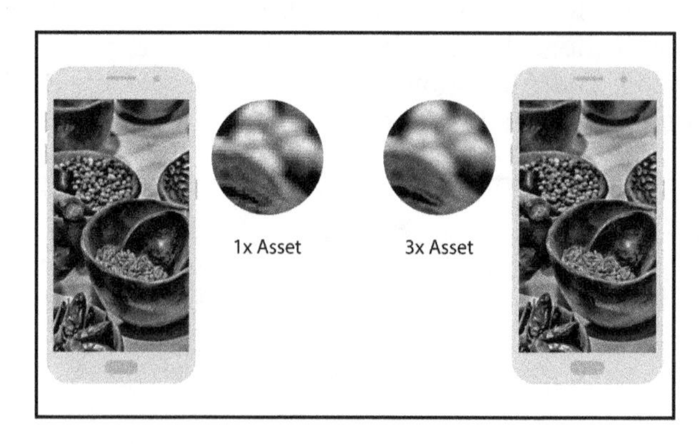

Scaling effect on a busy background where quality differences are not so evident but still appreciable.

(assets from https://pixabay.com/en/spice-chiles-paprika-chili-powder-370114/)

Also, keep in mind that formats such as JPG can help you to lower the weight of certain assets. Test the exported files on real devices to confirm whether they respond to the desired result. You should also confirm whether the colors are represented as expected in each type of screen.

Pixel perfect icons

The design is greatly affected by small details. Well designed and easily understandable icons are essential to make our application attractive and friendly. The icons we create will be finally rendered on screens with a given resolution. Some techniques can help us to create icons that render well on different screens, giving our design a more polished result.

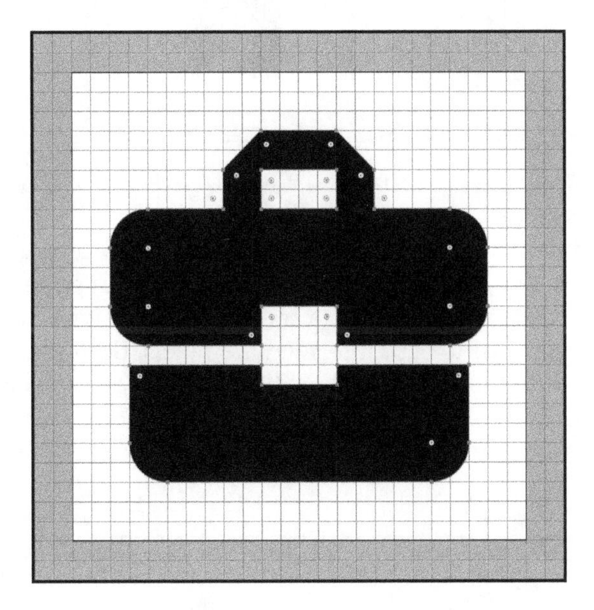

Icon from Material Design with their points placed on exact positions and with curves realized at 90 degrees angles (source: Screenshot from Illustrator)

The first thing we must do is choose one or several sizes of artboard for the icons we create for our application. For example, we can choose a size of 24x24dp for the general icons of our application and create a secondary size to represent certain states of some elements of 16x16dp.

In the same way, we must always work with a line thickness and similar types of curves throughout the icon family. This will help us achieve a uniform and elegant visual result.

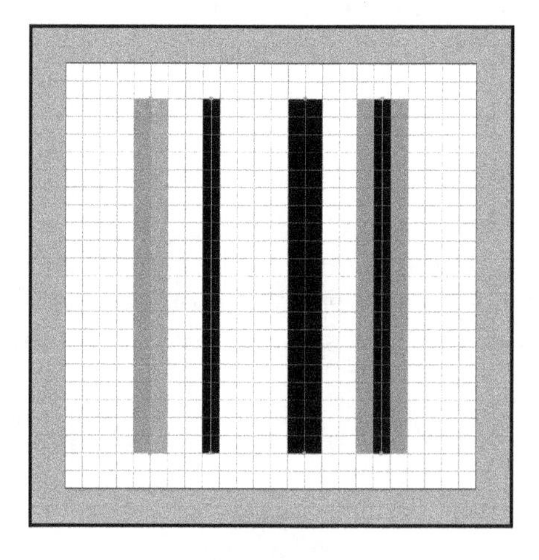

1px lines render different than 2px lines when exported to @1x (source: Screenshot from Illustrator)

Your vector design software usually allows the option to draw on a grid at the pixel level. When drawing polygons and lines, they must begin and end in positions that are multiples of 0.5px of our grid. Depending on the size of our lines and polygon borders, they will render better using integer positions or intermediate pixels. Both Illustrator and Sketch allow us to visualize a grid that corresponds to the pixels of our artboard. If our lines are to measure 2px thick, it is advisable to use rounded pixels in whole numbers, whereas if our lines are to measure 1px thick, intermediate pixel positions will give us better results when rendering.

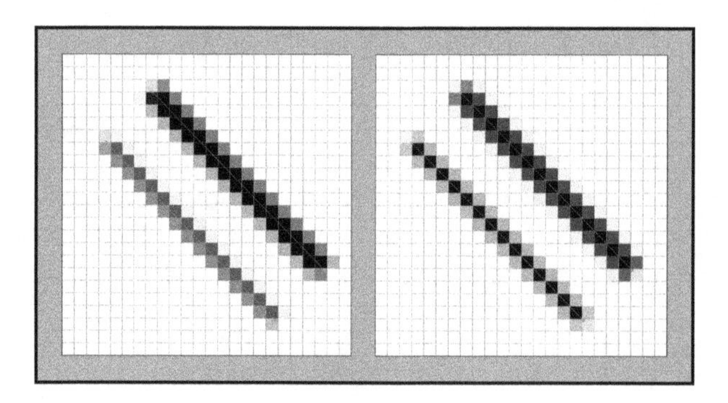

Draw the diagonal lines from exact positions so that they render well (left) and prevent the line from being rendered by dividing the weight between two lines of pixels (right) (source: Screenshots from Illustrator)

The diagonal lines will also be affected by the position of their initial and final points. The lines made in multiples of 45 degrees produce very homogeneous results visually.

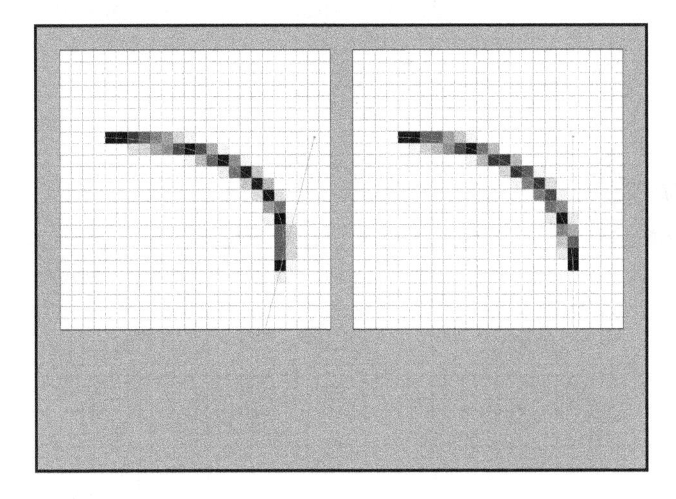

Curves that end in straight lines following axes are rendered nicely (right) (source: Screenshots from Illustrator)

In vector programs, we can draw curves using direction lines. The resulting curve will be tangent to the drawn line. The way we draw this tangent will also affect the final result of the icon. Curves tangent to lines parallel to the vertical and horizontal axes will produce more polished results.

Keep in mind that each curve is affected by both the start line and the finish line. Visualize the icon with the pixel preview option of your software; it will help you to visualize the final result before exporting your assets.

Being pragmatic

Build a close relationship with the development team and ask them for feedback on the material you create. They can give you a very practical and useful view of where to find ideas that may improve your workflow.

As an example, a functionality that you consider to be complex may integrate very easily with a native component. However, a functionality that you consider simple may require very specific specifications and a greater participation on your part to reach the level of detail expected.

When working with a new team, it is advisable to have conversations about the specifications themselves. Finding and understanding gaps in the early stages will help reduce development time and provide higher quality specifications. Help the team understand the different measurements and diagrams you use so that the whole team speaks the same language.

Learn how to code

Code is the ultimate material in which your ideas will be built. Try to have basic knowledge about how developers do their work when creating and placing elements in the different views of an app. You can find some nice videos about mobile and web application software tools they will likely use to produce the application. You don't need to be able to create production-ready code; however, understanding how the developers will do their work later on will help you create a good specification document and make your work more appreciated and followed with precision.

Test in real environments

Producing quality graphics is a skill that is learned by producing and testing. When you create an icon, use the option to display it in pixels to try to reduce the unwanted pixels, and when you consider that the result is good, take the design to a real mobile. This will give you an accurate vision of the result on the real device; it will be easier for you to appreciate small problems in rendering.

If you test the icons with a mockup of the actual application, you will be able to appreciate other aspects, such as the real size, or whether it represents the type of element that must be represented. When you have to create a family of icons, it is difficult to get the same level of detail in all of them, so it is best to try them visually alongside each other until you get a balanced visual result.

Stay up to date on the latest trends

The usability design community is an active community, generating content on an ongoing basis. This does not mean that you need to adopt any new approach. Some trends or new technologies will not have a direct application in your projects, but they will help you better understand how to find solutions to other problems you may find. Be aware of trends and analyze them critically on whether they could help you achieve your design goals better. Some trends will end up being so widespread that they will become part of regular user expectations. So, the sooner you know about them, the better you can experiment and make your own evaluations.

Summary

In this chapter, we covered how to detail our design solutions using wireframes and mockups. We have also explained how to prepare our specifications and assets for different screen resolutions.

Understanding all the concepts contained in this chapter will help us to prepare suitable materials for development teams. The use of common units will facilitate communication with different teams, making it easier for us to get the result we are looking for.

In the next chapter, we will focus on how to create prototypes to test our solutions in the early stages of the design process. Discovering changes sooner in the design process will avoid costly adjustments when the development process is further advanced.

6
Prototyping - Bringing Your Ideas to Life

"I don't explain, I don't tell, I show."

- Leo Tolstoy

Anticipating the success of a product is not an easy task. Human history is full of both successful and unsuccessful products. Although simple toys like the hula-hoop were a tremendous success, the swing-wing--a toy based on similar concepts--was not successful at all.

The Swing Wing was a toy designed to capitalize on the fun of moving your neck back and forth repeatedly. It was a big failure in terms of adoption, despite its similarities to the extremely successful, waist-moving hula-hoop (the preceding image was found from `https://en.wikipedia.org/wiki/Swing_Wing_(toy)`, `https://archive.org/details/swing_wing`).

Every app starts from an idea, and you never know for sure if that idea will work in practice. Waiting until your product gets built in order to validate your idea represents a big risk--if things don't go as expected, you'll have little room to change course. It would be more useful to know how users will react to your product much earlier.

Fortunately, you can evaluate your ideas earlier, thanks to prototyping. A prototype is a simulation of relevant parts of your solution that allows you to learn from your users before building the real product. In this way, you don't need to wait until your product is completed to check whether your idea works as expected. Prototyping will save you time and help you deliver a better product that is more likely to solve the real needs of your users.

Building prototypes is fast, but it requires you to understand the purpose of prototyping, pick the right tools, and plan the process. This chapter will provide guidance through those aspects so that you can bring your ideas to life as soon as possible.

Adopting the prototyping mindset

Prototyping is a common practice in many disciplines. Everybody understands the benefits of trying a scale plane in a wind tunnel before building the real aircraft. It is better to check and correct the aerodynamics of a smaller-scale plane model than discovering any issue once the real one is built and in flight. This is also true for apps.

Model of the supersonic transport in the NASA full-scale wind tunnel in 1973 (Source: https://commons.wikimedia.org/wiki/File:SST_model_in_Wind_Tunnel.jpeg)

A prototype may look similar to a real product, but they are very different in nature. A prototype does not have to work, it only has to look like it does. In addition, a prototype only tries to simulate a few aspects from those that the final product will have, in particular, those aspects the designer considers more important to learn about.

Prototyping takes advantage of the fact that *users do not care about the internals of your product*. They only care about how the product manifests to them. Simulating some superficial parts of a solution is often enough to recreate the experience users will have with the final product, and learn from it. While your real app may need to query a database or use some external services, your prototype can just fake the information that is presented to the user. Nobody will care about the difference, despite the different levels of effort required in each case. If the user taps on the search button of your prototype and some search results appear, the user won't question where these results came from.

The **prototyping mindset** is about creating an illusion with the minimum possible effort. If you try to prototype too many aspects at the same time, the level of complexity of your prototype will increase, eventually approaching the complexity of the final product. Keep prototypes focused, to quickly learn one aspect at a time.
Reducing the scope of the prototype is key to maximizing the prototyping benefits. In the case of prototyping a plane, you may want to focus on either the aerodynamics or the interior design, but not both aspects at the same time. In the preceding example, you can use a scale model to check the aerodynamics or you can rearrange the furniture of a room to recreate the interior of a plane in order to test your interior design ideas. However, it would be much harder to prototype both aspects at the same time with a single prototype.

Deciding the best prototyping approach for your needs

When prototyping, you need to constantly find *a balance between realism and speed*. On the one hand, you want your prototype to recreate the experience of your final product as much as possible. On the other hand, taking care of all the details requires time, and you will want to validate your ideas as quickly as possible.

The ideal balance between realism and speed will be different for each prototype. The following strategies will help you to find this balance in order to make the most of your prototyping efforts:

- Focus on a specific scenario
- Simplify the interactions according to their relevance
- Define what you want to learn in advance

Focusing your prototype on one specific scenario helps you to cut corners and keeps the prototyping process fast. You may want to limit the options the user has in the prototype to reduce complexity without making the prototype look incomplete to recreate a realistic experience.

Your prototype only needs to support the minimum number of steps for one particular representative instance, and you can pick that scenario in advance to your advantage. For example, you can make a prototype of a travel app that shows several destinations as options, but only allows users to actually select the city of Paris. When testing with users, you will introduce the scenario in a way that invites them to look for that destination.

Instead of supporting all user interactions at the same level of detail, consider *simplifying interactions according to their relevance*. Each interaction the user has with your prototype can be supported at different levels of detail according to their relevance. For example, if you want to learn about the user's perception of the general idea of your app, you can skip animated transitions when users move from one screen to another. Despite the lack of detail in those transitions, this basic prototype is all you need to learn whether the navigation across the different parts of the app makes sense to your users. When learning about more specific actions, such as discarding notifications, you may want to invest more time in supporting gestures, animations, and other aspects to recreate the experience with a greater level of detail.

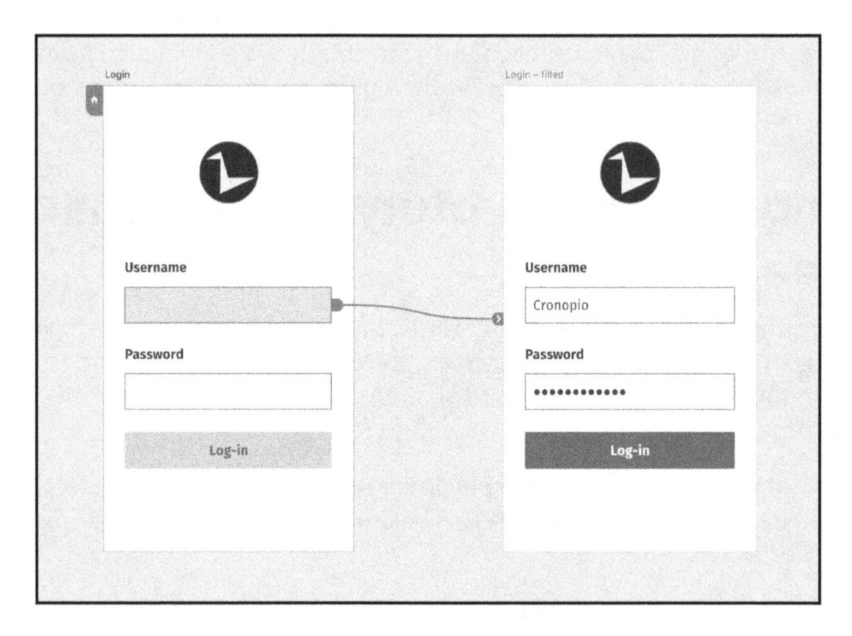

A prototype for the log-in process made of two screens with one interaction connecting them, as is represented in Adobe Experience Design. The resulting prototype will show the first screen initially, and by tapping on the username input, users will reach a view with the log-in information already filled-in, simulating the input process.

When simplifying interactions, you can even completely skip some intermediate steps. If your prototype includes the **Log-in** step, but it is not the main learning focus, you can include a simplified version of it. For example, showing a Login screen with information already filled in is less realistic, but may be good enough for the user to understand the overall process.

In the same way that a sequence of static images projected in a cinema is perceived as a continuous motion, many people will not notice such gaps in a prototype. The human brain is able to fill these gaps in many cases, and testing with users will tell you the right amount of steps you can skip without breaking the illusion.

Finally, you need to *define what you want to learn in advance*. Building your prototype becomes much easier when you explicitly state the purpose of the prototype before you start creating it. By specifying what you want to learn, you can ask yourself if the effort to build a specific part of the prototype will help to achieve that goal. Based on that, you can evaluate the costs and benefits and determine the simplest type of prototype that can help you learn the most.

Depending on the purpose of your prototype, you can pick a different style of prototype and tool. There are many different types of prototypes and many different tools to create them. In the following sections, you will learn some common options and times when it is more convenient to use them.

Deciding on the type of prototype

Prototypes can be very different depending on their purpose and the time available to create them. There is no limit to the kinds of prototypes you can create. At the end of the day, prototyping is about experimenting. However, here are some common approaches you can get inspired by to create your own approach to prototyping. These different existing approaches are characterized by two key aspects:

- The **fidelity level** defines how realistic the prototype looks
- The **interaction level** defines the degree to which the prototype responds to the user actions

Based on the fidelity level, you can find prototypes resembling real products to different extents:

- **Paper prototyping** is a low-fidelity approach to prototyping. It consists of cutting, combining, and moving around pieces of paper with different parts of the interface on them. You can sketch different screens of your app, show it to a user, and switch from one to another to simulate the interaction the user would have when the user touches the sketch on the paper.

Paper prototype where different parts of the UI have been combined in a collage (source: https://www.flickr.com/photos/21218849@N03/7984460226/)

You can use pre-designed templates such as those provided by `http://sneakpeekit.com/` to sketch on top the shape of a device or a browser frame, or print different UI widgets such as buttons or checkboxes to combine them. The flexibility of the paper medium allows you to quickly sketch new states in response to user actions that you didn't plan in advance. However, since users will be interacting with sketches on a piece of paper it is much harder for them to feel how using the final product would be.

The low entry barrier of paper can be very convenient for participatory design workshops where you can involve users to express their own ideas. Prototypes created by users may not capture ideas ready to be adopted, but they are useful for designers to learn more about the problems to solve and which aspects users care about in a solution.

- **Low-fidelity digital prototypes** use a similar idea of connecting multiple sketches to simulate interactions, but they apply the concept to the digital world instead. This allows prototypes to be used in a real device or shared digitally with people around the world. However, users will still be presented with sketches that show an abstracted view of the product.

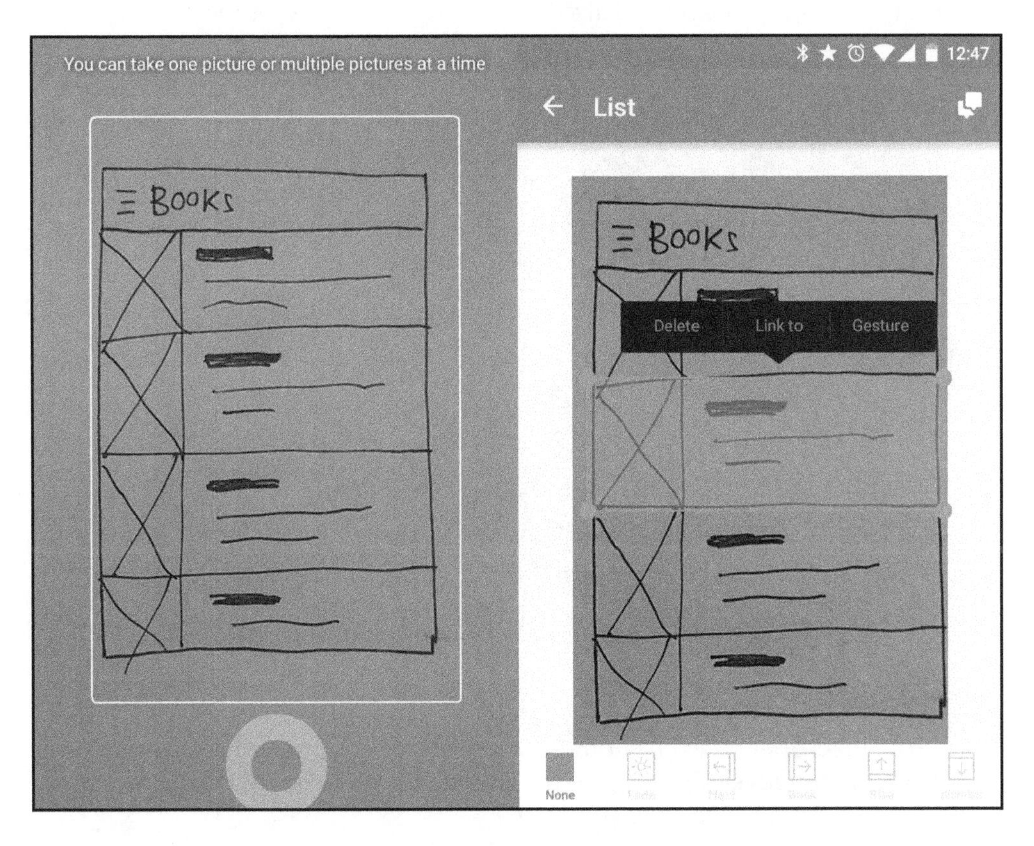

POP is a mobile prototyping tool that allows you to take pictures of your sketches (left screen) and define interactive areas and transitions between them (right screen)

You can make the sketches on paper and transfer them to a digital format by taking a picture or scanning them, or you can create them digitally. In any case, you will connect the sketches together in a prototyping tool to define how they will react to different user interactions.

- **High-fidelity prototypes** are realistic enough to be indistinguishable from a real product. Even if these prototypes cut some corners or skip some steps to approximate the intended experience, a user is able to get immersed in that experience. Users will communicate what they experience directly, without any effort of imagination Creating these prototypes requires more advanced tools to produce realistic assets and also combine them in a prototype.

Is this a real app or just a prototype? Not being able to tell the difference would help your users to get a more immersive experience

Apart from their fidelity level, another factor that determines the nature of a prototype is their **interaction level**. Prototypes can provide different levels of interaction, making the user take a more active or passive role.

- **Non-interactive prototypes** include static images showing how the product would look in a specific context, or videos showing what an interaction would look like. In these prototypes, users do not have the control, which avoids the need for you to prepare the prototype for potential user actions. The audience can comment on what they see or how they react to an idea represented in the prototype. These prototypes are very useful to get reactions from a wider audience, but you will not get feedback based on actual behavior.

- **Interactive prototypes** allow the user to act on the prototype in the same way they would do with the final product. Users get a more immersive experience and behave in a more natural way compared to noninteractive prototypes. Interactive prototypes make it possible to extract conclusions based on the actual user behavior instead of their initial impressions and opinions.

In this book, we will focus mainly on high-fidelity interactive prototypes since they allow you to get the most valuable feedback. Nevertheless, the techniques you'll learn will be useful in creating any other kind of prototype. For example, once you have created an interactive prototype, you can easily record a video showing a specific workflow to create a noninteractive prototype.

Selecting the appropriate tools

There are many different prototyping tools available, and probably, more will appear in the future. However, many of the existing tools follow similar approaches, making knowledge of one tool useful for another.

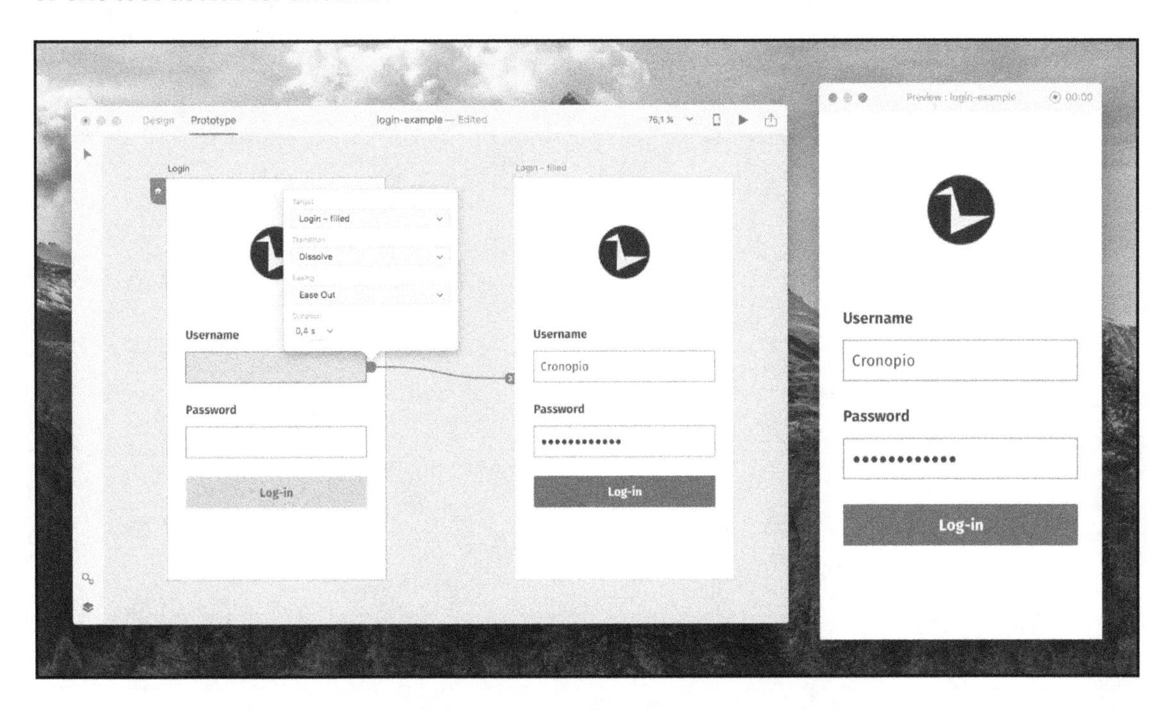

Adobe Experience Design is a combined design and prototyping tool that allows you to connect different pages visually by defining transitions. On the right side the simulator shows one view at a time allowing you to interact with the prototype. (source: Screenshot from Adobe Experience Design)

Tools based on **navigation between pages** make use of different pages and interactive areas. You can define a page to capture a specific view of your app. These pages can be made up of a single image of the UI you have designed in a separate tool, or a composition of different UI controls.

In order to create interactions, you can define interactive areas on a page and specify a transition to another page. In this way, you can specify that tapping on an area of the menu icon will trigger a transition to the menu view. In addition to capturing the navigation of your app, you can also define transitions to simulate changes of state, such as the transition between an unselected and selected checkbox.

A common limitation of these tools is that it is complex to deal with multiple simultaneous states because the state of the prototype needs to be captured to match the user path through different interactions. Thus, if your prototype allows you to take an optional action that needs to persist in some way, such as deleting an item of a list, you need to duplicate the many views to account for the case of the item being present and the case of the item being deleted from the list.

Tools based on **layer interactions** allow you to independently manipulate the different pieces that compose the prototype. In these tools, you can create a prototype with a list of items and control the visibility of each item in the list independently.

This provides greater control over the status of individual parts of the prototype.

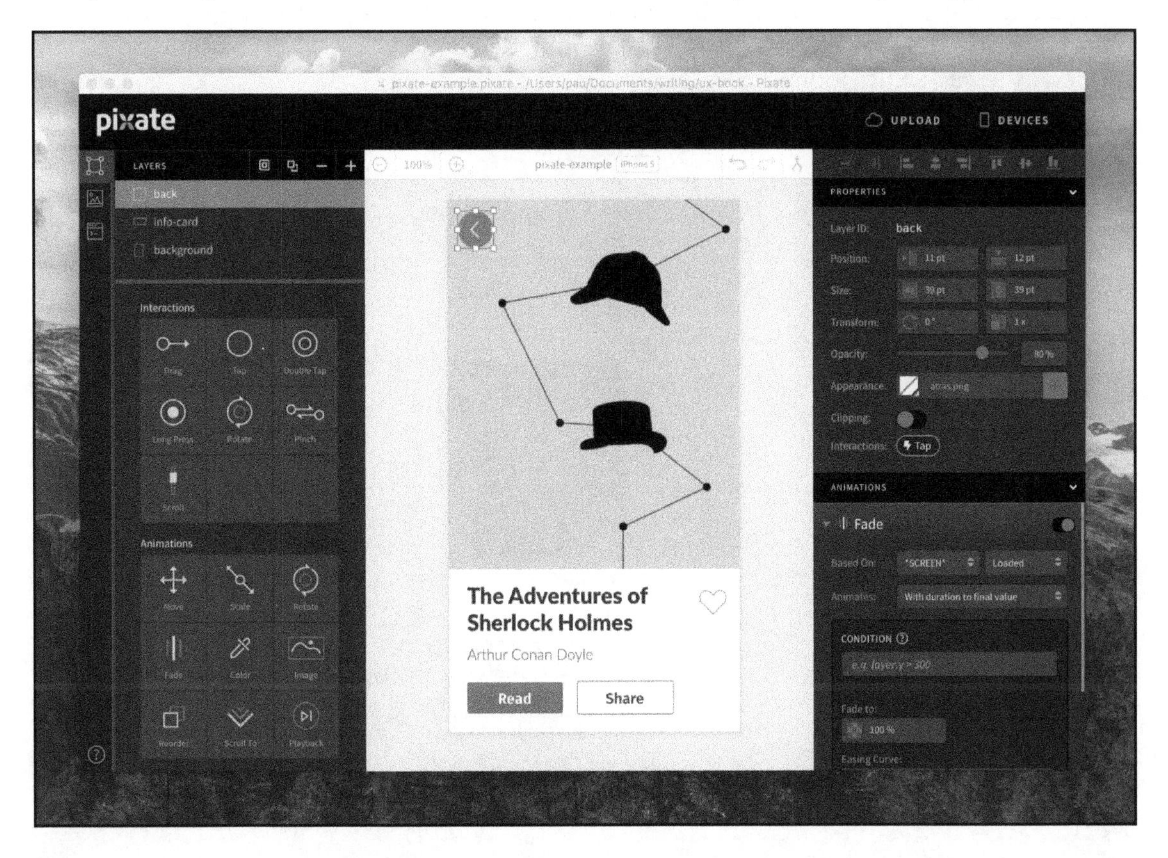

Pixate is based on layers--listed on the left--and different properties can be adjusted--on the right--including the definition of interactions and animations for each layer. (source: screenshot from Pixate)

A common inconvenience of these tools is that they often require you to decompose and reassemble the pieces of your prototype. Since mockups and prototypes are often created with separate tools, you need to export the relevant pieces from a graphic design tool and import them into the prototyping one. Some tools provide advanced importing tools to simplify the process and save a designer's time.

Timeline-based tools are also based on layers, but they give a prominent role to time. By using a timeline, they provide detailed control over animations and transitions in your prototypes. You can apply the principles of motion design to your prototypes and adjust all the details of each animation.

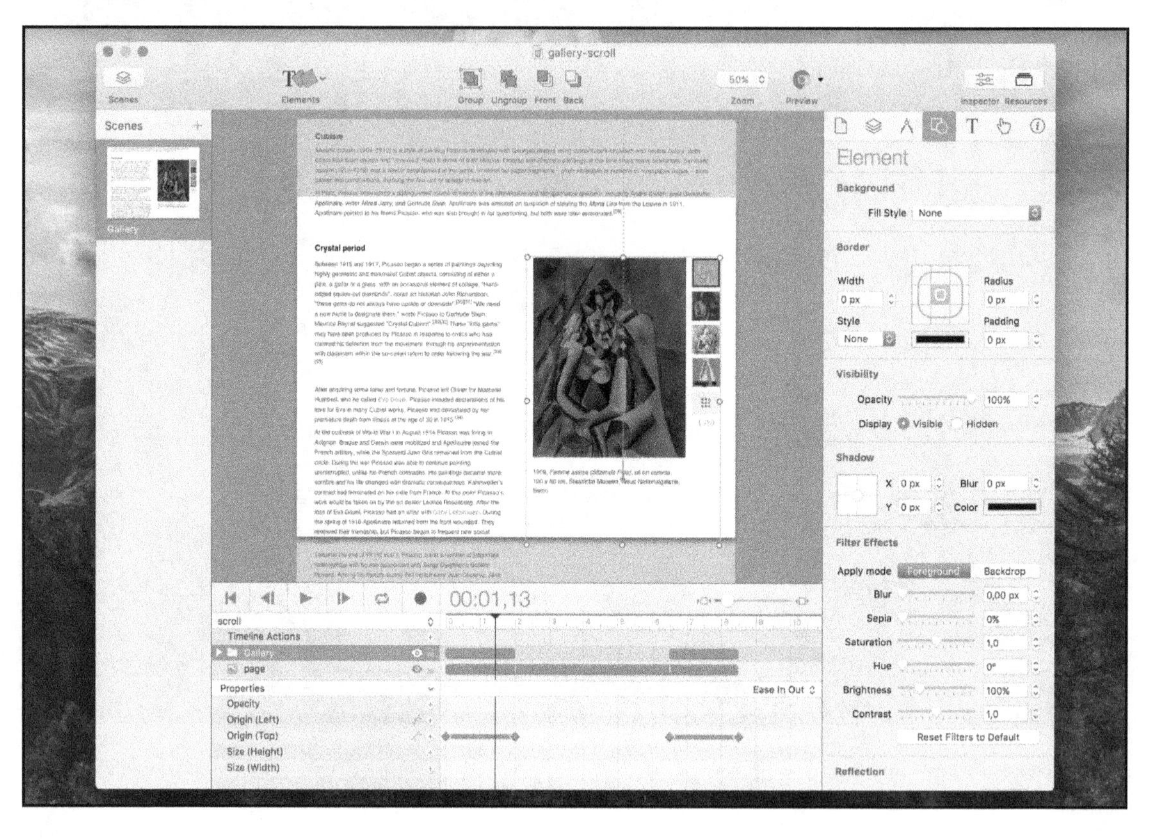

Tumult Hype makes use of a timeline at the bottom to visualize how the different elements and their properties are modified over time. (source: Screenshot from Tumult Hype)

Tools based on **component connection** follow a visual programming paradigm. You can connect blocks that represent interaction components, user interactions, or logical elements.

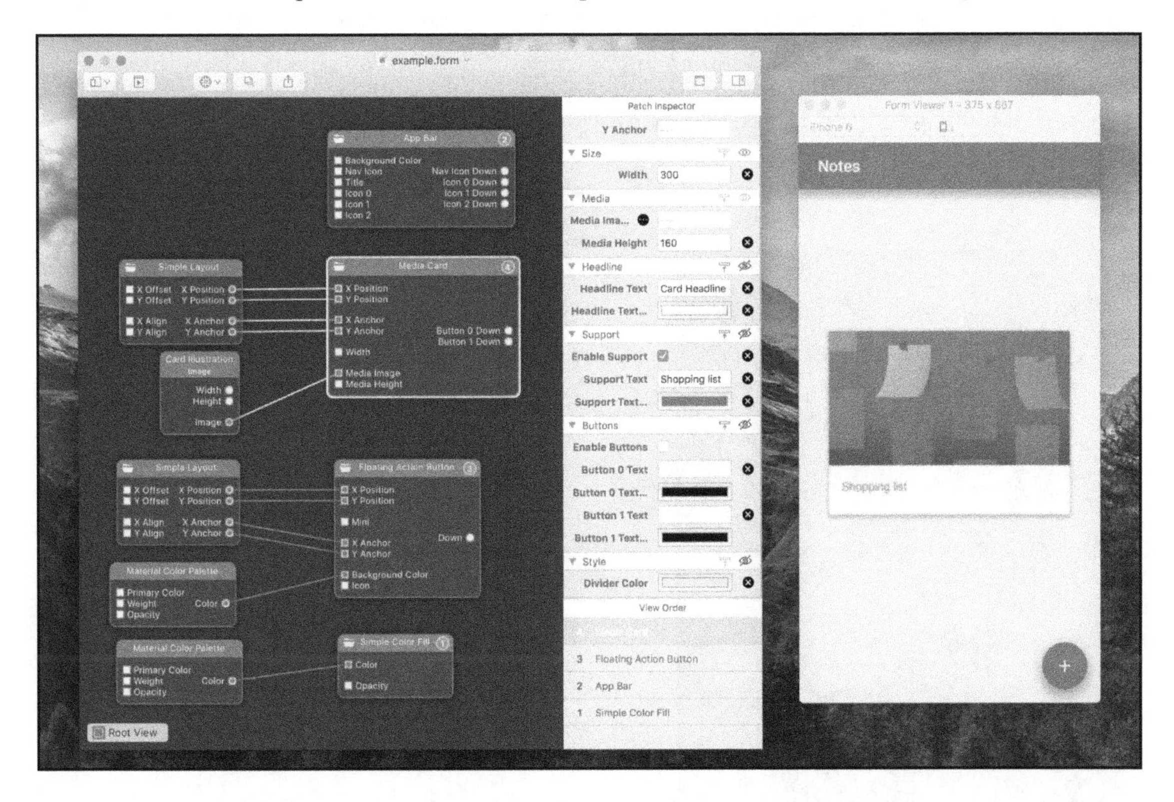

Form is a prototyping tool by Google that follows the component connection approach. On the left side, the editor allows the adding of blocks and connecting their properties. On the right side, the simulator shows the resulting prototype. (source: Screenshot from Form)

By connecting blocks, you can define the behavior for the prototype. A block representing the pinch gesture can be connected to the size property of an image to a zooming function. Some logical blocks can be added in between to limit the zoom range or control the transition speed.

Code-based tools allow you to define a prototype by using a programming language. These tools adopt some of the prototyping principles to provide facilities to transition between states and define animations and incorporate them into code. Code-based tools often provide integration with many other programming components, which allows great flexibility. However, this freedom makes it tempting to add unnecessary detail. When using code-based tools, you need to make an effort not to abandon the prototyping mindset, keeping the prototype focused.

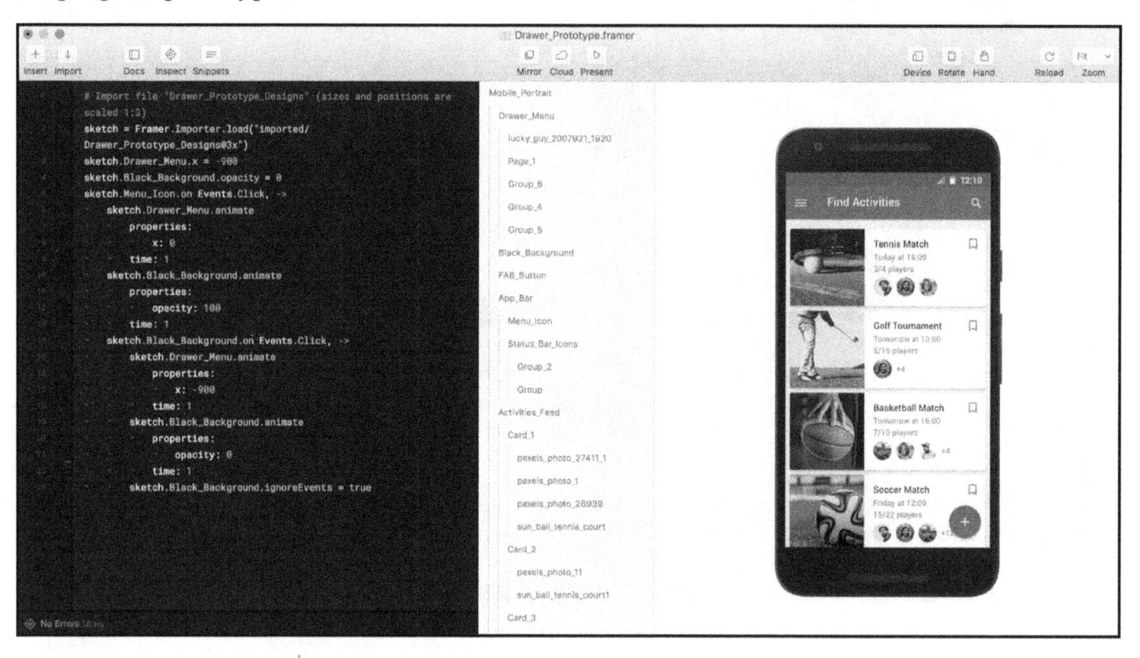

Framer is a prototyping tool based on code. Layers as well as their properties and interactions are defined textually. Additional tools help to visualize the resulting prototype. (source: Screenshot from Framer Studio)

In many cases, you may want to create a noninteractive version from your interactive prototype. Multimedia production tools can be of help. You can use screencast software to record your interactions with a prototype, and video editing tools to combine, cut, add audio, and adjust the final result.

Planning the prototype

Prototyping is a learning process, and you should not be afraid of making mistakes as long as you learn from them. It's perfectly fine to find unanswered questions about your design and solve them as you build your prototype. Experimentation is part of the process. A bit of planning, however, can help you to save some time.

When building your prototype, you need to take shortcuts and cut many corners to be efficient. These decisions may limit your future options, and it is good to anticipate their effects a bit. You don't want to find yourself in the middle of building a prototype and realize that the tool you chose does not support the interaction you absolutely need for a key part of your prototype.

In this section, we will provide some aspects to consider before starting your prototype. Plan a bit, but feel free to experiment as you prototype your solution.

Deciding what to prototype

Knowing the purpose of the prototype will help you to make key decisions during the prototyping process. At this point, you should have a clear idea of the following aspects:

- **The goal**: What do you need to learn with the prototype?
- **The audience**: Who do you need to learn from?
- **The scenario**: Which activity in a specific context will the prototype support?

This information will help you to decide on a prototyping approach and the tools to use.

Be specific when *defining the goal for the prototype*. You can decide to learn about the general understanding of your concept, the clarity of navigation, the discoverability of a specific activity, the fluency when completing a task, and many other aspects that contribute to the user experience. It is okay to have multiple goals, but avoid generic ones such as whether or not "the idea works". Otherwise, it won't be clear which aspects are more useful to prototype in order to answer your open questions.

You need to *help your audience provide you with a useful answer*. Consider whether the selected group of people will be able to answer your question and how the prototype can help them to do so. If you are creating a prototype to discuss concepts with other designers, a low-fidelity prototype may be enough, whereas a high fidelity prototype may be more appropriate when you need to observe specific details of real user behavior.

The prototype should be based on a context that is familiar to the audience in order to help them get into the situation. If you are prototyping a travel app, it may be better to use a well-known location as an example rather than a hard to pronounce, obscure destination--unless that is precisely what you want to test.

You also need to consider how to deliver your prototype to your audience. Depending on the size and location of your audience, you may provide them with a device prepared with the prototype, or share the prototype with them to use it on their own device. Many prototyping tools export to HTML, which makes it ideal for use in many kinds of devices thanks to the widespread availability of web browsers. However, other tools create prototypes for specific platforms, limiting the number of users you can reach and requiring some kind of installation process.

Based on the selected scenario, you can identify aspects of different relevance--the minimum core aspects to support the scenario, those needed for additional context, and those you don't need to prototype. Focus your efforts on the most important parts.

In some cases, it may not be clear what to prototype. You may not be sure about the most promising direction to take with your design. In those cases, you can create multiple prototypes to learn how your users react to different ideas. Due to the nature of time, given time to prototype, you will have to choose between building a more detailed prototype or several prototypes with a lower level of detail.

Deciding how to prototype

After picking a scenario to prototype, you need to capture all the interaction details for each step the user needs to take in the scenario. You can capture the steps to support in your prototype in a **sketchflow**. A sketchflow combines a sequence of sketches representing each step of a prototype and the different interactions to connect them.

Having a blueprint will help you as a reference for building your prototype. In addition, it will also be useful when reviewing your progress with the prototype. Since prototypes pretend to look like they work, it is easy to forget some interactions, and having a blueprint allows you to check them more systematically.

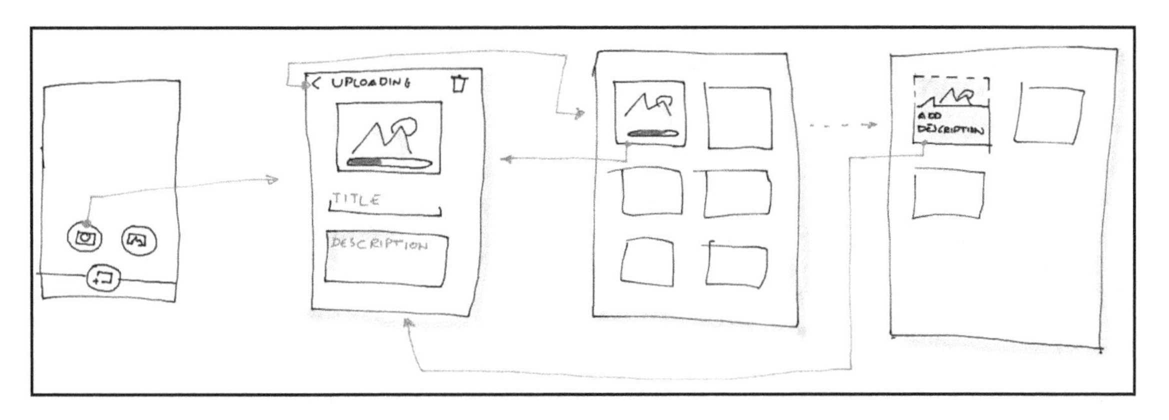

A sketchflow capturing the workflow of updating an image for a camera app prototype

Your scenario may have an ideal path representing the steps the user would take in an ideal situation. However, with interactive prototypes, you are not in control of the user actions, and they often don't follow the ideal path. Consider transitions to go back, and try to anticipate some of the places where users may go off track.

Providing a realistic context to the user will allow them to get immersed in the experience in which the prototype is being created. Avoid a placeholder text--no "Lorem Ipsum"--and use meaningful and relevant examples. You can also include additional steps in your prototype as a prelude to providing additional context. For example, instead of starting the prototype by showing your app, you can start prototyping from the app store screen where the user installs your app, if you want to reinforce the idea of a first-time experience.

Being pragmatic

Prototyping is an essential part of the design process. However, not everyone is familiar with the role it should play. Here are some considerations to help you ensure that prototyping is properly applied in practice.

A prototype is not an early version of your product

The term prototype is often used in many different ways. People may describe an early version of the product as a prototype since it has many edges to be polished. However, these half-baked products do not fully recreate the final experience (since they are incomplete), require additional effort to build, and represent a bigger commitment to a specific direction.

A prototype is built specifically to test an idea, and their missing parts are a result of a conscious decision to prioritize those elements that are exposed to the user and are relevant for the design questions to get answered. A prototype fakes as much as possible, to the point that it is useless to reuse. That's not a problem since learning from it is the biggest value; after that, it can be disposed of.

A prototype is worth a thousand meetings

> *"If a picture is worth 1000 words, a prototype is worth 1000 meetings" is a famous saying at IDEO.*

Meetings are often full of discussions based on opinions and speculations. Material often used in meetings, such as words and static images, still require a big mental effort to deeply understand how ideas would work in practice.

When presenting a prototype, focus on the story for the audience to get immersed in the situation. Ensure that you emphasize the problems your design solves instead of describing specific features. A prototype can act as a window into the future, showing how your product will work. It allows people to experience the solution directly, and helps them focus on a given context.

Summary

In this chapter, we introduced the fundamental principles of prototyping. By approaching prototyping with the right mindset, you will quickly be able to put any idea into practice and learn from it. This will help you to rapidly explore more innovative solutions for your apps and improve them based on what you learn from your real users.

Prototyping is a core step in the design process. However, some people may perceive it as optional. Understanding its principles and mastering the various prototyping techniques will help you prove that it is actually a time-saver and enable you to demonstrate its power.

In the subsequent chapters, we'll introduce specific tools to illustrate specific prototyping techniques. In particular, the next chapter is based on Hype, a tool with great animation capabilities where you will be able to coordinate the motion of the pieces of your future app to simulate how it works.

7

Prototyping with Motion - Using Tumult Hype

"If it can be written, or thought, it can be filmed."

- Stanley Kubrick

Motion can be a key element in storytelling. In theater and cinemas, directors pay a lot of attention to the position of actors on the stage and how they move; this planning process is known as **blocking** and was named after the technique of using wood blocks in a miniature stage that originated in the 19th century. The movement of the actors and, in the case of cinema, the camera helps to communicate emotions to the audience. The way an actor walks in and enters the scene can tell as much as what the actor says.

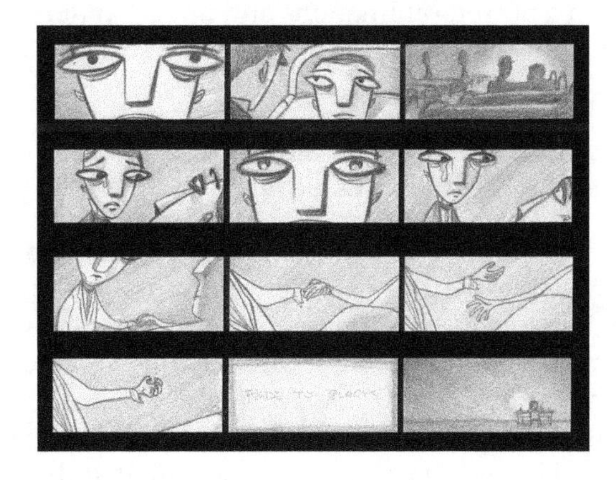

A storyboard capturing key camera angles, movements, and transitions--note the "FADE TO BLACK" sign--that contribute to telling the story

When building a prototype, you are also telling a story--the story of how your product will help your users--and you can use motion to tell that story better. Interactions are dynamic in nature and trying to describe them with static elements, such as sketches and mock-ups, leaves too much to the audience's imagination. When building a prototype, you can benefit from using tools that provide you a great degree of control of motion and time.

In this chapter, you will learn how to use Tumult Hype, a timeline-based prototyping tool. You will apply the general principles of prototyping from the preceding chapter with a specific tool. In particular, in this chapter, you will deal with the following:

- Understanding the role of motion and how to use motion to design better interactions
- Getting familiar with the basic principles of Hype
- Prototyping simple interactions based on manipulating layers with different gestures
- Supporting complex interactions by composing animations and reacting to the user input

The prototyping techniques that you will learn in this chapter will help you to quickly use Hype and also allow you to become familiar with concepts that are also available in many other prototyping tools you may find.

The role of motion in prototyping

An app normally has many moving parts, for example, transitions between views--panels that appear as you click on a button--animations and images that react to a touch gesture, and many more. Deciding how each of those elements will move is an important design decision to consider.

When prototyping, you can explore different approaches for using motion to help achieve your goals. Motion can be helpful at different levels:

- **Motion helps to explain**: The way items move can tell you about the rules of the digital world they live in, thus helping users to understand these rules better. Clarifying the information hierarchy or providing orientation cues can be more effective when it is communicated intuitively through motion rather than when explained with words. For example, friction in the scrolling movement of a list of items can be used to communicate that the user has reached the end of the list. When designing how elements move, make sure that they do so in a consistent way. Otherwise, they will communicate contradicting rules, which can lead to confusion.

- **Motion sets a tone**: The body language--including the movement of your hands, if any--affects how a message is received when you communicate. Similarly, the pace of transitions will give your app a different tone. For example, making elements bounce conveys a playful tone. Tools, such as Hype, provide a wide set of timing functions for you to easily adjust the pace of each movement.
- **Motion makes changes feel more natural**: Our brains are wired to have an intuitive understanding of basic physical laws. When elements move in a continuous way--as opposed to just disappearing or appearing suddenly--they make it easy for the user to connect the dots. For example, removing an item from a list is better communicated if the element fades away and the gap is closed gradually, rather than if the element just disappears all of a sudden.
- **Motion captures attention**: Moving elements capture our attention. This can be used to draw user attention to the relevant elements, such as the new element just added to a group. Even subtle animation details can also delight users and make the user experience more joyful. For example, loading indicators can contribute to make the wait less boring. Similar to the use of special effects in cinema, motion needs to be properly executed, and you should avoid overuse to prevent annoying your users.

The way elements change over time affects the user experience of your product. With appropriate tools, you can have control over the various types of motion and be able to explore the approaches that better suit the needs of your users.

The basic concepts of Hype

Tumult Hype is a tool to create interactive animations. Hype has been used to create functional applications, widgets for interactive e-books, interactive visualizations, entertainment videos, and games. Despite being a tool aimed at creating final products, it is also a very convenient prototyping tool, thanks to its interaction and time controls.

Hype falls into the same category as the classic Macromedia Flash, which was also used for prototyping purposes. However, Hype uses HTML5, which makes the resulting prototypes easy to use on different platforms. Hype is also able to export in video format--including animated GIF--which makes it easy to generate noninteractive prototypes.

Hype is available for Mac in two versions--regular and pro. Although the pro version provides features such as a physics engine and facilities to reuse components, the regular version should be enough for most of your prototyping needs. To facilitate the creation of mobile prototypes, Hype Reflect is available for iOS devices. You can find more about Hype and get the different apps at `http://tumult.com/hype/`

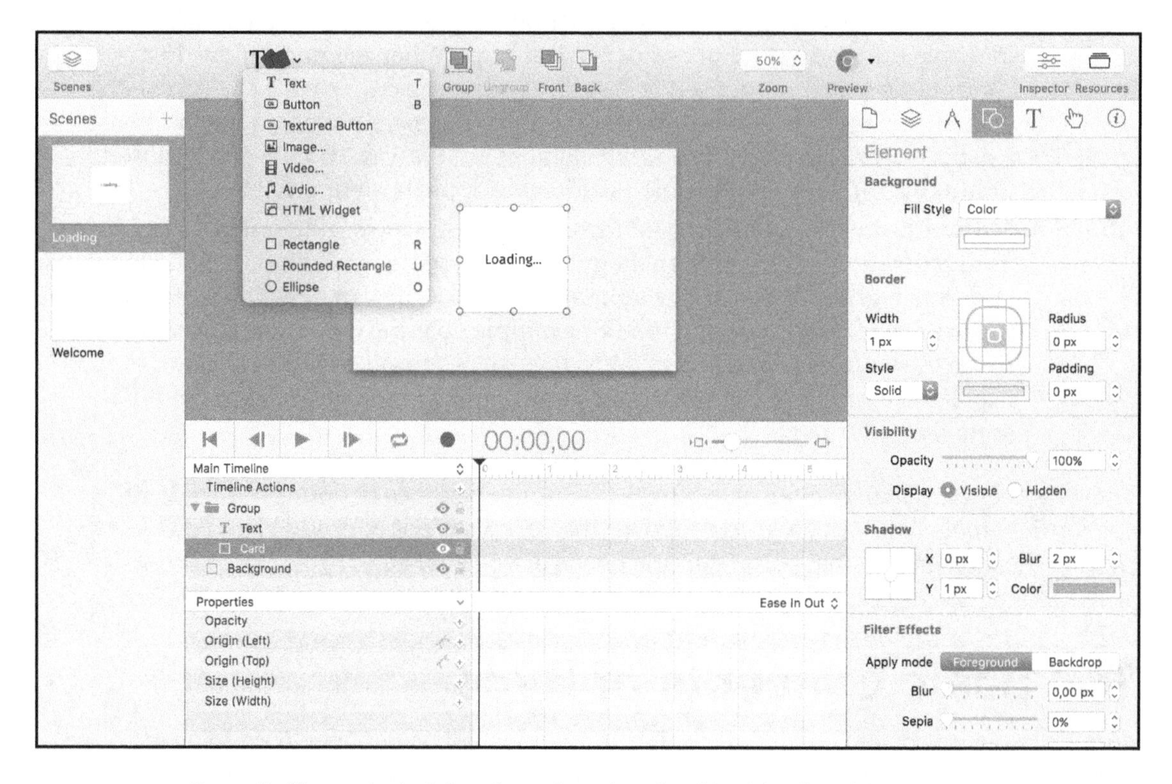

Hype provides different panels and tools. Scenes, layers, and properties are three of the main ingredients to build your prototype.

Hype is a very flexible tool. It provides as much complexity as the requirement of your prototype. You can create very simple prototypes really quickly, but it also allows you to keep adding more complex interactions as you need them. Finally, if you need to do something really complex for a particular part of your prototype, you can use HTML and JavaScript for just that part.

Hype provides many options and tools that you will be using to create your prototypes. We will introduce the main panels and views next.

Scene list

In Hype, you can organize your prototype into one or multiple scenes. Each scene contains its own multimedia elements, interactions, and animations. Although you can create a prototype in a single scene with multiple layers, breaking independent views of your prototype into separate scenes can help you to organize the complexity of your prototype better.

Hype shows a list of the current scenes in a panel on the left. You can create new scenes by clicking on the "+" sign, give them a name, and switch between them by clicking on their thumbnails. You can also drag them to change their order: the one on top will be the initial scene when you preview the result.

Scene editor

The central view of the tool shows the contents of the current scene. It shows a canvas where you can place and manipulate the different multimedia elements that will be used in the prototype.

At the top of the scene editor, you will find several controls to create and manipulate the elements. Hype allows for the creation of some basic elements, such as rectangles, ellipsis, or buttons. However, most of the time, you will be composing media created in external tools such as Sketch. For more advanced users, Hype also allows you to add HTML components directly.

You will also find various toolbar functions to control grouping, adjust the order of elements, preview the resulting prototype, and show or hide the different panels in Hype.

Property inspector

The property panel is available on the right. It shows the properties of the active element. Different properties tabs are available on the panel, depending on which aspect they address:

- **Document**: Includes general properties affecting the whole prototype, such as export and compatibility settings
- **Scene**: Shows properties of the current scene, such as the size of the canvas and interaction events for the whole screen area
- **Metrics**: Allows adjustments to the position, size, and rotation of the selected element

- **Element**: Includes properties related to the visual aspect of the selected element such as the color, border style, and visual effects
- **Typography**: This is relevant for textual content and defines the font, size, and alignment to be used
- **Actions**: Lets you define how an element reacts to a given event, such as tapping or dragging it
- **Identity**: Includes advanced properties, such as identifiers and classes, for the resulting HTML elements once the prototype is generated

Some animations will require changing some of these properties in order to manipulate the elements within the scene.

Timeline and layers

The timeline is a key component of many applications that deal with motion, such as multimedia editors. It captures how properties evolve through time. In order to change a property, you usually define the initial and final values, and the software will be in charge of computing all the in-between steps.

Following the cinema metaphor, Hype is able to generate every frame based on the few essential frames defined by the user--these are known as keyframes. For example, you can set an opacity to 0% initially and create a keyframe after half a second with the opacity at 100% in order to define a fade-in transition. The software will calculate all the intermediate frames needed for the animation.

The record button allows you to control when the new keyframes are created as you change properties. When you press the record button, you can just manipulate the objects of your prototype, and those changes will be captured in keyframes at the indicated point in time on the timeline.

In Hype, you can define multiple timelines. While the main timeline is played automatically, you have control of when any other timeline is played. Timelines are useful to define the different behaviors in your prototype. A timeline describes an animation that affects one or more properties of one or more layers. Making a panel appear, removing an element from a list, or zooming an image are some examples of animations you can define as timelines for your prototype.

In order to create different animations, you can define multiple timelines and switch between them. The player controls allow you to check that the animation works as expected.

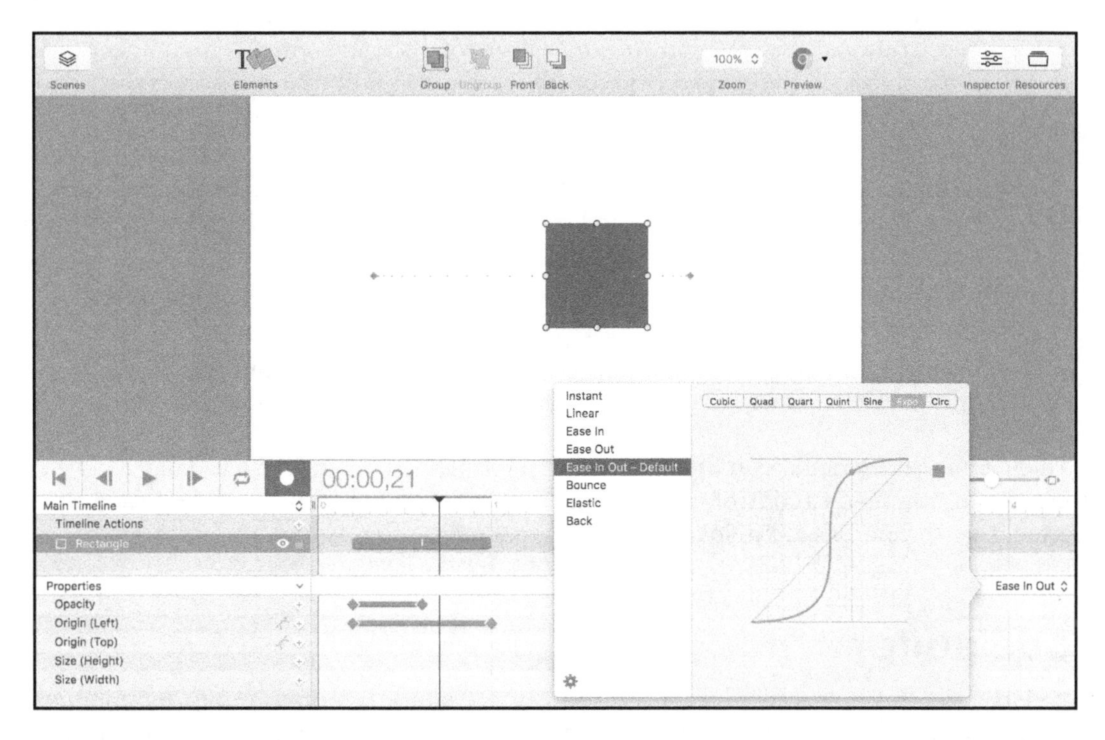

The timeline captures the transition in opacity and position for the rectangle layer. The object trajectory is shown in the scene editor and options to select a timing function are displayed in the timeline.

When defining a transition, you can select different timing functions. This will allow you to adjust the pace at which a property changes in an animation:

- **Instant**: This represents a sudden change instead of one that is gradual.
- **Linear**: This involves change happening at a constant pace. Elements moving at a linear pace will keep the same speed without any acceleration or deceleration.

- **Ease**: These functions take into account friction at the beginning, end, or both. An *ease in* will apply the changes more slowly at the beginning, whereas an *ease out* function will decelerate at the end. As you can expect, an *ease in out* function considers friction at both points, initially accelerating and ending with deceleration. Ease functions produce more realistic movements than linear ones since objects in the real world require some acceleration to reach their intended speed. Hype provides different variants for the ease functions to adjust the prominence of the movements.
- **Bounce**: This represents a change that reaches the intended point but bounces back. The value will never exceed the intended one, but it will go back and forth to create a bouncing effect.
- **Elastic**: This is similar to *bounce*, but the intended value will exceed initially, going back and forth like a spring.
- **Back**: This motion also exceeds the intended value initially but reaches it gradually in a more controlled way, with no back and forth movement.

The elements that participate in the scene are represented as layers in a list. They can be grouped and arranged to control which one is displayed on top of another. Once a layer is selected, their properties are displayed on the timeline.

Code editor

Hype lets you create your own JavaScript functions to support more complex interactions. A code editor is provided, where you can combine the Hype functionality with your own logic.

By writing code, you can access the same interaction options you can define visually with the tool. For example, you can play or pause a given timeline or move it to a different scene. The advantage of writing some functions in code is that you can define more complex logic about how to combine those functions. For example, you can switch to a different scene based on the value of a variable.

Importing and exporting

Importing media just requires you to drag and drop it into Hype. You need to take into account that Hype checks whether the original files added are updated and allows you to replace them with updated versions if there are changes. This facilitates the process of working with external tools. You can export all the prototype images from Sketch to the same folder as you make changes to them, and the prototype will remain in sync as long as the names are not changed.

Hype allows you to preview your prototype in a local browser. If you install Hype Reflect, you will find your mobile device as an option to preview the results. When you are happy with the results, you can export your prototype to an HTML or a video format.

Prototyping navigation

During the course of this chapter, we'll create several prototypes based on ideas for a social sports app. The application allows you to propose, discover, and coordinate sporting activities with your contacts with the aim of keeping you healthy, while having fun with your friends.

One of the main elements of the app is the list of the available activities for you to join. In this first example, we'll focus on a basic navigation for this process--moving from the list of different activities to the details of one of them.

Download a prototype from `[Asset_A6462_A07_A01_Navigation_prototype.zip]`.

The general steps we'll go through are as follows:

1. Creating images for each view.
2. Adding the images to new scenes in a prototype.
3. Defining the interactions to navigate between those scenes.

In order to prototype this navigation, we need images of the two views involved. The list view contains different sporting activities with a brief description. The detail view provides a more elaborate description for an activity--for example, a tennis match--as well as several actions. In Sketch, we define the two views as separate artboards and make them exportable to obtain the images.

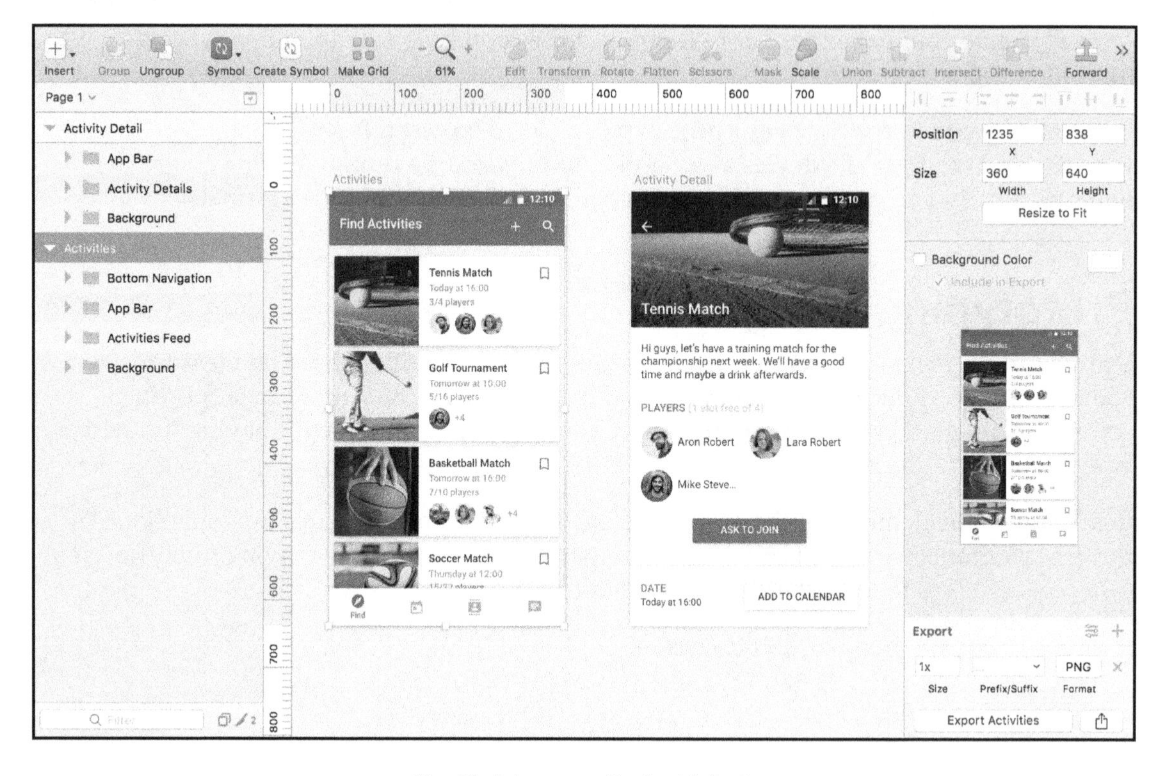

List and detail views as exportable artboards in Sketch

Once we have the images available, we need to combine them into a prototype with Hype. When we start Hype, we'll get a new document with a default scene. We need to adjust the size of the scene to the dimensions of our prototype--360x640 px, in this case. Since we want all the scenes in the prototype to be the same size, make sure that you leave the **Apply changes to all scenes** selected.

The initial scene will be the list of activities. You can add the image for the list by just dragging it from your filesystem. Alternatively, you can also access the **Elements** menu on the top toolbar and select the **Image...** option.

To complete our initial scene, we just need to give it a name. From the scene list on the left, we can rename our initial scene to `Activities` by double-clicking on the scene title or using the **Rename** option from the contextual menu that appears when right-clicking on the scene thumbnail.

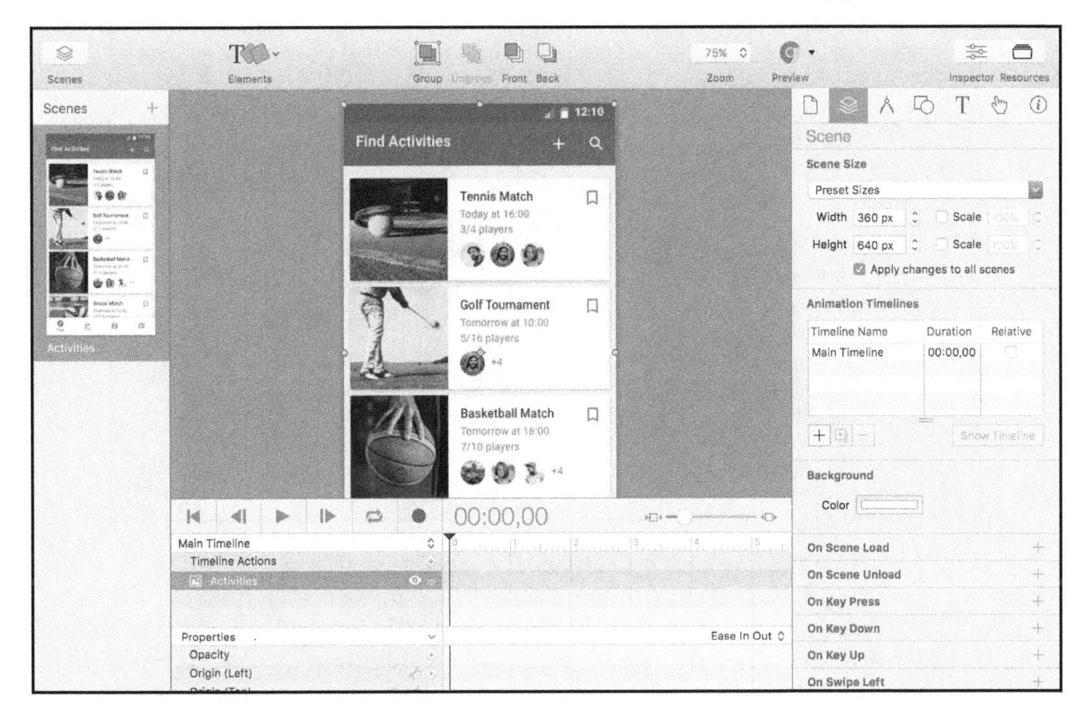

Initial scene for the activities list in Hype

Our navigation interaction requires moving between two screens, thus we need to add a new scene. We can click on the "+" in the scene list header to create a new untitled scene. We can then add the image to the second scene and rename the scene as `Activity Details`, as we did for the previous scene.

Once we have the two scenes, we need to define the navigation interactions. This will be supported in the following two steps:

1. Defining the active area that users are required to touch for the interaction to happen.
2. Specifying the resulting interaction.

To define interactive areas, we'll use a transparent rectangle. From the elements menu, we can create a new rectangle.

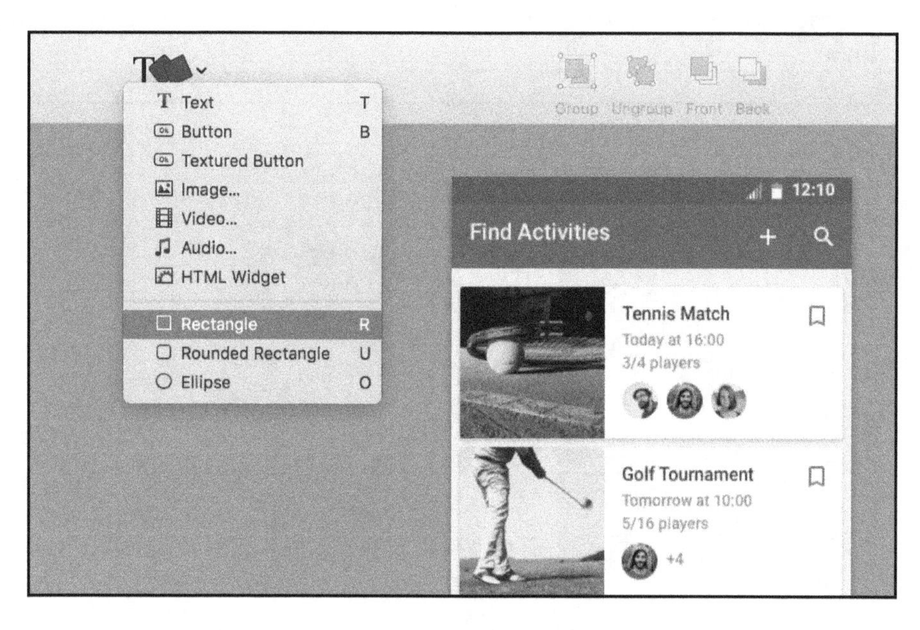

Adding a new rectangle allows you to set interactive regions for the underlying image

We'll adjust its size and position to cover the first item in the list of the **Activities** scene. In order to make it transparent, we'll adjust the style for the **Element** tab on the properties panel and set both the **Fill Style** and the **Border | Style** to **None**. In this way, we'll have an area that is invisible but can react to user interactions.

Since the active area is an invisible element, we rename it in the layer list to make it easier for us to find later. In the example, we have used the `act-` prefix to identify active areas, naming the current one as `act-tennis` since it is the active area representing the **Tennis Match** item.

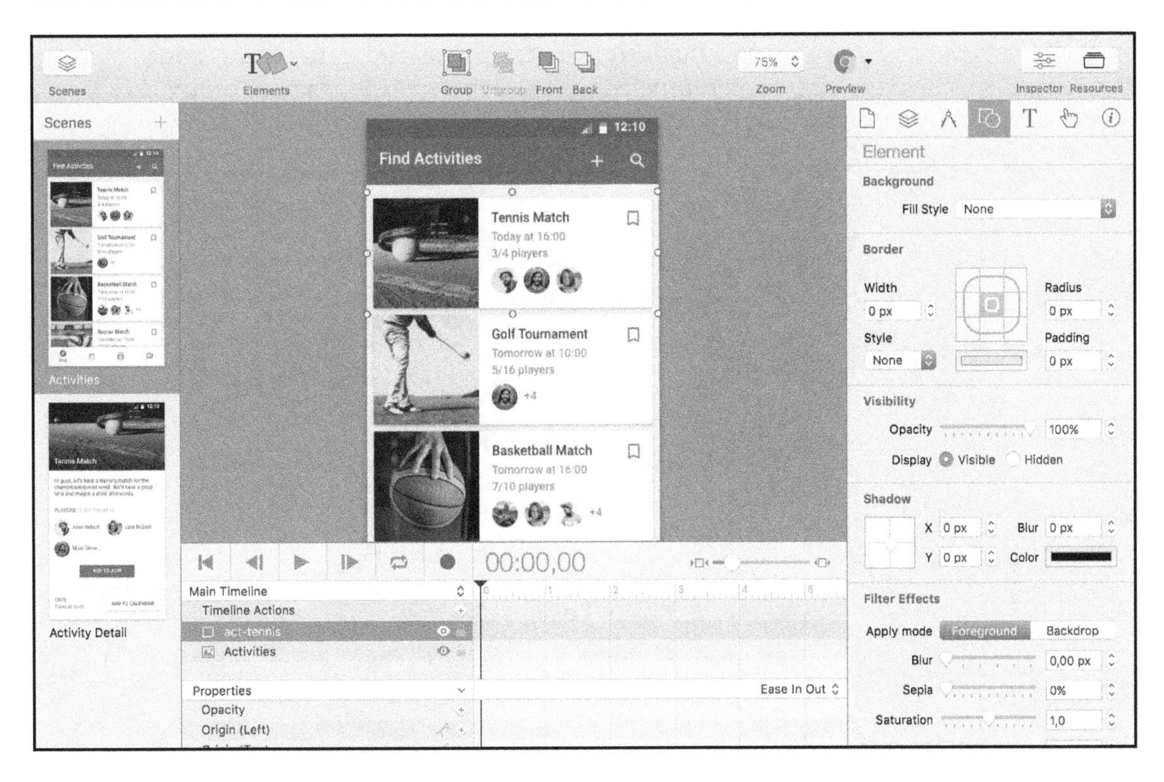

The act-tennis layer is a transparent rectangle without a fill or borders and is used to delimit an interaction area

Now that we have defined an active area, we can set an interaction for it. The actions section of the property inspector allows you to define interactions of different kinds for the selected element. In this case, we want to change the current scene when the user taps on the first item in the list.

We will add a new interaction on the **On Mouse Click (Tap)** section using the **+** icon, which is next to it. This is the event we'll use to react to the user clicks--when using a mouse or similar method or tapping--when using a touch device. From the different types of actions, we select the **Jump to Scene...** since it fits our purpose of navigating between scenes.

We also need to specify the target scene that we will navigate to and also the transition for the change. By default, the target is the next scene with an immediate transition.

To get better continuity, we'll use a **Push** style transition instead of the default one. With this transition, one view moves out of the current viewport as the new one enters. We'll adjust the speed for the transition to feel more fluent, setting it to 0.3 seconds.

The actions panel allows you to define the interaction that triggers a change of scene and to adjust its parameters

At this point, you can preview your prototype and try the navigation. By clicking on the preview option, you will see your prototype in a browser. In the prototype, you should be able to move from the list view to the detail view. However, once you reach the detail view, it is not possible to go back to the original list view, yet.

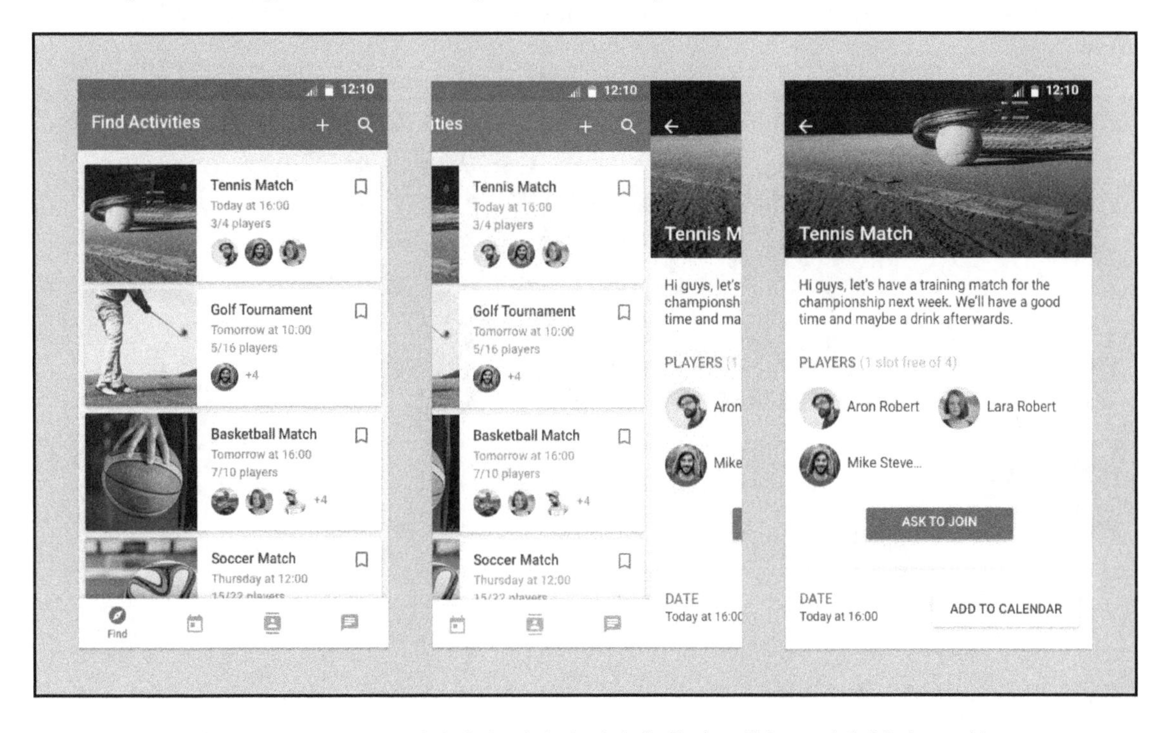

The first prototype allows you to access the details about the first item in the list. The views will change gradually following a transition.

The next step is to create a navigation back from the detail view. For this, we'll follow a similar process as we did to set up the previous interaction. We'll create a transparent rectangle over the back arrow area and specify a new transition. In this case, we will select the **Activities** scene as the target--or **Previous Scene** if you prefer--and use the push approach too; however, in this case, we will follow the opposite direction--using left to right.

Returning to the list view from the detail view requires you to define a new active area--act-back in the example--and a new transition

If you try the prototype at this point, you'll now be able to navigate back and forth between the two views. With this, we have reached our goal for the first prototype by supporting navigation between these two views, but let's just add a final touch to the prototype.

We saw how to add interactions to individual elements to trigger a change of scene. However, it is also possible to add interactions to the whole scene. We'll use this approach to provide an alternative way to return to the list using a touch gesture.

Select the scene menu for the **Activity Detail** scene, and create a new action for the **On Swipe Right** event. You can define the same transition you created before to switch scenes. In this way, when you are in the detail view, you'll be able to return to the list by quickly dragging your finger to the right.

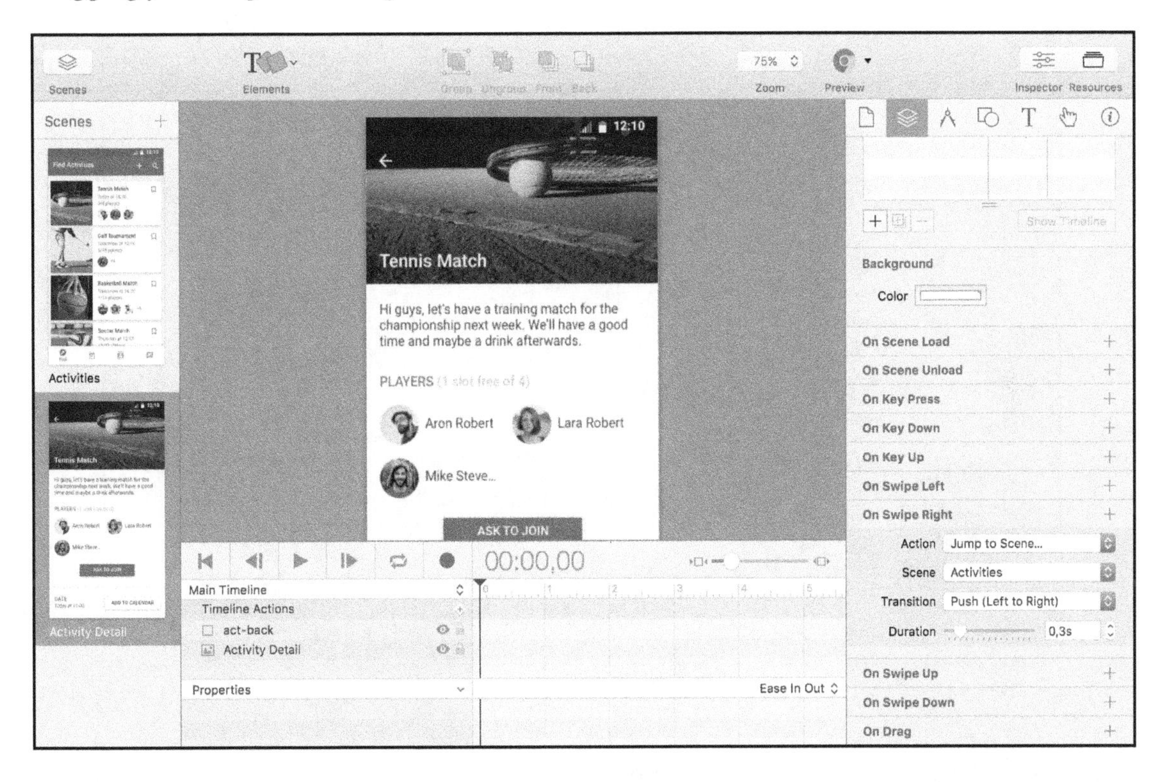

The scene panel allows you to define interactions for the whole scene. In this case, a swipe event will change the current scene to support going back with a gesture.

Try previewing your prototype with different kinds of transitions and adjust their speed. When you are happy with the result, you can export the prototype as an HTML document to share with the world. The **Export as HTML5** option in the **File** menu will allow you to get a version of the prototype that can be viewed with any web browser.

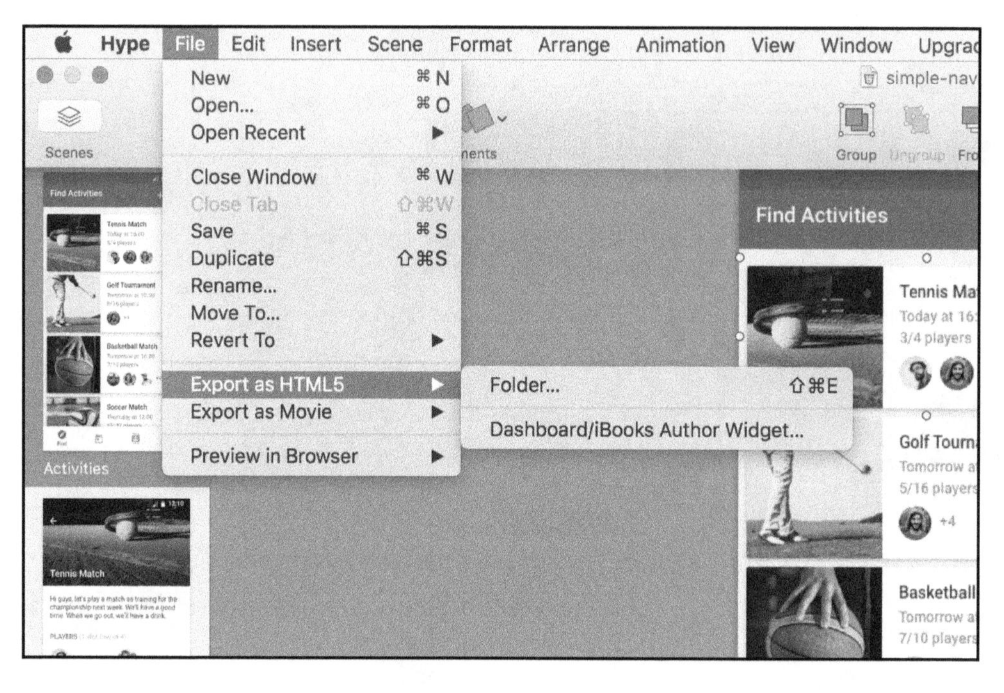

Although preview is useful for quickly testing your prototype, exporting it to HTML allows you to share it with the world

Combining scenes and transitions provides a quick way to prototype the navigation, but it is a limited approach. Quite often, you will need the various different parts of your views to move independently.

Manipulating layers with interactions

In the preceding example, we used a single image to represent a whole screen of an app. In this section, we will use layers to define separate behaviors for different parts of the prototype.

Manipulating layers

In this prototype, we'll explore a simple interaction that simulates the status change of an object. In the main list of activities on our example app, each element has a bookmark icon. We will build a prototype where you can activate and deactivate the bookmarked status of one item in the list.

We'll illustrate how to support this interaction through the following two different approaches:

- Using a single layer for the active state
- Using separate layers for each state

When preparing the images to export, we included a mock-up of the activity view with the bookmark icons and another without them, as well as separate images of the bookmark icons in both states.

Download a prototype from `[Asset_A6462_A07_A02-ManipulatingLayers.zip]`.

Sketch file with two versions of the activity view and bookmark icons

Using a single layer for the active state

The first approach consists of showing the filled-bookmark icons on top of the original ones when an item is bookmarked. In order to do so, we'll add a filled version of the bookmark icon on top of the empty one and control the opacity with an animation when the user clicks on the corresponding area.

First, we start by creating a new Hype prototype using a 360x640 px scene and adding the activities view mock-up as a layer in the background. Next, we add the filled-bookmark icon as a new layer, placing it on top of the bookmark icon of the first element in the list.

The layer representing the bookmark in an active state is placed over the original image, thus hiding it

Initially the bookmark icon will be empty, thus we set the opacity of the active bookmark layer to 0%. Now we need to define a transition to change the element opacity from 0% to 100%. In order to do so, we'll create a new timeline.

By clicking on the timeline selector on top of the list of layers--initially displaying "Main Timeline"--we have the option to create a new timeline. In this case, we'll create a timeline named "toggle-bookmark1". In the timeline, we need to capture the transition for the opacity property of the bookmark layer. So, click on the recording button and place the timeline to half a second from the starting point and change the opacity to 100% in the properties panel for the bookmark layer. This will generate two **keyframes** for the opacity property to represent the edge values of this transition from transparent to opaque. After you stop recording changes, you can still adjust them--feel free to play with the **keyframes** to make the transition longer, shorter, or introduce a delay.

When the recording is on, changing properties on a timeline creates new keyframes. In the example, a new keyframe is created to make the bookmark opaque.

The transition we defined in the timeline needs to be triggered by a user interaction. Since the bookmark icon has a small surface, we will create a transparent rectangle as the top layer above it. In the example, it is named **act-bookmark1**.

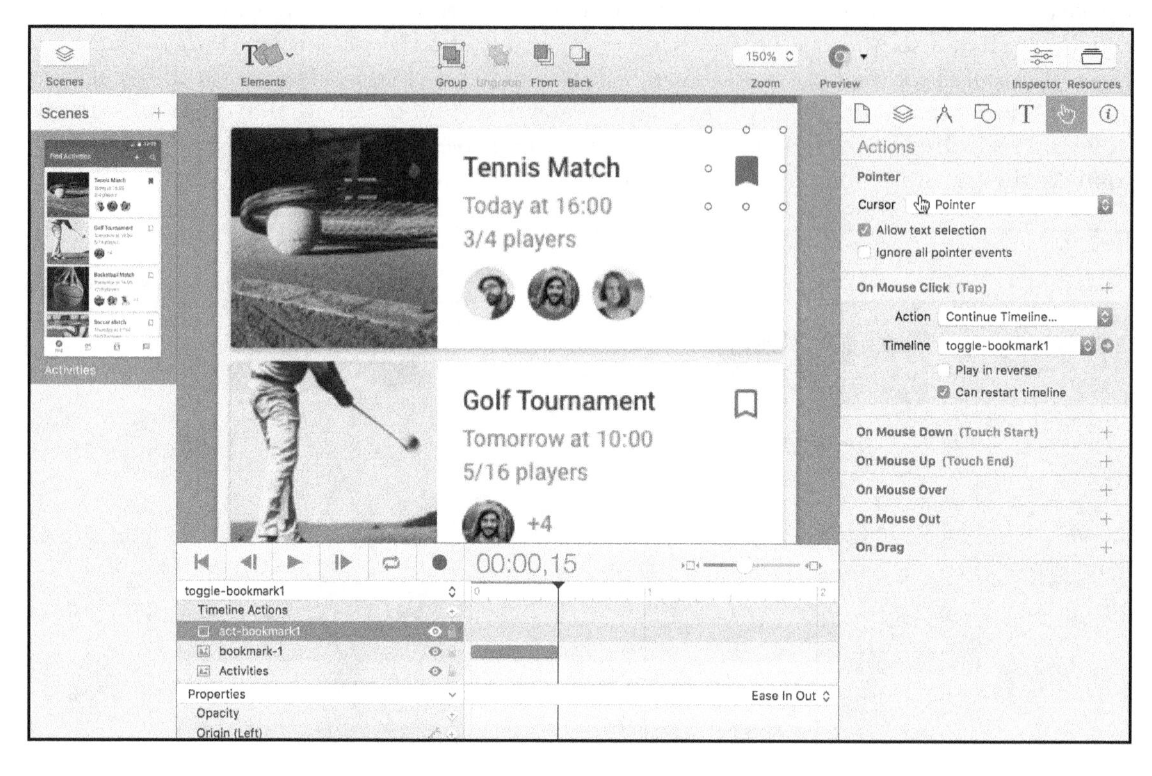

A "Continue Timeline" interaction associated to the tap event is defined for a transparent rectangle

By creating a new action, we can make the timeline play as the user clicks on the active area for the bookmark. To do this, we will create a **Continue Timeline...** action for the click event. If we preview the prototype at this point, we'll note that marking as a bookmark works, but unmarking it does not. In order to support the reverse interaction, we'll extend the timeline to include both transitions. In this way, the animation will be played in two steps--the first part will make the bookmark appear, and continuing to the second part will make it go away.

Since we want to play the animation in two steps, we'll add a pause action to separate both parts. In the timeline, there is a special row above all layers named **Timeline Actions**. You can use it to create actions for specific points in time. These actions can control the current or other timelines, as well as trigger more complex logic defined by the user in JavaScript functions. In this case, we want to add a pause action for the current timeline.

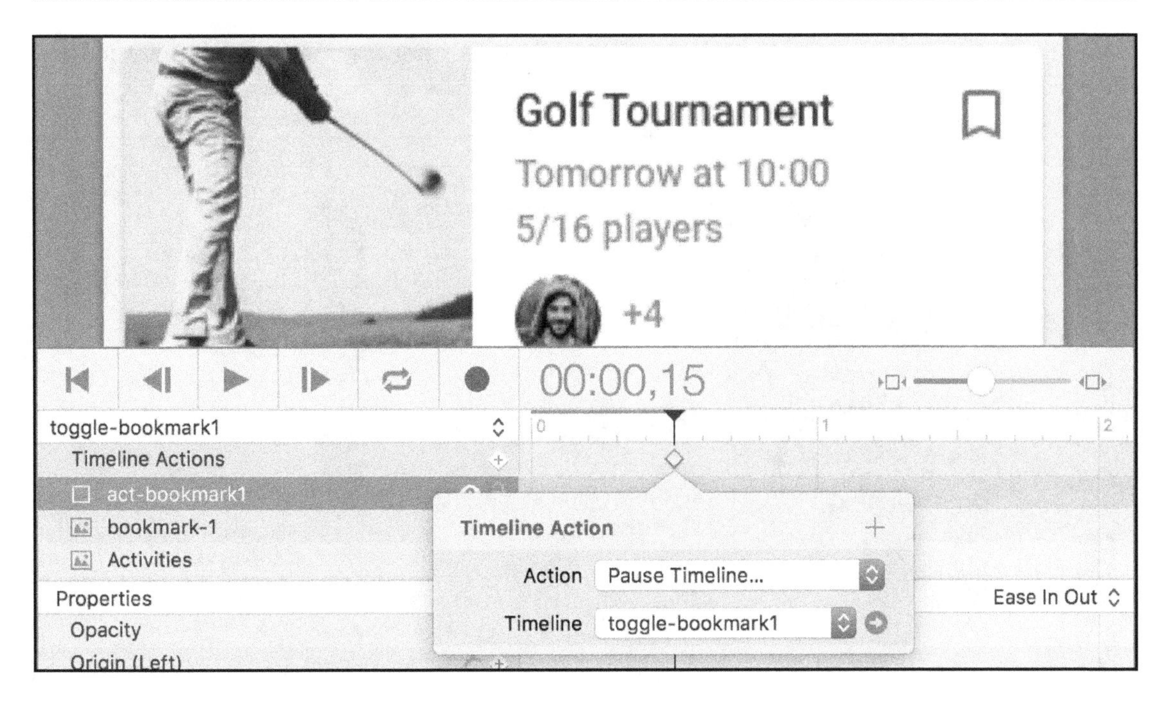

The "timeline actions" row allows you to create time-based events to control the current or other timelines

As a result, the animation will make the bookmark appear and pause at 0.5 seconds. The next time the user acts on the bookmark, the animation will continue playing, making the bookmark transparent again. Since the animation is played in two steps, it is important for the action that triggers the animation to be **Continue Timeline** instead of **Start Timeline**, otherwise the timeline will start from the beginning each time.

Now, the bookmark animation will work to set and unset the bookmarked state for the item as many times as you like.

Using separate layers for each state

As an alternative way to support this same example, we will use two different elements for the filled and empty bookmark states. To keep things simple, we'll create the alternative version as another scene in the same prototype, but feel free to create a new prototype if you prefer.

We will add the activities view mock-up version that does not contain the bookmark icons, and then add the icons as separate layers.

Bookmark icons are added as separate layers on top of the activities view

In order to make sure that we have a big enough touch area, we turn the bookmark layer into a group by right-clicking on the bookmark layer and selecting the **Group** option. This allows us to adjust the size of the group--without affecting the bookmark image size--and work with the group instead of the smaller bookmark layer.

Creating a group allows you to define an active area larger than the original element

We also need the filled version of the bookmark icon. We can follow the same approach to create a group containing the filled version of the bookmark icon--which we rename as **Bookmark-full-1**. In this case, the new group will be not only invisible, but it will also be disabled.

Making a layer invisible--by adjusting opacity to 0%--keeps it clickable. Since we want the full version of the bookmark to not interfere with the clicks on the empty version of the bookmark below it, we need to disable the layer by setting its display property to **Hidden**.

A new timeline will be in charge of switching the visibility of the layers. We can create a new timeline and make the **Bookmark-full-1** layer become active first and make the opacity **100%** later. In this way, the layer becomes active and gradually becomes visible. Optionally, we could also disable the empty version of the bookmark if it becomes problematic in terms of visibility (parts may remain visible despite having a layer on top), or interaction (parts of the active area are larger than the layer on top and could still be clicked).

A timeline making the layer with the filled bookmark visible, then have a gradual transition to 100% opacity

Finally, we'll add actions to the two groups of layers we created. The empty bookmark group will play the animation we just created for a tap. For the filled version of the bookmark, we'll lay the same timeline, but do it in a reverse order. Using the **Play in reverse** option allows us to support the opposite action without having to create a new specific timeline.

Play in reverse option allows you to reuse animations for symmetric actions

We've seen two different methods to change the status of elements using a different number of active areas and different approaches to building timelines. You can extend the example to make it possible to bookmark other items in the list and practice both approaches.

Supporting scroll and navigation

As it is common in many apps, our example app provides different views that users can select through a menu. We'll simulate the navigation across four different views: activities, calendar, contacts, and messages. In order to do that, we shall break those views down into different layers.

Download a prototype from
`[Asset_A6462_A07_A03-LayerNavigation.zip]`.

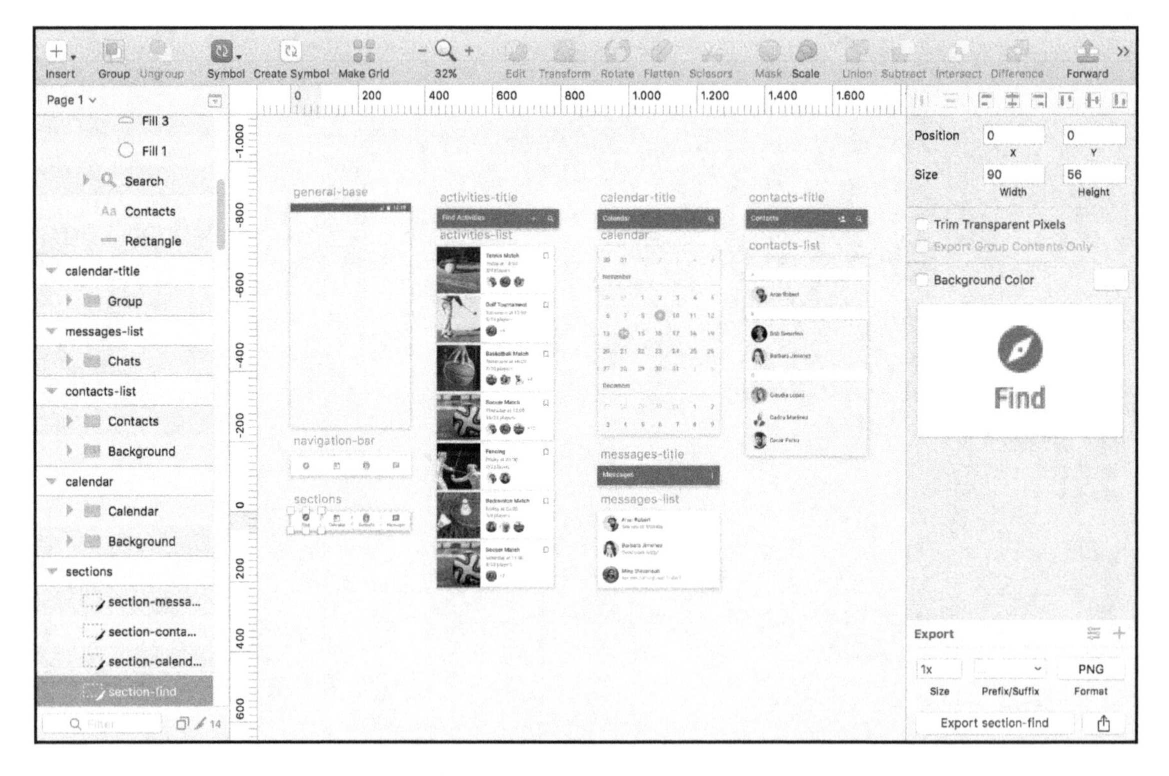

A sketch file with the different views and some common parts available in all of them

After we export the images from sketch, we can combine them into a Hype prototype. We start by placing the common elements--the background layer and the bottom navigation bar. The ordering of the layers is important since we want the menu bar to be placed on top of other layers in order to remain visible.

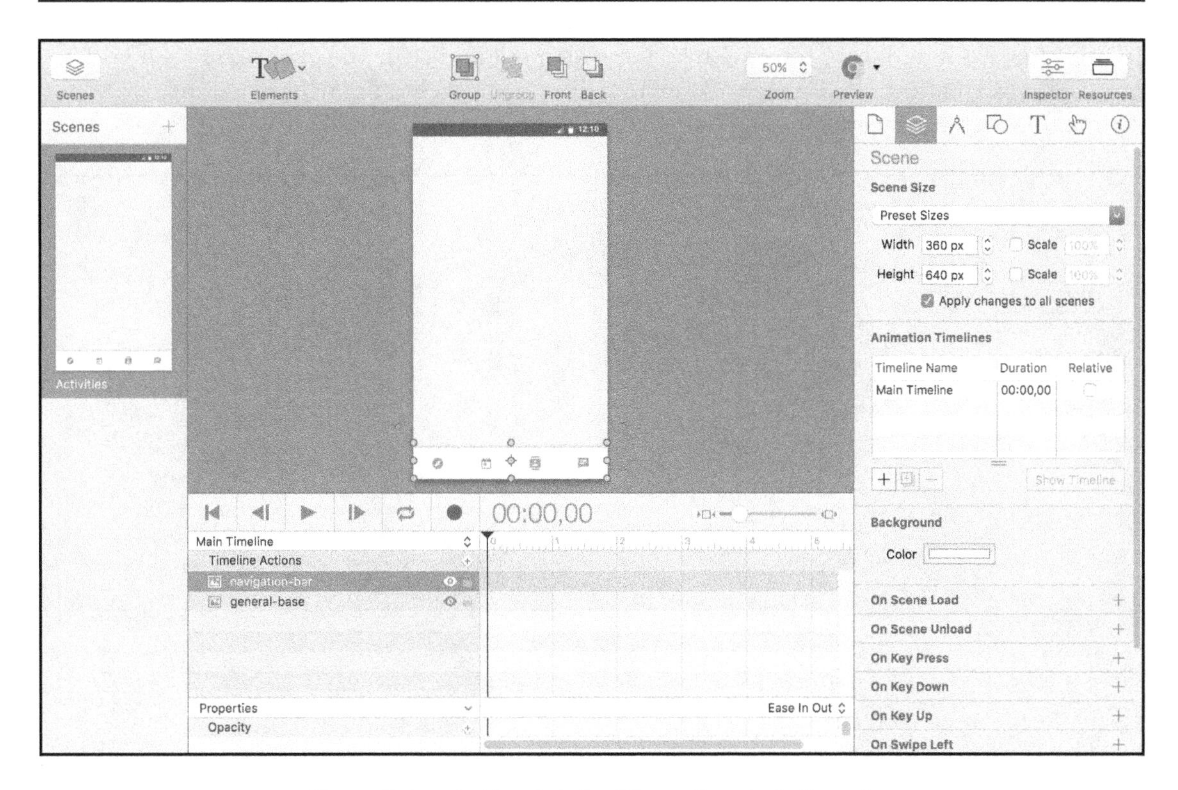

The general background and the navigation bar will be present in any view for this example

Then, we shall recreate the activities view. As part of that view, there is a long list of activities that are larger than the viewport, and we want to allow users to scroll through it. There are several ways to support scrolling in Hype.

One is simply to make the document larger. In that way, users can just scroll to reach the rest of the document. However, in this case, we want to scroll through the list, while other elements--such as the header and the navigation bar--remain in place. Fortunately, there are more options to support this scenario.

When adding large elements, Hype may scale them down. Make sure that you use the **Original Size** option to bring them back to their full size.

To support scrolling, we'll take advantage of the ability of Hype to specify the overflow property of groups. When grouping elements, Hype allows you to decide what to do with the elements that are placed outside the active area of the group.

In this case, we'll define a group with just one element and scale the group to fit the visible area of the list. Setting the **Content Overflow** property to **Auto Scrollbars** will provide scrollbars when it is needed to reach the rest of the content.

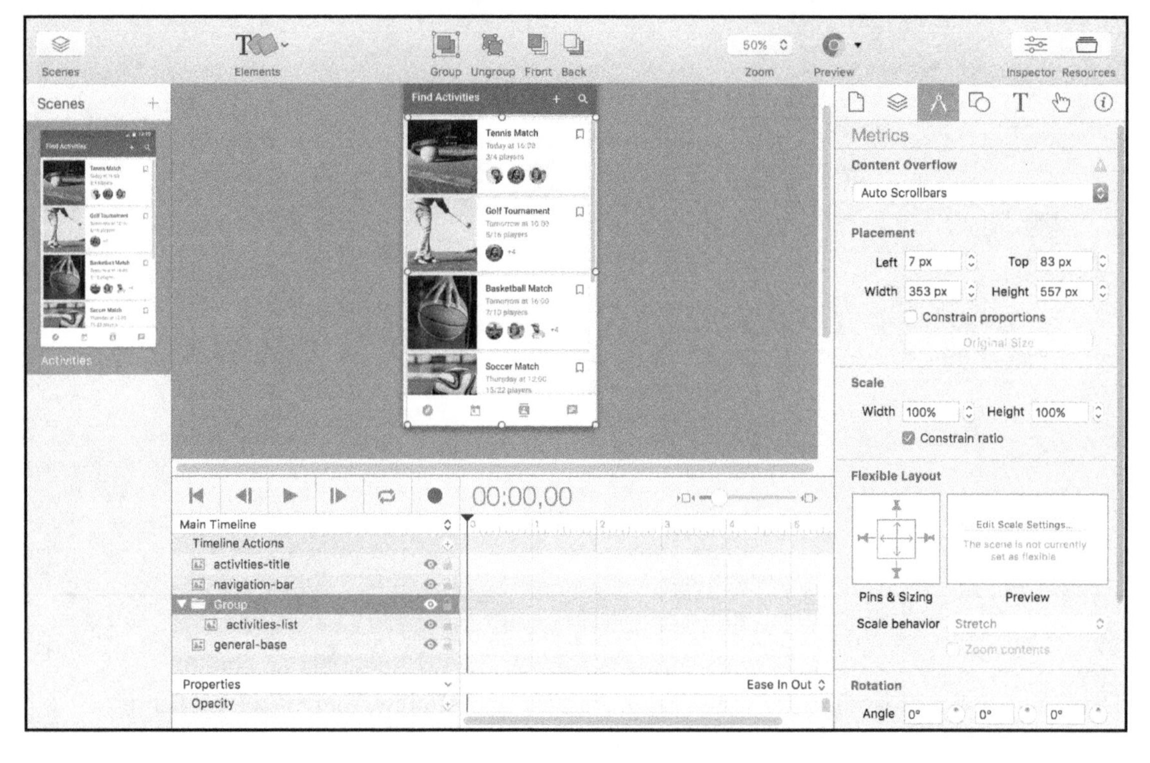

Making the size of groups smaller than their content allows you to specify how to deal with the content overflow--enabling scrolling, among other options

This technique uses the native scrolling support, which will work on both touch and nontouch devices. An alternative to supporting touch-based scrolling with greater control on the motion is illustrated in the subsequent examples.

In order to support users switching to a different view, we will need to do the following:

1. Change the active element in the navigation menu.
2. Switch the contents of the view.

The navigation bar highlights the current view. By default, we show a version with all options disabled. In order to support highlighting the currently selected view, we'll add a layer with an active version on top of each option. These layers will be fully transparent, except for the one that represents the selected view.

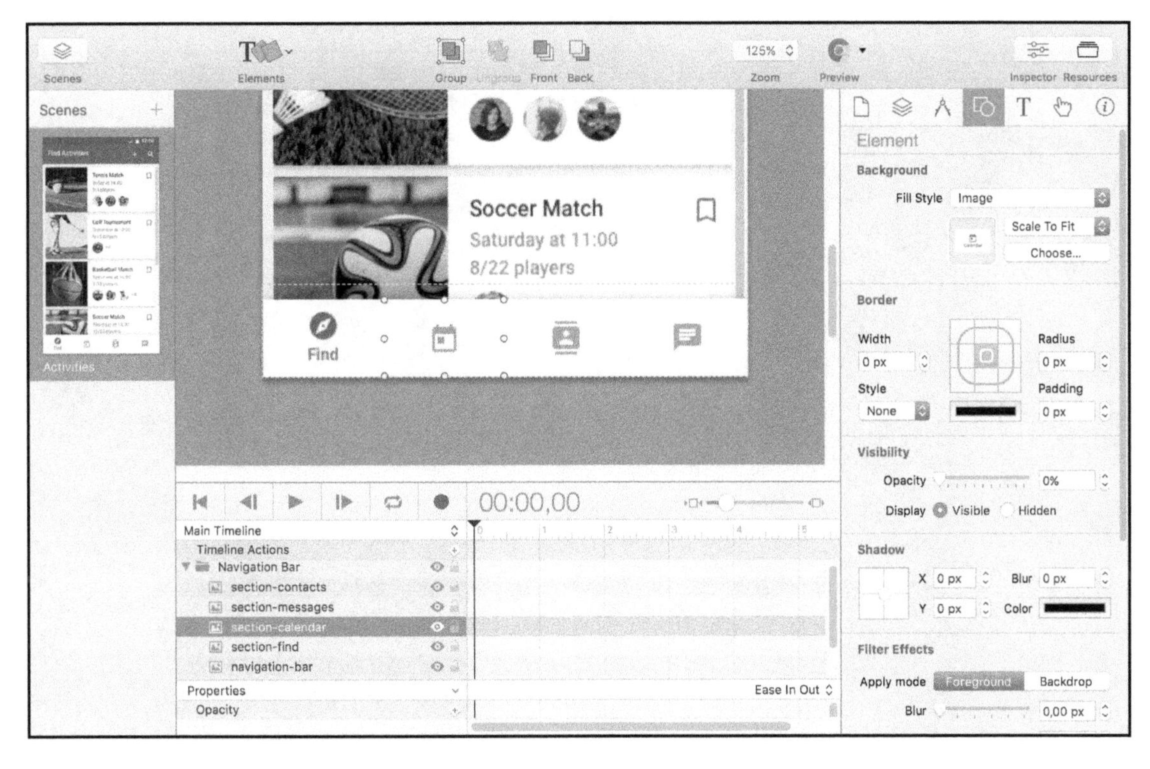

Active versions of the navigation menu options are placed on top of their disabled ones. Only one of the active versions remains visible at any time.

We'll also need the main contents of the view to change as we move to a different section. For example, when moving to the calendar view, the list of activities will be replaced by a calendar. In order to support this, we'll add the elements of the calendar view to the prototype. For convenience, we will add them in a group named **Calendar**:

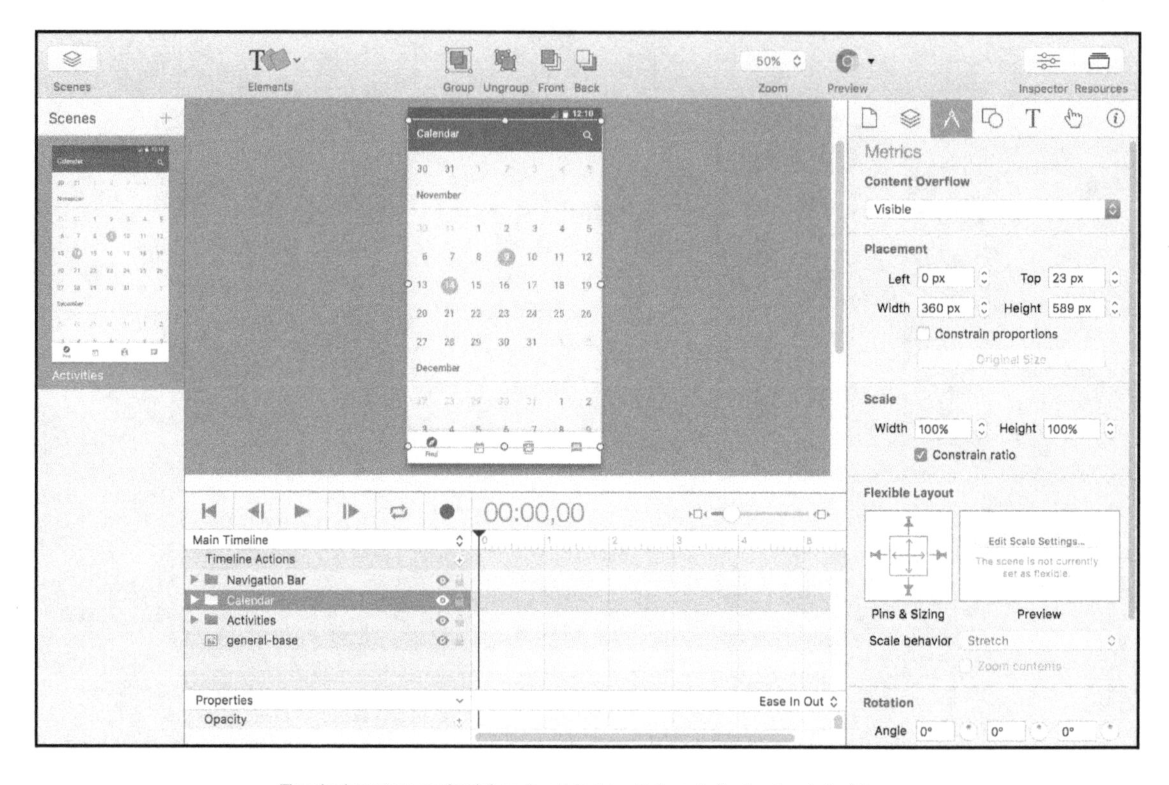

The calendar contents are placed above the activity list, with the navigation bar above both of them.

At this point, we have all the elements we need for the first transition--switching from the activities view to the calendar and updating the contents and the navigation menu. As it is common in Hype, we will specify those changes using a timeline.

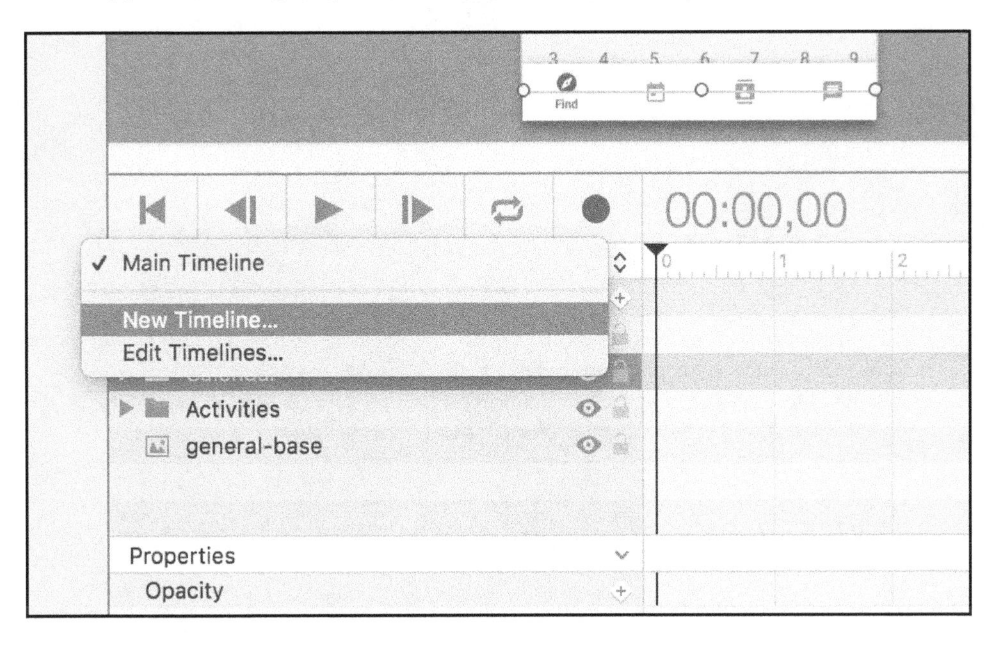

Creating a new timeline is the way to go when specifying changes in the properties of one or more elements

We'll create the **view-calendar** timeline where we can adjust the opacity to change the visibility of different elements in a half-second increment, making the calendar contents and active menu option visible, while making the former active option in the navigation bar fade away.

Finally, for the timeline to take effect, we will define a new action for the calendar option in the navigation bar. Tapping on it will start the new timeline to trigger the view change.

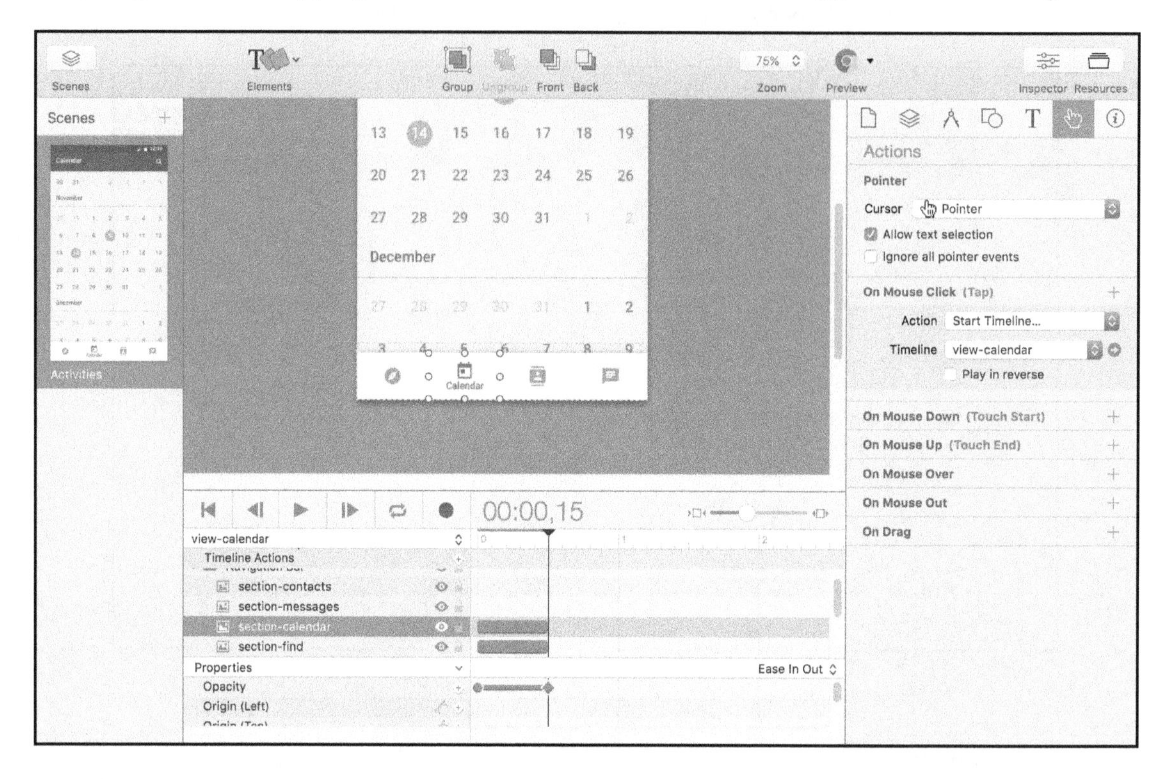

When the user taps on the calendar option, the view-calendar timeline will control the opacity of different layers in order to make the calendar the selected option.

If you preview the prototype, you'll see that the transition to the calendar view works. However, if you tap on the calendar again, you will experience a glitch--the view will change to the activities view for a moment before changing it back to the calendar view again. This makes sense since you are starting the transition again from the very beginning.

In order to make the transition more fluent, we can set the interaction as **Continue timeline...** instead. By continuing a timeline, an animation will be started if it is not already, but it won't restart later.

Another aspect we don't support yet is to move back to the initial view. In order to do so, we will need to create a new timeline. However, if we try to follow the same process, we'll find a small problem. Since the initial state already has the activities view as selected, the marker and the view that we want to make visible in the timeline are already visible.

In these cases, **relative timelines** come in handy. A relative timeline does not consider the initial properties as the starting point, ensuring the transition to the target state for the current state.

In the **Scene** tab from the properties panel, you'll find the list of the timelines. There, you can adjust which ones are **Relative**.

You can make timelines relative to one another if they capture a change from their current status to a specific target state. In the timeline, you will note that the initial status is presented with a circle to convey that.

By making the timelines relative, you can specify transitions focusing on only the target state, regardless of their initial status. In the example, you can indicate that clicking on an option makes the unrelated views transparent, regardless of their current visibility status. Since the target status is what matters, in this case, you can adjust the interactions to make them playable multiple times by either adjusting the interaction to use "Start Timeline" or marking the **Can restart timeline** option on the continue timeline event. In this way, users will be able to move back and forth between the views as many times as they want to.

In order to support the user switching between the other views, you only need to create a similar timeline for each of them.

Supporting gestures

For this prototype, we want to simulate a welcome tour for our app. The welcome tour consists of three panels that the user can move through in order to learn the basics of the app.

Download a prototype from `[Asset_A6462_A07_A04-Gestures.zip]`.

We will add each view as a separate layer next to each other. Only the first one will fit into the initial viewport at first. We can group the layers to make it easy to manipulate them together.

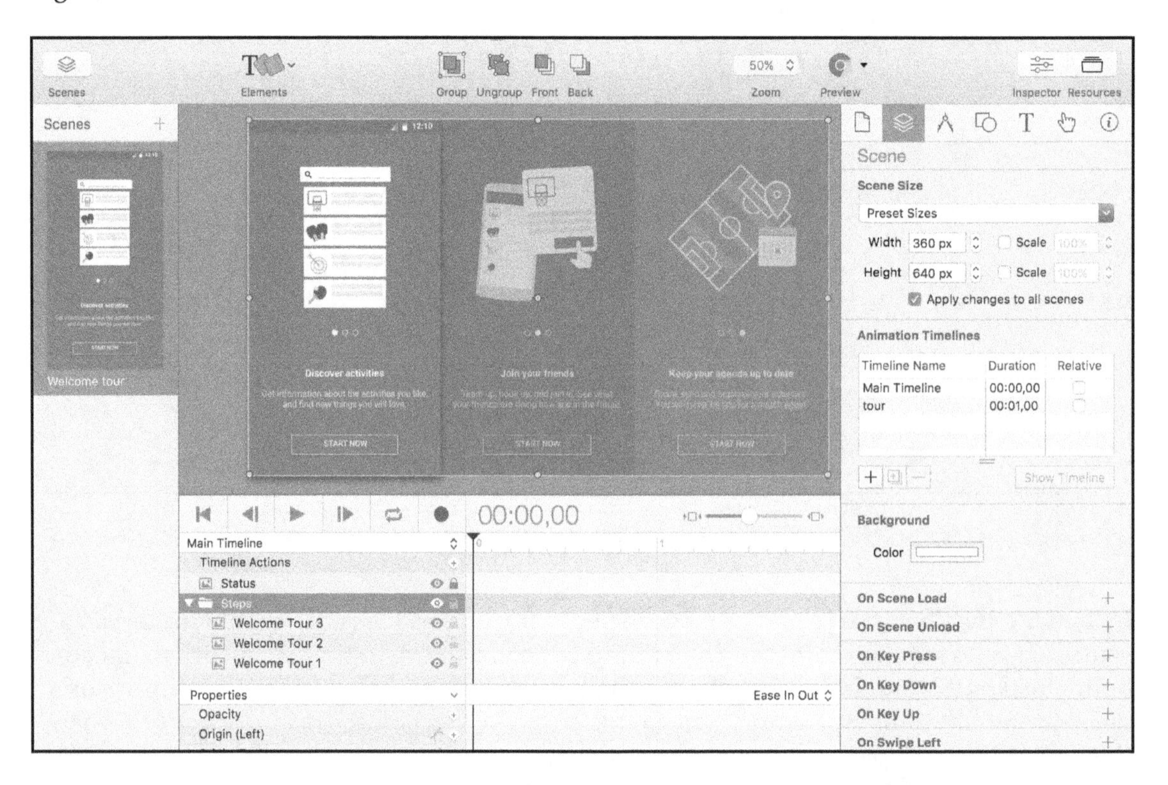

The three panels are organized in a group and placed next to each other, although initially only the first of them is visible.

We'll use a new timeline--named **tour--**to recreate the movement of the panels. In this timeline, we'll record two keyframes at regular intervals of 0.5 seconds where the group moves to the left making the next panel visible.

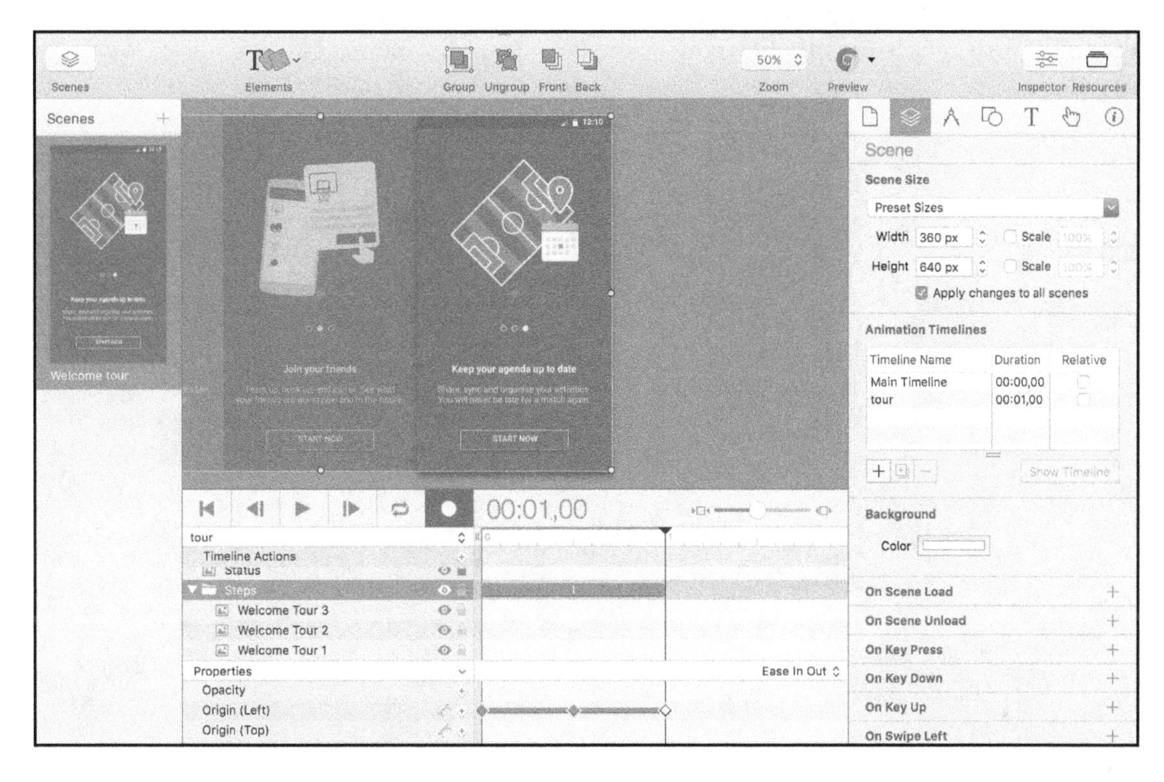

The tour timeline controls the movement of the three panels

In the preceding example, we are moving the three panels at the same time, but feel free to experiment moving them at different paces and creating some overlaps.

Unlike previous animations, this one won't be triggered when clicking or tapping on an element. We'll control this animation as we drag the panels. This will create the impression that we control their movement. In order to achieve this, we just need to create a new **Control Timeline...** action for the group of panels based on the **On Drag** event. This action allows us to play a timeline as we drag our fingers over an element.

There are some aspects we need to specify, for example, the dragging **Axis** indicates whether the dragging action is applied vertically or horizontally, and the **Direction** property indicates how the user needs to move their finger through the axis to make the timeline play. In our example, we'll set the action to use the horizontal axis in the reverse direction. This makes the timeline play as the user drags the element horizontally from right to left.

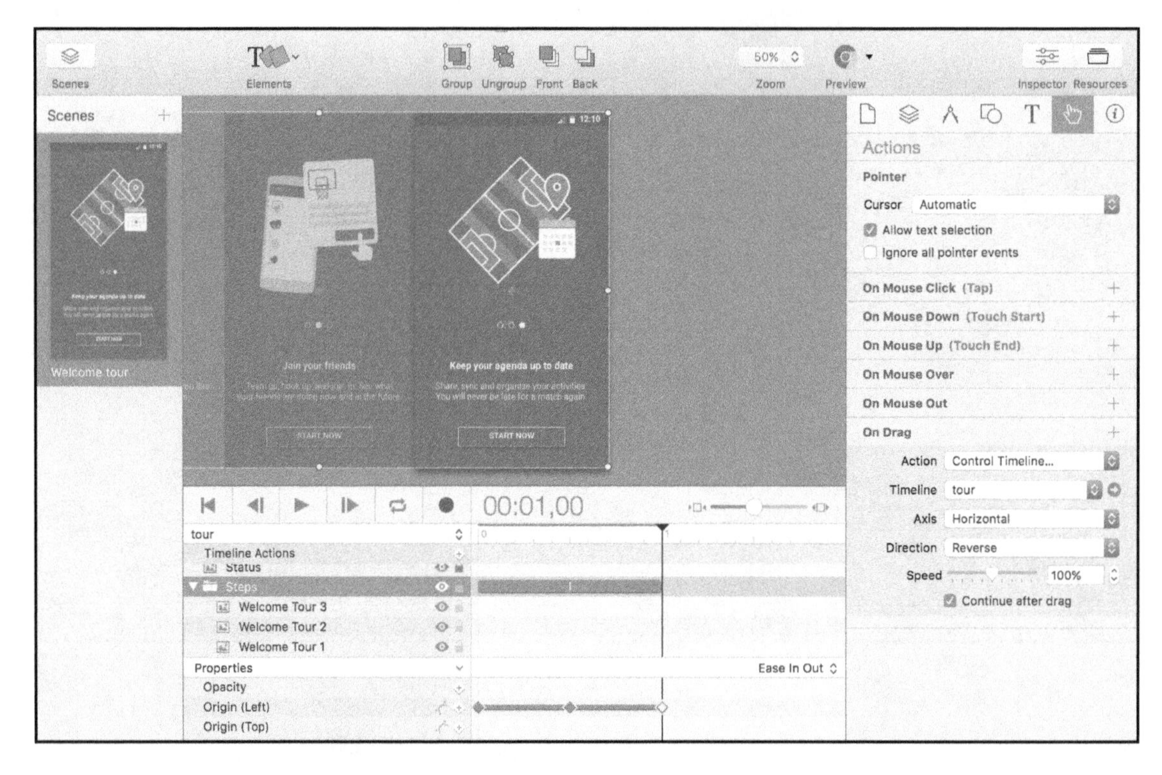

Controlling a timeline as the user drags an element allows you to create interesting transitions

For the drag action, you can also control the speed at which the timeline will be played as the user's finger moves and whether the animation can remain incomplete when the user stops dragging. The **Continue after drag** option prevents the timeline remaining at an intermediate point. This is very convenient for our example since we only want the views to remain at specific positions.

If we preview the prototype, we'll notice that dragging the tour view to reach the next panel leads to the last panel since the animation continues until the end of the timeline. One way to make sure that the second screen is considered is to add a pause action at that point.

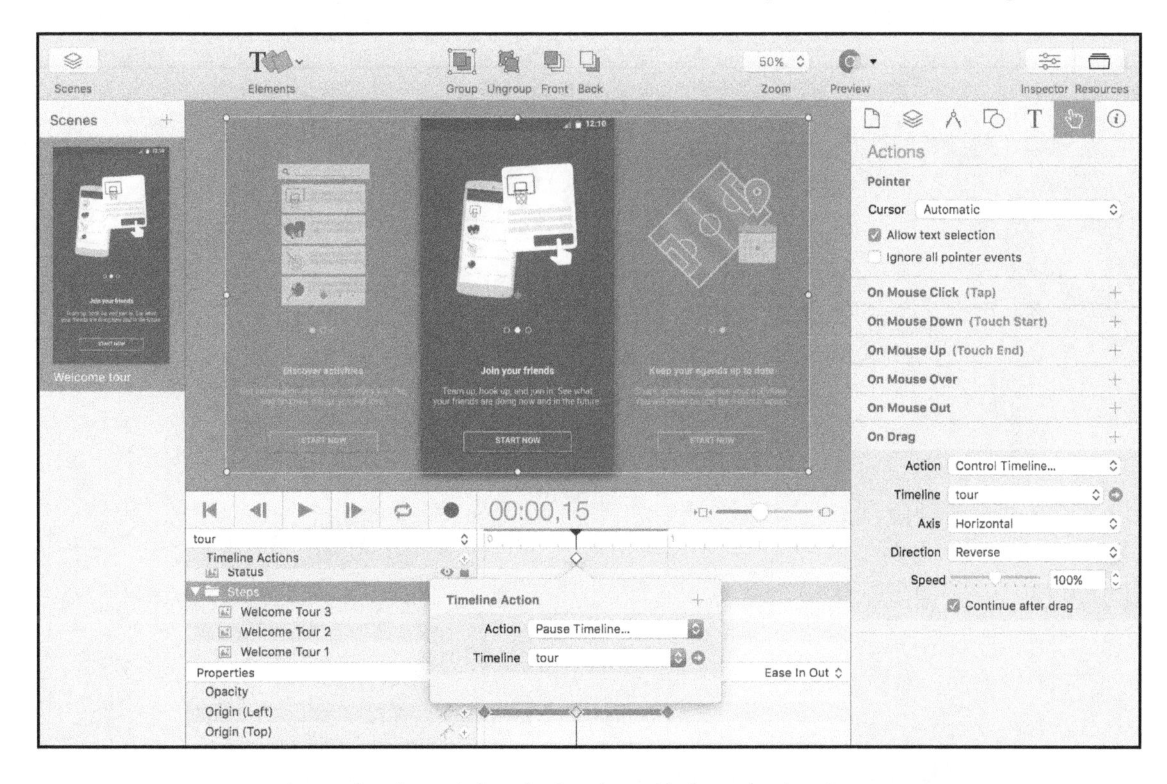

A pause action makes sure that incomplete drag actions consider the second panel as a place to stop

In this way, the animation will always stop at a point that makes sense. If you move to an intermediate point between the first and the second panel, the view will adjust to reach one of those steps, but won't remain in an in-between position.

Dragging to control a timeline allows any animation to happen as the user moves their finger. This is a powerful mechanism to create rich experiences. However, if we don't need such level of detail, there is a simplified way to get a similar result.

As an alternative, we can access the scene panel and use the general swipe right and swipe left actions. Those actions can continue the timeline to play backward or forward as a result of the user making a swipe gesture. In this case, the animation will only happen after the user completes the gesture.

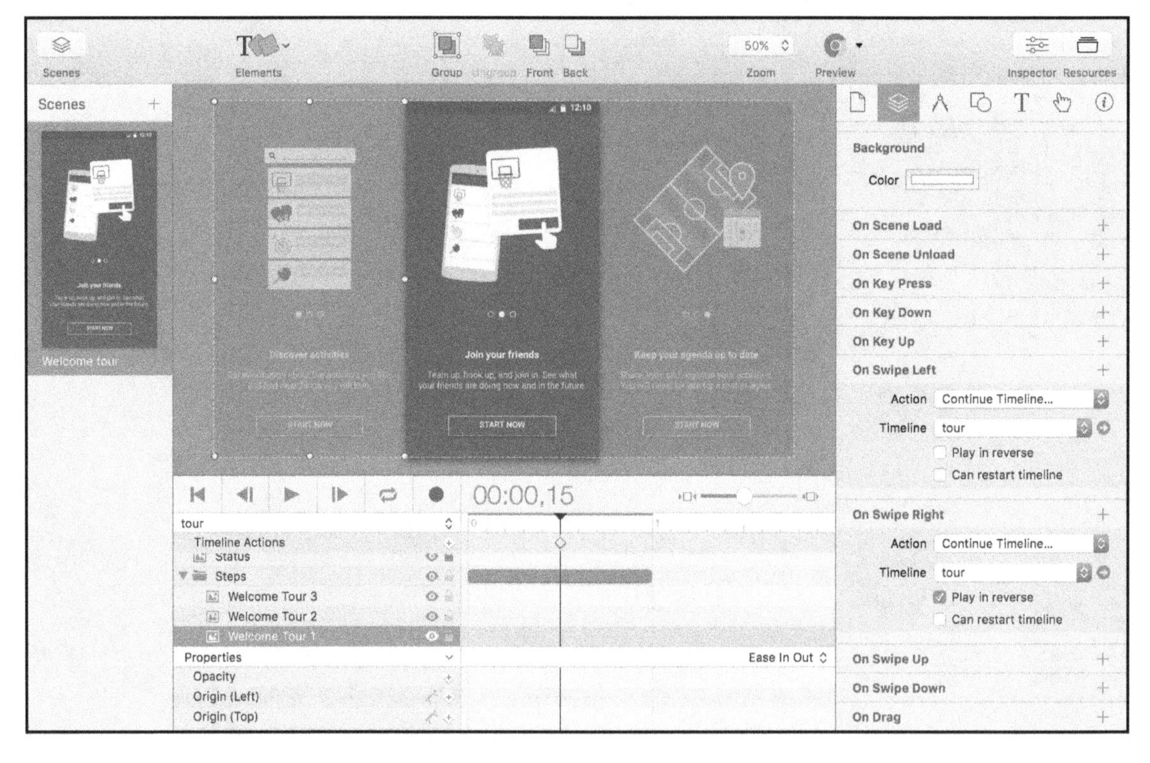

Using swipe gestures can simulate the movement through panels using the same timeline defined before

Feel free to use the more elaborate drag approach or a simplified swipe gesture depending on the specific needs of your prototype.

Prototyping complex behavior

The prototyping techniques you have already seen should allow you to prototype many diverse interactions. In this section, we'll see a few examples that can be useful in more specific situations. You can probably prototype the basic idea of your designs without them, but they can add an extra degree of realism in those cases where it is needed.

Composing animations

In the former examples, the animations defined have been quite simple. We have created transitions for a few properties such as opacity and position, but we haven't paid much attention to the timing and acceleration of those transitions. In this prototype, we will create a much more complex animation.

Download a prototype from `[Asset_A6462_A07_A05-Animations.zip]`.

Changing to a completely different view requires users to reorient. When transitions provide continuity between two views, it helps the user connect the dots. In our example, the list of activities and the detail activity both use an image to represent the specific activity. We can use that image to make the relationship between the two views easier to understand.

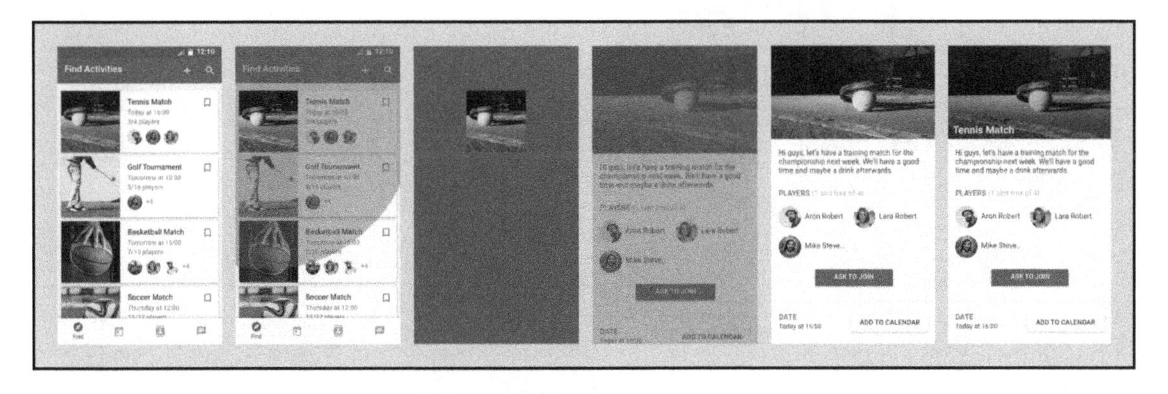

A transition between the list of activities and the detail of the tennis match where the image of the list item remains visible as the rest fades with a ripple effect, takes a central position and expands fading into the detail view.

The transition is organized in the following steps:

1. The activities view contents fade away as an expanding circle grows behind the activity thumbnail.
2. The activity image moves to the center of the view and grows in size.
3. As the image grows, it fades out, and the image from the detail view fades in.
4. Finally, the information panel of the detail view appears as it moves up in different stages--showing the content first and then the title.

Given this sequence of transitions, we'll need to break the views into different pieces to be able to move them independently. For the activities page, we can use a single image, but we'll need the thumbnail image as a separate layer placed on top of it.

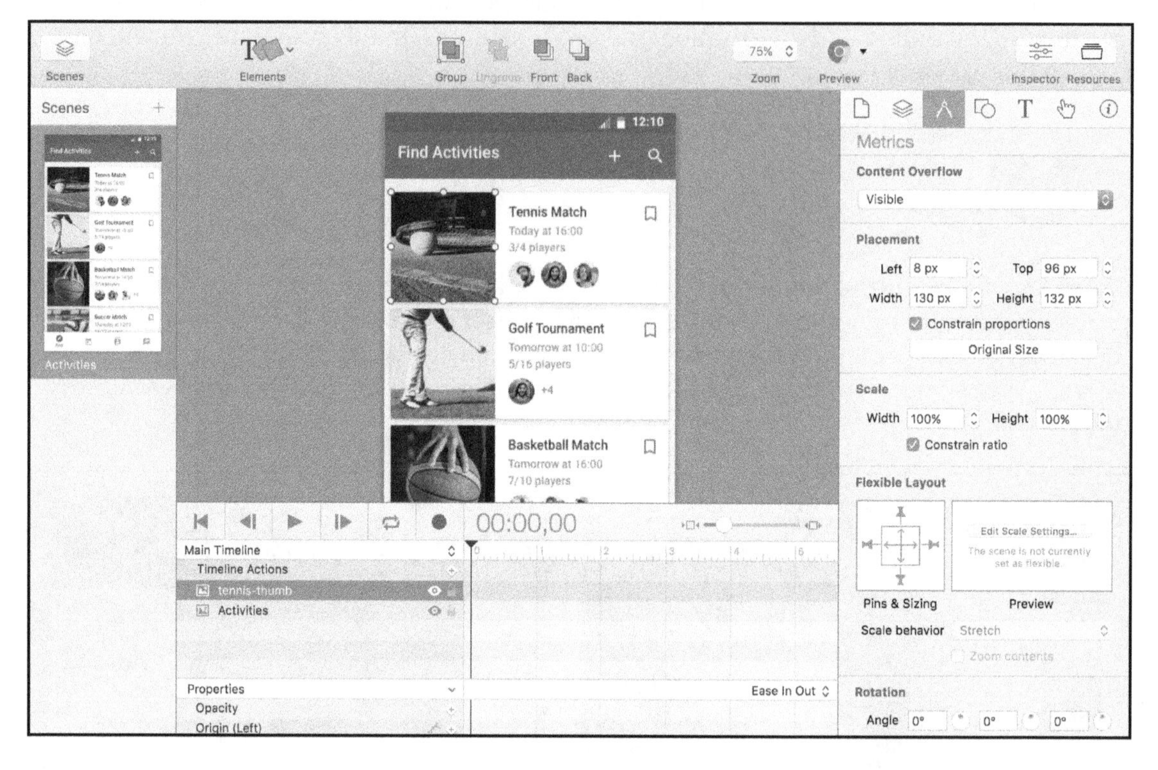

The thumbnail image for the first activity of the list is a separate layer since it is going to move independently

In order to fade the contents out and keep the focus on the image thumbnail, we'll use an expanding circle that grows from the thumbnail. We can either use an ellipse shape in Hype or just add a separate image of a circle. In this example, we are using an image of a circle big enough to cover most of the screen--979x979 px. We need to make sure that we set the circle to the original size, place it between the activities layer and the thumbnail, and center its position with the thumbnail image.

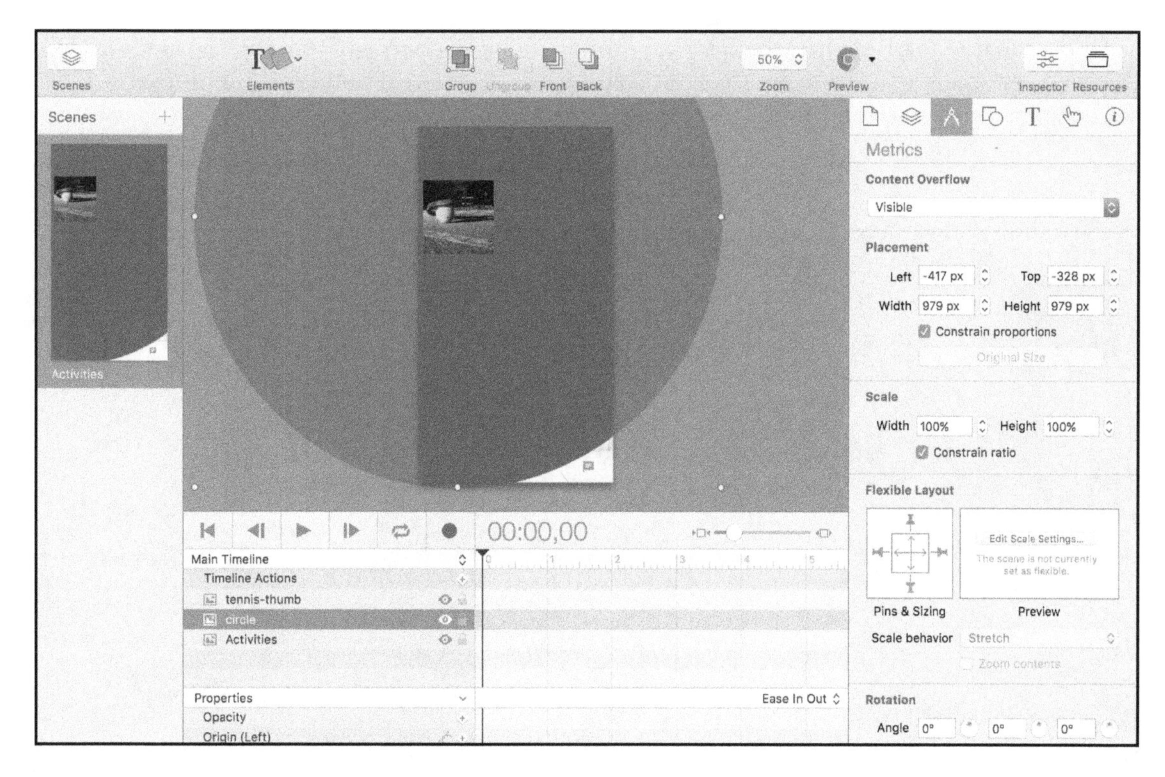

A circle emerging behind the thumbnail will be used to cover the rest of the contents

Initially, the circle will be hidden behind the thumbnail. We can use the **Scale** property from the **Metrics** tab of the properties panel to make the circle 10% of its original size. We'll also adjust the opacity to make it transparent.

Now that we have the initial state ready, we can create a new timeline to define the transition. We'll create the **transition** timeline and an active area over the first item in the list to play the timeline.

When recording the timeline, the first keyframe will be in charge of making the circle grow and become opaque at the same time. At 0.4 seconds after the timeline starting point, we will change the **Opacity** to **100%** and the **Scale** to **120%**.

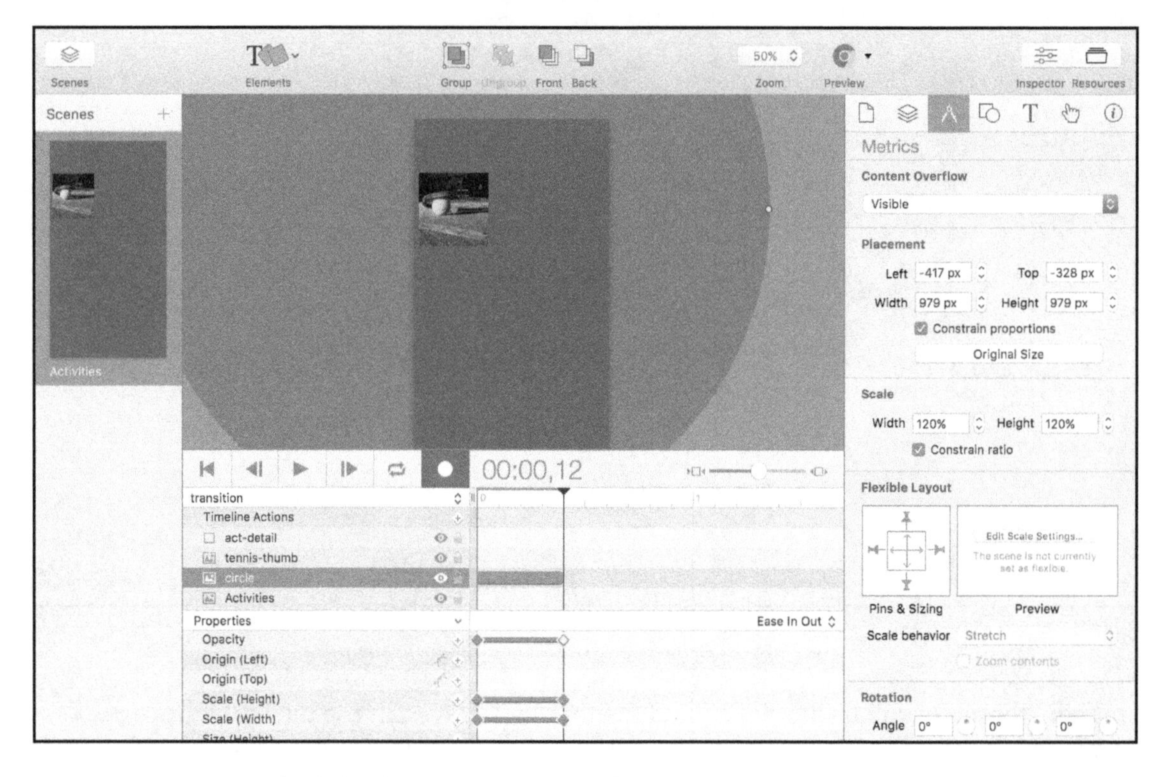

The opacity and scale--horizontal and vertical--properties are adjusted in the timeline for the growing circle transition

The next transition to support is for the thumbnail to move horizontally to the center of the screen. We want this movement to happen 0.3 seconds after the circle transition completes. By default, creating a new keyframe will define a transition starting from the previous keyframe for that property or the timeline origin. However, you can move the timeline recording origin to any point in order to control the starting point for the transition. To do this, you can drag the gray area that appears close to the origin of the timeline when recording.

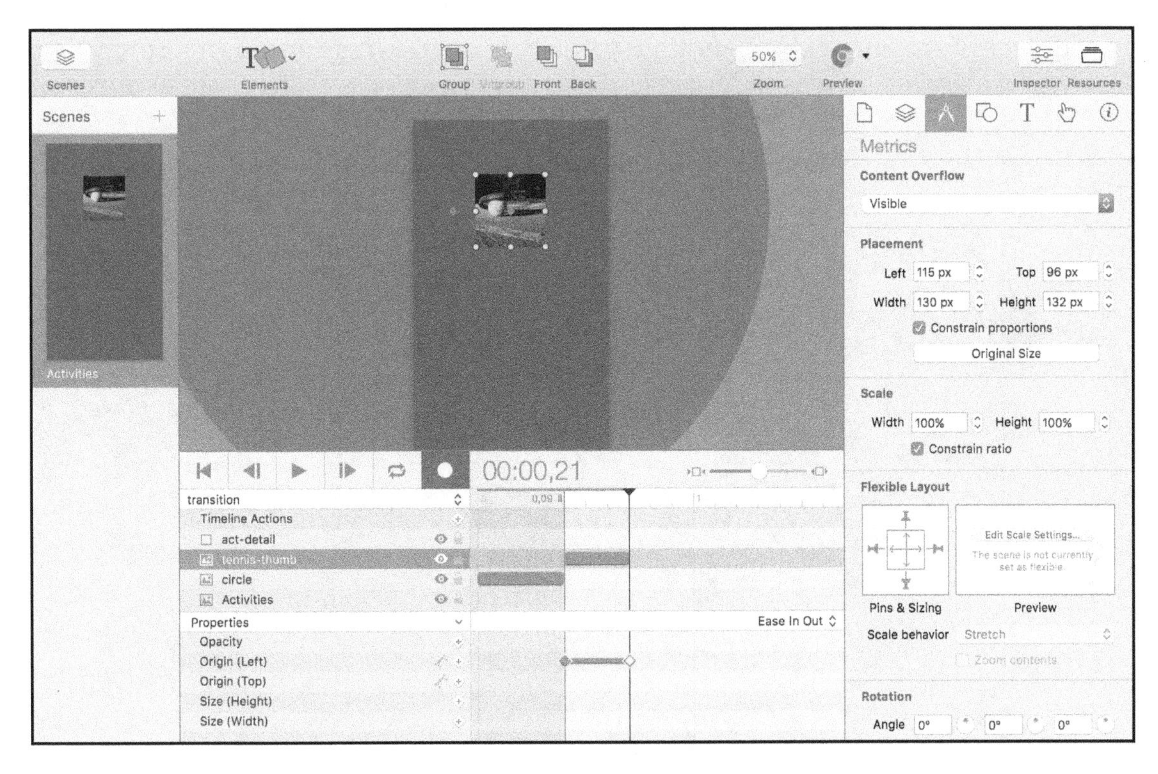

The timeline recording origin can be adjusted to control the starting point for a transition, in this case, making it start after the previous one ended.

In case you didn't set the timeline recording origin while creating the transition, you can always adjust its starting point afterward.

The next step in the animation is to make the thumbnail grow and vanish as the real background emerges. In order to support this, we'll add the background from the details view as a new layer on top of the thumbnail and initially set it as transparent. We add new transitions to the timeline to make the thumbnail scale to 180% and become transparent and the details background to become 100% opaque. In this case, the transitions won't happen both at the same time or strictly one after the other.

Rather, we overlap some of the transitions partially to create a more organic transformation, making the thumbnail scale, but they only start vanishing as the scaling transition reaches the end and the background starts to fade in.

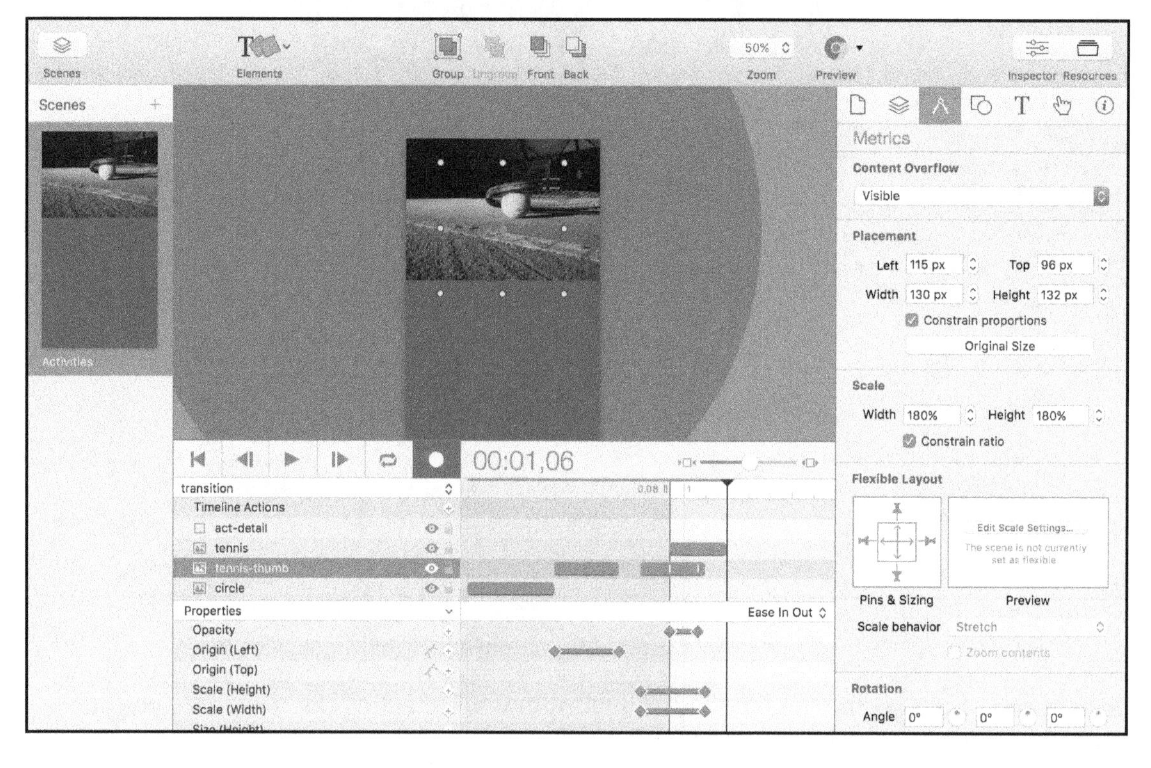

The thumbnail scales and fades out, and the larger background image fades in. Note the overlap between the different transitions in the timeline.

The only remaining part to complete this transition is to show the information details. We have organized the details in three pieces--the details panel, the title of the event, and a shadow gradient--that makes the title text more readable over the background image. To facilitate the manipulation of these pieces, we'll create a group for their layers called `Details`. Initially, the title and gradient layers will be placed behind the **Details** panel, so they will only be visible once they move above the **Details**.

For the details group, we want them to appear from the bottom. However, to make the transition more fluent, we don't want the details to move all the way from the bottom of the screen. Instead, we move the original position of the group a few pixels down, set their opacity to 0%, and define a transition where the group fades in as it moves up, reaching its intended position.

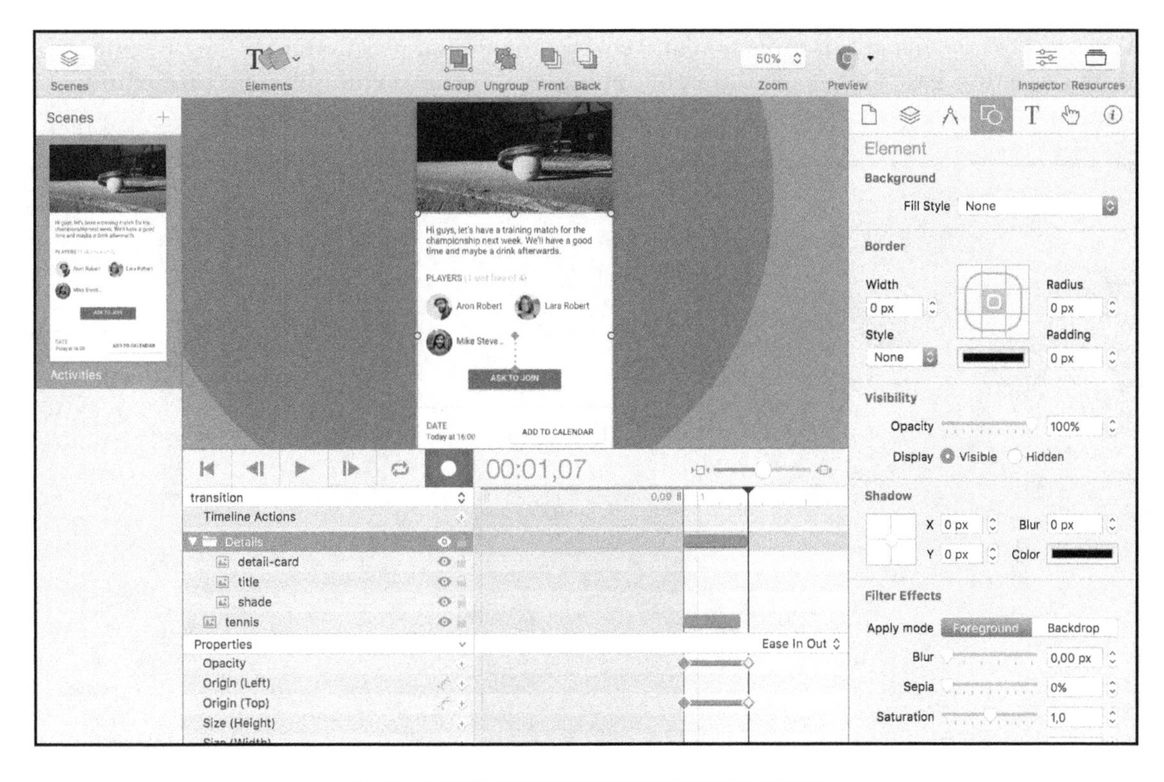

The group with details moves up to reach the intended position as it fades in.

The shadow gradient and the title will appear one after the other once the group reaches its final position. Moving individual elements inside a group is totally okay, but keep in mind that if the group is also moving, both movements will apply.

In the real world, objects are exposed to friction and inertia, and their motion often presents some initial acceleration and final deceleration, which corresponds to the ease in out timing function that Hype uses by default. However, in the case of the details panel, since it enters the scene as an object which is already in motion, it does not make sense to start with an initial acceleration, so we just use an **Ease Out** function instead.

We select the details group transition and change the timing function from the timeline. When selecting **Ease Out**, some different options are available with different acceleration patterns; we'll use the **Cubic** one.

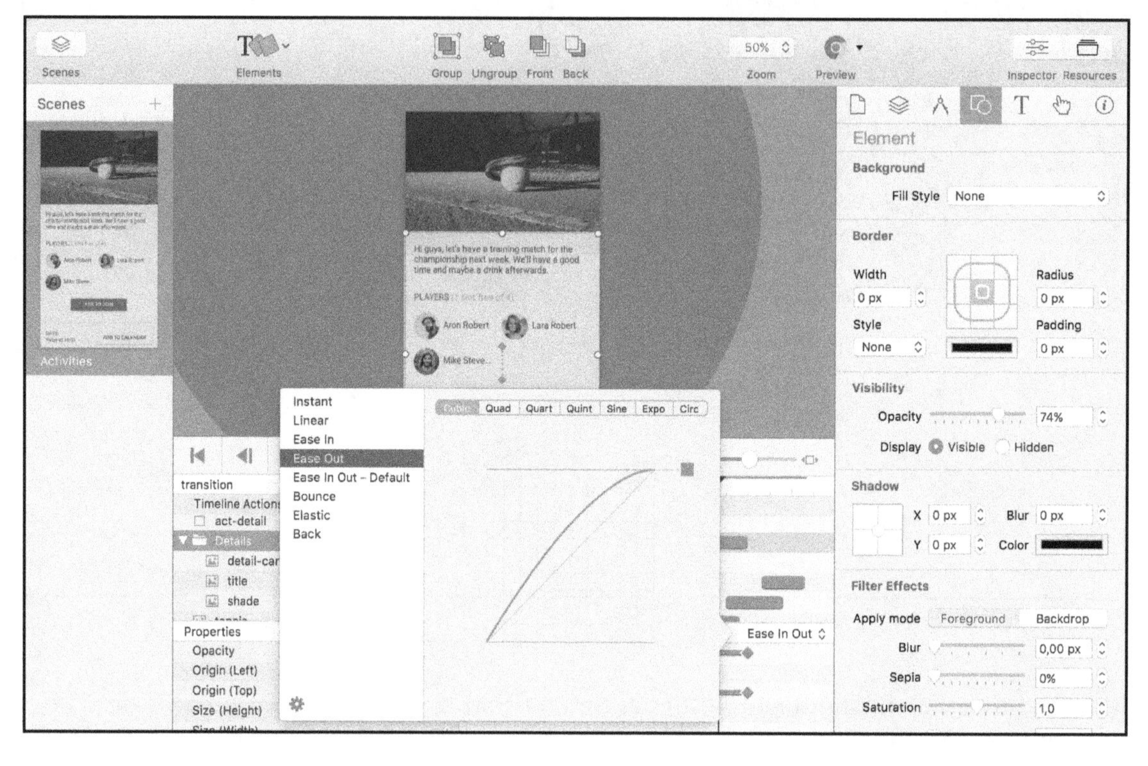

You can adjust the timing function for each transition in the timeline. In the example, a cubic Ease Out function is used to make motion decelerate when reaching the end of the transition.

At this point, we have completed a multi-step animation that helps orient the user in a pleasant way when they are changing views. Feel free to experiment with different timing functions and combine animations in different ways, such as presenting one after another, overlapping them, or introducing delays.

Supporting user input

Imagine that we want to prototype a search interface. One option to support this interaction would be to show an empty search field that gets filled with some predefined text when the user clicks on it. Since we just need to prototype a particular scenario, we can decide in advance which text to show. However, in some cases, you may need the user to actually type in the search field.

Download a prototype from [Asset_A6462_A07_A06-Input.zip].

The ability to integrate HTML elements into your prototypes is very useful in supporting user text input. To support the search scenario, we'll follow these steps:

1. Defining the search transitions.
2. Adding an invisible HTML input field on top of our prototype.
3. Making the search input field trigger the search transition when the user types.

When searching, users can access the search view by tapping the search icon in any view. In the **Search** view, as users type, they will get the **Results** view when matching results are shown.

We can support the first transition by switching between scenes. We create two scenes in a Hype prototype--**Activities** for the list of activities, and **Search** for the search view. In the activities view, we'll create a transparent rectangle over the search icon in order to define its active area, and an associated action to jump to the **Search** scene.

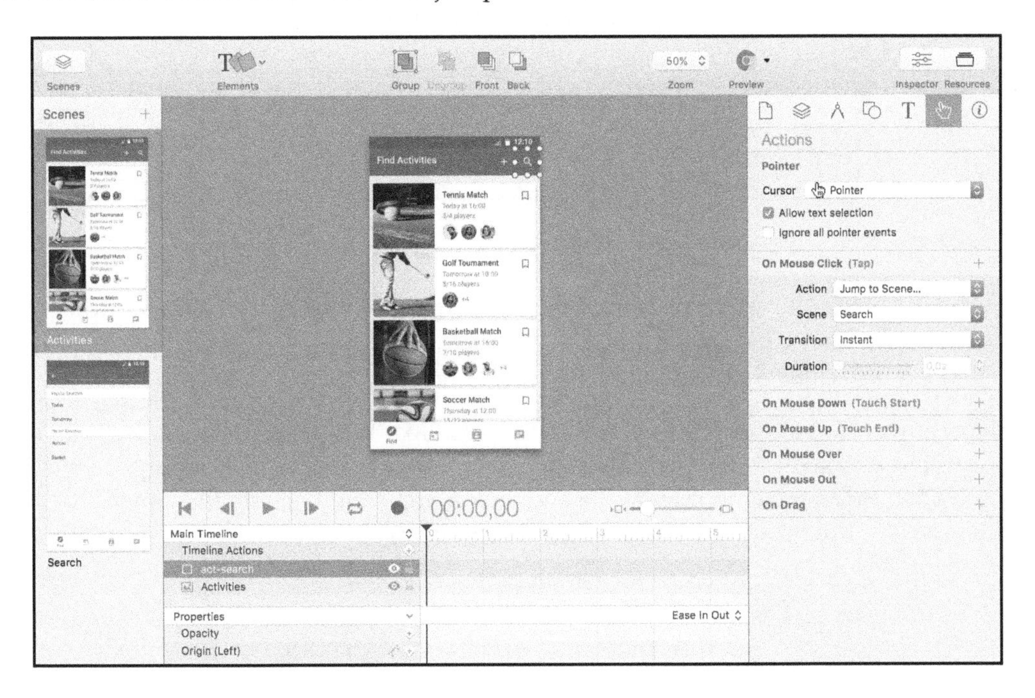

A transparent layer sets the active area with an associated action to change to the "Search" scene.

The **Search** scene will include the initial search state but also the one showing the results. We'll use different layers for each one. The **Results** view will initially be invisible and a new transition--named **show-results** in the example--will change its opacity to become 100%.

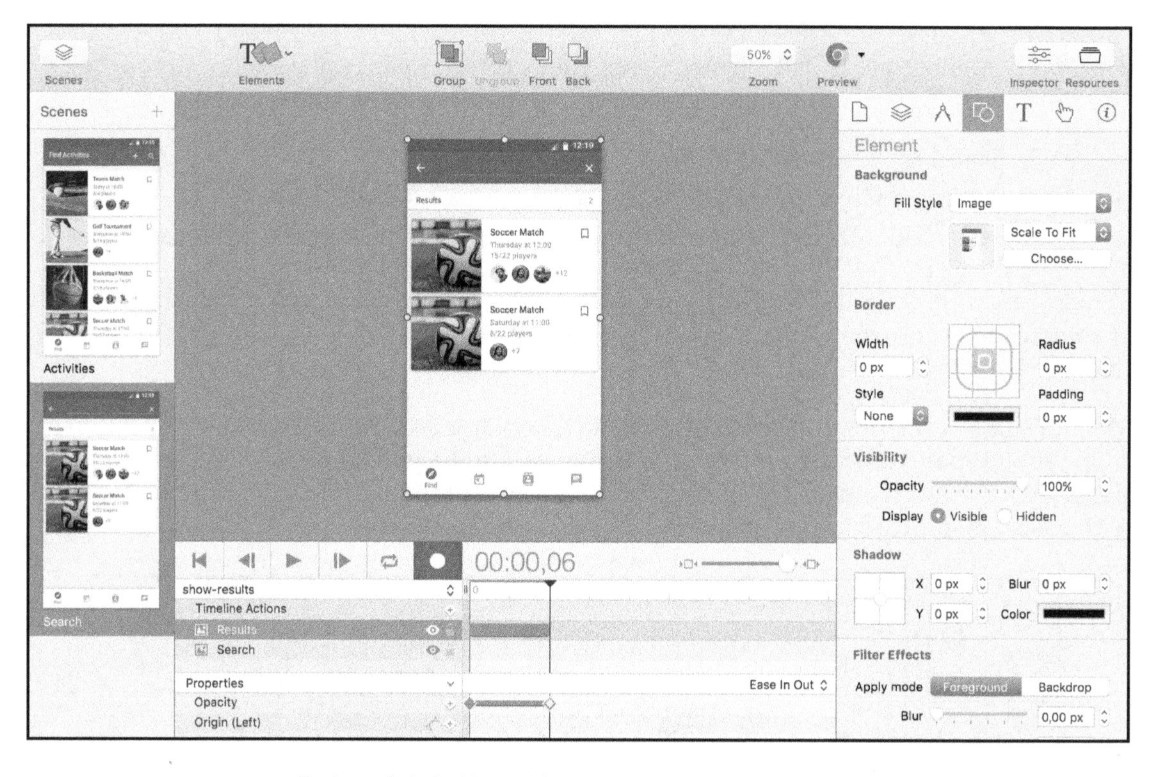

The show-results timeline is in charge of showing the results layer by making them opaque

So far, we have not done anything very different compared to the previous example. However, this new timeline will be played when the user types, and that requires a place in which to type and connect all the pieces together.

The **Element** menu in Hype allows you to add an **HTML Widget**. This is the way to add HTML content as a layer in the prototype to create a new object such as an input field. We'll add the **HTML Widget** element on top of the search area, and click on the pencil icon to add the code that will trigger the playback of the timeline.

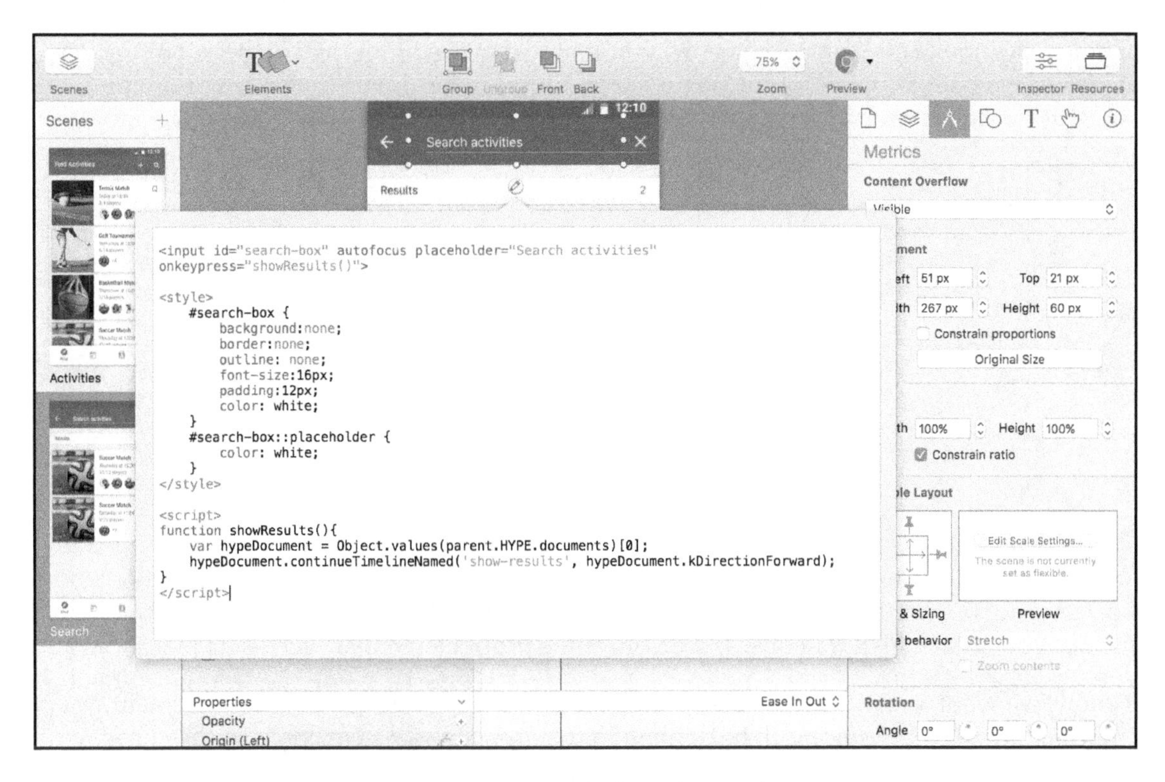

HTML Widget content can be edited from the Hype scene editor.

The HTML code is in charge of three different aspects: creating the input field (the **input** part), adjusting the aspect of the field to fit the prototype (the **style** part), and controlling the timeline (the **script** part).

First, we'll add the code to create the input field:

```
<input id="search-box" autofocus placeholder="Search activities"
onkeypress="showResults()">
```

This code defines a new input field, gives it an identifier to refer to it later--`search-box`--and specifies that the input should get the focus automatically so that the user can just start typing without having to select it first and a placeholder message to be displayed when there are no contents. Finally, it includes an `onkeypress` attribute that triggers a `showResults` function. This is a function we'll define in later steps to control the timeline.

If you take a look at the prototype now, you'll note that the input field is there, but the way it looks does not fit our prototype. We want the input to be almost invisible so that it integrates nicely on top of our prototype background. The `style` code allows us to do so:

```
<style>
    #search-box {
        background:none;
        border:none;
        outline: none;
        font-size:16px;
        padding:12px;
        color: white;
    }
    #search-box::placeholder {
        color: white;
    }
</style>
```

With this code, we are defining the aspect of the `search-box` input field. We are hiding the background, border, and the outline that appears around the element when it has the input focus. We also specified font size and color for the input element as well as its placeholder.

Finally, we want to make search results appear as the user types. In the input element, we indicated that this behavior will be defined in the `showResults` function, but we need to specify such behavior. For that purpose, we will use the following code:

```
<script>
function showResults(){
    var hypeDocument = Object.values(parent.HYPE.documents)[0];
    hypeDocument.continueTimelineNamed('show-results',
hypeDocument.kDirectionForward);
}
</script>
```

The `script` section defines a new function--we can use whatever name we want as long as it matches the one we use in the input element.

The function defines the `hypeDocument` variable to capture the representation of the prototype object in code. Hype provides objects in code to access its functionality.

The second line of the function uses the Hype functions to control a timeline. In this case, it uses a function to continue the show-results timeline we defined before and play it moving forward. This is analogous to what we did in other examples in Hype, but it is now expressed with code.

If you preview the prototype now, you'll be able to access the search function, and as soon as you type something, the results will appear. However, the arrow to go back and the **X** control to clear the search won't work. Supporting the back arrow is simple; you just need to create an active area with a transparent rectangle to trigger the scene change. Clearing the input is a bit more complex.

Since we need to access the input field inside the HTML Widget element, we need to give the widget a code identifier. By selecting the widget and selecting the **identity** panel from the property inspector, you can define `widget` as the **Unique Element ID**.

In order to clear the search box, you need an active area over it with an action associated with the tap event. In this case, we'll define two actions. One is to rewind the **show-results** timeline using the **Go to Time in Timeline...** action; the other will be defined in code. We'll use the **Run JavaScript...** option and create a new function.

In addition to rewinding the timeline, clicking on the clear button will trigger more advanced behavior in a JavaScript function

First, we give the function a descriptive name--`clearInput`. The function will be in charge of setting the input field with the empty value. The complexity of the code is mainly about extracting the element since the input field is inside an HTML iFrame.

From the following function code, only the last line is about manipulating the input field; the rest are about getting the `iframe`, the contents inside it, and the `input` field.

```
function clearInput(hypeDocument, element, event) {
     var iframe =
document.getElementById('widget').getElementsByTagName('iframe')[0];
     var contents = iframe.contentDocument || iframe.contentWindow.document;
     var input = contents.getElementById('search-box');
     input.value = "";
}
```

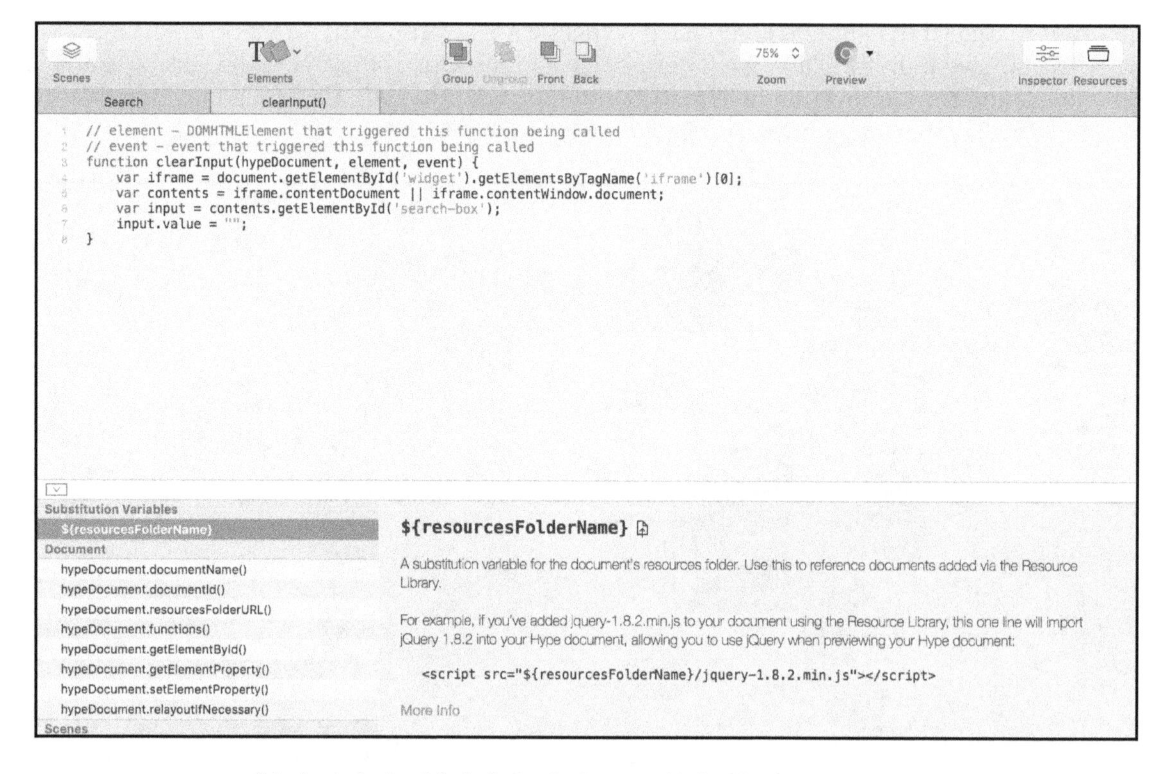

Code editor showing the code for the clearInput function on top and the list of Hype functions at the bottom

You can reuse most of the code used in this chapter to manipulate other HTML widgets just by giving identifiers to the corresponding elements. If you feel comfortable coding, you can add more complex logic, for example, to play a different timeline based on what the user typed.

Being pragmatic

Hype is a very powerful prototyping tool. It allows you to create all kinds of prototypes. However, the process of creating a prototype for a real project is not always a clear path. You cannot anticipate all the necessary steps in advance, and some changes are expected in the process. In this section, you'll find some advice to help you navigate the process of prototyping with Hype more fluently.

Organize your layers

Before you start your prototype, it is useful to spend some time planning how the different layers will work together. You'll need to break your mock-ups into different layers depending on which parts you need to manipulate. Sketching the basic interactions will help you to determine which pieces you need.

When building your prototype, it is also important to keep the different layers organized. Prototyping with Hype normally involves moving different layers around--even out of the current canvas--and changing properties, such as their opacity. This makes it hard to find and select some layers. Naming layers with a clear name will make the layer list a useful index for the different parts of your prototype, especially those that are not visible at some point.

When multiple layers work together, it is also convenient to group them. In this way, you can animate them as a block or as individual elements. This is especially relevant when these include interactive parts where you want them to keep their relative position to the element; this is something harder to achieve if you animate them independently without grouping them. Thinking about these groups from the beginning can help you keep the prototype simple.

Preview often

Prototypes are about recreating a user experience, not building features. As you make progress in building your prototype, you will need to check that experience. Preview the prototype often to get a better idea on what needs further adjustment, and focus the efforts in polishing the most important aspects. Feel free to experiment and tweak details such as the timing functions or duration of different transitions. Prototyping is also an experimentation exercise, and previewing the experience often will help you to decide which of the thousands of aspects that you can tweak with Hype are actually able to improve your prototype.

When creating prototypes for mobile devices, prototyping them in the real device also makes a big difference. For iOS devices, you can use Hype Reflect to quickly try out your prototype; for other devices, make sure that you set a quick export process that allows you to have new versions of your prototype available on the Internet or your local network. You can find multiple file hosting solutions that can serve the static HTML files that Hype generates.

Summary

In this chapter, we introduced Hype, a powerful prototyping tool. We illustrated how to support different prototyping patterns that we can use to simulate the behavior of our product. With examples of differing complexity, we will be able to support both quick rough prototypes and detailed interactions based on your specific needs.

Getting familiar with the concepts of motion design and how to use a timeline to support them will allow us to experiment with different kinds of interactions and communicate using motion with this or similar tools.

The next chapter introduces a very different tool that is equally powerful but approaches prototyping from a very different angle that relies mostly on prototyping with code.

8
Prototyping with Code - Using Framer Studio

"Success Comes Through Rapidly Fixing our Mistakes Rather than Getting Things Right the First Time"

- Tim Harford

A prototype simulates part of the behavior of your future app. An advanced and scalable way of describing the behavior of digital products is through code. There are different tools and libraries that try to reduce the time required to produce a prototype with a programming language. In this book, we will make use of `Framer.js`, a library based on JavaScript, and Framer Studio, a visual prototype development tool based on `Framer.js` and CoffeeScript.

This prototyping approach can be maintained and developed over time if it is planned properly. Also, thanks to `Framer.js`, our prototypes will be as realistic as required because we can use high-fidelity designs with advanced gestures and animations. It will allow us to obtain feedback very close to what we can have with the real product.

Framer.js

`Framer.js` is an open source framework based on JavaScript for the production of quick prototypes. It allows you to create both basic and more advanced prototypes with detailed interactions (`https://github.com/koenbok/Framer`).

`Framer.js` captures the basic building blocks you need to build a prototype in code. You can define and control layers, changes of state, and animations. `Framer.js` also allows you to import Photoshop and Sketch files using Framer Generator, an application distributed with the framework. This reduces the time you need to create the initial layers of your prototype and the time required to put them together in the right place.

You can start creating your prototypes directly with `Framer.js` using a general purpose code editor such as *Atom* or *Brackets*. However, Framer Studio is a commercial product that has been created with the specific purpose of creating prototypes with `Framer.js`. Framer Studio is used by many large companies and is the tool we'll use for our examples in this chapter.

Framer Studio

Framer Studio allows you to optimize your prototyping workflow, thanks to a desktop interface that shows the visual result of your code as you write it. In addition, it helps you keep your code simple, thanks to CoffeeScript, a programming language with a syntax for quick writing, which compiles behind the scenes into JavaScript.

In Framer Studio, the user interface is composed of several parts:

- The menu with main actions and some auto-code options to help you build your prototype
- The code editor where you will program your prototype
- The preview area where you will see the design in sync with your code
- Contextual panel with the layer inspector or properties related to a selected item

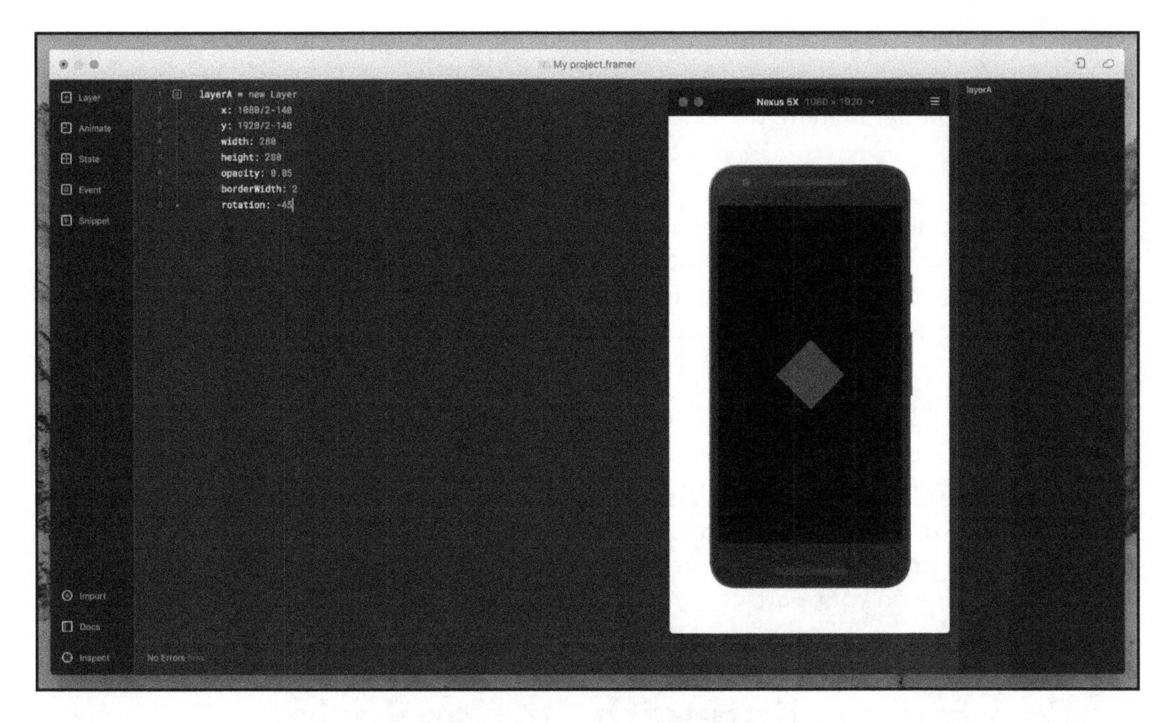

Screenshot of Framer Studio with a very simple project

Additionally, Framer Studio will allow you to import your designs from *Adobe Photoshop* and *Bohemian Sketch* with an easy-to-use wizard. This feature will allow you to change the visual design of your application, import again, and see the update in the preview area. You can see the results of your changes quickly and iterate over your design solution until it is pixel perfect. Using this tool will help you improve your prototyping workflow.

Understanding CoffeeScript

CoffeeScript is a programming language that compiles into JavaScript. JavaScript is a widely used and powerful language most notably used as the scripting language for the web. CoffeeScript provides a simplified syntax for JavaScript, making the resulting code simpler to write and understand.

With CoffeeScript, you will be able to write simple code describing your prototype, and it will be automatically transformed into JavaScript, so your prototype will work in browsers such as Firefox or Chrome, making your prototypes compatible with multiple platforms, simplifying the process of testing them with real users, and presenting your design ideas to your team and stakeholders.

Here's an example of a simple function in CoffeeScript that multiplies a given number by two. Do not worry if you do not understand the code perfectly as we will explain CoffeeScript grammar in more detail later in the chapter:

```
double = (x) -> x * 2
```

Below, you can find the compiled version in JavaScript code. As you can see, some words such as `function` or `return` and some curly brackets and semicolons have been added. Those are reserved words by programming languages such as JavaScript. They are used in the syntax of the language, and cannot be used as a name of variables or functions.

```
double = function(x) {
    return x * 2;
};
```

That sounds good, but then, do I need to perform an additional step to compile my code? Well, that is one of the best things about Framer Studio. This process will be transparent for you; you will be programming in CoffeeScript, and the result of your code will be shown without any action on your part.

Let's start coding with CoffeeScript

Although this is not a programming book, we will take a quick tour of some basic CoffeeScript syntax principles; however, you will need some programming knowledge to follow this chapter. If you have never programmed, it is recommended to complete the content of this chapter with a programming tutorial in CoffeeScript.

With the prototypes included in this book, you will be able to start using this prototyping solution and see whether it will be useful for your projects and workflow. You can expand your knowledge with the official documentation where all this content can be found in much greater detail, at `http://coffeescript.org/`.

Variables and operators

Some of the most basic elements of a programming language are variables and operators. **Variables** are storage locations where you keep information that you will use at some later point. For example, you can create a variable to track the number of notifications the user has in your prototype; that variable will determine how the notification badge is presented, and it will allow you to change its value according to the logic of your prototype.

It is important to give variables a clear name, normally using camelCase, for example, `numberOfNotifications`, or using underscore, for example, `number_of_notifications` notations since spaces are not allowed when naming the variables.

Operators allow you to perform arithmetic and logical operations using values and variables as input. You will be using those to define the logic of your prototype. The result of each operation can be also part of another operation, or can be stored in a variable.

Let's look at some simple examples. Let's say we have a variable called `players` where we will store the number `4`. In CoffeeScript, this will look like this:

```
players = 4
```

As you can see, we use the = symbol to assign a value to `players`. Now, imagine that we have a second variable called `tshirts`, where we will store the value `4` multiplied by `2`. This will look as follows:

```
tshirts = 4 * 2
```

However, we can also use the value stored in `players` to calculate the value of `tshirts`, leaving the code like this:

```
players = 4
tshirts = 4 * players
```

For the calculation, we have used an `*` to perform a multiplication. This asterisk is an operator and in CoffeeScript, we have many operators that we can use in our programs.

In CoffeeScript we can find arithmetic operators to do operations with values and variables. The most basic are +, -, *, / and they allow us to sume, substract, multiplicate and divide. You can also use `%`, ++, `--` to return the module of a division or to increase or decrease a value by one by typing less code.

There are also logical and comparison operators and they give us great potential for more advanced calculations. You can use == and `!`= to evaluate if two values are equal or different. Also you can use >, >=, > and <= to evaluate if a value is lower or higher than other. Conditions can be concatenated applying logical operators like `&&` and `||`.

Let's look at an example using these logical operators. Imagine that we want to store the value `TRUE` if `windowHeight` is less than `contentHeight`, two variables where we have stored some size values of our prototype. We can store the result of this conditional expression in `needsScroll` and use this variable to add the scrolling functionality to our prototype later. In CoffeeScript, it will look like this:

```
needsScroll = windowHeight < contentHeight
```

As you can see, the variables and the operators give us great potential since they allow us to calculate values, store them, and use them in other processes. For example, we can store the height of an element in a variable and calculate the position of a second element from the first position. Let's look at an example:

```
aux = square.height
square2.x = aux + 100
```

Well, let's pause for a moment; in the preceding example, we added the `height` value of the `square` element, and we accessed it using a dot notation. In Framer Studio, these are known as **properties** and **objects**; `height` would be a property of the `square` object. We will use objects to create our layers and animations in our prototypes, and they will have many properties whose values we can get and modify, but we will cover this later.

Types

The variables you define in your prototype will be able to contain different kinds of information. In CoffeeScript, we find different types of data with which we can work. These are common to many programming languages. In this chapter, we will also need to talk about numbers, strings, booleans, arrays, and objects:

- **Numbers** capture numerical values, such as 2, 100, and -250.
- **Strings** define textual information, and they are expressed in quotation marks, such as "welcome to your app".
- **Booleans** are logical binary values; they will take the value of TRUE or FALSE. They are useful for describing logic conditions to guide decisions in the behavior of your prototype.
- **Arrays** are collections of values, such as [3,5,2,9] or ["London", "Paris", and "Milan"].

- **Objects** represent more complex structured information. They have properties of any data type and set of functions describing their associated functionality that we will call methods. Elements such as the layers of your prototype will be represented by objects where you can access properties, such as their height, and methods, such as one to center the layer in the screen. We will cover the functions later.

Functions

A **function** is a set of instructions that perform a given action. They describe functionalities such as performing calculations, manipulating objects, using other functions, and more. Parameters can be used to make functions reusable. For example, a function to move objects can take the destination coordinates as parameters. When we call a function we will pass arguments for these parameters, and the function will perform its routine, being able to make use of these values. The syntax of a function in CoffeeScript is formed by a word, an equal symbol, a list of parameters between parentheses, a hyphen and a symbol of 'greater than' forming an arrow, and the body of the function.

Here's an example of CoffeeScript code. If you come from JavaScript, you might find it strange to not come across any curly brackets to enclose the body of the function. In CoffeeScript, multiline blocks of instructions can be delimited by indentation:

```
doubleIfOdd = (x) ->
    if x % 2 == 0
        x * 2
    else
        x
print doubleIfOdd 4
```

Download prototype from `Asset_A6462_A08_A01_Example_DoubleIfOdd.framer.zip`.

You can also call the function without parentheses when the function has parameters. In the following code, you will see the result provided by a `doubleIfOdd` function in the Framer Studio print console (you can instead use `console.log` in order to see the output by the browser console).

```
» 8
```

A function without parameters will be executed using parentheses, as you can see in the given example:

```
helloWorld = ->
    "Hello world"
print helloWorld()
```

Download prototype from `Asset_A6462_A08_A02_Example_HelloWorld.framer.zip.`

As you can see, the `helloWorld` function returns a `"Hello world"` string that we will print using the print console.

Loops and conditional structures

Conditional structures and loops will allow you to add advanced logic to your code. A conditional structure delimits a block of code that is executed only if a condition is met. Its syntax includes the reserved word `if`, and may include an alternative code block, for which we will use the reserved word `else`; that will be executed when the main condition is not met.:

```
x = 4
if x>2
    print "x value is bigger than two"
else
    print "x value is not bigger than two"
```

Download prototype from `Asset_A6462_A08_A03_Example_Conditional.framer.zip.`

As a result of the preceding code, you will see the string of the first print instruction by the print console as the value of `"x is bigger than two"`.

Loops help us write blocks of code that run repeatedly for a certain number of times or until a condition is no longer met. For example, they can be helpful for going over an array of elements. To create a *for loop,* we will use some reserved words; for example, a for loop can be created using `for` and `in`. To go over the elements of a contacts array, we can use `for name in contacts`, where name will be taking the value of the elements of the array:

```
contacts = [
    "John Walker"
    "Mark Roberts"
    "Jessica Plankton"
]

for name in contacts
    print name
```

The preceding code will show all the data elements contained in the array contacts via the print console, but we can add a condition in the loop and use the value of the array index.

```
for name, i in contacts when name isnt "Mark Roberts"
    print name + ' is in the position ' + i
```

Download prototype from `Asset_A6462_A08_A04_Example_For_Loops.framer.zip`.

This code will show all the data elements contained in the array of contacts except the element that is equal to `Mark Roberts`, adding the `is in the position` string and the index of the array. Take a look the following result:

```
» "John Walker is in the position 0"
» "Jessica Plankton is in the position 2"
```

We can also create *while loops* with the reserved word *while*. Here's an example of code where we will print the value of aux and decrease the number of aux until the condition returns false, that is, when aux is lower than 0:

```
aux = 4
printAndSubtract = ->
    print aux
    aux--
printAndSubtract() while aux > 0
```

Download prototype from
`Asset_A6462_A08_A05_Example_While_Loops.framer.zip`.

The result in the print console will be the numbers from 4 to 1:

```
» 4
» 3
» 2
» 1
```

Objects and methods

An **object** is a flexible type of data in which we can store a collection of properties consisting of pairs of keys and values, and **methods** are functions stored in the object. We can access the value of a property by calling the object and referencing its key. Here's an example of an object, created using the object literal definition, and how we access the `cardHeight` property using dot notation:

```
card =
    cardHeight: 10
    cardWidth: 10
    cardColor: 222222
print card.cardHeight
```

Download prototype from
`Asset_A6462_A08_A06_Example_Card_Object.framer.zip`.

With the print function, we get the value of the `cardHeight` property by the print console.

```
» 10
```

Functions stored in objects are called **methods**, and they can get parameters when called.

For example, we can create a function inside the `card` object that prints its properties values, and call it as we need it:

```
card =
    cardHeight: 10
    cardWidth: 10
    cardColor: 222222
    printCardDetails: (x) ->
            i = 0
            while i < x
                print "Height:  " + this.cardHeight + ", Width: " +
this.cardWidth + ", Color: " + this.cardColor
                i++

card.printCardDetails 3
```

Download prototype from `Asset_A6462_A08_A07_Example_Card_Object_PrintCardDetails.framer.zip`.

As a result, we will see the string generated by the `printCardDetails` method in the print console as many times as we define it with the `x` parameter, thrice in this case. As you can see, we have used the word `this` to access the values stored in the object where the method is executed.

```
» "Height: 10, Width: 10, Color: 222222"
» "Height: 10, Width: 10, Color: 222222"
» "Height: 10, Width: 10, Color: 222222"
```

Understanding the concept of properties and methods will help you understand how Framer has been built. In Framer, you will use objects to build your prototypes, so keep this concept in mind when reading the following pages of the chapter. You can find further information in the CoffeeScript documentation.

Understanding Framer.js

We are going to explain the main elements and concepts that you will need to start prototyping with Framer.

For further information, or as a reference guide, we recommend you to read the documentation offered by Framer Studio at `https://framer.com/docs/`.

Framer comes with a set of predefined elements that will help you create your prototypes. Framer.js provides several basic building blocks to build the structure of your prototype and help you control the events and actions you need to describe its behavior. Following the order of the official documentation those elements are the **Layers** that will be the base of our prototype, the **Animations** that allow us to move and change properties of our layers, the **Events** that will help us to make our prototype interactive, and the **States** that help us to create different states of our layers and change among them. We will also basically explain how to use some of the components that come with Framer.js which let us reduce steps to create some common design patterns.

Layers

Layers are the most basic elements you will use in your prototypes. They will contain your images, texts, and videos. They come with a set of properties you can modify according to your needs.

To create our first layer, we will use the word `new` and the name of the class, `Layer` in this case. This will create a new instance of the `Layer` class--by calling what is known as the constructor function of the class--and will assign it to the `myFirstLayer` variable. In the future, you can manipulate the `Layer` using the `myFirstLayer` variable:

```
myFirstLayer = new Layer
```

We can change its position by giving values to the `x` and `y` properties. Those values will be provided in pixels. As we will use an Android device for our prototype with a resolution of xxhdpi (@3x), our screen will be 1080x1920px, which is 360x640 at 3x resolution. To do this, you will need to select the **Google Nexus 5X** smartphone from the **Devices** menu. We can place the layer in the middle of the screen by changing the values of the `x` and `y` properties:

```
myFirstLayer.x = 1080/2
myFirstLayer.y = 1920/2
```

Download prototype from `Asset_A6462_A08_A08_Example_Prototype_Layer_v1.framer.zip`.

As you can see in the preview area, the layer has been placed in the middle of the screen, but with the top-left corner as the reference point to calculate the position. The code has been added in the code editor of the Framer Studio desktop interface:

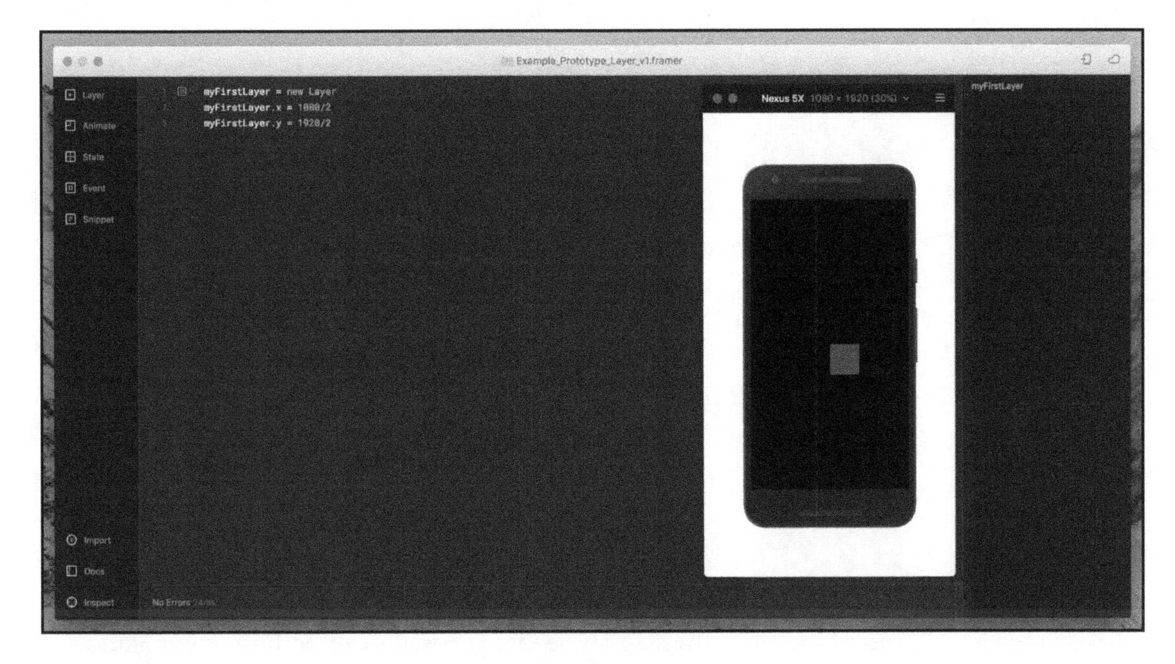

Framer Studio desktop user interface

To center the object from the center of the layer, we can use different options. For example, we can change its `midX` and `midY` properties to position the layer taking the center of the element as a reference:

```
myFirstLayer = new Layer
myFirstLayer.midX = 1080/2
myFirstLayer.midY = 1920/2
print myFirstLayer.x
print myFirstLayer.y
```

Download prototype from `Asset_A6462_A08_A09_Example_Prototype_Layer_v2.framer.zip`.

As a result of the preceding code, you will see the layer centered on the screen, and by the print console, the new position of the layer in the `x` and `y` properties.

```
» 440
» 860
```

We would obtain the same result using the `center()` method that comes with layers in Framer:

```
myFirstLayer.center()
```

We can also set other properties for our layers. For example, the size will be determined by the `width` and `height` properties, and should also be defined in pixels. We can create our layer with a size of 500x500 px:

```
myFirstLayer.width = 500
myFirstLayer.height = 500
print myFirstLayer.size
```

Download prototype from
`Asset_A6462_A08_A10_Example_Prototype_Layer_v3.framer.zip`.

We used the `size` property to print the size of the layer. It will print both the `width` and `height` values, as follows:

```
» {width:500, height:500}
```

Another useful example is the parent definition. We can nest layers, giving our project a structure. The layer behavior will be affected by their relation with other layers. For example, the `center()` method used before will center the layer in their parent layer, not on the screen:

```
mySecondLayer = new Layer
    parent: myFirstLayer
    x: 30
    y: 30
```

Download prototype from
`Asset_A6462_A08_A11_Example_Prototype_Layer_v4.framer.zip`.

In the preceding example, the definition of `mySecondLayer` makes it a child of `myFirstLayer`, and its position defined as `x: 30` and `y: 30` will bring the layer 30 px down and right from the top-left corner of its parent. Defining a hierarchy of layers allows you to create elements in groups where they are manipulated together.

Animations

You can create a new animation object to change the properties of a layer, such as the position or the color. The final state of the layer can be defined by setting the properties, or creating states for that layer, which will be another way of defining the value of the properties that will change their values during the animation. Additionally, we can define the time it will take to perform the animation and curve that will be applied to calculate the evolution of the values that change during the animation. In the next example, we will create an animation using the `animate` function to move our layer from its position to a new position, applying a *Bezier easeOut curve*:

```
myFirstLayer.animate
    x: 200
    options:
        curve: Bezier.easeOut
        time: 1
```

The same example can be carried out creating an animation object and calling the `start()` method:

```
animationGoTo200 = new Animation myFirstLayer,
    x: 200
    options:
        curve: Bezier.easeOut
        time: 1
animationGoTo200.start()
```

Download prototype from `Asset_A6462_A08_A12_Example_Prototype_Layer_v5.framer.zip`.

Events

Events allow us to give interactivity to our prototypes. You can associate functionality as a reaction to a given event. There are many kinds of events; for example, when the user interacts with an interface element or when an animation starts or ends.

In the following example, we will print the tap count number each time the user taps on it:

```
numberOfTaps = 0
numberOfTapsLayer = new Layer
    backgroundColor: "#123123"
numberOfTapsLayer.center()
numberOfTapsLayer.on Events.Tap, ->
    numberOfTaps++
    print numberOfTaps
```

Download prototype from
`Asset_A6462_A08_A13_Example_NumberOfTapsLayer.framer.zip`.

As you can see, we used the `Events.Tap` event, but we can listen to other events as `Swipe`, `LongPress`, `Pinch` or the `ForceTap`. You can also use some event shortcuts; for example, you can write `numberOfTapsLayer.onTap ->` instead of `numberOfTapsLayer.on Events.Tap, ->`.

Some gestures have more specific versions, such as "SwipeUp", where the event listener will react only when the swipe goes in the desired direction, up direction in this case. With this set of gestures provided by Framer Studio, we will be able to create a high-fidelity experience in our prototype, getting a very realistic response from the user.

States

A **state** is a set of values for some of the properties of a layer. We can use states, for example, to define the different positions an element can take, and use these states when the user makes an action on our user interface, to make the element visible on the screen area. In the next example, the `movingLayer` layer has two states--`up` and `down`--and changes from one to the other when the user taps on the layer:

```
movingLayer = new Layer
movingLayer.centerX()
movingLayer.states =
    up:
        y: 400
    down:
        y: 1200
movingLayer.stateSwitch("up")
movingLayer.onTap ->
    movingLayer.stateCycle("up", "down")
```

Download prototype from
`Asset_A6462_A08_A14_Example_MovingLayer.framer.zip`.

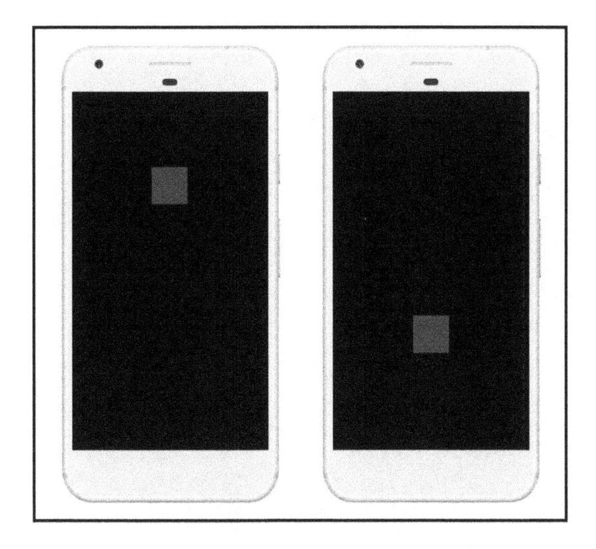

Our layer will have two states: 'up' and 'down'

Each time we call `stateCycle`, the layer will go through all the states one by one when the user taps on it, starting again when all the states have been visited. In this case, the layer will go up and down as we only have two states in this example.

Components

In Framer Studio, you will find some components to help you code your prototypes. They will save your time when creating common interaction design patterns.

When you create an instance of a component, it will come with preestablished interactions and behaviors. Let's talk about some of the components included in Framer Studio:

- **TextLayer:** This creates a layer with text on it. You can add the text using a string and define the text properties as you would do with CSS.

Here, we have a simple example of two text layers with different values for their properties:

```
myBackgroundLayer = new BackgroundLayer
    backgroundColor: "white"
myTextLayer1 = new TextLayer
    text: "Text Layer"
    color: "#333333"
    fontSize: 80
    x: 32
    y: 340
myTextLayer2 = new TextLayer
    text: "Lorem ipsum dolor sit amet, consectetur adipiscing elit. Etiam
quis vestibulum nisi, vitae imperdiet diam. In placerat felis erat, non
condimentum erat laoreet ultrices."
    color: "#888888"
    fontSize: 50
    x: 32
    y: 480
    width: 686
```

Download prototype from `Asset_A6462_A08_A15_Example_TextLayer.framer.zip`.

Example of a prototype using the TextLayer component

- **ScrollComponent:** This component allows you to create scrollable content in an area of your screen. You only have to encapsulate the content in a scroll component, and you will be able to define parameters, such as the direction in which it can be scrolled or the speed of scrolling when dragged.

In the next example, we will create a scrollable layer with a `TextLayer` inside it. Our scrollable layer will only allow horizontal scrolling:

```
myBackgroundLayer = new BackgroundLayer
    backgroundColor: "white"

myScroll = new ScrollComponent
    width: 750
    height: 1334
myScroll.scrollVertical = false
myTextLayer = new TextLayer
    text: "This layer is scrollable"
    color: "#333333"
    fontSize: 120
myLayer = new Layer
    width: 1500
    height: 1334
    backgroundColor: "#ffffff"
    parent: myScroll.content
myTextLayer.parent = myLayer
myTextLayer.center()
```

Download prototype from `Asset_A6462_A08_A16_Example_ScrollComponent.framer.zip.`

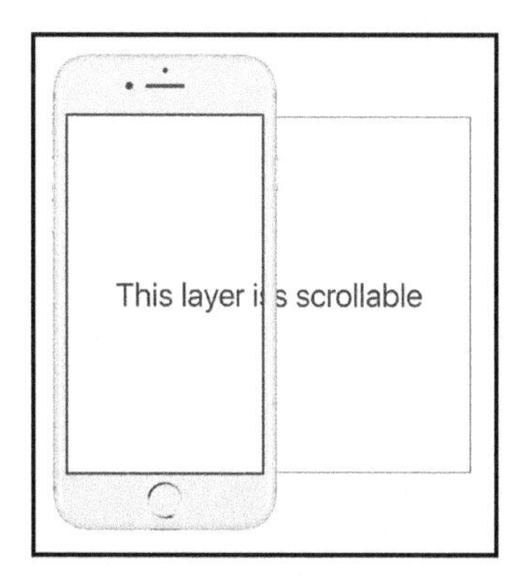

Example of a prototype using the scroll component

- **PageComponent:** This creates a navigation structure with paginated content. The user will be able to change the page by swiping the screen. You can add pages to access horizontally or vertically, which allows you to create a complex structure in a simple and functional way.

In the following example, we will create a `PageComponent` with three pages, each of them with a number to easily identify them. The user will be able to change the viewed page by doing a swipe gesture:

```
myLayer1 = new TextLayer
    text: "1"
    color: "#333333"
    fontSize: 200
    padding:
        top: 64
        left: 64
    width: 750
    height: 1334
    backgroundColor: "#ffffff"
myLayer2 = new TextLayer
    text: "2"
    color: "#333333"
    fontSize: 200
    padding:
        top: 64
        left: 64
    width: 750
    height: 1334
    backgroundColor: "#ffffff"
myLayer3 = new TextLayer
    text: "3"
    color: "#333333"
    fontSize: 200
    padding:
        top: 64
        left: 64
    width: 750
    height: 1334
    backgroundColor: "#ffffff"
myPage = new PageComponent
    width: 750
    height: 1334
myPage.addPage(myLayer1, "right")
myPage.addPage(myLayer2, "right")
myPage.addPage(myLayer3, "right")
```

Download prototype from
`Asset_A6462_A08_A17_Example_PageComponent.framer.zip`.

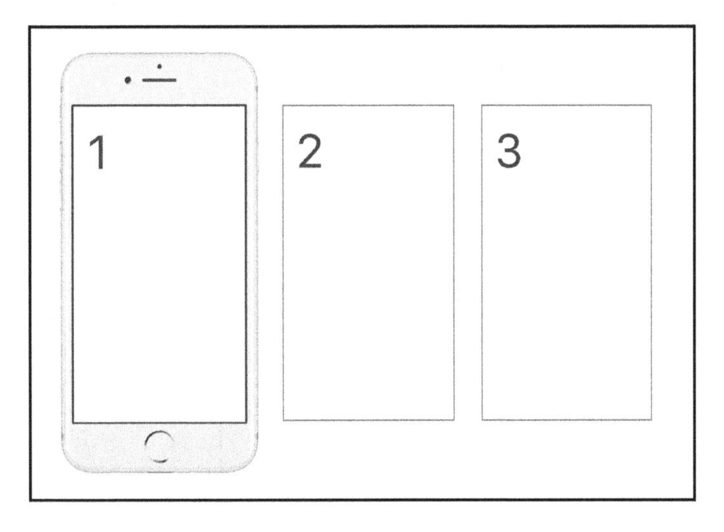

Example of a prototype using the page component

- **SliderComponent:** This will allow you to add a slider to our project. With a few lines of code, you can add a slider control that allows you to adjust a value according to the position of a knob in a line. The knob can be dragged, and the value will be adjusted according to its position.

This is an example of a slider centered on the screen:

```
myBackgroundLayer = new BackgroundLayer
      backgroundColor: "#dddddd"
mySlider = new SliderComponent
mySlider.backgroundColor = "#333333"
mySlider.knobSize = 80
mySlider.center()
```

Download prototype from
`Asset_A6462_A08_A18_Example_SliderComponent.framer.zip`.

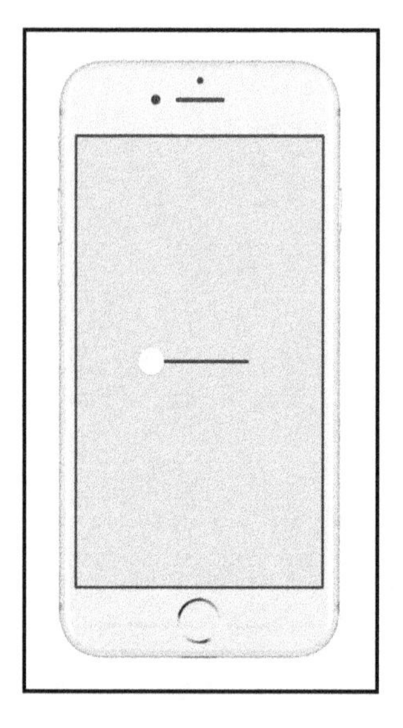

Example of a prototype using the slider component

- **RangeSliderComponent:** We will insert a range slider control in our prototype. Its behavior is similar to the slider component, but with two knobs. This controller will allow the user to choose a range within limits. The first of the knobs will indicate the lowest value of the selected range, and the second knob will indicate the highest value.

In this example, we will create a range slider centered on the screen:

```
myBackgroundLayer = new BackgroundLayer
    backgroundColor: "#dddddd"
myRange = new RangeSliderComponent
    min: 1
    max: 10
    minValue: 3
    maxValue: 8
myRange.knobSize = 50
myRange.fill.backgroundColor = "#333333"
myRange.backgroundColor = "#ffffff"
myRange.center()
```

Download prototype from
`Asset_A6462_A08_A19_Example_RangeSliderComponent.framer.zip`.

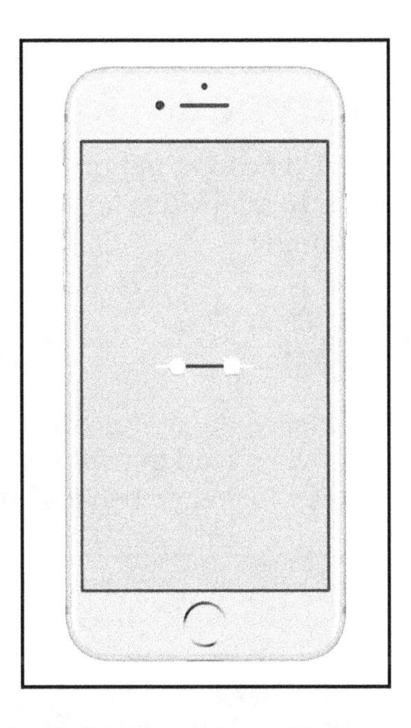

Example of a prototype using the range slider component

You can find further information about these components and others with use examples in the official Framer Studio documentation.

Creating prototypes with Sketch and Framer Studio

In this section, we will show some examples using designs created with Sketch and import them with Framer Studio. Although we can create the layers of our prototypes in code, using design software such as *Photoshop* or Sketch makes the process much more fluid. You can import the result in Framer as layers that we will use to create the prototype by adding interactivity to them.

In this section, we will include several prototypes and, although each one of them will be independent of the others, it is advisable to read them in the order presented, since some basic concepts will be explained in the first prototype in which they appear, and they will be treated with less detail in the subsequent prototypes.

Welcome Tour Prototype

In this prototype, we will create a welcome tour, importing designs made with Sketch. So, the first thing you need to do in order to follow this tutorial is to download the Sketch file that will be used in the prototype from the `Asset_A6462_A08_A20_Welcome_Tour_Prototype_Designs.zip` code bundle. You can also download this tutorial in Framer from the `Asset_A6462_A08_A21_Welcome_Tour_Prototype.framer.zip` code bundle.

As you can see in the following screenshot, the design consists of four screens that we have designed in four different artboards. When working with Sketch, remember to use easily recognizable names, since you will refer to them when you are codifying your prototype:

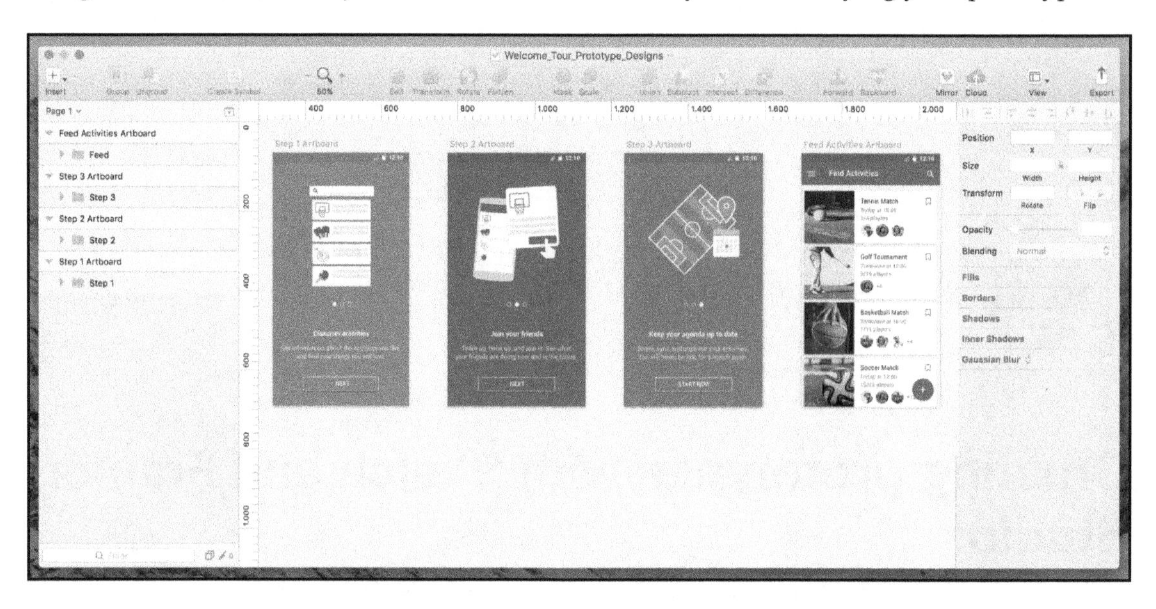

Welcome Tour prototype Sketch designs

Once you have the `Welcome_Tour_Prototype_Designs.sketch` file open in Sketch, you must import it into Framer. To do so, you will find the option to **Import** in the **Framer Studio** toolbar. When you click on **Import**, a dialog will appear where you can select the Sketch file that we previously had open in Sketch, select the option to import at **@3x**, and then click on **Import**. Remember that our Sketch file will only be available in Framer if we have it open in Sketch. The artboards will now measure 1080x1920 px in Framer, as we have chosen the **@3x** option, a size that corresponds to three times the size they were designed in Sketch, which was 360x640 px:

Import from Sketch at @3x

The following lines of code will appear in your project:

```
# Import file "Welcome_Tour_Prototype_Designs" (sizes and positions are
scaled 1:3)
sketch = Framer.Importer.load("imported/Welcome_Tour_Prototype_Designs@3x")
```

Framer will import your groups of layers from Sketch and will create a layer for each of them in Framer. Framer will ignore ungrouped layers in Sketch and will use the positions defined in Sketch to define the values of the *x* and *y* properties of the new layers.

Framer also allows you to ignore a *Sketch* group using the `-` symbol at the end of the group name, and you can also flatten a group by adding `*` to the group name; this group will be imported as a single layer without children.

Now that we have imported our design assets with which we will work, we have to adjust the preview so that it does not look oversized. For this, we will select a device in which to preview our prototype as we build it. The different devices that Framer offers us to preview our project can be found in the **Devices** menu:

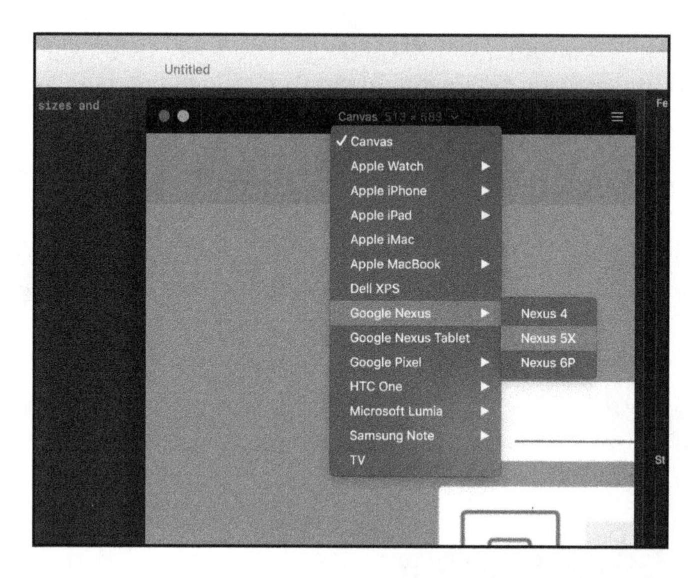

Select Google Nexus 5X device

For this tutorial, we will preview our prototype on a mobile device, so open the phone **Google Nexus 5X** in the selection menu. To see the prototype presented with a skin of the mobile, you may need to activate it with the **Toggle Device** option:

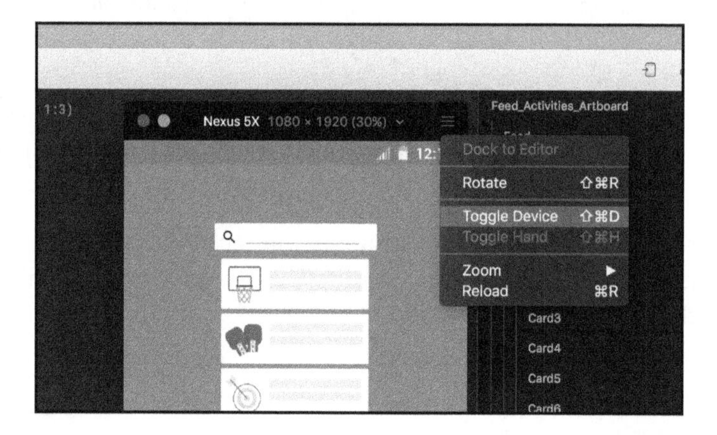

Toggle Device option

As a result, you should see the first artboard of the Sketch file, called **Step 1 Artboard**, presented in the selected mobile in the preview area of Framer Studio, the code to import it in the code editor, and the layer inspector with the groups of the Sketch file that will be our layers in Framer:

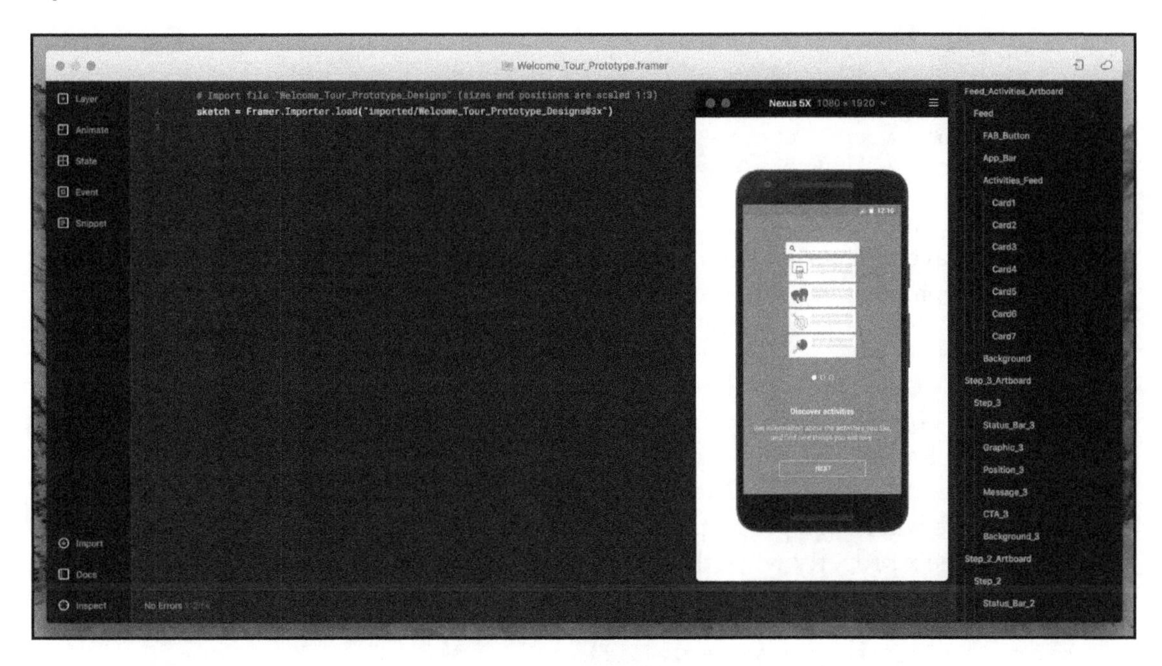

Framer Studio with Welcome_Tour_Prototype_Designs.sketch designs imported

Artboards states

The next thing we will do is to position the artboards that are not visible in the current view. These are the **Step 2 Artboard**, the **Step 3 Artboard**, and the **Feed Activities Artboard**. To do this, we will create two states for each of the artboards: one for when the artboard is off the screen, and another for when the artboard is located inside the screen and is visible to the user. We'll name these states `out` and `in` for the example, but different names can be used. We will also define the initial state of each artboard and the way it changes from one state to the other. For this purpose, we use the following code. Note that the lines that start with the # symbol are comments, and they will only serve to order and explain our code:

```
# STEP 2
# Step 2 states
sketch.Step_2_Artboard.states.out =
```

```
        x: 1080
        animationOptions:
            time: 0.3
            curve: Bezier.ease
sketch.Step_2_Artboard.states.in =
        x: 0
        animationOptions:
            time: 0.3
            curve: Bezier.ease
# Set default Step 2 state
sketch.Step_2_Artboard.stateSwitch("out")
```

In the preceding code, we refer to `Step 2 Artboard` with `sketch.Step_2_Artboard`. In Framer, all the layers imported from Sketch can be referenced with the word `sketch`, followed by the name of the artboard or the name of the group they have in the Sketch file. Note that spaces will be replaced by *underscores* during the import process.

To create the `out` state that we will use to move the artboard out of the screen view, we have used the `sketch.Step_2_Artboard.states.out =` instruction, where the reference of the layer is followed by `states.` and the name of the state that we want to create. In this case, we will have the `out` and `in` states, and so, we have two different declarations. With the `=` symbol, we will assign properties to each state. In our example, we have assigned the value `1080` to the `x` property when the `out` state is active, and `0` when the state of the layer is `in`:

```
sketch.Step_2_Artboard.states.out =
        x: 1080
sketch.Step_2_Artboard.states.in =
        x: 0
```

We can change the state of an artboard using an animation. The animation will change the layer properties from the current values to those of the new state gradually over time. In order to do so, you can just call `animate` with the name of the desired state:

```
sketch.Step_2_Artboard.animate("in")
```

You can also switch directly to a state without any animation, with `stateSwitch`:

```
sketch.Step_2_Artboard.stateSwitch("out")
```

Although we can use the default animation to change from one state to the other, we can also define our own animation. For this purpose, we will add indications in the state declaration by means of `animationOptions:`. In this case, we have defined the time of the animation in `0.3` seconds with the `time: 0.3`, time option, and we have indicated that the curve that will be used to change from the initial value to the end value will follow a `Bezier.ease` curve. Other animation curves, such as *Bezier.linear*, *Bezier.easeIn*, or *Spring* are possible:

```
sketch.Step_2_Artboard.states.out =
    x: 1080
    animationOptions:
        time: 0.3
        curve: Bezier.ease
```

The last line of code--`sketch.Step_2_Artboard.stateSwitch ("out")`--defines the state, from the two defined states, in which our artboard will start when running the prototype. In this case, this instruction will move the `Step 2 Artboard` artboard to the `out` state so that its initial position will have `x` equal to `1080`, as shown in the following image represented with a rectangle on the right side, and therefore it will be out of the screen:

Step_2_Artboard position

When using `stateSwitch`, the change is done automatically without following the options defined in the `animationOptions` block. As we are initializing the prototype, we don't need animations since we are only defining the initial positions of our layers. The options defined in the `animationOptions` block will serve to smooth the transitions later as the user advances through the welcome tour.

Now, we will do the same with `Step 3 Artboard`. As both the views will come from the right-hand side of the screen, their values and the code we will use will be very similar. Note that in the following block of code, only the name of the layer has been changed, in this case, `sketch.Step_3_Artboard`:

```
# STEP 3
# Step 3 states
sketch.Step_3_Artboard.states.out =
    x: 1080
    animationOptions:
        time: 0.3
        curve: Bezier.ease
sketch.Step_3_Artboard.states.in =
    x: 0
    animationOptions:
        time: 0.3
        curve: Bezier.ease
# Set default Step 3 state
sketch.Step_3_Artboard.stateSwitch("out")
```

To finish the states' declaration, we have to position the fourth artboard called `Feed Activities Artboard` in Sketch, and in Framer, converted to a layer called `sketch.Feed_Activities_Artboard`. This layer will appear from the bottom of the screen, so the `out` and `in` states for this layer will change the `y` property, and the layer will move vertically. This is the code we will use for this purpose:

```
# ACTIVITIES FEED
# Activities Feed states
sketch.Feed_Activities_Artboard.states.out =
    y: 1920
    animationOptions:
        time: 0.3
        curve: Spring(damping: 0.5)
sketch.Feed_Activities_Artboard.states.in =
    y: 0
    animationOptions:
        time: 0.3
        curve: Spring(damping: 0.7)
# Set default Activities Feed state
sketch.Feed_Activities_Artboard.stateSwitch("out")
```

```
# Set default x Activities Feed position
sketch.Feed_Activities_Artboard.x = 0
```

You will notice some differences from the earlier blocks of code where we defined the states for the other screens. There is a new line of code to define the position on the horizontal axis of the artboard. Since the change of state will only define a new value for the `y` property, we have added a new assignment to define the initial position of the artboard in the horizontal axis, assigning the value `0` to the `x` property. The `Sketch.Feed_Activities_Artboard.x = 0` instruction, along with the `sketch.Feed_Activities_Artboard.stateSwitch("out")` instruction, will bring the artboard right below the screen. This will be the position from which we will make the artboard appear onto the screen at the end of the welcome tour:

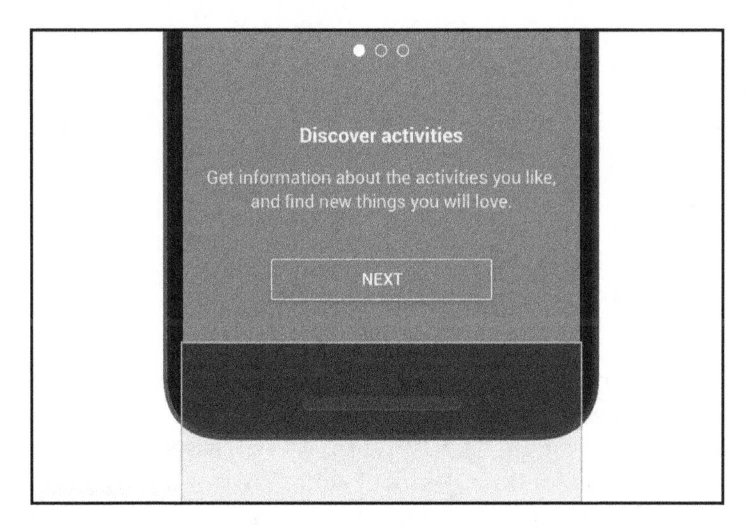

Feed_Activities_Artboard position

Also, we are using a different curve for the animation, `curve: Spring(damping: 0.7)` in this case. With this kind of curve, the transition of the `sketch.Feed_Activities_Artboard` layer will simulate the behavior of a spring.

Prototype behavior

Now, it's time to define the functionality of our prototype. Adding interactivity to the different elements of our design will allow the user to interact with it as if it were a real application. Let's go screen by screen, defining the different actionable elements and how our prototype reacts when the user interacts with them through a gesture:

```
# WELCOME BEHAVIOUR
# Step 1 Functionality
sketch.CTA_1.on Events.Tap, ->
    sketch.Step_2_Artboard.animate("in")
sketch.Step_1_Artboard.on Events.SwipeLeft, (event) ->
    sketch.Step_2_Artboard.animate("in")
# Step 2 Functionality
sketch.CTA_2.on Events.Tap, ->
    sketch.Step_3_Artboard.animate("in")
sketch.Step_2_Artboard.on Events.SwipeLeft, (event) ->
    sketch.Step_3_Artboard.animate("in")
sketch.Step_2_Artboard.on Events.SwipeRight, (event) ->
    sketch.Step_2_Artboard.animate("out")
# Step 3 Functionality
sketch.Step_3_Artboard.on Events.SwipeRight, (event) ->
    sketch.Step_3_Artboard.animate("out")
sketch.CTA_3.on Events.Tap, ->
    sketch.Feed_Activities_Artboard.animate("in")
```

In the first screen of our prototype, we will take two gestures into account. We will go to the **Step 2 Artboard** screen when the user taps on the **NEXT** button and when the user swipes left. To control the **Tap** event on the **NEXT** button, we will associate the action with the **sketch.CTA_1** layer using the following lines of code. We can reference each of the three buttons of our screens, the two **NEXT** buttons that appear in the first and the second screens, and the **START NOW** button of the third screen by accessing **sketch.CTA_1**, **sketch.CTA_2**, and **sketch.CTA_3**, according to the names we gave to their layer groups in Sketch:

```
sketch.CTA_1.on Events.Tap, ->
    sketch.Step_2_Artboard.animate ("in")
```

The `SwipeLeft` event will be associated with the `sketch.Step_1_Artboard` layer since we want the whole screen to react to the swipe gesture of our user:

```
sketch.Step_1_Artboard.on Events.SwipeLeft, (event) ->
    sketch.Step_2_Artboard.animate ("in")
```

We will do the same for the second screen, but we will add a behavior associated with the event when the user swipes right, since we want to allow the user to navigate back to our welcome tour. We will add a `sketch.Step_2_Artboard.on Events.SwipeRight, (event) ->` listener to our prototype and the `sketch.Step_2_Artboard.animate("out")` associated action that will take the `sketch.Step_2_Artboard` layer to its `out` state. This will position the artboard outside the screen and make the `sketch.Step_1_Artboard` visible again:

```
# Step 2 Functionality
sketch.CTA_2.on Events.Tap, ->
    sketch.Step_3_Artboard.animate("in")
sketch.Step_2_Artboard.on Events.SwipeLeft, (event) ->
    sketch.Step_3_Artboard.animate("in")
sketch.Step_2_Artboard.on Events.SwipeRight, (event) ->
    sketch.Step_2_Artboard.animate("out")
```

In the `sketch.Step_3_Artboard` screen, we will add only two listeners: one for when the user swipes right, to go back, and another for when the user taps the **START NOW** button, because we will make the **Feed Activities Artboard** screen appear from below the screen at this moment, simply changing the status of this new layer to `in`:

```
# Step 3 Functionality
sketch.Step_3_Artboard.on Events.SwipeRight, (event) ->
    sketch.Step_3_Artboard.animate("out")
sketch.CTA_3.on Events.Tap, ->
    sketch.Feed_Activities_Artboard.animate("in")
```

As you can see, adding functionality to your prototype is very simple. With the code added up until now, your welcome tour should be working. The user is able to move through the screens of the welcome tour. At the end of the tour, the user will be able to access the feed of your application.

Coordinating animations

Now, let's add a little more detail to the artboard entry transition **Feed Activities Artboard**. To do this, we will move each of the cards that make up the contents of this view independently.

Our transition will consist of moving each card 0.2 seconds after its predecessor. In this way, cards will appear in the list in a more organic way than if they were moving together as a single block. For this, we will define two states: the *start* state, which will position each of the cards at 200 pixels below their initial position on the design, and the *end* state, where we will define their final position as the position in which they appear in the design. In the *start* state, we will also change the `opacity` of the card to 0, and we will set it to 1 in the final state to create a fade-in effect while the card is moving:

```
# ACTIVITIES FEED
# Array of the cards
cardsInFeed = [sketch.Card1, sketch.Card2, sketch.Card3, sketch.Card4,
sketch.Card5, sketch.Card6];
# Loop to create card states
for card,i in cardsInFeed
    card.states.end =
        y: card.y
        opacity: 1
        animationOptions:
            time: 0.3
            curve: "ease-out"
            delay: i*0.2
    card.states.start =
        opacity: 0
        y: card.y+200
    card.states.switchInstant "start"
```

As you can see, instead of going through the cards one by one, we have created a card array that contains a reference to each of the cards of our prototype:

```
cardsInFeed = [sketch.Card1, sketch.Card2, sketch.Card3, sketch.Card4,
sketch.Card5, sketch.Card6];
```

Then, we will loop through the array and assign the `start` and `end` states to each of the elements of the array, in this case, our cards:

```
for card,i in cardsInFeed
```

To make each card appear 0.2 seconds after the previous one, we have added an index to our loop. We will use its value to increase the value of the delay for each card. The index grows in each iteration, and we will use its value, multiplied by 0.2, to define the delay for each card from the start of the transition, and that will be the number of seconds each card will be stopped before changing its state:

```
delay: i*0.2
```

The delay value will be 0 for the first card, and it will be increased 0.2 seconds for each new card.

With the states defined, we just need to add a tap event listener in the **sketch.CTA_3** layer, and start the transition of the screen and the cards. We will add a few more lines to add a loop that will `animate` each of the cards to the `end` state. We will add the *for loop* right after the preceding code, leaving it as follows:

```
sketch.CTA_3.on Events.Tap, ->
    sketch.Feed_Activities_Artboard.animate("in")
    for card in cardsInFeed
        card.animate("end")
```

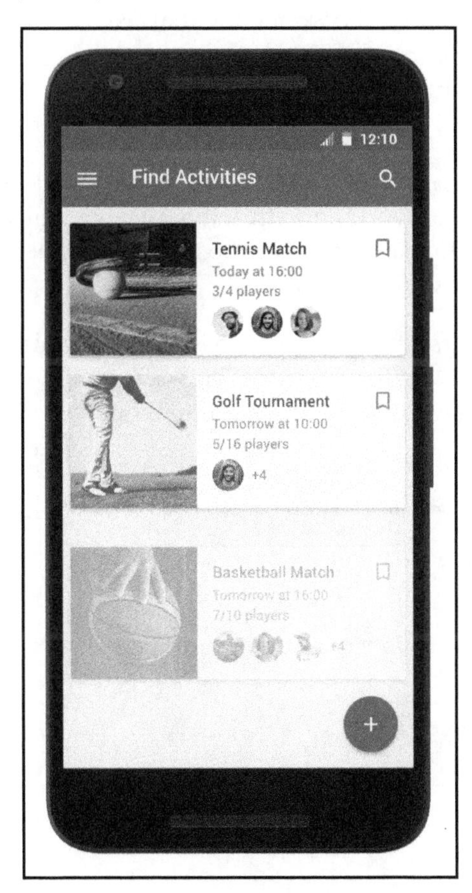

Activities feed cards animation effect

Your prototype will now be more visually appealing. With this prototype, we can test different ideas of a welcome tour and check how the users react to different approaches and different contents. Getting the attention of your users in a welcome tour is complicated, so it is advisable to try different versions before developing a definitive one in your application.

Drawer Navigation Prototype

In this prototype, we will create a **drawer** menu for our application. We will add some behavior for a FAB button, and we will add a simple example of how to prototype a search functionality to validate our flow. As in the previous tutorial, the first thing you need to follow this tutorial is to download the Sketch file that will be used in the prototype from the `Asset_A6462_A08_A22_Drawer_Navigation_Prototype_Designs.zip` code bundle. You can also download this tutorial in Framer from the `Asset_A6462_A08_A23_Drawer_Navigation_Prototype.framer.zip` code bundle.

In this example, all our screens are placed in the same artboard in Sketch, grouped by functional elements. Instead of working with artboards, we will work with the layers that are generated when importing each of the groups. These will be accessible using `sketch.`, followed by the group name with underscores.

As in the last example, the first thing we will do is to import our Sketch designs into Framer. To do this, open the `Drawer_Navigation_Prototype_Designs.sketch` file in Sketch and, with the file open, go to the **Import** menu option in Framer Studio, select **@3x**, and click on **Import**.

The following code will appear in Framer:

```
# Import file "Drawer_Navigation_Prototype_Designs" (sizes and positions
are scaled 1:3)
sketch =
Framer.Importer.load("imported/Drawer_Navigation_Prototype_Designs@3x")
```

Now we will choose the device we will work with. Click on the **Devices** menu and look for the `Google Nexus 5X`. Once these steps are done, we should see the layers in the layer inspector of Framer, and a preview of the prototype with the **drawer** menu open in the preview area, as illustrated:

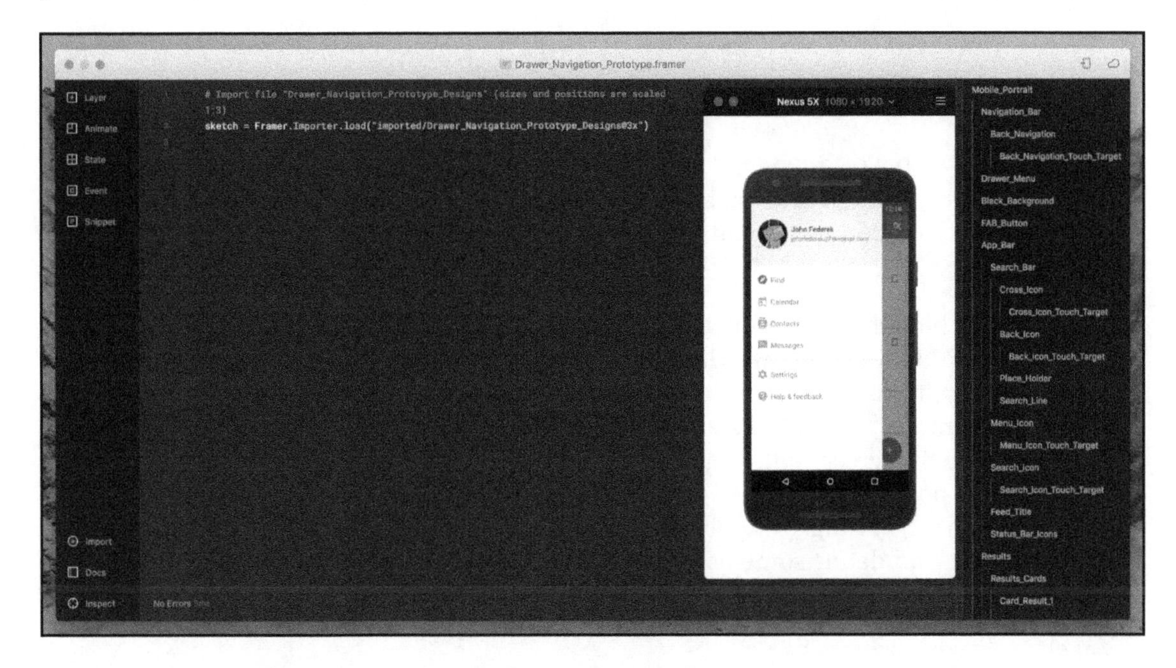

Framer Studio with Drawer_Navigation_Prototype_Designs.sketch designs imported

Since all elements of the prototype are located in the same artboard, the first thing we have to do is to hide all the elements that do not belong to the initial view of our prototype. For this, we will initialize all the elements that must be hidden by assigning the value 0 to its `opacity` property or moving them from their current position in the design to a position outside the screen:

```
# HIDE ELEMENTS INIT
# Hide Result view
sketch.Results.opacity = 0
# Hide Suggested Search view
sketch.Suggested_Search.opacity = 0
# Hide Search Bar view
sketch.Search_Bar.opacity = 0
sketch.Place_Holder.opacity = 0
sketch.Search_Line.scaleX = 0.2
sketch.Search_Line.x = sketch.Search_Line.x + sketch.Search_Line.width*0.4
sketch.Cross_Icon.opacity = 0
# Hide Drawer Menu
```

```
sketch.Drawer_Menu.x = -900
# Hide Black Background
sketch.Black_Background.opacity = 0
# Hide touch target elements
sketch.Cross_Icon_Touch_Target.opacity = 0
sketch.Search_Icon_Touch_Target.opacity = 0
sketch.Menu_Icon_Touch_Target.opacity = 0
sketch.Back_Icon_Touch_Target.opacity = 0
sketch.Back_Navigation_Touch_Target.opacity = 0
```

As you can see, we have added a `_Touch_Target` layer for the icons that will be actionable because, due to its small size, it can be complicated to tap on the icon itself. As these layers will only be used to add functionality to our prototype, we will also hide them, reducing their `opacity`.

We are going to hide the **drawer** menu by taking it off to the left, out of the screen, so the appearing transition will bring the **drawer** on to the screen by sliding. The **drawer** menu will have two positions: one at x = 0 and another at x = -900 . The **drawer** menu will be at x = -900 when the prototype is initialized. When the user taps on the menu icon, the **drawer** will animate from off the screen to its final position in the design, at x = 0. We can create states for the different positions of a layer, or we can just modify its values and animate the transition if wanted. For this example, we will create a function that will bring the layer inside the screen and define some listeners that will be active only while the layer is inside the screen:

```
sketch.Drawer_Menu.x = -900
```

When hiding the line of the search input, you will see that we have applied a transformation to it. We have changed its scale to `scaleX = 0.2` and have placed it to the right. When we show it later, the field will appear from that position, growing as if the line was drawn from right to left:

```
sketch.Search_Bar.opacity = 0
sketch.Place_Holder.opacity = 0
sketch.Search_Line.scaleX = 0.2
sketch.Search_Line.x = sketch.Search_Line.x + sketch.Search_Line.width *
0.4
```

Note that the `scaleX` property scales the element, maintaining its center position. This is why, to set it to the right, we have set the x value using the `Sketch.Search_Line.x = sketch.Search_Line.x + sketch.Search_Line.width * 0.4` instruction.

Using the ScrollComponent

The next thing we will do is to make our feed scrollable. For this, we will use the Framer `ScrollComponent`, which helps us do this task in a simple and fast way. We will do it with the following code:

```
# SCROLLABLE ELEMENTS INIT
# Wrap Activities Feed
scroll = ScrollComponent.wrap sketch.Activities_Feed
scroll.scrollHorizontal = false
scroll.scrollVertical = true
scroll.y -= 42
scroll.contentInset =
    bottom: 182
    top: 42
```

We have created an instance of `ScrollComponent` with `scroll = ScrollComponent.wrap sketch.Activities_Feed`, where `sketch.Activities_Feed` is the layer we will wrap with the scroll component. The `ScrollComponent` will be inserted between this content layer and its superlayer. With `scroll.scrollHorizontal = false` and `scroll.scrollVertical = true`, we are defining the scrolling directions of our component. In this case, the user will only be able to scroll the content vertically.

We will define a `contentInset` of `182` at the bottom of the component. This will allow us to scroll the content of the scroll component above the `sketch.Navigation_Bar` layer. We also displaced the `42` px scroll component previously with the `scroll.y -= 42` instruction and added a `contentInset` of `42` at the top to allow the content to scroll until the **App Bar**. If we do not add it, the scroll component will end at the top of where the cards appear in the design, that is, `42` px below the **App Bar**, creating an unrealistic effect.

FAB button event reacting

A common behavior for the **FAB** button is to move out of the screen when the user scrolls down and reappears when the user scrolls up. Let's encode that behavior in our prototype:

```
# FAB BUTTON
# Fab Buttons States
sketch.FAB_Button.states =
    stateIn:
        y: 1551
        animationOptions:
            time: 0.2
    stateOut:
        y: 1551+400
```

```
        animationOptions:
            time: 0.2
```

To define this behavior, we have created two states for this button: one off the screen that we will call `stateOut`, and another inside the screen that we will call `stateIn`:

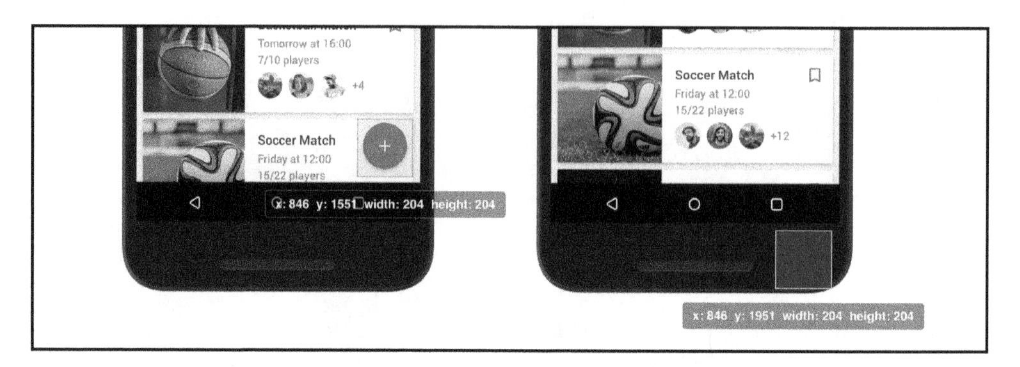

The FAB button has two states, inside of the screen (left) and out of the screen (right)

Now, we will add the behavior by creating listeners for some of the scroll events. The scroll component we created for the feed earlier will generate events when the user scrolls up and down the content, and we will add some listeners to react to them:

```
# FAB Button Behaviour
scroll.on Events.Scroll, ->
    if scroll.direction == "up"
        sketch.FAB_Button.animate('stateIn')
    if scroll.direction == "down"
        sketch.FAB_Button.animate("stateOut")
```

Each time the user scrolls, the component triggers an event and, by reading the value of `scroll.direction`, we can tell whether it has been triggered because the user has scrolled up or down. For each of these cases, we will add a condition that will change the state of the FAB button according to the desired behavior.

Drawer menu functionality

To create the **drawer** menu functionality, we will declare two functions.: one for the opening transition and another for the closing transition. These transitions will be in charge of showing and hiding both the menu and the dark overlay that de-emphasizes the contents behind the menu. Each function will make all the changes needed in the `sketch.Drawer_Menu` layer and the `sketch.Black_Background` layer. In the following code, we can find both the functions: their names will be `openMenu` and `closeMenu`:

```
# DRAWER MENU
# Open Menu Function
openMenu = ->
    sketch.Drawer_Menu.animate
        properties:
            x: 0
        time: 0.2
    sketch.Black_Background.animate
        properties:
            opacity: 100
        time: 0.2
    sketch.Drawer_Menu.on Events.SwipeLeft, (event) ->
        closeMenu()
    scroll.scrollVertical = false
    sketch.Search_Icon_Touch_Target.off(Events.Tap, showSearch)
# Close Menu Function
closeMenu = ->
    sketch.Drawer_Menu.animate
        properties:
            x: -900
        time: 0.2
    sketch.Black_Background.animate
        properties:
            opacity: 0
        time: 0.2
    scroll.scrollVertical = true
    sketch.Search_Icon_Touch_Target.on(Events.Tap, showSearch)
```

The first block of code of each function moves the drawer layer, referenced as `sketch.Drawer_Menu`, in and out of the screen, and makes the `sketch.Black_Background` layer visible when the **drawer** menu is on the screen view. We have also defined a listener for the `swipe left` event, which will call the `closeMenu()` function, moving the drawer out of the screen.

The `scroll.scrollVertical = false` and `scroll.scrollVertical = true` instructions, one of each function, make the scroll component, which is placed behind the **drawer** menu, stop reacting to the user gestures while the menu is open to avoid involuntary actions.

When the menu is open, the search icon will not react to the user's gestures. To do this, we activate and deactivate the listeners of the `sketch.Search_Icon_Touch_Target` layer, depending on whether the menu is visible or not. The `showSearch` function will be defined later.

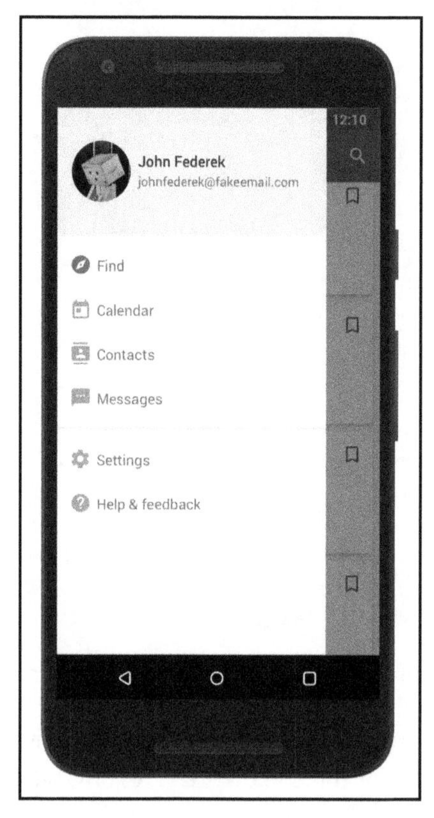

Drawer menu visible state

We will bring the **drawer** menu onto the screen with two actions: when the user makes an `EdgeSwipeLeft` event, and when the user taps on the **menu** icon. In the following code, we add an event listener for the screen when the user makes a swipe from the edge of the screen. We have also added a listener to the `sketch.Menu_Icon_Touch_Target` layer for the `Events.Tap` event. As you can see, we created the event connected to the touch target layer of the **menu** icon, which has a size of 48x48 dp and will be easier to hit by the user, instead of the **menu** icon itself, which has a smaller size:

```
# Drawer Menu Behaviour
Screen.on Events.EdgeSwipeLeft, (event) ->
    openMenu()
sketch.Menu_Icon_Touch_Target.on(Events.Tap, openMenu)
```

We will also call the `closeMenu()` function when the user taps on the **back** button of the lower navigation bar:

```
# Back Navigation Functionality
sketch.Back_Navigation_Touch_Target.on Events.Tap, ->
    closeMenu()
```

Input field search functionality

We will add the search functionality to our prototype by adding an `HTML` input. As this is a quick prototype, we do not need to actually search through a set of elements or a database; it will be enough to simulate its behavior by showing some fixed results. Framer allows us to add layers that contain code written in HTML by assigning value to the `html` property of a layer.

For this example, we will include some inline CSS in the HTML tag so that we can set the `size`, the `font`, and some visual adjustments to make it invisible. As the visual design is already included in the Sketch design, the input field can be hidden in the HTML tag. Here's the code:

```
# SEARCH FUNCTIONALITY
# Add Input Field
inputSearchField = new Layer
    html: "<input style='width: 690px; height:144px; font-size:60px; color:
#ffffff; background: transparent; border: none;' type='text'
id='searchInput' name='inputName'>"
    backgroundColor: null
    x: 218
    y: 82
document.getElementById('searchInput').style.display = 'none';
```

The user will now be able to write in the `HTML input` field with the smartphone virtual keyboard. As you can see, we used `getElementById` to access the input element of the HTML document.

We will now create two new functions; they will allow us to `show` and `hide` the searching functionality. These functions are a little long, so read them carefully:

```
# Show Search Bar Function
showSearch = ->
    layersToHide = [sketch.Activities_Feed, sketch.Menu_Icon,
sketch.Feed_Title, sketch.FAB_Button, sketch.Search_Icon]
    for layer in layersToHide
        layer.animate
            properties:
```

```
                opacity: 0
            time: 0.4
    layersToShow = [sketch.Search_Bar, sketch.Suggested_Search]
    for layer in layersToShow
        layer.animate
            properties:
                opacity: 1
            time: 0.4
    sketch.Place_Holder.animate
        properties:
            opacity: 1
        time: 0.4
        delay: 0.5
    sketch.Search_Line.animate
        properties:
            opacity: 1
            scaleX:  1
            x: sketch.Search_Line.x - sketch.Search_Line.width*0.4
        time: 0.8
    document.getElementById('searchInput').style.display = 'inline'
    sketch.Cross_Icon_Touch_Target.on(Events.Tap, cleanInput)
    sketch.Search_Bar.bringToFront()
    sketch.Search_Icon_Touch_Target.off(Events.Tap, showSearch)
    sketch.Menu_Icon_Touch_Target.off(Events.Tap, openMenu)
    sketch.Back_Icon_Touch_Target.on Events.Tap, (event) ->
        hideSearch()
```

In the preceding lines, we first made all the layers of the `layersToHide` array disappear and made all the layers included in `layersToShow` appear.

For the input field represented by the line in the `sketch.Search_Line` layer, we will scale to its design size `scaleX: 1` from the 0.2 scale we defined in the code earlier. By changing its `scaleX` and `x` values, we are creating an effect as if the line was being drawn from right to left. After a small delay, the `sketch.Place_Holder` will appear. It will happen about the same time the line is getting its final position.

The `document.getElementById('searchInput').style.display = 'inline'` line displays the field input. The `sketch.Search_Icon_Touch_Target.off(Events.Tap, showSearch)` and `sketch.Menu_Icon_Touch_Target.off(Events.Tap, openMenu)` instructions will disable the listeners of these layers. They will not be active while the search screen is visible.

We assign a function to the `sketch.Cross_Icon_Touch_Target` layer that we will define later, and whose purpose will be to empty the search box and hide the results shown.

We bring all the elements of the search functionality to the foreground with `sketch.Search_Bar.bringToFront()`.

We also add the functionality of hiding the search screen with `sketch.Back_Icon_Touch_Target.on Events.Tap, (event);` it will create a listener of the `Event.Tap` event in the `sketch.Back_Icon_Touch_Target` layer.

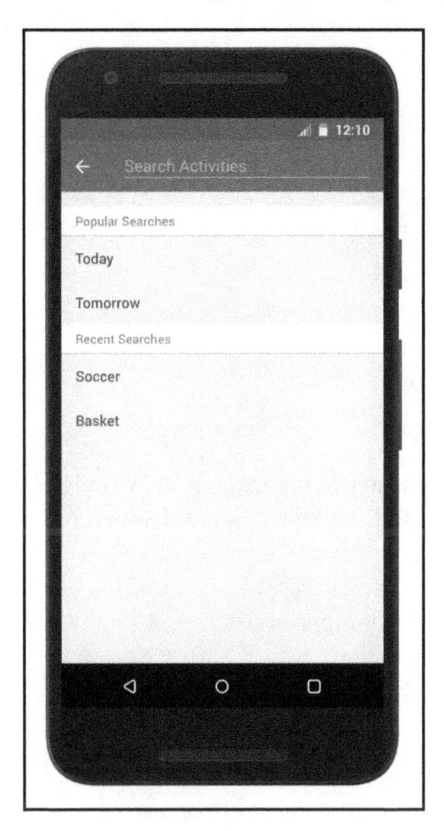

Search feature with searching suggestions

The `hideSearch()` function will have similar behavior; let's go for it:

```
# Hide Search Bar Function
hideSearch = ->
    layersToShow = [sketch.Activities_Feed, sketch.Menu_Icon,
sketch.Feed_Title, sketch.FAB_Button, sketch.Search_Icon]
    for layer in layersToShow
        layer.animate
            properties:
                opacity: 1
            time: 0.4
```

```
    layersToHide = [sketch.Search_Bar, sketch.Place_Holder,
sketch.Suggested_Search]
    for layer in layersToHide
        layer.animate
            properties:
                opacity: 0
            time: 0.4
    sketch.Search_Line.animate
        properties:
            opacity: 0
            scaleX:  0.2
            x: sketch.Search_Line.x + sketch.Search_Line.width*0.4
        time: 0.4
    document.getElementById('searchInput').style.display = 'none'
    document.getElementById('searchInput').value = ''
    sketch.Results.opacity = 0
    sketch.Cross_Icon.opacity = 0
    sketch.Cross_Icon_Touch_Target.off(Events.Tap, cleanInput)
    sketch.Search_Bar.sendToBack()
    sketch.Search_Icon_Touch_Target.on(Events.Tap, showSearch)
    Utils.delay 1, ->
        sketch.Menu_Icon_Touch_Target.on(Events.Tap, openMenu)
```

In this function, we will first show the layers that we previously hid in the transition to the search screen, and will also hide the elements we showed in the same transition. With `document.getElementById('searchInput').style.display = 'none'` and `document.getElementById('searchInput').value = ''`, we will also hide the search input and put its value to null. The next time it appears, it will not have any string inside.

With `sketch.Search_Bar.sendToBack()`, we return the search bar behind the other elements.

In the `sketch.Search_Icon_Touch_Target.on(Events.Tap, showSearch)` instruction, we make the search icon actionable again.

Finally, after a second, we return the functionality to the touch target of the menu icon. In Framer, you can use some utilities as the delay we used in `Utils.delay 1, ->`. You will find more at `https://framer.com/docs/#utils.utilities`.

When the user types in our search box, we will show results simulating a search. To do this, we will define some behaviors. This is the code:

```
# Input Field Behaviour
document.getElementById('searchInput').onfocus = ->
    sketch.Place_Holder.opacity = 0
document.getElementById('searchInput').onkeyup = ->
```

```
if document.getElementById('searchInput').value != ''
    sketch.Suggested_Search.opacity = 0
    sketch.Place_Holder.opacity = 0
    sketch.Cross_Icon.opacity = 1
    sketch.Results.animate
        properties:
            opacity: 1
        time: 0.5
else
    sketch.Suggested_Search.opacity = 1
    sketch.Results.opacity = 0
```

When the user taps on the **input**, it will get the focus, and we will make the placeholder disappear. That will be done with the `document.getElementById('searchInput').onfocus = ->` and `sketch.Place_Holder.opacity = 0` lines.

When the user types something, we will analyze whether the search field has a string or has been emptied. If it is empty, we will show the placeholder again. If it has a value, we will show the `sketch.Results` results layer. We will also show the `sketch.Cross_Icon` layer, which will allow the user to empty the search box, and we will hide the search suggestions with `sketch.Suggested_Search.opacity = 0`.

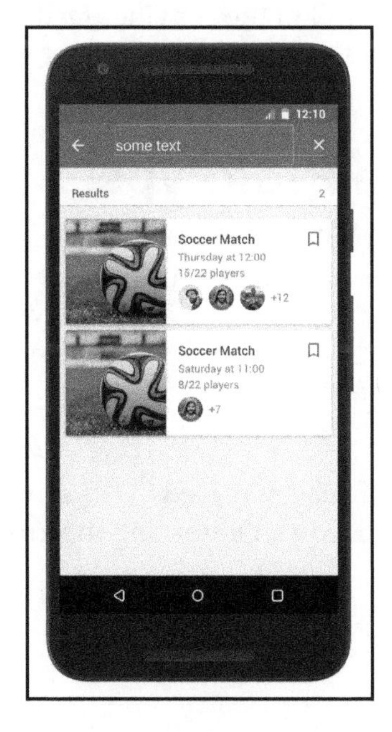

Search feature with results

We will now create the function we will call when the user taps on the **cross** icon. Remember that we added a listener earlier, with `sketch.Cross_Icon_Touch_Target.on(Events.Tap, cleanInput):`

```
# Clean Input Field Function
cleanInput = ->
    document.getElementById('searchInput').value = ''
    sketch.Suggested_Search.opacity = 1
    sketch.Results.animateStop()
    sketch.Results.opacity = 0
    sketch.Place_Holder.opacity = 1
    sketch.Cross_Icon.opacity = 0
```

In the `cleanInput()` function, we empty the search box, return to show the search suggestions and the placeholder, stop the animation that shows the results if it is in progress, and also hide the **cross** icon.

Finally, we will make the `showSearch()` function be called when the user taps on the **search** icon, (well, actually on the touch target we created for this purpose). Here's the code:

```
# Search Bar Behaviour
sketch.Search_Icon_Touch_Target.on(Events.Tap, showSearch)
```

Now, the user should be able to scroll in the activities feed, display the **drawer** navigation by tapping on the menu icon, and simulate a search to get some results.

Bottom Navigation Prototype

In this prototype, we will create a bottom navigation using the `PageComponent` included in Framer Studio. As in the previous tutorial, the first thing you need to follow this tutorial is to download the Sketch file that will be used in the prototype from the `Asset_A6462_A08_A24_Bottom_Navigation_Prototype_Designs.zip` code bundle. You can also download this tutorial in Framer from `Asset_A6462_A08_A25_Bottom_Navigation_Prototype.framer.zip`.

In this example, all our screens have been placed in the same artboard in Sketch, grouped by functional elements. So, we will work referencing the groups as we did in the previous prototype.

Now, we need to open the `Bottom_Navigation_Prototype_Designs.sketch` file in Sketch and import it into Framer Studio. To do this, you need to click on **Import** in Framer, select **@3x,** and click on **Import**. This code should appear in your Framer project:

```
# Import file "Bottom_Navigation_Prototype_Designs" (sizes and positions
are scaled 1:3)
sketch =
Framer.Importer.load("imported/Bottom_Navigation_Prototype_Designs@3x")
```

Now, we will select the device for the preview. Click on the D**evices** menu and select **Google Nexus 5X**; you can activate the **Toggle device** option to preview the prototype with the phone skin. After these steps are done, you should see the imported code in the code editor, the Sketch groups imported into layers in the layer inspector, and the preview of the prototype in the preview area, as seen in this screenshot:

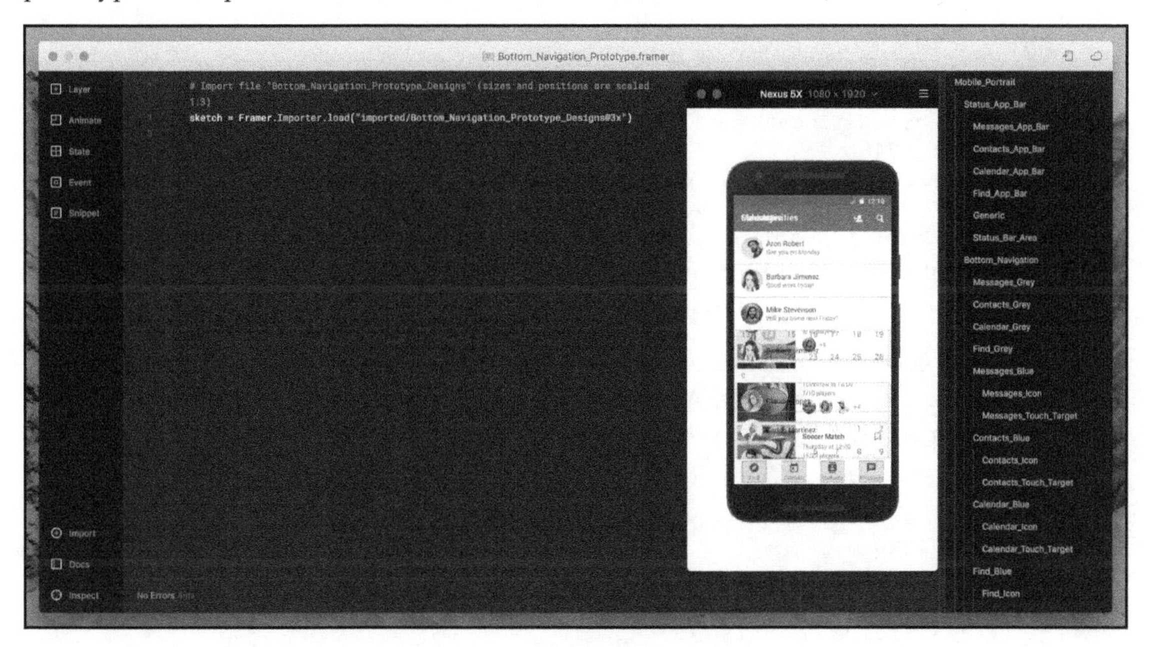

Framer Studio with Bottom_Navigation_Prototype_Designs.sketch designs imported

The first thing we will do is to hide all the `Touch Target` layers that should not be visible when loading our prototype:

```
# HIDE ELEMENTS INIT
# Hide Touch Target Buttons
sketch.Find_Touch_Target.opacity = 0
sketch.Calendar_Touch_Target.opacity = 0
sketch.Contacts_Touch_Target.opacity = 0
sketch.Messages_Touch_Target.opacity = 0
```

As we will create this prototype using the `PageComponent` provided by Framer, we need to create an instance of this component and add all our section layers to it. However, we will first create a `ScrollComponent` for the **Find Activities** layer. We will nest this new scroll layer inside the `PageComponent`:

```
# PAGE COMPONENT INIT
# Scroll Find Activities Creation
scrollFind = ScrollComponent.wrap(sketch.Find)
scrollFind.contentInset =
    bottom: 204
scrollFind.scrollHorizontal = false
```

We have added some `contentInset` in order to allow the user to drag the content of the scroll component above the bottom navigation. Also, we force the scrolling to vertical direction, blocking the horizontal scrolling.

In the following code, we create a new instance of `PageComponent` and put it inside the `sketch.Mobile_Portrait` layer. We will only allow horizontal scrolling on this component with `page.scrollVertical = false`:

```
# Page Componen Creation
page = new PageComponent
    width: 1080
    height: 1920
page.superLayer = sketch.Mobile_Portrait
page.scrollVertical = false
sketch.Background.sendToBack()
sketch.Status_App_Bar.bringToFront()
sketch.Bottom_Navigation.bringToFront()
page.addPage scrollFind
page.addPage sketch.Calendar
page.addPage sketch.Contacts
page.addPage sketch.Messages
```

We have also rearranged the layers to ensure that the `sketch.Background` background layer stays behind, and the `sketch.Status_App_Bar` and `sketch.Bottom_Navigation` layers are in front:

```
sketch.Background.sendToBack()
sketch.Status_App_Bar.bringToFront()
sketch.Bottom_Navigation.bringToFront()
```

Then, we will add the four views to the component, which will leave only the first one visible. The navigation between views will be handled by the component itself, allowing users to change from one view to another with a swipe gesture. You can disable the swipe event listener by adding `page.content.draggable = false`. Also, you can disable the animation when changing between views with the `snapToPage` method by adding false as the animate parameter in the call of the method. The syntax of the method will be `page.snapToPage(page, animate, animationOptions)`.

```
page.addPage scrollFind
page.addPage sketch.Calendar
page.addPage sketch.Contacts
page.addPage sketch.Messages
```

Bottom navigation

Now that we have our `PageComponent` working, it's time to add functionality to the bottom navigation. For this, the first thing that we will do is to create a function that will hide and show the necessary elements so that the **App Bar** and the bottom navigation represent the view in which we are. The function will show the elements of one or the other view according to a parameter that we will have to pass on the call.

The function we created first puts all the elements of the bottom navigation in the deselected state, making the gray state of each one visible and hiding all the elements of the **App Bar** from all the views.

After analyzing the parameter that we passed to the function with a `switch` structure, and according to the view that we have said is visible, it will hide the unselected state of the bottom navigation in the corresponding view, showing its blue state, which represents the selected state. It will also show the elements of the **App Bar** corresponding to that view:

```
# CHANGE VIEW FUNCTIONALITY
# Change View Function
changeView = (view) ->
    sketch.Find_Blue.opacity = 0
    sketch.Find_Grey.opacity = 1
    sketch.Calendar_Blue.opacity = 0
    sketch.Calendar_Grey.opacity = 1
    sketch.Contacts_Blue.opacity = 0
    sketch.Contacts_Grey.opacity = 1
    sketch.Messages_Blue.opacity = 0
    sketch.Messages_Grey.opacity = 1
    sketch.Find_App_Bar.opacity = 0
    sketch.Calendar_App_Bar.opacity = 0
    sketch.Contacts_App_Bar.opacity = 0
    sketch.Messages_App_Bar.opacity = 0
    switch view
        when 'find'
            sketch.Find_Blue.opacity = 1
            sketch.Find_Grey.opacity = 0
            sketch.Find_App_Bar.opacity = 1
        when 'calendar'
            sketch.Calendar_Blue.opacity = 1
            sketch.Calendar_Grey.opacity = 0
            sketch.Calendar_App_Bar.opacity = 1
        when 'contacts'
            sketch.Contacts_Blue.opacity = 1
            sketch.Contacts_Grey.opacity = 0
            sketch.Contacts_App_Bar.opacity = 1
        else
            sketch.Messages_Blue.opacity = 1
            sketch.Messages_Grey.opacity = 0
            sketch.Messages_App_Bar.opacity = 1
changeView 'find'
```

After the function definition, we initialize our prototype with the **Find** view. Therefore, the **Calendar**, **Contact**, and **Messages** views will show their gray tab in the bottom navigation and have their items hidden in the **App Bar**.

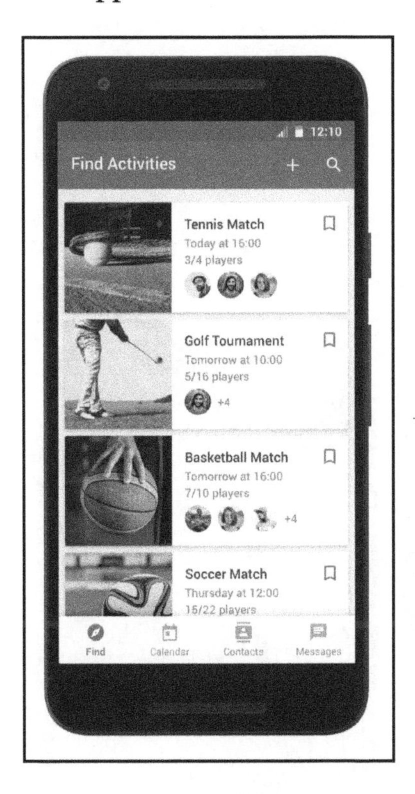

Bottom navigation with Find section active

With all these elements, we only need to relate the state of the `PageComponent` with the bottom navigation. To do this, the first thing we will do is to select the page chosen by the user when tapping on an element of the bottom navigation. Each time the user taps on an element of the bottom navigation, we will call `page.snapToPage`, indicating the page to which it should move. As argument, we will tell the name of the layer to which we want it to move:

```
# BOTTOM NAVIGATION
# Bottom Navigation Behaviour
sketch.Find_Blue.on Events.Tap, ->
    page.snapToPage(sketch.scrollFind)
    changeView 'find'
sketch.Calendar_Blue.on Events.Tap, ->
    page.snapToPage(sketch.Calendar)
    changeView 'calendar'
```

```
sketch.Contacts_Blue.on Events.Tap, ->
    page.snapToPage(sketch.Contacts)
    changeView 'contacts'
sketch.Messages_Blue.on Events.Tap, ->
    page.snapToPage(sketch.Messages)
    changeView 'messages'
```

Note that in addition to the changes to the `PageComponent`, we have also added a call to our `changeView` function so that the bottom navigation also represents the new status of our prototype.

Currently, our bottom navigation allows us to navigate between the different layers that we have added to the `PageComponent`.

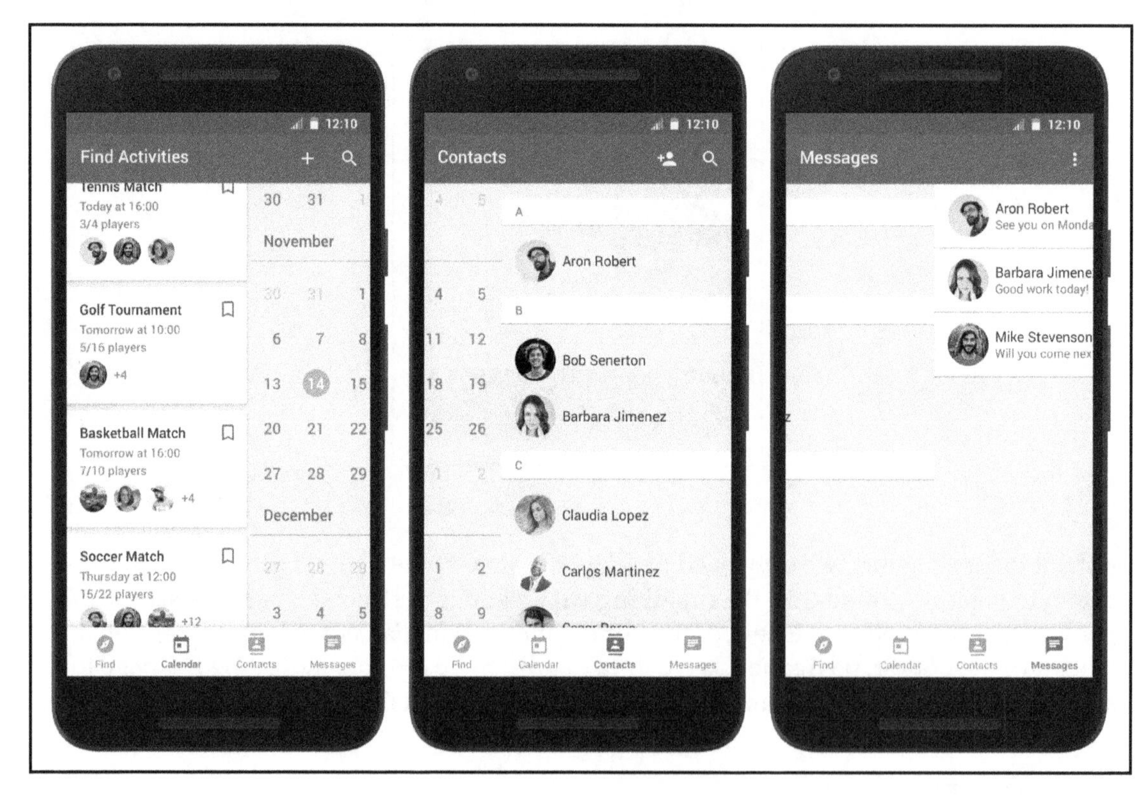

Prototype screenshots changing section

Finally, we also want the new state reflected in the bottom navigation area when the user changes page by swiping on the PageComponent. To do this, we will add a listener to the PageComponent.

```
# Page Behaviour Control
page.on "change:currentPage", ->
    if page.currentPage == scrollFind
        changeView 'find'
    if page.currentPage == sketch.Calendar
        changeView 'calendar'
    if page.currentPage == sketch.Contacts
        changeView 'contacts'
    if page.currentPage == sketch.Messages
        changeView 'messages'
```

With this, we will have the basic structure of our application making use of the page component.

Being Pragmatic

Programming a prototype is simple when done slowly. It is common to follow a trial and error strategy while learning a new programming language.

CoffeeScript is designed to be easy to read and program, so it is advisable to look for examples on the internet as you are learning. They will be easy to understand and will teach you new ways to codify your prototypes.

Remember that a prototype should be a fast method of learning as much as possible with minimal effort, and it is better not to go into too complex developments. When developing any functionality in a very detailed way does not contribute anything to your study, opt for developing a functionality that is as simple as possible.

Sometimes, it is better to think of different low-fidelity prototypes that allow you to clarify whether one solution is better than another, looking for clearly differentiated elements in your design. From the conclusions, you can create prototypes closer to the final version.

Be part of the community

Framer has a very broad user community behind it. There is documentation on the internet that you can consult to prepare your prototypes. Probably any doubts you have will have been met by someone else before. If you are stuck with a new problem, you can also ask, and there are chances that someone will come up with a helpful answer.

You may also wish to look in the official documentation and in the *Facebook* groups of the program. By simply reading solutions that others bring to the same problem, you will learn new ways to create your prototypes.

Learning resources

To learn more about framer, you can get this book written by Tes Mat, The Framer book (`https://framerbook.com/`) or take a look to this video created by Kenny Chen, Rapid Prototyping with Framer (`http://shop.oreilly.com/`).

You can find extra CoffeeScript tutorials at Framer web (`https://framer.com/getstarted/programming/`), or in this book written by Tessa Thornton, CoffeeScript for Framer.js (`https://coffeescript-for-framerjs.com/`).

Test with your mobile phone

Framer makes it easy to preview your prototypes as you create them on your desktop. While that is very useful to check the progress of the prototype, it cannot be compared to the experience of using the prototype on the intended final device. Framer allows you to see your prototype on a real mobile device too. The difference of testing a prototype on a mobile phone can be huge. Look for an app that lets you test your prototype on Android and iOS. Currently, you can find applications working in the following links:

- Framer App Android
  `https://play.google.com/store/apps/details?id=com.framerjs.android`
- Framer App iOS
  `https://itunes.apple.com/app/framer-preview/id1124920547?ls=1&mt=8`

Stay up to date with Framer news

Framer is regularly updated to include new gestures, components, and functionalities. It is useful to stay in touch with the latest developments in order to create prototypes that respond to the latest trends.

Visit the Framer website regularly and include your email in your newsletter list. You can register at `https://framer.com/newsletter/`.

Summary

In this chapter, we learned the basic principles for building prototypes with CoffeeScript and Framer. We also created some sample prototypes, including many basic elements of Framer Studio.

Framer Studio has become a popular professional prototyping program, so learning how to use it will become a valuable skill. Creating prototypes with Framer Studio will also help you validate solutions with users and present ideas to your teammates.

In the next chapter, we will explain what user testing is and how it can help us improve our application. We will also learn how to organize testing sessions with real users.

9
User Testing

"We try to develop products that seem somehow inevitable. That leave you with the sense that that's the only possible solution that makes sense."

- Jonathan Ive

The users are the ultimate judges of your product, but predicting their behavior in advance is really hard. Even if you ask your users what they want, it is not guaranteed that what they say is what they really need. There are many examples of organizations that have made product decisions by interpreting their users input literally, leading them to unsuccessful results. For example, Coca-Cola adjusting the flavor of the *new Coke* based on thousands of sip tests and Walmart spending millions in reorganizing their aisles are just two of the most well-known examples.

As research shows, people are affected by the **introspection illusion**, a cognitive bias that limits our capabilities to explain our own behavior and predict our future attitudes.

In order to deeply understand how your ideas work in practice, you need to observe how people actually use them. You need to focus on the reactions of your users, not their opinions.

Even with their best intentions, users may not be able to tell you what they need. You should focus on what they do rather than what they say. (source: https://www.flickr.com/photos/sophotow/16559284088/)

You would want to get quality feedback from your users as early as possible. The sooner you check how well your solution works for your users, the better. Learning from your users as you design your product allows you to make course corrections when necessary, reducing the risks of moving too far in the wrong direction.

Testing your ideas with users is a key step in the design process. In this chapter, we'll describe a testing approach to get useful feedback early in the process. By recreating realistic-enough scenarios, you can test your ideas before you start building your product.

Observing your users with your product in their hands is a powerful learning tool. However, in order to get quality feedback that helps improve your designs, you will need to organize the testing process appropriately. This requires you to understand the purpose of the testing process, plan the testing steps to avoid any interference, and learn how to observe your user's behavior in order to extract relevant conclusions.

Understanding the role of testing usability

We want our users to achieve their goals with minimal friction. **Usability** is defined as the quality of a product's ease of use. Usability depends on how your product design aligns with the different user needs: the needs from our human condition, the needs from general expectations, and those from the specific context of use. There are usability guidelines that capture general principles, but they cannot include all the context-specific considerations that make your product unique.

In order to check whether your ideas work in a specific context, you need to test them in such context. **Usability testing** is a process used to identify the most relevant issues in the usability of a product. Usability testing is not aimed at discovering all issues, or to provide you with accurate statistics on how many users are affected by a given issue. It will help you to understand why users have problems, and to which extent these problems prevent users in achieving their goals in their context.

The steps you normally follow in a usability test are as follows:

1. Deciding what to test and the right approach to do so.
2. Defining a plan to provide users with context and the right questions.
3. Observing how participants interact with the product.
4. Identifying and summarize the findings.

The specific steps of the process will depend on what you are exactly testing and the kind of results you are interested in.

Deciding what to test

Testing your ideas with users helps you to improve your ideas. In order to test these ideas, you will need something to be tested. Fortunately, you don't need to have a complete product to be able to test your ideas. At any point of the development process, you should have something valuable to test and learn from. For example, you can test the following:

- **Existing products**: You can test previous versions of your product if they exist, or even similar products from your competitors. This is an opportunity to learn more about your users, and better understand how previous ideas worked at a very low cost--since these products already exist.

- **Early designs**: Sketches and mock-ups won't get the user immersed in the experience you are designing, and you cannot expect to learn how well a solution will work just based on their feedback. However, they can help you learn about the user mental model and their expectations. You can ask users to reinterpret the idea of your sketches in order to learn about the terms and concepts that are familiar to them. Mock-ups can be used to check user expectations by asking them to describe the result they would expect if they interacted with the product that the mock-up describes.
- **General interaction concepts**: Using basic prototypes, you can test the general concept or the approach for a specific workflow of your app. Even if interactions are not polished, a prototype will help you to learn how well the concept works for the user. Depending on how confident you are in your concept, you can either focus your test on a single concept or compare alternative approaches to identify the most promising direction.
- **Detailed interactions**: Using detailed prototypes, you can evaluate how to better support a specific activity. With more polished prototypes, you can recreate interactions in more detail, thus getting very close to the interaction that users would have with your final product. In this way, you can focus on whether specific aspects in the interaction work as expected, such as the discoverability, the motion pace, the feedback provided to the user, and many more.
- **Versions of your product**: As your product is developed, each version can be used to get feedback from your users. This is useful to identify gaps between the intended design and its execution. It is also very helpful for prioritization, in order to polish the aspects that can most improve the user experience.

Even in an informal setting, you can learn from users by observing how they use your product in practice (source: https://www.flickr.com/photos/stevevosloo/4918831135)

Testing should be a continuous learning process. You may always feel tempted to wait to have something more polished to show users, but the earlier you start testing, the better. If you have a continuous stream of user feedback from the beginning of the project, you will be able to polish your ideas before committing to building them.

Using the right method

In physics, the **observer effect** indicates that the act of observation has an effect on the physical phenomenon observed. Observing users can have a similar effect. Although there is no perfect method to learn everything from your users, user researchers have developed many different methods to learn from different angles in order to reduce the noise as much as possible. These research methods can be organized in two big families--generative and evaluative research.

- **Generative research**: This is aimed at learning about the user needs and turning these observations into ideas on how to solve their problems. In previous chapters, we described some of the methods used in generative research, such as contextual inquiry, interviews, or surveys. These are methods that you would apply in the initial iterations of the project.
- **Evaluative research**: This is focused on learning about how effective the solutions are. As you have ideas, you will need to check how well they will fit with the users; you will want to evaluate them. Some of these methods are based on the user attitude, whereas others focus on the actual user behavior:
    - **Behavioral methods** try to understand what the user does with minimal intervention, in contrast to the **attitudinal methods** where users provide the information themselves. Although observing requires an effort to get the user immersed in the experience and interpret the user actions, we find it more reliable to trust what users do rather than what they say.

- **Qualitative methods** are based on direct observation, and their processing is not mathematical. **Quantitative methods** are based on measuring and aggregating data such as those obtained by surveys or server logs. With the numbers, you can understand what happens, but the observations used in qualitative methods will tell you why. For example, if your measurements for the time users spend in your app goes up, your metrics are not going to tell you whether this was caused by users being more engaged with your content--which may be positive--or users taking more time to find the information they were looking for--which may not be positive.

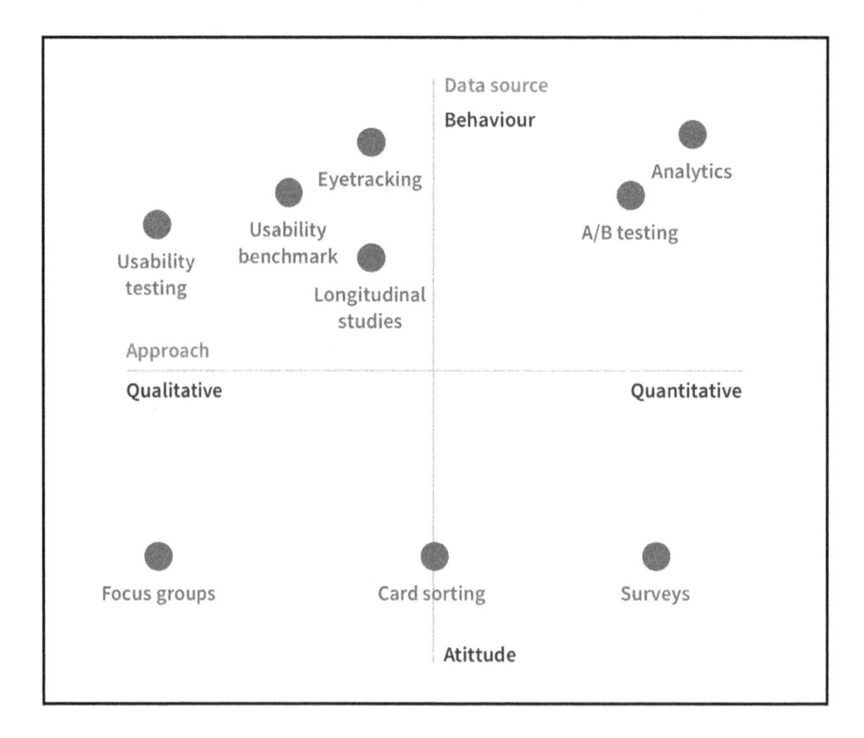

There is a vast variety of research methods; this diagram shows just a few, organized based on the information they rely on (user behaviors or attitudes) and the approach used to learn from them (qualitative or quantitative)

Among the different behavioral and qualitative methods, we'll focus on usability testing in this chapter. Usability testing is a research method based on observing the user behavior. It allows you to identify problematic usability patterns and helps you to understand why your design does not serve the user goals.

In usability testing, you look for user reactions, not their opinions. Thus, you want to recreate a situation that resembles as much as possible the real context of use for your product and get some participants to go through such experience, observing how well your solution meets the user needs. It is not a complex process, especially if you are familiar with prototyping. There are multiple flavors of the process:

- **Moderated usability testing**: The person conducting the test interacts with a participant on a one-to-one basis. The conductor can participate in person or remotely and provides context information about the goal of the test. The participant will use a product or prototype while describing their thoughts for some tasks in order to achieve the set goals. Meanwhile, the person conducting the test observes the participant's interactions in order to learn about the different usability problems the user finds and asks follow-up questions to learn more about the origin of the issues and the user's mental model.
- **Unmoderated usability testing**: In the unmoderated version of usability testing, the person conducting the test is not present when participants complete it. The person conducting the test prepares a script in advance, and the participants will follow it without further intervention. The script can be provided to participants on paper or digitally. This helps to automate the process, since a script can be distributed to many people at the same time, and many online services, such as `https://www.usertesting.com/`, allow you to automate the process. However, it has also drawbacks, since the lack of a conductor prevents learning from digging deeper into an unexpected situation or helping the participants if they go off-track. This requires the scripts to be detailed, take into account any possible deviations, set time limits for some tasks, and make sure that the prototype is polished enough to avoid causing distractions.
- **Usability benchmarks**: When defining benchmarks, the goal is to compare how different products or versions of a product support a given task. Participants will complete a set of tasks with a product or prototype while some measurements are taken. Common measurements are the time spent on the task, whether the task was successfully completed, and the number of errors found. Participants don't talk while working on the task to keep the time precise. Since the goal is to get statistically significant results, such as *80% of the participants completed the flight reservation under 3 minutes*, you need to consider testing with a high enough number of participants to get accurate results. In order to get overall results for a specific group of users, you need to provide them with the same exact version of a product--although it is totally fine to have multiple groups with different versions, if that is what you are comparing. In addition, you may want to take several measurements of the main tasks in order to identify the learning factor of users.

- **Longitudinal studies**: Usability testing sessions are relatively short, normally around 1-hour long. However, some products have goals that are related to long-term activities for the user. For example, an *activity tracking* product to encourage people to exercise involves the user in experiences that could span through months. While it is possible to organize usability tests to evaluate specific interactions by providing the user with enough context--telling them to imagine what they achieved during the last month or choosing a scenario that actually matches what they did in some cases--you may want to have a more continuous observation of the user interactions through time. Different software tools, such as appsee (`https://www.appsee.com/`), support the recording of user interactions, as they use your product, allowing you to analyze them as if it was a month-long unmoderated usability test.
- **Eye tracking:** Capturing what the user sees can be a useful data point for a usability study. An eye tracking software allows you to know where participants focus their eyes, which can be very useful during usability testing. For example, thanks to eye tracking, you can distinguish a user who cannot find the button they need (a discoverability problem) from another user who finds the button and reads the label, but considers it as not providing the needed functionality (a labeling problem). You need to consider that what users see is very dependent on their task, and you should not consider this information in isolation. Eye tracking provides you with another data point to consider in the context of what users do and what they say.

In the subsequent sections, we'll guide you through the steps for planning and conducting moderated usability tests. However, the process can be adapted to accommodate different variants.

Planning the test

You can learn a lot by just casual observations of how people use your products or prototypes. However, testing with users requires some previous planning in order to get the best results.

Defining the goals

Although you may consider that your ultimate goal is to check whether your ideas work, having more specific goals will be helpful. There are many different aspects that contribute to a good user experience, depending on the nature of your solution you may want to focus on differing goals.

Defining what you want to obtain from the test allows you to define a more focused testing process with more chances to provide a clear response.

These are some aspects you may be interested in evaluating:

- **Visual hierarchy**: Do users understand the relationship among the different pieces of information provided?
- **Navigation**: Can users orient through the different parts of the application?
- **Workflows**: Can the user fluently complete an activity?
- **Compare two different approaches**: Which aspects make one alternative preferred over another?

Once you have identified what you need to learn, you can define the scenarios that will put users into the context you need to get your answers.

Scenarios and tasks

The next step is to decide what users will be doing for you to learn from their interactions and any issues they may find on their way. Unfortunately, we cannot tell users exactly what to do. If you direct your users too much, they will be just following instructions, and you won't learn about the issues they may find when using the real product, and you will not be there to help.

When defining the testing scenarios, you need to provide enough context for the user to understand what needs to be achieved. The user will be in charge of figuring out the steps to achieve a specific goal.

You can adapt your scenarios to be presented in one of these forms:

- **General scenarios**: Ask the users to give their initial impression of what they see. This is helpful to clarify the purpose of what the user imagines for the product and how that matches their mental model.
- **Gymkhana**: Present the participant with a clear objective to be achieved and let them find it, for example, ask them to find the cheapest way to visit your holiday destination.
- **Reverse Gymkhana**: Provide the participant with an instance of the result. You can show the participants an image of a promotional pack to visit Paris and let them work out the way to find it.

- **User-defined tasks**: You can propose activities based on initial questions about the normal activities for the participant. This helps you learn more about a relevant and familiar context for the user, but it also requires the tested product to support those. This may be less likely for specific prototypes compared to real products.
- **Unexpected tasks**: When testing spontaneous or error situations, it does not make sense to anticipate the activity the user is expected to perform. For example, if you want to test how users react to a notification of a message or an incoming call, you can ask the user for a secondary task and prepare the primary one to appear as the user completes the secondary one.
- **Impossible tasks**: Proposing a task that cannot be achieved can be useful in some cases too. For example, asking the user to call someone not present in the phone contacts can help you determine how clear it is that the said information is not available, depending on whether the user is confident about it or assumes that the contact is there, but has not been found.

These are just some ideas on how to present your testing scenarios; feel free to experiment with new ways that suit your specific context.

Identifying the user goals and illustrating them in scenarios have already been useful in designing solutions for your product. You can also use those scenarios as a general base for the testing scenarios. You just need to decide how to present them, which contextual information to provide, and which specific tasks to ask for.

Defining a script

Writing a script for your test allows you to think on the best strategy to get the user to do what you want, without directly telling them. It also allows you to have a guide to keep you on track as you test with them.

For each scenario you want to test, a usability testing script normally consists of the following aspects:

1. **Introduction**: This describes how to present the scenario to the participant.
2. **Questions**: Questions for the participant before, during, and after the test allow you to learn from the participant--initial questions to further understand the problem and the user expectations, followed by asking the user to do certain tasks during the test, and finally collecting general impressions at the end of the test.

3. **Expected results**: For each task, you will want to describe the steps you expect the user to take. This will help you to identify any deviation from the successful path. You can also mention important aspects to be observed, in order to focus on them as you observe the user interactions.
4. **Scenario variants**: Based on the expected results, you may anticipate some possible alternative action paths. In some cases, you would want to consider proposing modifications to the scenario.

The script is just an initial guide. You should allow some room for the unexpected. In the case of unmoderated tests, you will need to define a more detailed script.

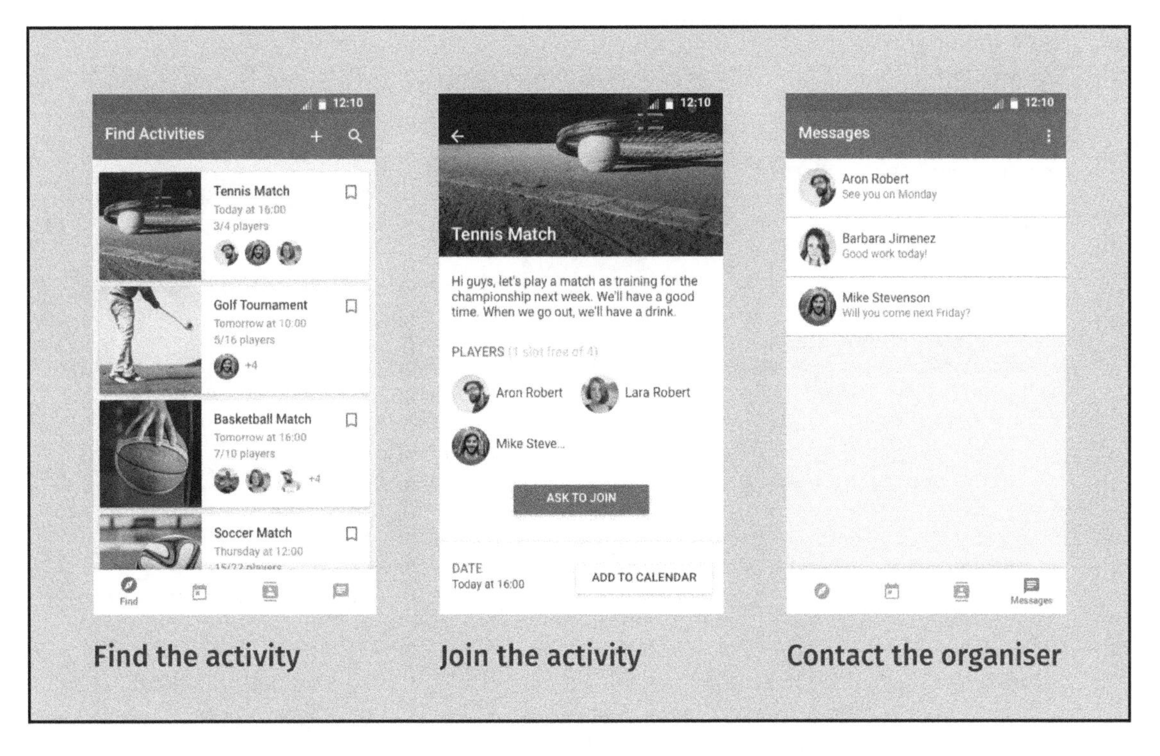

The three steps in the example workflow we want to test with users (source: screenshots from Sketch)

Here, you can see an example script to test the social sports app prototype we created in previous chapters:

```
Goal. Evaluate whether users can fluently join a sporting event created by
their friends and participate in it.

Introduction. Imagine four colleagues from the office are organizing
regular tennis matches using a mobile app. Today, one player may not be
able to attend the match, and they may need one more player. You, as a
tennis fan will be happy to join the game.

Questions before the test:
- Do you often participate in sports with friends or work colleagues?
- Can you tell us which are the steps that are needed for organizing such
events? In which of those steps do you participate?

Questions during the test:
- In an informal conversation with your colleague Mike Stevenson at the
office, he told you that a tennis player may be needed for today. You want
to check if they are missing a player for today's tennis game and play with
them if possible. What would you do?
- [Expected: The user finds the tennis activity, notices that there are
just three players and selects the "ask to join" option]
- What would you do now?
- [Expected: the user understands they need to wait for the confirmation,
and will notice when the confirmations appears in a few seconds]
- [Variant: If the user does not notice the confirmation] As the time to
the match approaches, how would you know if you should go there or not?
- Ok, now you only need to go there and play some tennis. Imagine that due
to the traffic state, you expect to be 10 minutes late. What would you do
to let your colleagues know?
- [Variant: If the user suggests contacting them through another
communication means such as calling them or SMS] Is there any way to
contact them from the app itself? Does this seem more convenient to you
than the previous method you suggested?
- [Observation: Did the user notice that they can tap on the participants
from the activity description to contact them? If not, are users able to
find them through the contacts view?]

Questions after the test:
- How was your experience in general? Were you able to participate in a
sporting activity with colleagues and coordinate with them fluently?
- Were the steps to find and join an activity easy to follow?
- Did you encounter any issue in coordinating with other people?
```

Defining good questions is the most important skill for usability testing. Focus on what the user wants to achieve, provide enough context for the user to understand why they want to achieve that, and let the user take the specific steps. You should be careful with the terms you use since mentioning terms that literally appear in the product can become clues that makes users get there blindly. Also, note that in the preceding example, we are talking about the final activities and not specific actions. We ask how to play tennis today with your colleagues, and it is up to the user to figure out that tapping on the *ask to join* button is the way to achieve the goal--while phrasing of the question, we avoided to use the term *join* to avoid directing the user.

It is convenient to run a **pilot test** before starting the process with the real users. A pilot test consists of organizing a session with one of your teammates. Since the participant does not represent the target audience, you won't be interested in finding usability issues with the product. The purpose of this test is to find issues in the script: verifying that the script is clear and that the users understand what they are asked to do. A pilot test is also useful to avoid an underestimation of the time it takes to complete the set of activities that you are asking users to do.

Setting up the environment

In order to observe a user behavior that is realistic, you would want to get as close as possible to the real user environment. However, the need for observations does create some logistical issues. You need to observe the user interactions in detail and keep recordings in order to analyze them and use fragments when summarizing relevant outcomes.

In a traditional usability lab setting, you'd have a room where the participant and the person conducting the test meet with a testing device and a recording system. The recording system will capture the user interactions with the device and also may capture the user facial expressions. In a separate room, other members of the team can view the recorded session.

You can use screen sharing software to record and share what is displayed on the user screen. AirPlay for iOS and Google Cast for Android are general solutions for sharing the screen of a mobile device. Several specialized apps and services focused on usability testing allow you to do more advanced recording where user tap areas are recorded and even the camera of the device can be used to capture their facial expression.

Alternatively, you can also use a separate device for the recording; this can help you capture more detailed interactions, such as the user's fingers touching the device screen; however, the close-range interaction with mobile devices makes it hard for the recording device not to interfere too much. Some options include document cameras--which force you to keep the device flat on a table while being used, not the most usual way to hold the phone for most users--cameras attached to the device, cameras attached to the participant, and recording devices, such as laptops or tablets, placed between the user and the mobile device.

The device itself can also be a point of distraction. Use mobile devices that will be as familiar as possible to the final resulting device experience that your participants had. If the user tests a new product on a new device, some issues can be caused or influenced by the differences in hardware or the operating system. Using devices that are as close as possible to those that the user normally uses or allowing the participant to use their own devices can help. You don't want the differences in the placement of buttons or an unusual way to *copy and paste* to interfere with the results. HTML prototypes allow you to support a wide variety of devices.

Conducting usability tests

Once you have a plan, you can consider finding people, put your ideas into their hands, and observe them. Each of these steps requires you to also have some consideration in order to find the right people, guide them through the process, and extract useful conclusions.

Recruiting participants

With usability testing, your goal is to identify the biggest rocks in the user's path that prevent them from achieving their goals successfully. You don't need to test with a large number of users to identify those big problems. Studies have shown that testing your product with 3 to 5 users is enough to catch most of the big usability issues. Testing with more users quickly results in diminishing returns, and it is much better to organize a new study instead.

For example, if you have the resources to test your solution with 15 different people, it is much better to organize three rounds with 5 users each than a single testing round with 15 of them. Having multiple rounds allows you to solve the bigger issues and verify that your solution does not introduce new ones, and keep iterating. Having a single round with lots of users will result in a longer list of issues to solve with many repeated issues, and there will be a lack of confirmation on whether the proposed solution for those issues will be effective or will introduce new issues.

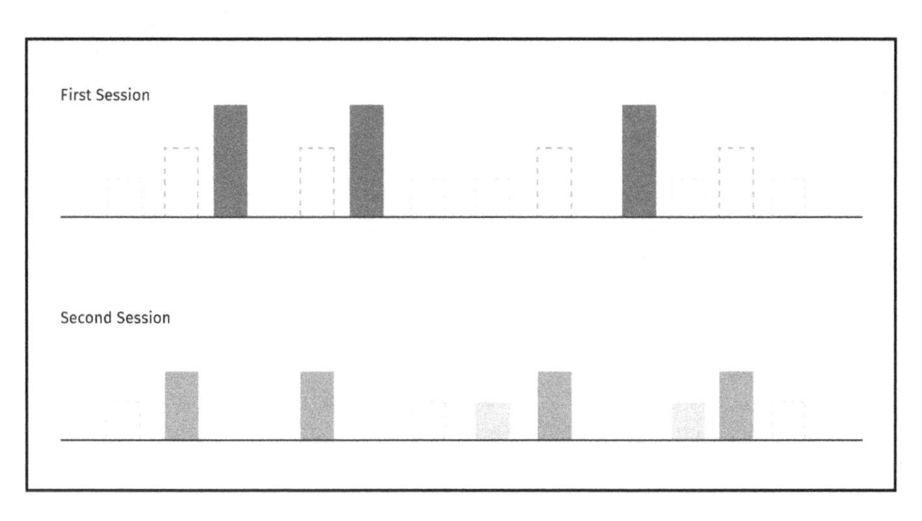

On a first session, we could detect only some of the main problems (top), whereas on a second session, with them solved, we could find new issues that were not so visible before (bottom)

Although you will need only few people to test with, it is important that those people are representative of your target audience. During the research of your project, you defined your target audience, capturing the characteristics in a persona document. You can use those as screening criteria to select the testing candidates. For the example of the social sports app, you may want to target people that practice sport regularly, but are not professionals. You can ask how often they practice sports each week and whether they do it alone or with friends. Using an online survey, you can capture those screening questions as well as the contact details, and distribute such form through the channels where you expect your users to be. Providing participants an incentive as an appreciation for their time also helps them to be committed throughout the process.

Introducing the process

You don't want to make your users feel as if they were being abducted by aliens at the center of an experiment. Making users feel relaxed and comfortable helps them behave as close as possible as they would normally do when nobody is observing them.

1. First, welcome the participants, thank them for their time, and explain the process as a very simple exercise will help to remove any pressure.
2. Explain the purpose of the test, making it clear that it is about testing the ideas behind the prototype. Emphasize that they are not being tested, but the product is. Make it clear that the purpose is to find issues, so it is perfectly fine if they have problems using it because that is precisely what you want to find out.
3. You also want to avoid the tendency of people to agree or keep negative comments to themselves. You can emphasize that the product to be tested is just an early prototype created by a team that you are not connected to. Even if that is not completely accurate, it will help to set some safety distance for the user to express their thoughts honestly.
4. Encourage participants to *think aloud*. Make sure that you insist that the participants talk as they interact with the prototype, describing what they do, what they see, what surprises them, and what matches their expectations. Making them talk aloud is the best way available to read their mind in order to understand exactly what originated the issues. If users stop doing this at some point during the test, remind them gently to describe what they are thinking.
5. If the session is being recorded, inform the participant but clarify its purpose. Explain that recording will be only used for the team with the purpose of improving the products. If you consider making the session recording or parts of it publicly available, you can inform the participant that they will have the opportunity to review and approve before it gets widely distributed. In this way, users feel in control and are less worried about their recording being the next viral video on the Internet.
6. Give participants the opportunity to ask any questions about the process, then you are ready to start following your testing script.

Observing users behavior

During the test, you'll be asking the participant questions according to the script you defined previously. As participants encounter problems, don't make a literal interpretation of what users do or say. You need to look for the underlying problems that caused the issue. If a user didn't tap on a button, you need to figure out whether that was because the user didn't pay attention to the button, the user recognized the button but the user thought it was for something else, or the user didn't expect the functionality to be provided in such a way.

Some users may even suggest a specific solution to you. For example, the user having problems in finding a button may suggest to make it bigger. However, that may or may not be the best possible solution. Use the suggestion to understand what is the root cause and what is the user trying to achieve. Ask in which ways the proposed alternative would help the user to achieve their goals and try to rephrase the suggestion to connect it to a more general problem--is the request intended to make the button easier to access since it supports a functionality that is often used.

As users experience issues during the testing session, you may be tempted to provide them some help. Remember that the goal is not for the user to succeed, but rather for you to learn what fails and why. Even if users get blocked for a while, use that to understand why they are blocked and let them find alternative paths. Users may ask you for confirmation--should I tap there?--or help--where can I find the map?. In those cases, you can turn the question to them--what do you think? where do you expect to find the map?

If users get really off-track, you can move on to the next task. Make sure that you remain positive and not make them feel like they failed or are doing something wrong.

As participants are answering your questions or describing their thoughts, try not to interrupt them. Give participant enough time to express themselves. You can also use any silences to your advantage. After a participant answers your question, you need to keep quiet, as at that point, some more details about the previous idea may come to the participants mind, including details, nuances, exceptions, and other useful information for you to learn.

If the participant digresses, starts providing feedback based on their opinions, or guesses how the product would work for other people, make sure that you direct the session to focus on the participant behavior and experience, not their opinions. Ask them to show how the aspect that they describe would work for them in the current scenario.

Identifying key aspects and summarizing the results

As you test with different users, you'll see patterns emerge as the same issues keep repeating. You want to focus on those issues with a bigger impact for the user experience. Focus on the big issues that prevent users completing their tasks or that cause friction in their experience. If the user is able to recover their track or seems affected by some small confusion, it may not be worth updating your designs. Even if a team has enough resources to fix all issues, it will be helpful to have a clear sense of the priorities.

The outcomes of the study are normally presented in a report. This is a very important piece of information that can help your product improve significantly. Avoid creating a report that is long and boring, which nobody will be interested in reading. You want to make it as lightweight and interesting as possible. Capture your conclusions in a succinct way. You can include screenshots and compile short videos based on the recordings to emphasize some key points.

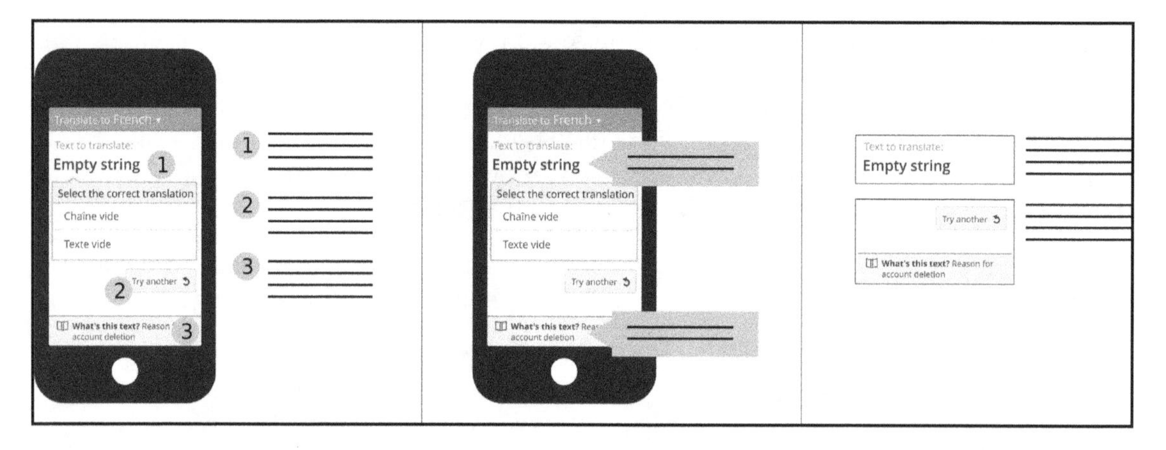

Three different ways to capture usability issues associated with different parts of the UI: using annotations, callouts, and using cropped screenshots embedded in a document

Keep the information organized since your findings are not useful only in the present moment. You are likely to look back at some point in future iterations of the design to check some specific aspect you were not considering before. Keeping links to the specific minutes where some of the observations were made in the recording of the sessions can be very helpful.

Being pragmatic

Getting feedback from users based on their actual behavior is one of the most valuable parts of the design process. However, it is also a step that often gets skipped in many projects. Some teams that may be too confident about how people will use their product may rely on self-reported feedback or may perceive the testing process as too complex.

Despite requiring time to prepare, you need to make your teams understand that testing is actually a way to save time. Since the earlier problems are caught, it is easy to fix them.

Inviting people from your team to view the research sessions

Viewing research sessions becomes an eye-opener for many teams. As they see that users struggle to accomplish basic tasks that they expected to be quite easy, they often better understand the purpose of the whole design process.

Establishing a routine of testing with users helps to move the discussion from what team members like to what works best for users. In this way, concerns and suggestions can be defined as hypotheses to test or aspects to observe during the next round of tests.

The testing process can help make the relation more fluent between designers and the rest of the team in both directions. As you get feedback from your team about your design decisions, you can be open to observing how well those work with your users. As the team decides to cut some corners in the product for an initial version, you can emphasize the importance of checking how those changes will affect users when you test your product with them.

Learning is more important than validating

One of the worst settings for the usability test is when a team has already decided to go into one particular product direction and usability testing is used with just the intention to confirm that decision.

In order to avoid that, you need to push for usability testing to happen as early as possible, before the team is committed to any particular direction for the product.

If you are working with very limited resources, keep in mind that some testing is often better than no testing. Even if you can afford to do only a small round of testing with three users and send a text-only report in a short e-mail, it is worth doing. When making the process lightweight, you will need to be careful to keep some rigor to avoid invalidating the results, since getting misleading results can be worse than having no results at all. Even for lightweight versions of the testing process, make sure that you select users that align with your target audience and avoid leading questions. Picking random people at the nearest coffee shop may not work well--unless that is actually your audience, of course.

Check you are answering the research questions

Making your research questions explicit at the beginning of the process is useful to clarify your goals, but it is also very useful at the end. At the end of the process, you want to check whether you were able to answer those questions.

If you were not able to do so in all cases, you'll be able to retrospectively identify what to improve on the upcoming studies. This will be very helpful to improve the process the next time, either by making the research questions clearer or by improving the process to get better answers.

Combining research with measurements

In this chapter, we put the emphasis on qualitative research since it provides key data to improve your product. However, combining qualitative and quantitative approaches will provide you a wider perspective.

Quantitative methods allow you to reach a higher volume users and compile data about their general behavior.

As you explore design ideas, you can use **A/B testing** to compare approaches for a larger audience. A/B testing consists of presenting a small subset of your product users with a variant of your software with some modifications you want to test. In order to know which one is more successful, you need to define a metric in advance, for example, whether people click on the *buy* button. A/B testing software will tell you which variant got better results--on which one did more people clicked on the *buy* button. Services such as Google Analytics or Optimizely automate this process to make it easy for you to set-up A/B test experiments in your project requiring minimal instrumentation code.

A/B testing works better when the metric defined works as a real indicator of the user behavior that you want to learn about, and especially for small variations where the cause of the difference in behavior is clear. In any case, A/B testing is not going to tell you why one option works better by itself, or whether the improvement comes with other associated issues not captured by the metric.

Once your product is working, you may want to instrument some **key metrics**. In order to define useful metrics, ensure that you consider the design goals you have already defined and explore indicators that can signal when those are achieved, or if the product fails to achieve them. For example, measuring the search terms that lead to no results can be useful to identify what people are unsuccessfully trying to search most. Then, you can explore better ways to support those cases and learn more about how these ideas work.

Summary

In this chapter, you looked at the importance of learning as early as possible from your user's behavior. You also learned how to organize a usability testing session and get quality feedback to improve your product before building it. This ensures that you only build a product when you are confident enough that you are moving in the right direction.

This is the last chapter that describes the stages of the design process. However, you should understand that the process is not a set of linear steps. Testing is just another step that may complete one more iteration; depending on the results, it can lead you to any of the previous stages to learn more from your users, explore new ideas, prototype different approaches, or adjust the test script. Design is a never ending process; what is important is to serve your users better on each iteration.

10
Bibliography and References

General

- Dan M. Brown. Communicating Design. New Riders, 2006.

- Leah Buley. The User Experience Team of One: A Research and Design Survival Guide. Rosenfeld Media, 2013.

- Jake Knapp, John Zeratsky, Braden Kowitz. Sprint: How to Solve Big Problems and Test New Ideas in Just Five Days. Simon & Schuster, 2016.

- Cennydd Bowles. Undercover User Experience design. New Riders, 2010.

- Jason Mander. "Mobile-Only Users by Country". Last modified December 06, 2016. `http://blog.globalwebindex.net/chart-of-the-day/mobile-only-users-by-country/`

- Jason Mander. "15% of Internet Users are Mobile-Only". Last modified December 05, 2016. `http://blog.globalwebindex.net/chart-of-the-day/15-of-internet-users-are-mobile-only/`

- Jared M. Spool. "The $300 Million Button". Last modified January 14, 2009. `https://articles.uie.com/three_hund_million_button/`

Kano model

- Karl T. Ulrich. Design: Creation of artifacts in society. University of Pennsylvania, 2011

Gestalt principles

- Susan M. Weinschenk. 100 Things Every Designer Needs To Know About People. New Riders, 2011.

Mental model references

- Jakob Nielsen. "Mental Models". Last modified October 18, 2010. https://www.nngroup.com/articles/mental-models/

- Wikipedia. "Mental model." Last modified 17 June 2017. https://en.wikipedia.org/wiki/Mental_model

- Susan Weinschenk. "The Secret to Designing an Intuitive UX". Last modified October 8, 2011. http://uxmag.com/articles/the-secret-to-designing-an-intuitive-user-experience

Conceptual model references

- The Interaction Design Foundation. "We Think Therefore It Is – Conceptual Modelling for Mobile Applications". Last modified 2016. https://www.interaction-design.org/literature/article/we-think-therefore-it-is-conceptual-modelling-for-mobile-applications

- Wikipedia. "Conceptual model". Last modified 2 June 2017. https://en.wikipedia.org/wiki/Conceptual_model

Persona document references

- Alan Cooper. The origin of personas. 2008.

Retrieved from https://www.cooper.com/journal/2003/08/the_origin_of_personas

- Alan Cooper. The Inmates Are Running the Asylum. 1998.

Retrieval from https://www.cooper.com/journal/2003/08/the_origin_of_personas

- Alan Cooper, Robert reimann, and David Cronin. About Face 3. Willey, 2007.

Retrieved from http://eu.wiley.com/WileyCDA/WileyTitle/productCd-1118766571.html

- Shlomo Goltz. "A Closer Look At Personas: What They Are And How They Work". Last modified August 6th, 2014. https://www.smashingmagazine.com/2014/08/a-closer-look-at-personas-part-1/

- Usability.gov. "Personas". https://www.usability.gov/how-to-and-tools/methods/personas.html

Card sorting references

- Jakob Nielsen. "Usability Testing for the 1995 Sun Microsystems' Website". Last modified 1995, May 25. https://www.nngroup.com/articles/usability-testing-1995-sun-microsystems-website/

- UserTesting. The UX Research Methodology Guidebook. http://www.usertesting.com/

- Wikipedia. "Card sorting". Last modified 4 April 2017. https://en.wikipedia.org/wiki/Card_sorting

- UsabilityNet. "Card sorting". http://www.usabilitynet.org/tools/cardsorting.htm

Tree testing (Reverse card sorting) references

- Donna Spencer. "Card-Based Classification Evaluation". Last modified April 7th, 2003. http://boxesandarrows.com/card-based-classification-evaluation/

- Wikipedia. "Tree testing." Last modified 9 January 2017. https://en.wikipedia.org/wiki/Tree_testing

Affinity diagram references

- Wikipedia. "Affinity diagram". Last modified 29 March 2017. https://en.wikipedia.org/wiki/Affinity_diagram

- Wikipedia. "Seven Management and Planning Tools". Last modified 12 April 2017. https://en.m.wikipedia.org/wiki/Seven_Management_and_Planning_Tools

- American Society for Quality. "Affinity Diagram". http://asq.org/learn-about-quality/idea-creation-tools/overview/affinity.html

- UsabilityNet.org. "Affinity diagramming". http://www.usabilitynet.org/tools/affinity.htm

Crazy eights references

- Jake Knapp. "The product design sprint: diverge (day 2)". Last modified Oct 26, 2012. https://library.gv.com/the-product-design-sprint-diverge-day-2-c7a5df8e7cd0

- Dave Gray. 6-8-5. Last modified May 17, 2011. http://gamestorming.com/games-for-fresh-thinking-and-ideas/6-8-5s/

- Jake Knapp. "The product design sprint: diverge (day 2)". Last modified Oct 26, 2012. https://library.gv.com/the-product-design-sprint-diverge-day-2-c7a5df8e7cd0

Survey references

- Susan Farrell. "Open-Ended vs. Closed-Ended Questions in User Research". Last modified May 22, 2016. https://www.nngroup.com/articles/open-ended-questions/

- Wikipedia. "Closed-ended question". Last modified 15 June 2017. https://en.wikipedia.org/wiki/Closed-ended_question

- Wikipedia. "Open-ended question". Last modified 27 November 2016. https://en.wikipedia.org/wiki/Open-ended_question

- Bert Markgraf. "Short-Term, Medium-Term & Long-Term Planning in Business". http://smallbusiness.chron.com/shortterm-mediumterm-longterm-planning-business-60193.html

- Chris Thelwell. "How to quickly create a powerful survey". https://www.invisionapp.com/blog/how-to-create-a-survey/

- Gerald Linda. Guerrilla Marketing Research: Marketing Research Techniques that Can Help Any Business Make More Money. 2006.

- Jeanne Grunert. "Differences Between a Short- & Long-Term Period of a Marketing Plan". http://smallbusiness.chron.com/differences-between-short-longterm-period-marketing-plan-74826.html

User journey references

- Kate Kaplan. "When and How to Create Customer Journey Maps". Last modified July 31, 2016. https://www.nngroup.com/articles/customer-journey-mapping/

- Wikipedia. "User journey". Last modified 28 February 2017. https://en.wikipedia.org/wiki/User_journey

- Jennifer Havice. "A Step By Step Guide To Building Customer Journey Maps". https://conversionxl.com/customer-journey-maps/

- Chris Risdon. "The Anatomy of an Experience Map". Last modified November 30, 2011. http://adaptivepath.org/ideas/the-anatomy-of-an-experience-map/

Scenarios references

- Usability.gov. "Scenarios". https://www.usability.gov/how-to-and-tools/methods/scenarios.html

- Nielsen Norman Group. "Turn User Goals into Task Scenarios for Usability Testing." Last modified January 12, 2014. https://www.nngroup.com/articles/task-scenarios-usability-testing/

Progressive disclosure

- Jakob Nielsen. "Progressive Disclosure". Last modified December 4, 2006. https://www.nngroup.com/articles/progressive-disclosure/

- Frank Spillers. "Progressive Disclosure". https://www.interaction-design.org/literature/book/the-glossary-of-human-computer-interaction/progressive-disclosure

- Nick Babich. "Design Patterns: Progressive Disclosure for Mobile Apps". Last modified May 27, 2016. https://uxplanet.org/design-patterns-progressive-disclosure-for-mobile-apps-f41001a293ba

Reciprocity effect

- Gamberini L., Petrucci G., Spoto A., Spagnolli A. Embedded Persuasive Strategies to Obtain Visitors' Data: Comparing Reward and Reciprocity in an Amateur, Knowledge-Based Website. Springer, Berlin, Heidelberg, 2007. Retrieval from https://link.springer.com/chapter/10.1007/978-3-540-77006-0_24

- Raluca Budiu. "The Reciprocity Principle: Give Before You Take in Web Design". Last modified 2014, February 16. https://www.nngroup.com/articles/reciprocity-principle/

- Susan M. Weinschenk. Neuro Web Design: What Makes Them Click? New Riders, 2009.

Lazy login

- Luke Wroblewski. "Sign Up Forms Must Die". Last modified March 25, 2008. https://alistapart.com/article/signupforms

- Anders Toxboe. UI-Patterns.com. http://ui-patterns.com/patterns/LazyRegistration

- Janko Jovanovic. "10 UI Design Patterns You Should Be Paying Attention To". Last modified June 23rd, 2009. https://www.smashingmagazine.com/2009/06/10-ui-design-patterns-you-should-be-paying-attention-to/

User testing

- Steve Krug. Don't make me think. New Riders, 2005.

- Steve Krug. Rocket Surgery Made Easy: The Do-It-Yourself Guide to Finding and Fixing Usability Problems. New Riders, 2009.

- VWO. "The Complete Guide to A/B Testing". https://vwo.com/ab-testing/

- Optimizely. "A/B Testing". https://www.optimizely.com/ab-testing/

- Wikipedia. "A/B testing". Last modified 6 June 2017. https://en.wikipedia.org/wiki/A/B_testing

Mobile patterns

- Luke Wroblewski. Mobile first. A Book Apart, 2011.

- Google Material Design guidelines. Retrieval from https://material.io/guidelines/

- iOS Human Interface Guidelines. Retrieval from https://developer.apple.com/ios/human-interface-guidelines/

- Luke Wroblewski. Retrieval from https://www.lukew.com/

- Chris O'Sullivan. "A Tale of Two Platforms: Designing for Both Android and iOS". Last modified 15 Apr 2015. https://webdesign.tutsplus.com/articles/a-tale-of-two-platforms-designing-for-both-android-and-ios--cms-23616

Information architecture

- Wikipedia. "Information architecture". Last modified 7 May 2017. https://en.wikipedia.org/wiki/Information_architecture

- Usability.gov. "Information Architecture Basics". https://www.usability.gov/what-and-why/information-architecture.html

- Jennifer Cardello. "Low Findability and Discoverability: Four Testing Methods to Identify the Causes". Last modified July 6, 2014. https://www.nngroup.com/articles/navigation-ia-tests/

Visual design

- Andrei Stefan. "How to Create Pixel-Perfect Artwork Using Adobe Illustrator". Last modified 19 May 2015. https://design.tutsplus.com/tutorials/how-to-create-pixel-perfect-artwork-using-adobe-illustrator--cms-23907

- Icons8. "How to Make Pixel Perfect Icons". Last modified May 17, 2017. https://icons8.com/articles/make-pixel-perfect-icons/

- Abhijeet Wankhade. "How to create pixel perfect icons in Illustrator". Last modified Mar 19, 2014. https://medium.com/@sokratus/how-to-create-pixel-perfect-icons-in-illustrator-6b3a188b4292

Prototyping

- Todd Zaki Warfel. Prototyping. Rosenfeld Media, November 2009.

Tumult Hype

- Tumult Hype documentation. Retrieval from `http://tumult.com/hype/`

CoffeeScript

- CoffeeScript documentation. Retrieval from `http://coffeescript.org`
- Tutorials Point. Retrieval from `https://www.tutorialspoint.com/coffeescript`

Framer

- Framer documentation. Retrieval from `https://framer.com/docs/`
- Framer documentation. Retrieval from `https://framer.com/getstarted/programming/`
- Tes Mat. The Framer Book. March 2017
- Tessa Thornton. CoffeeScript for Framer.js.

JavaScript

- JavaScript documentation. Retrieval from `https://www.javascript.com`
- W3Schools JavaScript documentation. Retrieval from `https://www.w3schools.com/Js/`

jQuery

- jQuery documentation. Retrieval from `https://jquery.com`
- W3Schools jQuery documentation. Retrieval from `https://www.w3schools.com/jquery/`

Image sources

Chapter 1

Source: https://www.flickr.com/photos/colalife/14624508474/ by Abraham Piper is licensed under CC BY-SA 2.0 https://creativecommons.org/licenses/by-sa/2.0/

Source: https://www.flickr.com/photos/phrawr/6655550583/ by phrawr is licensed under CC BY 2.0 https://creativecommons.org/licenses/by/2.0/

Source: https://www.flickr.com/photos/afoncubierta/3003286245/ by Antonio Foncubierta is licensed under CC BY-SA 2.0 https://creativecommons.org/licenses/by-sa/2.0/

Source: http://www.flickr.com/photos/ajmexico/3281139507/ by ajmexico is licensed under CC BY 2.0 https://creativecommons.org/licenses/by/2.0/

Source: Screenshot from http://www.nick.com/

Source: Screenshot from http://www.un.org/

Source: Screenshot from Instagram

Source: Screenshot from Facebook

Source: https://www.flickr.com/photos/chrisandhilleary/153059898/ by Chris Conway, Hilleary Osheroff is licensed under CC BY 2.0 https://creativecommons.org/licenses/by/2.0/

Source: Screenshot from LinkedIn

Source: Screenshot from TripAdvisor

Source: Screenshot from Google

Source: Screenshot from iOS Maps

Source: Screenshot from iOS Maps

Source: Screenshot from iOS Maps

Source: Screenshot from iOS Maps

Chapter 2

Source: https://commons.wikimedia.org/wiki/File:Redstair_GEARcompressor.pngby Klaus Göttling is licensed under the Creative Commons Attribution-Share Alike 3.0 Unported https://creativecommons.org/licenses/by-sa/3.0/deed.en

Source: https://commons.wikimedia.org/wiki/File%3AAffinity_wall.pngby Goldenratio is released into the public domain https://en.wikipedia.org/wiki/Public_domain

Source: https://commons.wikimedia.org/wiki/File:Grouped_Post-Its.jpgby Lil 81 is licensed under the Creative Commons Attribution-Share Alike 3.0 Unported https://creativecommons.org/licenses/by-sa/3.0/deed.en

Source: Screenshot from Google Gmail App

Source: Screenshot from Gmail App

Assets from https://pixabay.com/en/man-red-hair-beard-red-beard-1848452/ by nastya_gepp is licensed under CC0 Public Domain https://creativecommons.org/publicdomain/zero/1.0/deed.en

Chapter 3

Source: https://www.flickr.com/photos/bygenejackson/3112404581/ by Gene Jackson is licensed under CC BY-SA 2.0 https://creativecommons.org/licenses/by-sa/2.0/

Source: https://www.flickr.com/photos/jackdorsey/182613360/ by Jack Dorsey is licensed under CC BY 2.0 https://creativecommons.org/licenses/by/2.0/

Source: Screenshot from MyPaint

Chapter 4

Source: Screenshot from YouTube

Source: Screenshot from YouTube

Source: Screenshots from iOS Settings

Source: Screenshot from Twitter

Source: Screenshot from Twitter

Source: Screenshot from Google Drive

Source: Screenshot from LinkedIn

Source: Screenshot from Twitter

Source: Screenshots from YouTube

Source: Screenshot from Google Maps

Source: Screenshot from TripAdvisor

Source: Screenshots from Facebook

Source: Screenshots from LinkedIn

Source: Screenshots from Instagram

Source: Screenshots from Facebook

Chapter 5

Assets from https://www.pexels.com and https://pixabay.com

Assets from `https://pixabay.com/en/sports-games-fun-holiday-parks-679594/` by `maptango3600` is licensed under CC0 Public Domain `https://creativecommons.org/publicdomain/zero/1.0/deed.en`

Source: Screenshot from Sketch with Sketch Measure

Assets from `https://pixabay.com/en/sports-games-fun-holiday-parks-679594/` by `maptango3600` is licensed under CC0 Public Domain `https://creativecommons.org/publicdomain/zero/1.0/deed.en`

Source: Screenshot from Sketch with Sketch Measure

Assets from `https://pixabay.com/en/sports-games-fun-holiday-parks-679594/` by `maptango3600` is licensed under CC0 Public Domain `https://creativecommons.org/publicdomain/zero/1.0/deed.en`

Source: Screenshot from Photoshop with Ink

Assets from `https://pixabay.com/en/camera-photography-lens-equipment-801924/` by `Unsplash` is licensed under CC0 Public Domain `https://creativecommons.org/publicdomain/zero/1.0/deed.en`

Assets from https://pixabay.com/en/spice-chiles-paprika-chili-powder-370114/ by babawawa is licensed under CC0 Public Domain https://creativecommons.org/publicdomain/zero/1.0/deed.en

Source: Screenshot from Zeplin

Source: Screenshots from Illustrator

Chapter 6

Source: https://en.wikipedia.org/wiki/Swing_Wing_(toy) , https://archive.org/details/swing_wingis licensed under Public Domain, Prelinger Archives

Source: https://commons.wikimedia.org/wiki/File:SST_model_in_Wind_Tunnel.jpeg by Unknown is licensed under the Public Domain https://en.wikipedia.org/wiki/Public_domain

Source: https://www.flickr.com/photos/21218849@N03/7984460226/ by Samuel Mann is licensed under CC BY 2.0 https://creativecommons.org/licenses/by/2.0/

Source: Screenshot from Adobe Experience Design

Source: Screenshot from Pixate

Source: Screenshot from Tumult Hype

Source: Screenshot from Form

Source: Screenshot from Framer Studio

Chapter 7

Source: Screenshots from Tumult Hype

Source: Screenshots from Sketch

Chapter 8

Source: Screenshots from Framer Studio

Source: Screenshots from Sketch

Chapter 9

Source: `https://www.flickr.com/photos/sophotow/16559284088/` by `Wassim LOUMI` is licensed under `CC BY-SA 2.0 https://creativecommons.org/licenses/by-sa/2.0/`

Source: `https://www.flickr.com/photos/stevevosloo/4918831135` by `stevevosloo` is licensed under `CC BY-SA 2.0 https://creativecommons.org/licenses/by-sa/2.0/`

Source: Screenshots from Sketch

Index

U

V

W